INVENTORY SYSTEMS

INVENTORY SYSTEMS

Eliezer Naddor

Professor of Operations Research
The Johns Hopkins University

JOHN WILEY & SONS, INC.
New York · London · Sydney

Library of Congress Catalog Card Number: 65-26850
Printed in the United States of America

To Sedelle, Danny, and David

Preface

In writing this book I have set myself a rather ambitious task. I am trying to achieve three goals within the confines of one book. My first goal is to present the results of my research work in the study and solution of inventory systems. I have been working in this field since 1953 and have accumulated considerable research material. Most of it is being presented here for the first time. My second goal is to teach. It is for this reason that the book is in text form and contains numerous examples and problems for solution. My third goal is to provide a reference for people actively engaged in solving inventory problems. Since, at the moment, most of these problems exist in the business and industrial environment, the book has been somewhat slanted in this direction.

Most of the material presented in this book is based on notes which I have been using in teaching the subject to seniors and to graduate students at The Johns Hopkins University and at Case Institute of Technology. The notes themselves are an outgrowth of research work in industrial inventory problems and of theoretical investigations carried out at Hopkins and at Case.

The material in certain sections of the book has been presented at short courses and conferences in Operations Research at Case Institute of Technology during the period 1953–1956, at intensive courses and seminars in Operations Research and Systems Engineering at The Johns Hopkins University since 1955, and at special courses and lectures in Finland, Israel, England, Sweden, and Germany in 1964–1965. Presentations have also been made at national and chapter meetings of The Institute of Management Sciences, Operations Research Society of America, American Chemical Society, International Federation of Operational Research Societies, American Society of Mechanical Engineers, American Institute of Electrical Engineers, and the Association for Computing Machinery. Some of the material in this book has been presented to management and technical personnel of the General Electric Company, Cleveland Graphite Bronze Company, American Airlines Inc., Office of the Quartermaster General, Royal McBee Corporation, North American Aviation, Chesapeake and Potomac Telephone Company of Maryland, the General Motors Corporation, and the Osuustukkukauppa, International Business Machines, and Kesko Companies of Finland.

In writing the book I have attempted to meet the needs of two groups of potential users, college students and practitioners in industry. The book should be useful to advanced undergraduates and to graduate students in industrial engineering, production engineering, operations research, management science, business administration, economics, and related fields. In industry it will be found useful to personnel in departments handling production scheduling, inventory control, market research, forecasting, cost accounting, budgeting, etc.

The book is divided into four parts. Part 1 deals with introductory material and with definitions, Part 2 with the analysis of systems in which the demand for inventory is known with certainty. In Parts 3 and 4 the demand for inventory is not known with certainty but the knowledge of the probability distribution of demand is assumed. In Part 3 replenishments occur at equal intervals; in Part 4 they occur when a reorder point is reached.

The mathematical background required for Part 1 is a knowledge of algebra. For Part 2 the elements of differential and integral calculus are needed. For Parts 3 and 4 the reader will also need some mathematical statistics and an introductory knowledge of Markov chains. An introductory knowledge of differential equations is necessary for Chapters 15 and 16.

The chapters of the book are rather closely related and should be studied in the order presented. Chapters 6, 7, 11, and 12 deal with special topics which are only mentioned occasionally in subsequent chapters. They may be omitted on first reading without affecting continuity.

Equations in each section are numbered consecutively from equation (1) up. Within the section they are referred to only in this form. When an equation not belonging to a current section is referred to, however, its section is also stated, for example, equation 13–1(2) at the beginning of Section 14–1. Figures, tables, and examples in each section bear the number of that section. If more than one figure, table, or example is dealt with in one section, a letter is added to the number, for example, Figures 3–2a, 3–2b, etc., in Section 3–2.

I wish to acknowledge the generous and extensive help I have received from Ronald Rubel of the Harvard Graduate School of Business Administration. Mr. Rubel has read the entire manuscript and has pointed out a number of errors and inconsistencies. He has also contributed the write-up on judgmental probabilities in Section 2–1.

I am also indebted to Mrs. Joyce Franke, Mrs. Dorla Hall, and Mrs. Helen Macaulay. Mrs. Franke and Mrs. Hall typed portions of early versions of the manuscript, and Mrs. Macaulay has expertly typed the final copy.

A wonderful environment for teaching, research, and writing has been provided by The Johns Hopkins University. In particular, I wish to thank Dean Robert H. Roy, my chairman and colleague.

ELIEZER NADDOR

Baltimore, Maryland
October 1965

Contents

Part 1

INTRODUCTION

This book is devoted to the study of inventory systems. Interest in the subject is constantly increasing, and its development in recent years closely parallels the development of operations research in general. Some authors even claim that "More operations research has been directed towards inventory control than toward any other problem area in business and industry" (Churchman [14], p. 195).

In the past, attempts have been made to define such terms as the "inventory problem" (Dvoretzky et al. [15], p. 187), "inventory control" (Simon and Holt [52], p. 289), and "inventory process" (Ackoff [1], p. 271). And more recently we find the terms "inventory theory" (Starr and Miller [53], p. 3), "inventory management" (Buchan and Koenigsberg [13], Foreword), and "inventory systems" (Naddor [38]). We can readily conclude that no accepted terminology yet exists in this area. Not only do we not have commonly accepted terms, but there also seem to be numerous views on what the inventory research field should encompass.

Some people consider inventory systems the systems of keeping records of the amounts of commodities in stock. An inventory problem, for these people, is the problem of determining what details should be recorded, who should make the entries in the records, where and when entries should be made, etc. Others look at inventory systems from a general over-all point of view. For them the inventory system usually involves not specific commodities but rather the totality of the commodities and the investments in all the stocks in inventory. Their problems are inventory turnover, financing investments tied up in stocks, etc. They are the people who are often concerned with inventories that are too high and the problem of reducing them.

Other groups consider inventory systems from still another point of view. Their problems are what items to stock, when to stock them, how many to stock, etc. Usually, they are also concerned with problems of labor stability, utilization of equipment and facilities, customer relations, etc.

Because of this wide range of points of view, it is necessary to devote some time to the definitions of the inventory terms used in this book, many of which are used here for the first time. They do not contradict or conflict with other known inventory definitions. Chapters 1 and 2 deal with these definitions. In Chapter 1 we define terms pertaining to inventory systems in general. In Chapter 2 we define specific terms pertaining to the detailed properties of inventory systems.

Chapter 1

Terminology

1-0 An *inventory system* is a system in which only the following three kinds of costs are significant, and in which any two or all three are subject to control:

1. The cost of carrying inventories.
2. The cost of incurring shortages.
3. The cost of replenishing inventories.

A production system is one in which these costs arise, and are subject to control. In this system the costs may be controlled by making appropriate decisions about ordering raw materials, manufacturing semi-finished and finished goods, and inventorying goods in readiness for shipment to consumers.

The first kind of cost in this production system, that of carrying inventories, is the cost of the investment in inventories, of storage, of handling items in storage, of obsolescence, etc.

The second kind of cost, that of incurring shortages, is the cost of lost sales, of loss of good will, of overtime payments, of special administrative efforts (telephone calls, memos, letters), etc.

The third kind of cost, that of replenishing inventories, is the cost of machine setups for production runs, of preparing orders, of handling shipments, etc.

These three kinds of costs will be referred to in general as the *carrying cost*, *shortage cost*, and *replenishing cost*, respectively. The sum of these costs will be referred to as the *total cost*.

The term *cost* is used in a broader and more general sense than the dollars and cents usually associated with the word. Cost is the measure of performance used for the systems under study. We assume that carrying inventories, incurring shortages, and replenishing inventories can all be measured by some common measure, so that meaningful comparisons can be performed. It seems natural that the measure in this case should be referred to as cost.

By defining inventory systems as systems in which the costs of carrying, shortage, and replenishing are significant and subject to control, we imply that other costs are not pertinent in inventory systems. If they are pertinent in some system, we do not call it an inventory system. We do not mean that the methodology and results presented in this book do not apply to a wide range of systems in which, in addition to the carrying, shortage, and replenishing costs, there are other significant costs. On the contrary, the methods and results do indeed apply and examples will be given to show how they apply. The definition of inventory systems just given is necessary as a frame of reference and as an indication of the scope of the subject matter to be studied. Many systems encountered in practice are inventory systems in the sense just defined.

The three kinds of costs that characterize inventory systems are generally closely related. When one cost is decreased, one of the other two costs, and sometimes even both, may increase. The total cost may thus be affected by suitable decisions. It is only in this sense that we mean that the costs are controllable. Any one cost may be decreased (or increased), but this will usually tend to increase (or decrease) the other costs. The following example provides a simple illustration of how the three kinds of costs can be controlled.

Example 1-0

The inventory records of an item at a depot for a year are given in Table 1-0a. The depot operates as follows. Every 3 months, on January 1, April 1, July 1, and October 1, a delivery of 60 lb is made to the depot. This amount is then added immediately to stock. The depot is required to fill orders at the beginning of every month, orders being filled from stock on hand. If insufficient stock is available, outstanding orders are filled when new deliveries to the depot are made. This system will be referred to as Case I.

The amounts in inventory on hand are given in the last column of Table 1-0a. Therefore the average amount carried during the year is

$$(50 + 30 + 10 + 40 + 20 + 0 + 50 + \cdots + 20 + 0)/12 = 26\tfrac{2}{3} \text{ lb}$$

A shortage of 10 lb exists only during June; hence the average shortage during the year is $\frac{10}{12} = \frac{5}{6}$ lb. In addition, there are four stock replenishments during the year.

Let us now assume that the cost of carrying 1 lb in inventory per month is $0.20, that the cost of incurring shortages is $5.00 per pound per month,

TABLE 1–0a

Case I

*Inventory Records of an Item at a Depot,
Deliveries of 60 lb Every Three Months*

Date	Quantity delivered to depot	Quantity required from depot	On hand at end of day
Jan. 1	60	10	50
Feb. 1		20	30
Mar. 1		20	10
Apr. 1	60	30	40
May 1		20	20
June 1		30	−10
July 1	60	0	50
Aug. 1		0	50
Sept. 1		40	10
Oct. 1	60	30	40
Nov. 1		20	20
Dec. 1		20	0

and that the cost of ordering and handling a delivery at the depot is $10.00 per delivery. The yearly costs of the inventory system are therefore

Carrying cost: $26\frac{2}{3}$ lb × 0.20 × 12 = $64.00 per year
Shortage cost: $\frac{5}{6}$ lb × 5.00 × 12 = 50.00 per year
Replenishment cost: 4 deliveries × 10.00 = 40.00 per year
                            Total cost $154.00 per year

Now consider Case II in which orders are placed so that instead of deliveries of 60 lb every 3 months, there are deliveries of 40 lb every 2 months. The inventory records of the item at the depot would be as in Table 1–0b. The yearly costs of the inventory system in this case are now

Carrying cost: $16\frac{2}{3}$ lb × 0.20 × 12 = $40.00 per year
Shortage cost: $\frac{5}{6}$ lb × 5.00 × 12 = $50.00 per year
Replenishing cost: 6 deliveries × 10.00 = $60.00 per year
                            Total cost $150.00 per year

TABLE 1–0b

Case II

*Inventory Records of an Item at a Depot,
Deliveries of* 40 *lb Every Two Months*

Date	Quantity delivered to depot	Quantity required from depot	On hand at end of day
Jan. 1	40	10	30
Feb. 1		20	10
Mar. 1	40	20	30
Apr. 1		30	0
May 1	40	20	20
June 1		30	−10
July 1	40	0	30
Aug. 1		0	30
Sept. 1	40	40	30
Oct. 1		30	0
Nov. 1	40	20	20
Dec. 1		20	0

TABLE 1–0c

Case III

*Inventory Records of an Item at a Depot,
Deliveries of* 40 *lb Every Two Months,
Additional* 10 *lb Available at Beginning
of the Year*

Date	Quantity delivered to depot	Quantity required from depot	On hand at end of day
Jan. 1	40	10	40
Feb. 1		20	20
Mar. 1	40	20	40
Apr. 1		30	10
May 1	40	20	30
June 1		30	0
July 1	40	0	40
Aug. 1		0	40
Sept. 1	40	40	40
Oct. 1		30	10
Nov. 1	40	20	30
Dec. 1		20	10

By changing the frequency of delivery of orders from Case I to Case II the carrying cost was decreased and the replenishing cost was increased. The shortage cost was unchanged. The total cost was reduced from $154.00 per year to $150.00 per year.

Suppose now that, in addition to the change of frequency of delivery of orders, an additional quantity of 10 lb was available at the beginning of the year. This leads us to Case III and the inventory records would be as in Table 1–0c. The yearly costs of the inventory system in this case are

Carrying cost: $25\frac{5}{6}$ lb × 0.20 × 12 = $62.00 per year
Shortage cost: 0 lb × 5.00 × 12   = $ 0.00 per year
Replenishing cost: 6 deliveries × 10.00 = $60.00 per year

Total cost $122.00 per year

Compared to Case II, the replenishing cost of Case III is unchanged; however, the carrying cost is increased and the shortage cost is decreased. The results of the three cases considered are summarized in Table 1–0d.

TABLE 1–0d

Comparison of Annual Costs for Different Decisions

	Case I	Case II	Case III
Carrying cost	64.00	40.00	62.00
Shortage cost	50.00	50.00	0.00
Replenishing cost	40.00	60.00	60.00
Total cost	154.00	150.00	122.00

Our definition of an inventory system is clearly illustrated by comparing all three cases simultaneously. There are three types of significant costs that can be suitably controlled by making appropriate decisions.

TYPES OF INVENTORY SYSTEMS

1–1 An inventory system has been defined as a system in which two or all three kinds of costs are subject to control. We now distinguish among several *types* of inventory systems:

In a type (1, 2) inventory system only the carrying cost and the shortage cost are subject to control. In systems of this kind the replenishing cost is *not* subject to control.

In a type (1, 3) inventory system only the carrying cost and the replenishing cost are subject to control. The shortage cost is *not* subject to control.

(All systems in which shortages do not occur are type (1, 3) systems. In these systems the shortage cost is thus zero.*)

Similarly, in a type (2, 3) inventory system only the shortage cost and the replenishing cost are subject to control. In such a system the carrying cost is *not* subject to control. (Type (2, 3) systems are rarely encountered in practical applications.)

A type (1, 2, 3) inventory system is a system in which all three costs are subject to control. (The preceding Example 1-0 illustrates such a system.)

By using this classification, inventory systems can be grouped into four classes: type (1, 2), type (1, 3), type (2, 3), and type (1, 2, 3). We shall see that there is practically no difference between type (1, 3) and type (2, 3) inventory systems. We shall also see that in some special circumstances type (1, 2) and type (1, 3) systems are special cases of type (1, 2, 3) systems. Since this is not true in general, we cannot content ourselves with the study of type (1, 2, 3) systems alone but will have to study the other types of systems as well.

Inventory Problems

An *inventory problem* is a problem of making optimal decisions with respect to an inventory system. In other words, an inventory problem is concerned with the making of decisions that minimize the total cost of an inventory system. We have pointed out that when one cost is decreased (or increased) the other costs may increase (or decrease). There is thus the problem of controlling the costs so that their sum will be the lowest. The inventory problem is thus defined in terms of making *optimal decisions* with respect to costs.

Decisions that are made always affect the costs, but such decisions can rarely be made directly in terms of costs. Decisions are usually made in terms of time and quantity, for example,

1. When should the inventory be replenished?
2. How much should be added to inventory?

The time element and the quantity element are the *variables* that are *subject to control* in an inventory system. (They are also referred to as the *controllable variables*.) They affect the carrying cost, the shortage cost, the replenishing cost, and the total cost. The inventory problem is to find the specific values of the variables that *minimize* the total cost.

Although finding the variables that give the minimum total cost is the main purpose of the inventory problem, there are other questions of interest. One of these is finding the minimum cost of the system. Not only

---

* These inventory systems occur whenever the unit shortage cost is infinite or when management prescribes that no shortages be allowed.

should the research worker developing decision rules to be used by operating personnel be able to say "This is the rule"; he should also be able to to state ". . . this is the minimum it is going to cost you to use it".

Example 1–1

A customer orders from a manufacturing company shipments of parts at a uniform rate of 2400 parts per year. The company makes the parts on a machine that can produce any number of parts at a time. The cost of setting up the machine for a production run is $42.00. The cost of carrying

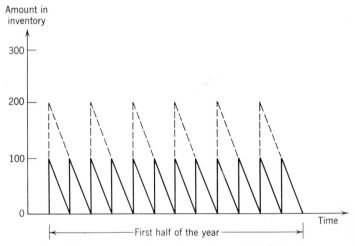

Figure 1–1   Inventory fluctuations of parts in Example 1–1.

inventory is $0.56 per part per year. No shortages are allowed to occur. The manufacturing company's inventory problem is to find how many parts should be produced for each production run.

In this case the controllable variable is the number of parts in a production run. This variable is sometimes referred to as the *lot size*. Let us call this variable q.

If q is 100 parts, the inventory fluctuations during the first half of the year may be represented by the full lines in Figure 1–1.

There will be 50 parts on the average in inventory during the year. Hence the carrying cost will be $50 \times 0.56 = \$28.00$ per year. In addition, if q is 100, then there will be 24 setups during the year. These will cost $24 \times 42.00 = \$1008.00$ per year. Since no shortages occur in this case, the total cost of the inventory system for a lot size of 100 will be $1036.00 per year.

Now suppose that the lot size is 200, that is, q is 200 parts. The inventory fluctuations during the first half of the year may be represented by the

broken lines in Figure 1–1. The total cost per year of the inventory system
in that case will be

$$100 \times 0.56 + 12 \times 42.00 = 56.00 + 504.00 = \$560.00 \text{ per year}$$

Table 1–1 gives the total cost of the inventory system for various values
of the variable q.

TABLE 1–1

*Total Cost per Year of an Inventory System
for Various Lot Sizes*

Lot size q	Average inventory	Carrying cost per year	Average number of setups per year	Replenishing cost per year	Total cost per year
100	50	$28.00	24	$1008.00	$1036.00
200	100	56.00	12	504.00	560.00
300	150	84.00	8	336.00	420.00
400	200	112.00	6	252.00	364.00
500	250	140.00	4.8	201.60	341.60
600	300	168.00	4	168.00	336.00
700	350	196.00	$3\frac{3}{7}$	144.06	340.06
800	400	224.00	3	126.00	350.00
900	450	252.00	$2\frac{2}{3}$	112.14	364.14
1000	500	280.00	2.4	108.00	388.00
1100	550	308.00	$2\frac{2}{11}$	91.56	399.56
1200	600	336.00	2	84.00	420.00

The table indicates that a lot size of 600 parts will minimize the total
cost of the system and this minimum is $336 per year. (Later we shall show
how answers can be obtained without computing the total cost for numerous values of the variable q.)

In this example the two decisions when to replenish and by how much
are answered as follows: replenish whenever inventory reaches a zero level,
and make a lot of 600 parts at that time. These decisions will result in a
minimum yearly total cost of $336.00.

Balancing of Costs

It will be recalled that an inventory system was defined as a system in
which three types of costs were subject to control. An inventory problem
can also be considered a problem of *balancing* these costs. In other words,
an inventory problem can be defined as a problem of balancing the three
types of costs so that their sum will be minimized.

It is interesting to note that in Example 1-1, the minimum cost is obtained when the carrying cost and the replenishing cost are literally balanced—when they are equal. We shall see later that this result is not a coincidence and that it holds for a certain class of inventory systems.

Solution of Inventory Systems

When we speak about the *solution of an inventory system* we mean the solution of the inventory problem. That is, the solution is a set of specific values of the controllable variables that minimize the total cost of the inventory system. In some cases specific values cannot be obtained because of the general nature of the problem studied or because of some other reasons. In these cases the solution is given by a set of decision rules. The rules specify how the exact values of the controllable variables can be obtained. We refer to these rules as the *optimal decision rules*. The word "optimal" is added as a reminder that the inventory problem and its solution are concerned with an optimization process. In our inventory systems this process is a minimization process, but rather than using the phrase "minimum decision rules," which may have several connotations, we prefer the phrase "optimal decision rules."

INVENTORY POLICIES

1-2 It will be recalled that the decisions pertaining to an inventory problem deal with two questions, "When?" and "How much?" The first question is usually answered in one of two ways:

1. Inventory should be replenished when the amount in inventory is equal to or below s_o quantity units.*

2. Inventory should be replenished every t_o time units.

The second question is also usually answered in one of two ways:

1. The quantity to be ordered is q_o quantity units.

2. A quantity should be ordered so that the amount in inventory is brought to a level of S_o quantity units.

The quantities s, t, q, and S will be used extensively in this book. They will also be referred to as the reorder point, scheduling period, lot size, and order level, respectively.

When the time interval between placing of an order and its addition to inventory is significant, the reorder point will be designated by z. In this case an order is placed when the amount on hand *and* on order is equal to or below z. The order level is then designated by Z. The quantity ordered will raise the amount on hand and on order to the level Z. The interval

---

* The subscript o indicates that s_o is an optimal quantity.

between placing an order and its addition to inventory will be referred to as *leadtime*. Thus in systems with zero leadtime we use the quantities s and S, and in systems with non-zero leadtime* we use the quantities z and Z.

An inventory system in which we attempt to find s and q will be called an inventory system with an (s, q) *inventory policy*. Similarly, we can define a (t, S) *policy*, an (s, S) *policy*, and a (t, q) *policy*.**

In systems with non-zero leadtime the corresponding policies are (z, q), (t, Z), and (z, Z),

In certain inventory systems one of the two variables in the inventory policy may be prescribed in some manner. For example, consider the system described by Example 1–1. This system may be viewed as a system with an (s, q) policy. However, since no shortages were allowed in that system, the reorder point was taken to be $s = 0$. Thus only q was controllable, and on this basis it was found that $q_o = 600$ parts.

To indicate that one of the variables in a policy is prescribed in some manner we use the subscript p. Thus we speak about such policies as $(s_p, q) (t_p, Z)$, etc.

In most applications we shall find that systems with prescribed reorder points or order levels will be type $(1, 3)$ systems whereas systems with prescribed lot sizes or scheduling periods will be type $(1, 2)$ systems. Systems in which neither of the policy variables is prescribed will be type $(1, 2, 3)$ systems.

The policies discussed thus far by no means exhaust all possible policies applicable to inventory systems. Several other policies will also be discussed in the appropriate sections in this book, and many more are described in the vast literature on inventory systems.

ANALYSIS OF INVENTORY SYSTEMS

1–3 What method should be used to find the solution of an inventory system? In Example 1–1, the problem was to find the optimal lot size. In Table 1–1 we listed 12 alternative lot sizes and found the total cost of the system for each alternative. We noticed that when $q = 600$ the total cost was least, and we thus concluded that the optimal lot size should be 600. This method of approach, though suitable in some instances, is generally not the best method for finding the optimal lot size (a) because it does not insure that the best alternative is actually included in the list of alternatives and (b) because it is lengthy and time consuming.

---

* Systems with zero leadtime will also be referred to as systems without leadtime. Similarly, systems with non-zero leadtime will be referred to as systems with leadtime.

** But see problem 1-5(5).

Many inventory systems can be solved by another method that is generally more effective: a mathematical model describing the system is obtained and then optimal decision rules are derived from the model.

A *model* is a representation of a system under study. A mathematical model is one in which the system is represented by symbols that can be manipulated by using mathematical rules.

Consider, for example, the inventory system in Example 1-1. If the lot size is q and the annual total cost of the system is C, the mathematical model of this system is

$$C = \frac{q}{2} \times 0.56 + \frac{2400}{q} \times 42.00 = 0.28q + \frac{100800.00}{q} \qquad (1)$$

The first term on the right side of equation (1) represents the carrying cost of the system per year. The second term represents the replenishing cost per year. The shortage cost is zero in this system. Thus equation (1) essentially gives the three types of costs of the inventory system, in symbolic terms. Here the controllable variable and the total cost C per year can be manipulated mathematically. That is, by the use of mathematical techniques it is possible to find what value of q will give the minimum total cost per year. The techniques of analytical geometry and calculus are useful for this purpose.

Using analytic geometry we plot the graph of the curve $C = 0.28q + 100,800/q$ as shown in Figure 1-3.

From the graph we find by inspection that the optimal lot size is 600 parts and that the minimum total cost is \$336 per year. Actually there is almost no difference between using this method of solution and that employed in the derivation of Table 1-1.

Using the calculus ($dC/dq = 0$ etc.*) we obtain the following results:

$$q_o = \sqrt{100800.00/0.28} = 600 \text{ parts}$$

$$C_o = 2\sqrt{0.28 \times 100800.00} = \$336 \text{ per year}$$

Most of the models to be discussed in this book are of the form

$$C = C_1 + C_2 + C_3 \qquad (2)$$

where C_1 designates the carrying cost per time unit, C_2 the shortage cost per time unit, C_3 the replenishing cost per time unit, and C the total cost per time unit. Generally each cost will be a function of one or more controllable variables (as q in Example 1-1) and of some *parameters* of the system (as 2400 parts, \$0.56, \$42.00 in the Example 1-1).

* For the detailed derivation see Section 3-1.

The primary purpose of the models will be to obtain solutions of inventory systems. That is, (1) to develop optimal decision rules and (2) to determine minimum total costs. They will also be used (3) to analyze the sensitivity of results, and (4) to compare different inventory policies.

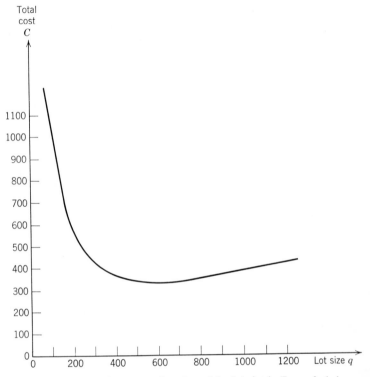

Figure 1–3   Total cost as a function of the lot size in Example 1–1.

Properties of Inventory Systems

In order to develop a model of an inventory system it is first necessary to know the *properties* of the system.

In Example 1–1 a customer orders shipments at a uniform rate. "A uniform rate" is a property of the system. Systems in which the rate of shipments is not uniform may have different optimal decision rules as compared with optimal decision rules in systems with uniform rate. In Example 1–1 the customer orders 2400 parts per year. There is no indication that he is expected to order 2400 parts. If there were such an indication it would mean that he might possibly order other quantities or perhaps nothing at all. Whether customer demands are known exactly or whether an expectation is involved is another property of an inventory system. Similarly, the fact that no shortages are allowed to occur, that the cost of carrying inventories is $0.56 per part per year, and that the setup cost is $42.00, are all properties of the system.

The knowledge of the properties of a system is essential for obtaining a model that represents the system under study. Omitting properties, or making wrong assumptions about properties, will usually lead to incorrect decision rules. It should be mentioned, though, that correct (optimal) decision rules are sometimes obtained although wrong assumptions are made about a system. Similarly, the cost difference between the incorrect and correct decision rules may sometimes be rather insignificant. Only a knowledge of the properties of a system will determine whether the decision rules are correct and whether the cost difference between correct and incorrect rules is significant.

Analysis of Inventory Systems

An *analysis* of an inventory system consists of the following steps: (1) determination of the properties of the system, (2) formulation of the inventory problem, (3) development of a model of the system, (4) derivation of a solution of the system. These steps will be followed in the analysis of most of the systems presented in this book. They are also recommended for use in the analysis of inventory systems occurring in practice. In actual applications, however, this order of analysis need not be strictly adhered to. Frequently, in formulating the inventory problem, for example, it is necessary to redetermine the properties of the system. Or, after deriving a solution, the inventory problem may have to be reformulated. However, the student or practitioner will find the preceding order satisfactory for the analysis of most inventory systems. In the first step he acquaints himself with the subject matter and finds out as much as possible about the inventory system. In the second step he decides precisely what the problem is and he identifies the variables that are subject to control. In the third he prepares the means to answer the problem by mathematically relating the controllable variables and the total cost of the system. In the fourth step he finds the optimal values of the variables and the minimum total cost of the inventory system.

SELECTION OF SYSTEMS FOR ANALYSIS

1–4 Selecting inventory systems for analysis is not a simple problem. When the properties of inventory systems in general are studied, we recognize immediately that there are an infinite number of different systems. Which are the systems that deserve analysis?

Several approaches to the selection of inventory systems for analysis are possible. We may attempt to select the most general inventory system, analyze it in detail, and hope to be able to apply the results to any specific inventory system. A second approach is the case study approach. The users of this approach select and analyze specific inventory systems and suggest that other inventory systems can be analyzed in a similar way. Still another approach is possible. Relatively simple inventory systems are analyzed first, and then more and more complex systems. We have found the third approach the most suitable. It is certainly the most suitable as an introduction to the subject. And it is equally good as a basis of research work. It provides the "building blocks" on which the analysis of any system can be based.

Brief Historical Review

The earliest known analysis of an inventory system was by F. W. Harris in 1915 (Raymond [49], p. 121). Harris is assumed to be the person who first published the classical lot size formula

$$q_o = \sqrt{2rc_3/c_1} \tag{1}$$

where q_o is the optimal lot size, r is the rate of demand per time unit, c_1 is the cost of carrying one unit in inventory per time unit, and c_3 is the cost of replenishing inventory. In the past this formula has had more applications than any other single result obtained from the analysis of inventory systems.

The system for which this formula holds is a very special system. The precise rate of demand must be known, no shortages are allowed to occur, leadtime is assumed to be insignificant, etc. The formula should therefore be used only for systems in which these assumptions hold; otherwise it may not give the minimum cost of the system.

Researchers have recognized the shortcomings of Harris's formula for quite some time. Benjamin Cooper in 1926 analyzed an inventory system in which the rate of production was considered. (In Harris's system the rate of production was assumed to be infinitely higher than the rate of demand.) In 1928 Thornton C. Fry studied an inventory system in which requirements were not known precisely. He showed now the theory of probability can be used to solve some inventory problems. The first attempt to deal with a large variety of inventory systems and to present the beginning of a theory of inventory systems was made by Fairfreld E. Raymond in his *Quantity and Economy in Manufacture* published in 1931.

Interest in the study of inventory systems has increased since World War II, and numerous publications have been devoted solely to this subject. An excellent review of the systems that were studied until 1951 is given by

Whitin in *The Theory of Inventory Management*, published in 1953. Whitin's bibliography contains 180 entries and covers the period from 1923 to 1951. (A new edition, published in 1957, has 43 additional bibliographic entries which cover publications up to 1956.)

The publication of the paper "Optimal Inventory Policy" by Arrow, Harris, and Marschak in 1951 marks the beginning of what may be called the modern analysis of inventory systems. This paper constitutes a considerable advance in the study of inventory systems and has influenced numerous research workers in their approach to inventory systems. In the conclusion of their paper, the authors outline the general nature of other systems that should be studied.

An attempt to analyze the general systems proposed by Arrow, Harris, and Marschak was made by Dvoretsky, Kiefer, and Wolfowitz in their two papers on "The Inventory Problem" which were published in 1952. In these papers very powerful mathematical and statistical tools were employed, and the systems studied were of a very general nature.

Since 1952 more and more work has been devoted to inventory systems. Most of this work has been carried out by operations researchers. Many articles on the subject now appear regularly in *Operations Research, Management Science, Journal of Industrial Engineers, Naval Research Logistics Quarterly*, and many other journals.

The references and bibliography at the end of the book include reviews, books, and articles pertaining to inventory systems which have appeared in recent years.

1–5 PROBLEMS

1. What are the definitions of such terms as inventory system, inventory problem, inventory control, inventory process, given by the following authors:
    (a) Arrow, Harris, and Marschak in 1951 [3]
    (b) Dvoretzky, Kiefer, and Wolfowitz in 1952 [15]
    (c) Whitin in 1953 [55]
    (b) Simon and Holt in 1954 [52]
    (e) Whitin in 1954 [56]
    (f) Ackoff in 1956 [1]
    (g) Morse in 1958 [35]
    (h) Arrow, Karlin, and Scarf in 1958 [4]
    (i) Magee in 1958 [31]
    (j) Holt, Modigliani, Muth, and Simon in 1960 [27]
    (k) Fetter and Dallack in 1961 [18]
    (l) Hanssmann in 1962 [24]
    (m) Buchan and Koenigsberg in 1963 [13]
    (n) Hadley and Whitin in 1963 [23]

2. Indicate which of the following systems associated with a university may be considered as inventory systems:
    (a) Waiting lines at the cafeteria.
    (b) Parking facilities on the campus.
    (c) The enrollment, training, and graduation of undergraduate students.
    (d) Acquiring and disposing of books at the library.
    (e) Scheduling of courses by days and hours of the week and by rooms.
    (f) Stocking (paper, pencils, etc.) in the bookstore.
    (g) Ordering fuel for heating the campus buildings.
For each system considered an inventory system state the inventory problem and indicate the appropriate costs (or other measures) which are involved and which correspond to the carrying cost, the shortage cost, and the replenishing cost.

3. Table 1-5 and Figure 1-5 describe the amounts in inventory of a product during one year. The policy during this year was to order every month a

TABLE 1-5

Amounts in Inventory (Problem 3)

Day	Order quantity	Demand on day	On hand at end of day
Dec. 16	–	50	150
Jan. 1	50	0	200
Jan. 16	–	50	150
Feb. 1	50	150	50
Feb. 14	–	150	−100
Mar. 1	300	50	150
Mar. 16	–	200	−50
Apr. 1	250	150	50
Apr. 15	–	150	−100
May 1	300	50	150
May 16	–	50	100
June 1	100	250	−50
June 15	–	100	−150
July 1	350	0	200
July 16	–	50	150
Aug. 1	50	100	100
Aug. 16	–	50	50
Sept. 1	150	0	200
Sept. 15	–	0	200
Oct. 1	0	50	150
Oct. 16	–	250	−100
Nov. 1	300	0	200
Nov. 15	–	0	200
Dec. 1	0	0	200
Dec. 16	–	50	150
Jan. 1	50	100	100

quantity that would raise the inventory to a level of S = 200 lb. Leadtime was insignificant. Demand for the product occurred at the beginning and at the middle of each month. Assume that the carrying cost was $0.10 per pound per month, the shortage cost was $0.50 per pound per month, and the ordering cost was $25.00 per order (this cost was incurred for every order even when the order quantity was zero).

(a) What are the three types of costs of the inventory system during the period January 1 to December 31?

(b) What are the costs if S is not 200 lb but 250 lb? 300 lb? 350 lb?

(c) What are the costs if the policy is not to order every month but every 2 months and S = 300 lb? 350 lb? 400 lb?

(d) What are the costs if the policy is to order every 3 months and S = 400 lb? 450 lb? 500 lb?

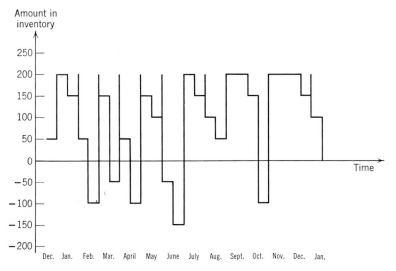

Figure 1–5   Amounts in inventory in the system of problem 1–5(3).

4. How would you classify the inventory policy in Example 1–0?
5. Show that the inventory policy (t, q) does not fully specify all controllable variables in an inventory system.
6. Can the inventory policy in Example 1–1 be considered an (s, S) policy? A (t, S) policy? A (t, q) policy?
7. Discuss the relations between inventory systems and queueing systems? In particular compare carrying costs with cost of idle facilities and shortage costs with costs associated with queues. What are the controllable variables in queueing systems?
8. The problems associated with hiring, training, and employing airline stewardesses are sometimes classified as inventory problems. Can this be justified?

9. In Example 1–0 assume that the demands are known in advance and that they repeat from year to year. Can you suggest an optimal ordering policy? (Note, for example, that in Case II, if the quantities ordered are 30, 50, 50, 0 70, and 40 the total cost of the system is only $76.00, a considerable reduction as compared to the costs in Table 1–0d.)

10. In Example 1–1 assume that leadtime is 2 months and that a (z, q) policy is used. What are the optimal z_o, q_o? What is the solution if leadtime is 7 months?

11. Classify the inventory policy of a housewife shopping for food in a supermarket.

12. The definition of an inventory system given in Section 1–0 may seem rather restrictive. Attempt a broader definition. Indicate some of the pertinent inventory problems under your new definition.

Chapter 2

Properties
of Inventory Systems

2-0 For an inventory system to be analyzed, its properties must be established. This chapter deals with the identification of the various components and properties of inventory systems.

Four components are recognized for every system: demands, replenishments, costs, and constraints. Briefly stated, demands are what is taken out of inventory; replenishments are what is put in; costs are the pertinent measures associated with positive and negative* inventories (the carrying and shortage costs) and with raising the level of inventories (the replenishing costs); and constraints are various administrative, physical, and other factors that place limitations (constraints) on demands, replenishments, and costs.

The properties discussed in this chapter should not be regarded as an exhaustive list of the possible properties of inventory systems—to prepare such a list would be impossible. Instead, the properties listed should be regarded only as illustrations.

DEMAND PROPERTIES

2-1 Demand properties will be discussed before other components of inventory systems because they are the most important component in the properties of an inventory system. Inventories are kept so that demands may be met, orders filled, requirements satisfied. Inventory problems exist only because there are demands; otherwise, we have no inventory problems.

---

* Positive inventory is also referred to as overage, surplus, etc. Negative inventory is also referred to as shortage, stockout, etc.

Generally, demands cannot be controlled directly, and in many cases they cannot be controlled even indirectly. They usually depend on decisions of people outside the organization which has the inventory problem. Although demands themselves are generally not controllable, their properties may be studied. When do customers place their orders? How much do they require? Is demand higher at the beginning of the month or at the end of the month? Do we have accurate information on future requirements, or do we have to estimate average demands and ranges of demand? All these properties are significant, and they affect the solutions of inventory systems.

Demand Size

The quantity required to satisfy the demand for inventory will be called the demand size. The size may be 20.3 lb of some chemical, or 531 nails, or 37 automobiles, etc. We denote the size by x. The dimension of x is thus the quantity dimension. This can be expressed as

$$[x] = [Q] \tag{1}$$

where the brackets refer to dimension and Q refers to quantity.*

In Example 1–0 demands occur at the beginning of each month. The demand size x in pounds has the values 10, 20, 20, 30, 20, 30, 0, 0, 40, 30, 20, and 20. In this example the demand size varies from month to month. Since this property of demand size is common to most inventory systems, we denote the size by x to indicate that x may be a variable.

When the demand size is the same from period to period we say that it is constant. Otherwise we refer to it as variable. When we have precise advance information about the demand size we say that it is known. Inventory systems in which the demand size is known will be referred to as *deterministic systems*. Sometimes when the demand size is not known, it is possible to ascertain its *probability distribution*. This distribution will usually be denoted by $P(x)$. Inventory systems with this property will be referred to as *probabilistic systems*.

Probability Distributions

In probabilistic systems $P(x)$ will designate the probability of the occurrence of a demand size x. For short we shall call $P(x)$ the probability distribution of demand. Let x_{min} designate the least possible demand, and let x_{max} designate the maximum demand. Therefore

$$\sum_{x=x_{min}}^{x_{max}} P(x) = 1 \tag{2}$$

* The other dimensions to be used in the book are those of time $[T]$ and cost $[\$]$.

The cumulative distribution of demand will be designated by $F(S)$, that is,

$$F(S) = \sum_{x=x_{min}}^{S} P(x) \tag{3}$$

The average demand size, or average demand, or mean demand, will be designated by $\bar{x}$, that is,

$$\bar{x} = \sum_{x=x_{min}}^{x_{max}} x P(x) \tag{4}$$

An illustration of a probability distribution may be derived from Example 1–0. If we assume that the quantities required in that example are typical of future requirements, that they are random, etc., the probability distribution $P(x)$ and the cumulative distribution $F(x)$ can be given as in Table 2–1.

TABLE 2–1

The Probability Distribution and the Cumulative Distribution of Requirements in Example 1–0

x lb	0	10	20	30	40	50 and over
$P(x)$	2/12	1/12	5/12	3/12	1/12	0
$F(x)$	2/12	3/12	8/12	11/12	1	1

In this case, then, the probability that no demand occurs is 2/12, that there is a demand for 10 lb is 1/12, and so on. The corresponding average monthly demand, by equation (4), is 20 lb.

Judgmental Probabilities

In actual practice, the probability distributions are not known for certain and must be ascertained. An obvious recourse is to rely on historical data. If the decision maker is *certain* that the past distribution of demand will continue into the future, he may use that as $P(x)$. It may also be possible to use the results of a sampling survey if the decision maker feels that a distribution derived from this source adequately represents the future.

Often, possibly most of the time, historical data or marketing research or both will not provide a picture of future demand adequate for the needs of the decision maker. For example, he may be concerned with a new product or with the introduction of a technological change by a competitor. The decision maker may then turn to so-called "judgmental" or "Bayesian" probabilities; methods exist whereby he can develop *his own* probability distribution of future demand based on his own judgment. It is also possible to incorporate into these distributions past data, marketing research, and the judgmental probabilities of his associates. (For further details see [48].)

Although there is still controversy over the use of judgmental probabilities, we can see at once that they represent an attempt to quantify information that the decision maker already has and *should* use, namely, his own past years of experience and the experience of the people who work with him. By formulating judgmental probabilities, it is possible to apply the analytic tools developed in this book; otherwise the decision maker may have to rely on non-scientific methods.

Demand Rate

Demand rate is the demand size per unit time. This rate will be denoted by r. If a demand of size x quantity units occurs over a period of t time units, the demand rate is given by

$$r = x/t \tag{5}$$

The dimension of the demand rate is thus

$$[r] = [Q]/[T] \tag{6}$$

where Q refers to quantity and T refers to time.

In Example 1–1 the customer required 2400 parts per year. This is the demand rate, and we can write $r = 2400$ parts per year. Here the unit quantity is a part and the unit time is a year. The numerical value of the demand rate depends on the units involved. If, for example, the parts come in boxes of 100 parts each, the demand rate can be given as

$r = 2400$ parts per year $= 24$ boxes per year $= 200$ parts per month

$= 2$ boxes per month, etc.

In probabilistic systems we shall use the average rate of demand. Let $\bar{x}(t)$ be the average demand size during some period t. Thereafter average rate of demand is given by

$$r = \bar{x}(t)/t \tag{7}$$

Demand Patterns

If we consider a period of time over which a demand of size x occurs, it is possible to recognize numerous ways by which quantities are taken out of inventory. All x units may be withdrawn at the beginning of the period; they may all be withdrawn at the end of the period; they may be withdrawn uniformly throughout the period; etc. These different ways by which demand occurs during a period will be referred to as demand patterns. Figure 2–1 illustrates five such patterns. In all five patterns there are S quantity units in inventory at the beginning of the period, the length of the period is t time units, and the demand size is x quantity units. Illustrations (i), (ii), (iii), and (iv) can be considered to belong to a general class of patterns which can be represented by

$$Q(T) = S - x\sqrt[n]{T/t} \tag{8}$$

where $Q(T)$ is the amount in inventory at time T

S is the amount in inventory at the beginning of the period (i.e., when $T = 0$)

x is the demand size during the period t

n is the demand-pattern index.

The patterns belonging to this class will be referred to as *power patterns*. Their nature is entirely determined by n, the *pattern index*.

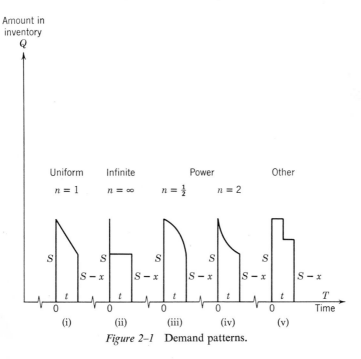

Figure 2-1   Demand patterns.

When $n = 1$, as in Figure 2-1(i), we say that demand is *uniform*. When $n = \infty$, Figure 2-1(ii), we say that demand is *instantaneous*; this pattern occurs when demand is entirely at the beginning of the period. Figures 2-1(iii) and 2-1(iv) illustrate power patterns with $n = \frac{1}{2}$ and $n = 2$ respectively. When n is larger than 1, a larger portion of demand occurs toward the beginning of the period. When n is smaller than 1, a larger portion of demand occurs at the end of the period. When $n = 0$, the entire demand occurs at the end of the period and the quantity S is carried in inventory throughout the period.

REPLENISHING PROPERTIES

2-2　The replenishing properties of inventory systems are generally the properties that can be controlled by decision makers. Generally speaking, replenishing refers to the quantities that are scheduled to be put into inventories, to the time when decisions are made about ordering these quantities, and to the time when they are actually added to stock. It has already been pointed out that the inventory problem is the problem of determining when and how much to order or produce. Thus the inventory problem may also be considered a replenishing problem.

　　In considering the replenishing properties we identify the following elements.

　　1. The *scheduling period* is the length of time between consecutive decisions with respect to replenishments.

　　2. The *replenishment size* is the quantity scheduled for replenishment.

　　3. The *leadtime* is the length of time between scheduling a replenishment and its actual addition to stock.

The scheduling period is not always controllable. The replenishment size is, in general, controllable. Leadtime is generally not subject to control.

Scheduling Period

　　The scheduling period is the length of time, measured in time units, between consecutive decisions with respect to replenishments. The scheduling period will be denoted by t. Dimensionally, then, we have

$$[t] = [T] \tag{1}$$

　　Consider an inventory system in which decisions are made at times $T_i, i = 1, 2, 3, \ldots$. The first scheduling period t_1 is of length $T_2 - T_1$, the second t_2 is of length $T_3 - T_2$, etc. In general, the ith scheduling period t_i is given by

$$t_i = T_{i+1} - T_i \tag{2}$$

These relations may also be illustrated as in Figure 2–2a.

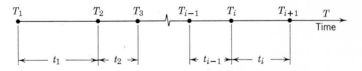

Figure 2–2a　Scheduling periods.

Scheduling periods may be prescribed or they may not be prescribed. When the scheduling periods are prescribed, the decision maker cannot control them. Then the t_i are not variables subject to control, but they are given parameters. The only variables that can be controlled then are the replenishment sizes. When the t_i are prescribed, we usually find that they all have the same magnitude. These equal and prescribed scheduling periods are called the *prescribed scheduling periods* and are denoted by t_p, that is,

$$t_p = t_i = \text{const.} \tag{3}$$

When the scheduling periods are not prescribed, the t_i are variables subject to control. Here again we may have equal scheduling periods. These will be called *constant scheduling periods* and will be denoted by t.

When the scheduling periods are not prescribed and when they are not equal, we say that they vary and we distinguish between varying scheduling periods subject to deterministic control and varying scheduling periods subject to statistical control. Deterministic control occurs when it is possible to decide exactly the future scheduling periods t_i. Statistical control occurs when the scheduling periods cannot be determined precisely, but their statistical distribution can be predicted. An illustration of scheduling periods subject to statistical control is given in Example 2–2a.

Example 2–2a

In an inventory system the demand size x during any week follows the probability distribution: $P(1) = 0.4$, $P(2) = 0.3$, $P(3) = 0.2$, and $P(4) = 0.1$.

The demand pattern during the week is uniform. Whenever the amount in stock at the end of the week is at or below s quantity units, the inventory is immediately replenished so that the amount at the beginning of the following week is S quantity units. That is, this is an inventory system with an (s, S) policy.

Here decisions can be made only with respect to the quantities s and S. The scheduling period t is subject only to statistical control. If it is decided to have s equal to 1 quantity unit and S equal to 3 quantity units, then t can be determined as follows.

Suppose a replenishment has just been scheduled, that is, suppose there are $S = 3$ units in stock. During the coming week there will be a demand of 1, 2, 3, or 4 units. If there is a demand of 2, 3, or 4 units, the inventory at the end of the week will be equal to or below the reorder point $s = 1$, and hence another replenishment will be scheduled. In that case the scheduling period is $t = 1$ week. Since this occurs when demand is 2, 3, or 4 units, it follows that the scheduling period will be 1 week for 60% of the time.

Similarly, when there is a demand for only 1 unit, it can readily be seen that the scheduling period will be 2 weeks long for 40% of the time. Thus 60% of the time the scheduling period will be 1 week long and 40% of the time it will be 2 weeks long. A numerical example given in Table 2–2 further illustrates the point.

TABLE 2–2

Inventory Fluctuations for an (s, S) Policy
When s = 1 and S = 3

Week	Inventory at beginning of week	Demand	Inventory at end of week	Replenishment size	Scheduling period
1	3	2	1	2	1
2	3	1	2	–	
3	2	3	−1	4	2
4	3	2	1	2	1
5	3	2	1	2	1
6	3	4	−1	4	1
7	3	1	2	–	
8	2	1	1	2	2
9	3	4	−1	4	1
10	3	2	1	2	1
11	3	1	2	–	
12	2	3	−1	4	2
13	3	1	2	–	
14	2	2	0	3	2
15	3	3	0	3	1
16	3	2	1	2	1
17	3	1	2	–	
18	2	1	1	2	2
19	3	1	2	–	
20	2	3	−1	4	2

The inventory fluctuations and the scheduling periods corresponding to Table 2–2 can also be illustrated graphically as in Figure 2–2b. In the 20-week period a scheduling period of 1 week occurred 8 times and a scheduling period of 2 weeks occurred 6 times. Thus a period of $t = 1$ occurred with a relative frequency of $\frac{8}{14} = 0.57$, and a period of $t = 2$ occurred with a relative frequency of $\frac{6}{14} = 0.43$. (For an interval longer than 20 weeks, these relative frequencies would have approached the probabilities 0.6 and 0.4, respectively.)

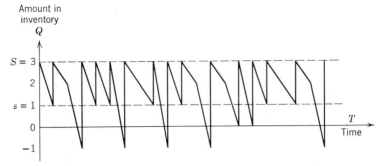

Figure 2–2b   Amounts in inventory in a system with an (s, S) policy.

Leadtime

Leadtime is the length of time between the making of a decision to replenish an item and its actual addition to stock. Leadtime will be denoted by L. Its dimension is that of time, namely

$$[L] = [T] \tag{4}$$

In Figure 2–2c we illustrate two scheduling periods. Decisions about replenishments are made at times T_{i-1}, T_i, T_{i+1}. Consider the decision at time T_i and assume that a quantity q_i is ordered then and that this quantity is actually added to stock at time T_i'. Then, in general,

$$L_i = T_i' - T_i \tag{5}$$

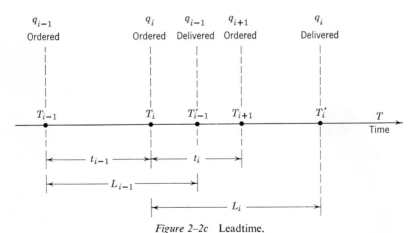

Figure 2–2c   Leadtime.

Leadtime is generally prescribed and thus is not subject to control. It is therefore one of the parameters of the inventory system. When leadtime is very small, we say that it is insignificant and we treat it as if $L = 0$. In practice this can never occur because between the decision made to replenish and the time at which it is effected some time always elapses. However, it is instructive to deal with hypothetical systems in which $L = 0$.

When leadtime is significant we write $L \neq 0$. If leadtime is the same for each decision we say that it is constant. If leadtime is not the same for each decision we say that it varies, and we can speak about the probability distribution of leadtime in the same way that we speak of the probability distribution of demand. An illustration of inventory fluctuations with varying leadtime is given in Example 2–2b.

Example 2–2b

In an inventory system the uniform demand rate r is constant and equal to 10 parts per week. Whenever the amount in inventory reaches a level of $z = 30$ parts, a lot size of $q = 40$ parts is ordered. Leadtime varies and is either 2 or 3 weeks with equal probabilities.

For this system typical inventory fluctuations over a 25-week interval are given in Figure 2–2d. It is interesting to note here that although leadtimes vary, the scheduling periods are constant because the demand rate and the replenishment size are constant, so that $t = q/r = \frac{40}{10} = 4$ weeks.

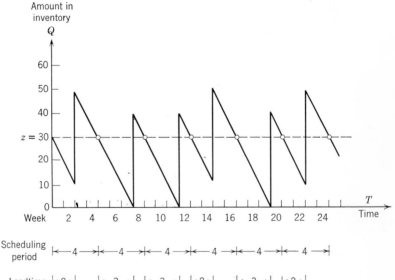

Figure 2–2d   An inventory system with varying leadtimes.

Leadtime generally has considerable effects on the solutions of probabilistic systems. However, when the exact demand and leadtime are known, leadtime will only have a minor effect on the solutions. This point will be discussed presently. In Chapters 9, 11, 14, and 16 we deal in detail with probabilistic systems in which leadtime is significant.

Leadtime in Deterministic Systems

When demand is known and when leadtime is a known constant, the demand during the leadtime period is also known. The decisions in systems with such properties can be derived easily from the decisions in systems with known demands and zero leadtime. This can be explained as follows.

Let system A have deterministic demand and zero leadtime. Let the controllable variables in this system be s_A, t_A, q_A, and S_A, as the case may be. Let system B be an identical system, except that leadtime is significant, say L time units. Let the total demand during L be R quantity units. Since demand is known R is also known. Let the controllable variables in system B be z_B, t_B, q_B, and Z_B.

Now let the variables of the two systems be related as follows

$$z_B = s_A + R$$
$$t_B = t_A$$
$$q_B = q_A \tag{6}$$
$$Z_B = S_A + R$$

A study of the behavior of the two systems will now reveal that the amounts in inventory in both systems are identical. It is true that in system B replenishments are ordered L time units before they are ordered in system A. But the amounts ordered are the same, they are added to the stock at the same time, and the amounts on hand when stock is replenished are also the same.

Thus in deterministic systems we really do not have to worry about leadtime. If leadtime is significant, we analyze the system by first assuming that leadtime is zero. Then the corresponding controllable variables are adjusted using equation (6).

Replenishment Size

In analogy to the demand size we define the replenishment size as the quantity scheduled for replenishment. This quantity will be denoted by q_i. It is scheduled at time T_i, the beginning of the ith scheduling period, and is added to stock at time T_i', as in Figure 2–2c. Dimensionally we have for the replenishment size

$$[q_i] = [Q] \tag{7}$$

Whenever the replenishment size is the same for every scheduling period, we denote it by q and refer to it as the *lot size*. The problem then is to find the *optimal lot size* q_o. A simple illustration of such a problem was given in Example 1–1.

In most systems to be analyzed in this book it is assumed that when a replenishment q_i is ordered this exact amount is delivered and added to stock. However, there are also systems in which the quantity delivered is subject only to *statistical control*. In these systems the amount delivered, q_i', has a probability distribution, one of whose parameters is the replenishment size q_i.

Replenishment Period, Replenishment Rate, and Replenishment Patterns

The replenishment period is the length of time during which the replenishment q is being added to inventory. Let this period be denoted by t'. The *average replenishment rate* p is the ratio of the replenishment size and the replenishment period. That is,

$$p = q/t' \qquad (8)$$

Dimensionally we also have

$$[p] = [Q]/[T] \qquad (9)$$

When the replenishment period is insignificant, we assume that $t' = 0$ and we say that the corresponding rate is infinite (i.e., $p = \infty$). We also say then that replenishment is instantaneous; all replenishments in Figures 1–1, 2–2b, and 2–2d, for example, are instantaneous.

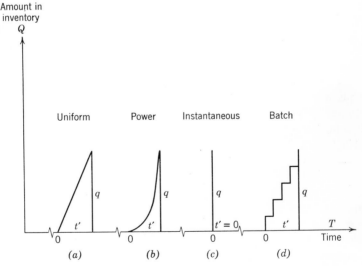

Figure 2–2e Replenishment patterns.

When the replenishment is not instantaneous, we may be interested in the manner in which it is put into inventory. This manner will be referred to as the *replenishment pattern*. Figure 2–2e gives a few illustrations of replenishment patterns.

Replenishment—Demand Interactions

Often the amounts in inventory have to be determined when demand and replenishment occur concurrently.

Figure 2–1 illustrates the amounts in inventory when only demands are considered. Figure 2–2e illustrates the amounts in inventory when only replenishments are considered. Many combinations of simultaneous demands and replenishments are possible, and the amount in inventory will depend on the corresponding patterns.

Example 2–2c

Consider a scheduling period t. At the beginning of this period there are s quantity units in inventory. The demand during the period is x. The demand pattern is uniform. Replenishment begins at the beginning of the period with a uniform pattern at a rate of p quantity units per unit of time and lasts t' units of time. By that time a replenishment of size q has been added to inventory.

The amounts in inventory during the scheduling period are described in Figure 2–2f. If there were no demand during the period t', inventory

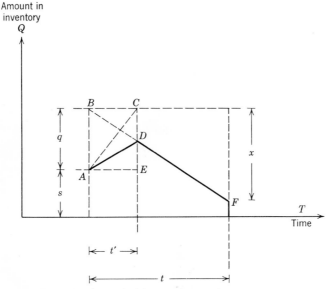

Figure 2–2f Replenishment–demand interaction.

would have increased along line AC at the rate of p. On the other hand, if all the replenishment q were instantaneous, the amount in inventory at the beginning of the period would have been $s + q$ and would have reached the level at B. Then demand would have caused inventories to be along the line BDF, the amounts decreasing at a rate of x/t. If both input and demand occur simultaneously, then during t' inventory will increase at a rate of $p - x/t$ along the line AD. During the remainder of period t it will decrease at a rate x/t along the line DF.

Reorder Point and Reviewing Period

The reorder point is used in inventory systems with (s, q), (s, S), (z, q), and (z, Z) policies (see Section 1–2). It refers in general to a specific amount in inventory. When leadtime is zero the reorder point will be denoted by s; otherwise it will be denoted by z. Dimensionally we have

$$[s] = [z] = [Q] \tag{10}$$

In systems in which a reorder point is used, a replenishment is scheduled whenever the inventory on hand *and* on order is equal to or below the reorder point.

The *reviewing period* is a time period associated with systems in which a reorder point is used. In these systems there is a question when to review the amount of inventory on hand and on order so that a decision may be made whether to order a replenishment. The reviewing period is the time interval between consecutive reviews. Obviously, the scheduling period will always be composed of an integral number of reviewing periods. (In Example 2–2a the reviewing period is 1 week; the scheduling period is sometimes 1 week and sometimes 2 weeks.)

The reviewing period will be denoted by w. Its dimension is the time dimension

$$[w] = [T] \tag{11}$$

For most systems to be analyzed, the reviewing period will be *prescribed* and denoted by w_p. Frequently it will be instructive to analyze systems in which the amounts in inventory are *reviewed continuously*. In such systems, then, $w_p = 0$.

Order Level

The order level is used in inventory systems with (t, S), (s, S), (t, Z), and (z, Z) policies (see Section 1–2). Like the reorder point, the order level also refers to a specific amount in inventory. When leadtime is zero the order level will be denoted by S, otherwise it will be denoted by Z. Its dimension is the quantity dimension

$$[S] = [Z] = [Q] \tag{12}$$

In systems with leadtime in which the order level is used let T be a point in time at the end of a reviewing period, let $Q(T)$ be the amount on hand at time T, and let $P(T)$ be the total amount on order at time T. Then the replenishment size is

$$q = Z - [Q(T) + P(T)] \tag{13}$$

Similarly, when leadtime is zero, then

$$q = S - Q(T) \tag{14}$$

COST PROPERTIES

2-3 An inventory system has been defined as a system in which only the following three types of costs are significant, and in which any two or all three are subject to control: (1) the carrying cost, (2) the shortage cost, and (3) the replenishing cost. To use these costs as measures of the performance of controllable variables of an inventory system, they all have to be computed for the same period of time, generally a year, but any unit of time is equally suitable. The corresponding measures of performance can be defined as follows:

C_1 the carrying cost per unit of time
C_2 the shortage cost per unit of time
C_3 the replenishing cost per unit of time
C the total cost per unit of time $(C_1 + C_2 + C_3)$

The dimension of each of these measures is

$$[C] = [C_1] = [C_2] = [C_3] = [\$]/[T] \tag{1}$$

The properties of an inventory system should enable us to determine the relations between the controllable variables and these measures of performance of the system. The demand and replenishment properties establish the quantities carried in inventory, the amounts short, and the number of replenishments as a function of the controllable variables. Thus, in order to find C_1, C_2, and C_3, we must know something about the unit costs of carrying inventory, of shortage, and of replenishing. These *unit costs* will be denoted by c_1, c_2, and c_3, respectively.

The dimensions of the unit costs differ from system to system. For many systems, however, the unit costs are constant and their dimensions are

$$[c_1] = \frac{[\$]}{[Q][T]} \tag{2}$$

$$[c_2] = \frac{[\$]}{[Q][T]} \tag{3}$$

$$[c_3] = [\$] \tag{4}$$

In these systems, then, the unit cost of carrying inventory is $\$c_1$ per quantity unit per unit of time; the unit cost of incurring a shortage in inventory is $\$c_2$ per quantity unit per unit time; the unit cost of replenishing is $\$c_3$ for each replenishment; and c_1, c_2, and c_3 are constants.

Thus for these systems we also have

$$C_1 = I_1c_1 \tag{5}$$

$$C_2 = I_2c_2 \tag{6}$$

$$C_3 = I_3c_3 \tag{7}$$

where I_1 is the average amount carried in inventory, I_2 is the average shortage in inventory, and I_3 is the average number of replenishments per unit of time. The dimensions of I_1, I_2, and I_3 are thus

$$[I_1] = [I_2] = [Q] \tag{8}$$

$$[I_3] = 1/[T] \tag{9}$$

A numerical example best illustrates how I_1, I_2, I_3, C_1, C_2, C_3, and C can be obtained in a simple inventory system.

Example 2–3

The amounts in inventory in an inventory system are described graphically in Figure 2–3. The behavior of the system during the period T_1 to T_3

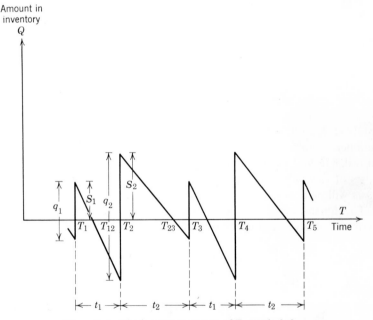

Figure 2–3   The inventory system of Example 2–3.

is assumed to be repeated continuously. The average amount carried during the period from T_1 to T_{12} is $S_1/2$. During the period T_2 to T_{23} it is $S_2/2$. Therefore the average amount carried I_1 is given by

$$I_1 = \frac{(S_1/2)(T_{12} - T_1) + (S_2/2)(T_{23} - T_2)}{t_1 + t_2} \tag{10}$$

Similarly, the average shortage, is given by

$$I_2 = \left[\frac{q_2 - S_2}{2}(T_2 - T_{12}) + \frac{q_1 - S_1}{2}(T_3 - T_{23})\right] \bigg/ (t_1 + t_2) \tag{11}$$

During the period T_1 to T_3 there are two replenishments. Hence the average number of replenishments per unit time is

$$I_3 = \frac{2}{t_1 + t_2} \tag{12}$$

Now if the unit costs c_1, c_2, and c_3 and their dimensions are as in equations (2), (3), and (4) respectively, we have

$$C = C_1 + C_2 + C_3 = c_1 I_1 + c_2 I_2 + c_3 I_3 \tag{13}$$

$$= \left\{ c_1\left[\frac{S_1}{2}(T_{12} - T_1) + \frac{S_2}{2}(T_{23} - T_2)\right] \right.$$

$$\left. + c_2\left[\frac{q_2 - S_2}{2}(T_2 - T_{12}) + \frac{q_1 - S_1}{2}(T_3 - T_{23})\right]2c_3 \right\} \bigg/ (t_1 + t_2)$$

The Unit Carrying Cost

The unit carrying cost usually covers the following cost elements: the costs (1) of money tied up in inventories, (2) of storage, (3) of taxes on inventories, (4) of obsolescence, (5) of insurance of inventories, and other costs.

It is customary to compute this unit cost as a fraction of the cost of the item carried in inventory per unit time. Thus in many systems, if the cost of a unit quantity is b and if the carrying cost fraction is f per unit time, we have

$$c_1 = fb \tag{14}$$

where the dimensions of b and f are

$$[b] = [\$]/[Q] \tag{15}$$

$$[f] = 1/[T] \tag{16}$$

The fraction f, usually referred to as a percentage per year, depends on the nature of the cost elements just given. For many industrial applications its numerical value varies from about 5% to about 25% per year.

The Unit Shortage Cost

This unit cost is usually the most difficult to determine. Some of the costs associated with the unit cost of shortage may include (1) overtime costs, (2) special clerical and administrative costs, (3) loss of specific sales, (4) loss of goodwill, (5) loss of customers, and other costs.

In many inventory systems the cost of shortage depends both on the quantities short and on the duration of time over which shortages exist. For such systems an appropriate unit of shortage is the unit whose dimension is given by equation (3).

However, when the shortage cost is the cost of the loss of specific sales, the unit cost of shortage is the value of lost profit per quantity, say g per unit quantity short. In this case

$$[c_2] = [g] = [\$]/[Q] \tag{17}$$

Equation (6) still holds, but I_2 is now the average number of shortages per unit time, namely

$$[I_2] = [Q]/[T] \tag{18}$$

Thus, if in Example 2–3 the shortage cost is the profit lost, we would have

$$I_2 = \frac{(q_1 - S_1) + (q_2 - S_2)}{t_1 + t_2} \tag{19}$$

and hence

$$C_2 = \frac{g[(q_1 - S_1) + (q_2 - S_2)]}{t_1 + t_2} \tag{20}$$

Many managers do not allow any shortages to occur in the inventory systems under their control. They assume that the unit cost of shortage is infinite. It seems that such a cost is not realistic. These managers believe that the unit shortage cost is relatively high and they therefore endeavor not to have any shortages. In many systems to be discussed in this book we will show how the unit cost of shortage affects optimal solutions of these systems. We will show that although this cost may be very high, an optimal solution may nevertheless require some shortages to occur!

Many managers also state categorically that the unit cost of shortage cannot be measured. It is true that this unit is very difficult to measure. However, this does not mean that the unit does not have some specific value. Decisions affecting inventories are made all the time by managers. Shortages do occur in most inventory systems. If the decisions are good ones (and the managers claim that they are), it is evident that in making the decisions the managers are actually placing a value on the unit cost of shortage. They may not be able to state numerically what this value is, but their decisions imply that such a value exists.

The Unit Replenishment Cost

Two classes of costs must be distinguished in discussing the unit cost of replenishment: (1) costs in which a replenishment refers to ordering of q units from an agency outside the organization studied (the *ordering cost*), and (2) costs in which a replenishment refers to manufacturing of q units within the organization itself (the *setup cost*).

In the first class the costs associated with the unit cost of replenishment may include clerical and administrative costs, transportation costs, unloading costs, and other costs. In the second class the costs associated with the unit cost of replenishment may include labor setup costs, cost of materials used during setup testing, cost of time during which production cannot take place because of setups, and other costs.

The dimension of the unit replenishing cost is usually given by equation (4).

In some systems c_3 is not constant but depends on the replenishment size, for example, when discounts are given (see Section 6–1).

An important consideration in determining the unit cost of replenishment is the number of different items pertaining to one order. Whenever two or more different items may be ordered simultaneously and only one replenishment cost is incurred, the solutions *cannot* be obtained by considering each item individually and solving its inventory system. Only one inventory system exists in such a case, and several items affect the costs of the whole system (see, for example, Sections 3–5, 6–3, and 17–3).

Other Costs

There are numerous costs, in addition to those mentioned thus far, that can be classified into one of the three types of costs of inventory systems. Examples of such costs appear in several sections and problems in this book.

There are many systems in which certain significant costs cannot be considered as inventory costs, however. These systems can therefore not be classified as inventory systems, even though they may include significant inventory costs. For example, in production systems involving utilization of men and machines there are costs associated with maintaining a stable labor force, with allocation of machines to product lines, with replacement of equipment, etc. Although such production systems also have significant carrying, shortage, and replenishing costs, they are not inventory systems. Instead, production systems can be considered as extensions of inventory systems.

The methods of analysis of inventory systems are usually quite helpful in analyzing extensions of inventory systems. However, they may not be sufficient in themselves. For example, analysis of production systems may require the methods of linear programming, queueing theory, sequencing, etc., in addition to the methods of analyzing inventory systems covered in this book.

CONSTRAINTS

2-4 Constraints in inventory systems deal with various properties that in some way place limitations on the components discussed in the previous three sections. These constraints have to be considered in setting up models of inventory systems and in solving them. We consider in turn unit constraints, demand constraints, replenishment constraints, and cost constraints.

Unit Constraints

The kind of mathematical analysis used in solving an inventory system depends to a large extent on whether the *units* involved are *continuous* or *discrete*. Automobiles, for example, are represented by discrete units. We speak of the sale of 3 automobiles, but we do not speak of the sale of 3.7 automobiles. Gasoline, on the other hand, can be represented by continuous units. We can sell 3.7 gallons, or any other amount for that matter, if we so desire.

When demand is in discrete units, the demand size x can take only the values x_{min}, $x_{min} + u$, $x_{min} + 2u$, ..., x_{max}, where u is some basic unit. We can then speak about the probability that a demand of size x will occur. (This we have done in Table 2-1 where the basic unit was $u = 10$ lb and x took the values 0, 10, 20, 30, and 40.)

When demand is in continuous units, x can be any quantity and it is meaningless to speak about the probability of occurrence of x. We can speak only about the probability of x being in some interval. This can be done if the probability density of demand $f(x)$ is known. The probability that the demand is between a and b is $\int_a^b f(x)\, dx$. The cumulative distribution and the average demand, by analogy with equations 2-2(3) and 2-2(4), are

$$F(S) = \int_{x_{min}}^{S} f(x)\, dx \tag{1}$$

and

$$\bar{x} = \int_{x_{min}}^{x_{max}} x f(x)\, dx \tag{2}$$

Unit constraints also apply to the replenishment component of inventory systems. The replenishment size q may be in either discrete units or continuous units. So can the scheduling period t, the reviewing period w, leadtime L, etc.

Demand Constraints

Some constraints associated with demand are the following.

1. *Making up of shortages.* In some systems any shortages accumulated during a period can be made up immediately after a replenishment has occurred at the end of the period. In other systems, for example, when sales are lost, shortages cannot be made up. This property of demand has a significant effect on the shortage cost and hence on the solution of inventory systems.

2. *Negative demand.* When returns by customers are allowed and when they exceed shipments during some period, the total effect is the same as a negative demand. For many systems negative demand does not have an effect on the analysis. Sometimes, though, the analysis is indeed affected if we allow the possibility for the occurrence of negative demands [see, for example, problem 8–5(14)].

3. *Dependent demand structures.* Demand during any period may depend on demand in the previous period(s) and on the amounts in inventory in the previous period(s). Analysis of systems with such dependent demand structures is rather complex [see, for example, problem 8–5(15)]. This is also true of systems in which the demand forecast is an integral part of the inventory system (see, for example, Chapter 12).

Replenishment Constraints

Some constraints associated with replenishments are the following.

1. *Space constraints.* In some systems the amount of space for storing inventories is limited so that the amount in inventory at any time may not exceed some specified amount.

2. *Scheduling and reviewing constraints.* We have already mentioned that scheduling periods and reviewing periods may be prescribed in some systems. Such prescriptions should be considered as constraints.

3. *Inventory levels.* In some systems management may place certain specifications on inventory levels. Section 8–1 provides an illustration of such a system. In that system the inventory level S at the beginning of any scheduling period is required to be A times as much as the average demand during that period, and A is such that no shortages can occur.

4. *Inventory policy.* An inventory policy may be prescribed by management. The researcher may be required to find optimal solutions for this policy, even though less costly solutions exist for other policies. Thus a (t, S) policy may sometimes be prescribed even though an (s, S) policy can be shown to be the better policy. (For details see Chapter 17.)

Cost Constraints

Several cost constraints have already been mentioned. In some systems no shortages are allowed (i.e., $C_2 = 0$), and in others no inventories are carried (i.e., $C_1 = 0$). When the scheduling periods are prescribed, the replenishment costs may be constant and are not then subject to control (i.e., $C_3 = $ constant). The fact that one replenishment cost may be used for one commodity only is another important constraint.

In some systems the probability that shortages occur may be required to be below some specified amount, say 0.05. In other systems the inventory problem may be stated as: "Given a total amount of C per unit time, what should be done to minimize shortages?"

2–5 PROBLEMS

1. Every t units of time a production run of q units is made. The rate of production is p units per unit time. Withdrawals are uniform at a constant rate of r per unit time. Assume that production is started whenever the inventory reaches a level of s units.
   Describe graphically the amounts in inventory when
      (a) s refers to a positive quantity (no shortages occur),
      (b) s refers to a negative quantity (inventories are carried and shortages occur).
   In the graphs indicate all appropriate magnitudes as functions of t, q, p, and r.

2. The cost of carrying Q units in inventory is $c(Q)$ per unit time, where

$$c(Q) = \begin{cases} 3Q & \text{when} \quad Q \geq 0 \\ 2Q^2 & \text{when} \quad Q < 0 \end{cases} \tag{1}$$

   Find C_1 and C_2 for cases (a), (b), (d), (h), and (i) in Figure 2–5.

3. The demands in pounds for the coming year are known to be as in Table 2–5a.
   At the beginning of week 1 there are 15 lb in inventory. During any week the demand has a uniform pattern. The unit cost parameters are $c_1 = \$1.00$ per pound per week, $c_2 = \$10.00$ per pound per week, $c_3 = \$30.00$ per order.

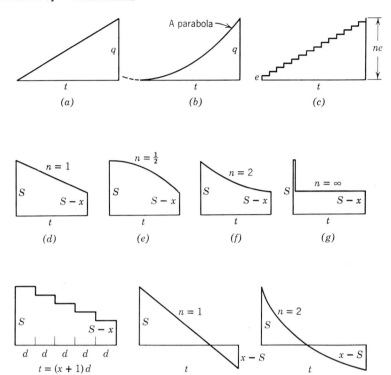

Figure 2-5 Amounts in inventory for various demand and replenishment patterns.

TABLE 2-5a
Weekly Demands

Week	Demand	Week	Demand	Week	Demand	Week	Demand
1	0	14	4	27	0	40	3
2	1	15	4	28	1	41	1
3	2	16	1	29	1	42	1
4	2	17	0	30	2	43	1
5	1	18	3	31	3	44	2
6	0	19	1	32	2	45	2
7	1	20	2	33	0	46	3
8	5	21	1	34	4	47	0
9	3	22	0	35	2	48	1
10	1	23	3	36	1	49	1
11	4	24	1	37	0	50	1
12	1	25	1	38	2	51	1
13	0	26	0	39	0	52	3

Describe graphically the amounts in inventory and the corresponding annual carrying, shortage, and replenishing costs for each of the following policies.

(a) An (s, q) policy, when $w_p = 0$ weeks, $s = 0$ lb, $q = 15$ lb.

(b) A (t, S) policy, when $t = 4$ weeks, $S = 15$ lb;

(c) An (s, S) policy, when $w_p = 1$ week, $s = 0$ lb, $S = 15$ lb.

(d) A (z, q) policy, when $w_p = 1$ week, $z = 6$ lb, $q = 14$ lb, $L = 3$ weeks.

4. Show that the length of the reviewing period is irrelevant in systems in which demand is known.

5. In addition to the three types of costs of inventory systems, the unit cost of reviewing in a system is c_4 and its dimension is $[c_4] = [\$]$.
In this system there is the question of balancing four costs: C_1, C_2, C_3, C_4. What variables are subject to control in this system?

6. Find the probability distribution of the scheduling period in Example 2–2a for

(a) $s = 1$, $S = 4$,

(b) $s = 1$, $S = 5$,

(c) $s = 1$, $S = 6$.

7. Find the average amounts in inventory I_1 and the average shortage I_2 during the period t in Figure 2–5. For cases (d) to (g) and (i) and (j), assume the relation given by equation 2–1 (8).

8. Describe the inventory fluctuations in the six systems with leadtime given in Table 2–5b. Indicate with broken lines the amounts on hand and on order, and with full lines indicate the amounts on hand.

TABLE 2–5b

System	Type	Policy	Demand	Reviewing period	Leadtime
A	1, 2, 3	z, Z	Constant	Irrelevant	L
B	1, 2	t, Z	Variable	t	$2t$
C	1, 3	t, Z	Variable	t	$2t$
D	1, 3	z, q	Variable	w	$3w$
E	1, 2, 3	z, Z	Variable	0	L
F	1, 2, 3	z, Z	Constant	0	Variable

9. What are the properties of an inventory system associated with the stocking of candy bars in a vending machine?

10. (a) Under what conditions are the (s, q) and (s, S) policies identical?

(b) Under what conditions are the (s, q), (t, S), and (s, S) policies identical?

Part 2

DETERMINISTIC SYSTEMS

Each of the following five chapters deals with inventory systems in which the demand is known. In Chapters 3, 4, 5, and 6 the demand is constant but in Chapter 7 it varies. In Section 7–1 demand is increasing at a known constant rate. In Section 7–2 demand varies from period to period but the precise demands are known in advance.

In reality we rarely encounter systems in which demand is known. However, much insight is gained through the analysis of such systems. They serve as starting points for analysis of probabilistic systems. They illustrate the methods used in developing models of inventory systems and their solution, and they can be used as standards against which the solutions of probabilistic systems can be compared.

In all the systems in this part leadtime is zero. It is relatively quite easy to extend the results to systems with significant leadtime. Since demand is known, the remarks of Section 2–2 apply. In particular, the relations in equations 2–2(6) can be used to derive solutions of deterministic systems with significant leadtime.

Chapter 3

Lot-Size Systems

3–0 Lot-size systems are deterministic systems with constant demands and with an (s_p, q) policy in which $s_p = 0$. They are $(1, 3)$ type systems, that is, carrying costs are balanced against replenishing costs.

All cost equations in lot-size systems are therefore of the form

$$C(q) = C_1(q) + C_3(q) \tag{1}$$

Several lot-size systems are analyzed in following sections. In Section 3–1 the classical* lot-size system is described. For this system we reserve the designation "*the* lot-size system." (In contrast, every other lot-size system will be referred to as "*a* lot-size system.") We solve the system both for continuous units and discrete units. In Section 3–2 we describe the type of analysis that can be made on the sensitivity of an inventory system. For the lot-size system we determine the effect of deviating from the optimal solution and the effect of using estimates rather than the true values of some of the parameters.

In Sections 3–3, 3–4, and 3–5 we analyze several lot-size systems, each of which has a property somewhat different from the lot-size system. In the lot-size system the demand pattern is uniform. In Section 3–3 a more general demand pattern is considered. In the lot-size system the replenishment rate p is infinite; in Section 3–4 the rate may be any amount p. Finally, in the lot-size system only one item is dealt with; in Section 3–5 several items have a common replenishment cost.

* See Section 1–4 and the comments on equation 1–4(1).

Lot-size systems may have many other properties. Some of these are explored in the problems at the end of the chapter. Some of the properties relating to special cost structures are dealt with in Chapter 6.

THE LOT-SIZE SYSTEM

3-1   The inventory fluctuations in *the* lot-size system are illustrated by Figure 3-1a.

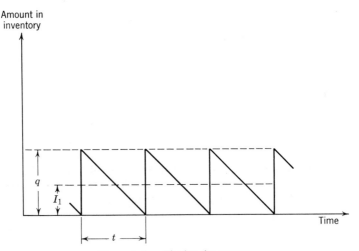

Figure 3-1a   The lot-size system.

In this system

1. Demand is deterministic at a constant rate of r quantity units per unit time.

2. Replenishments are made whenever the inventory reaches the prescribed zero level so that no shortages can occur.

3. The replenishment size is constant; the lot size is q.

4. The replenishment rate is infinite.

5. Leadtime is zero.*

6. The unit carrying cost c_1 is a constant whose dimension is $[\$]/([Q][T])$.

7. The unit replenishing cost c_3 is a constant whose dimension is $[\$]$.

On the basis of these properties it follows immediately that the scheduling period is given by

$$t = \frac{q}{r} \tag{1}$$

* However, see the pertinent comments in Section 2-2 for extending the results to systems with significant leadtime.

The average amount carried in inventory is $I_1 = q/2$, and the average number of replenishments per unit time is $I_3 = 1/t = r/q$. Hence the total-cost equation of the system is

$$C(q) = \frac{c_1 q}{2} + \frac{c_3 r}{q} \tag{2}$$

Graphically, this cost equation can be described as in Figure 3-1b.

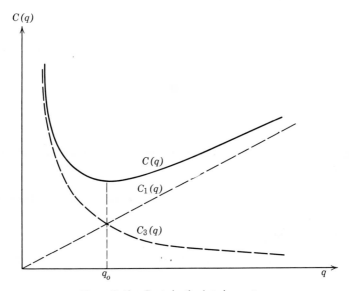

Figure 3-1b   Costs in the lot-size system.

To find the optimal lot size we differentiate $C(q)$ with respect to q giving

$$\frac{dC(q)}{dq} = \frac{c_1}{2} - \frac{c_3 r}{q^2} \tag{3}$$

Now solving for the optimal lot size q_o it is necessary that

$$\frac{c_1}{2} - \frac{c_3 r}{q_o^{\,2}} = 0 \tag{4}$$

or that

$$q_o = \sqrt{2 r c_3 / c_1} \tag{5}$$

Equation (5) is also a sufficient condition since $d^2C/dq^2 = 2c_3 r/q^3$, and this is positive for the lot size of this equation.

Substituting the optimal lot size in the total-cost equation (2) gives the minimum cost of the system:

$$C_o = \frac{c_1\sqrt{2rc_3/c_1}}{2} + \frac{c_3 r}{\sqrt{2rc_3/c_1}} \tag{6}$$

$$= \frac{\sqrt{2rc_1c_3}}{2} + \frac{\sqrt{2rc_1c_3}}{2} = \sqrt{2rc_1c_3}$$

The results in equations (5) and (6) thus constitute the solution of the lot-size system.

Cost Equations of the Form $C(y) = ay + b/y$

Cost equations similar to equation (2) appear in the analysis of many inventory systems. Their general form can be expressed as

$$C(y) = A(y) + B(y) = ay + b/y \tag{7}$$

where y is the controllable variable and where a and b are given constants. In the special case of the lot-size system $A(y)$ is the inventory carrying cost per time unit and $B(y)$ is the replenishing cost per time unit.

Let y_o be the value of y that minimizes C. Let the values of $A(y_o)$, $B(y_o)$, and $C(y_o)$ be designated respectively by A_o, B_o, and C_o. It can be readily verified (using the methods given earlier in this section) that

$$y_o = \sqrt{b/a} \tag{8}$$

$$A_o = B_o = \sqrt{ab} \tag{9}$$

$$C_o = \sqrt{4ab} \tag{10}$$

We will use these results whenever equations of the form of equation (7) are encountered.

In passing, we should note the result in equation (9). This result indicates that in cost equations of the form of equation (7) the costs $A(y)$ and $B(y)$ for the optimal y are equal. A graphical interpretation of this result can be seen in Figure 3–1b. The optimal lot size is the lot size for which $C_1(q)$ and $C_3(q)$ are equal.*

Discrete Units

When the lot size q is restricted to discrete units, we cannot use the differential calculus to find q_o as we did earlier in this section. The following procedure may then be adopted.

---

* In this connection see the comments on balancing of costs in Section 1–1.

Let the lot size q be constrained to the values u, $2u$, $3u$, etc. The necessary conditions for q_o to be the optimal lot size are

$$C(q_o) \leq C(q_o + u) \tag{11}$$

$$C(q_o) \leq C(q_o - u) \tag{12}$$

From equations (2) and (11) we obtain

$$\frac{c_1 q_o}{2} + \frac{c_3 r}{q_o} \leq \frac{c_1(q_o + u)}{2} + \frac{c_3 r}{q_o + u} \tag{13}$$

Rearranging equation (13) leads to the result

$$\frac{2rc_3}{c_1} \leq q_o(q_o + u) \tag{14}$$

Similarly equations (2) and (12) lead to

$$(q_o - u)q_o \leq \frac{2rc_3}{c_1} \tag{15}$$

Hence the necessary conditions for the optimal lot size when q is restricted to u, $2u$, $3u$, etc., are

$$q_o(q_o - u) \leq \frac{2rc_3}{c_1} \leq q_o(q_o + u) \tag{16}$$

It can be readily shown that these are also sufficient conditions [see problem 3–6(14)]. Therefore equation (16) constitutes the desired solution.

Example 3–1

Demand in an inventory system is at a constant and uniform rate of 2400 lb per year. The carrying cost is $5 per pound per year. No shortages are allowed. The replenishing cost is $22 per order. The lot size can be only in 100-lb units. What is the optimal lot size and what is the minimum cost of the system?

This system is the lot-size system with constraints on the lot size. Here $r = 2400$ lb per year, $c_1 = \$5$ per pound per year, $c_3 = \$22$, and $u = 100$ lb.

Hence, by equation (16), $(q_o - 100)q_o \leq 21{,}120 \leq q_o(q_o + 100)$. Therefore $q_o = 200$ lb. Substituting this value in equation (2) gives the minimum cost of $C_o = \$764$ per year.

It is interesting to compare this system with a similar one in which no constraints are imposed on the lot size. In the latter, using equations (5) and (6) we obtain $q_o = 145$ lb and $C_o = \$727/\text{year}$. Thus, because of the constraints, the cost of operating the inventory system is increased by about 5%.

SENSITIVITY OF THE LOT-SIZE SYSTEM

3–2 The total cost of the lot-size system as a function of the controllable variable q has been seen to be, by equation 3–1(2),

$$C(q) = c_1 q / 2 + c_3 r / q \tag{1}$$

The optimal solution of the system, by equation 3–1(5), is

$$q_o = \sqrt{2 c_3 r / c_1} \tag{2}$$

and the corresponding minimum total cost of the system, by equation 3–1(6), is

$$C_o = \sqrt{2 c_1 c_3 r} \tag{3}$$

Suppose now that instead of the optimal q_o in equation (2) the decision maker used another lot size q', which is related to q_o by

$$q' = b q_o \qquad b > 0 \tag{4}$$

Let C' designate the total cost of the system when q' is used. Let the ratio C'/C_o be used as a *measure of sensitivity*.

TABLE 3–2a
Sensitivity of the Lot-Size System,
Values of C'/C_o When $q' = b q_o$

b	0.5	0.8	0.9	1.0	1.1	1.2	1.5	2.0	3.0
C'/C_o	1.250	1.025	1.006	1.000	1.005	1.017	1.083	1.250	1.667

Substituting q' of equation (4) into equation (1) and dividing by the corresponding terms of equation (3) eventually leads to

$$C'/C_o = (1 + b^2)/(2b) \tag{5}$$

Thus the measure of sensitivity of the lot-size system is only a function of b and does not depend on r, c_3, and c_1.

Some numerical values of C'/C_o for various values of b are given in Table 3–2a. According to this table, for example, if $q_o = 600$ tons but the lot size chosen is half as much, that is, $q' = 300$ tons, or $b = 0.5$, the additional cost as a result of deviating from the optimal solution is 25% of the minimum cost.

Effects of Estimates

There are several circumstances that can lead to the deviation from the optimal lot size as in equation (4). One such possibility arises when the decision maker uses estimates for the parameters of the system and these differ from the true values.

Let the estimated values of the parameters in the lot-size system be r', c_1', c_3' and let the true values be r, c_1, c_3. The lot size chosen will be

$$q' = \sqrt{2c_3'r'/c_1'}$$

Then, by equations (2), (4), and (6), we obtain

$$b = \frac{\sqrt{2c_3'r'/c_1'}}{\sqrt{2c_3r/c_1}} = \sqrt{(c_3'/c_3)(r'/r)/(c_1'/c_1)} \tag{7}$$

Some numerical values of C'/C_o are given in Table 3–2b to indicate the effect of estimates on the sensitivity of the lot-size system. The table gives

TABLE 3–2b

Sensitivity of The Lot-Size System,
Values of C'/C_o When Estimates Are Used

r'/r	1.20	0.80	1.20	1.20	0.80	0.80	1.20	0.80
c_1'/c_1	1.20	1.20	0.80	1.20	0.80	1.20	0.80	0.80
c_3'/c_3	1.20	1.20	1.20	0.80	1.20	0.80	0.80	0.80
q'/q_o	1.10	0.90	1.35	0.90	1.10	0.73	1.10	0.90
C'/C_o	1.005	1.006	1.042	1.006	1.005	1.050	1.005	1.006

results when the parameters are overestimated or underestimated by 20%. The effect of such estimates thus leads to additional costs ranging from 0.5 to 5%.

POWER DEMAND PATTERN

3–3   Thus far we have examined the lot-size system in which demand is uniform, as in Figure 3–1a. We will now study a system in which the inventory fluctuations are as in Figure 3–3a. In this system there is a basic prescribed period V during which there is a power demand pattern with index n which was described in Section 2–1. An example of such a system occurs when the demands toward the beginning of the week are smaller than the demands at the end of the week. Then V is 1 week and $n < 1$.

Two other examples of systems of this kind are given in Figure 3–3b. The inventory fluctuations represented by the full line correspond to the case when demands occur at the beginning of each basic period V and the index n is ∞. Similarly, when demand occurs at the end of each basic period we have the inventory fluctuations represented by broken lines; then $n = 0$.

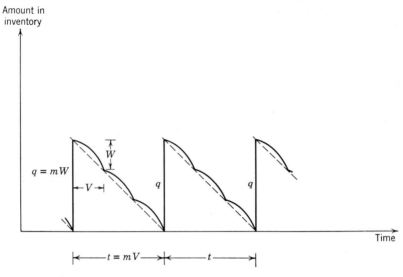

Figure 3–3a   A lot-size system with a power demand pattern.

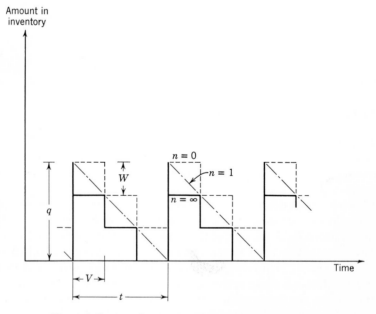

Figure 3–3b   Lot-size systems with specific power indices.

Let W be the known demand during V. Let m be a number such that

$$q = mW \tag{1}$$

Hence

$$t = mV \tag{2}$$

and also

$$r = W/V \tag{3}$$

We will now solve the system assuming that m must be an integer.

Referring to Figure 3-3a and using the definition of power demand pattern in equation 2-1(8), we can express the average amount carried in inventory by

$$I_1 = \frac{q}{2} + \frac{1}{t} m \int_0^V (Q_n - Q_1)\, dT \tag{4}$$

where

$$Q_n = W - W \sqrt[n]{T/V} \tag{5}$$

Substituting the corresponding values of equation (5) for Q_n and Q_1 in equation (4) and evaluating the integral leads to

$$I_1 = \frac{q}{2} + \frac{(W/2)(1 - n)}{1 + n} \tag{6}$$

The average number of replenishments per time unit is as in the lot-size system: $I_3 = r/q$. Hence the total cost is now

$$C(q) = \frac{c_1 q}{2} + \frac{c_1(W/2)(1 - n)}{1 + n} + \frac{c_3 r}{q} \tag{7}$$

where $q = W, 2W, 3W, \ldots$.

We can now use the results of the lot-size system with discrete units to find the optimal lot size. In fact, since the term $c_1(W/2)(1 - n)/(1 + n)$ in equation (7) is independent of q, then, by analogy with equation 3-1(16), we have immediately the result

$$q_o(q_o - W) \leqq \frac{2rc_3}{c_1} \leqq q_o(q_o + W) \tag{8}$$

The optimal lot size is therefore independent of the index n. Thus, even for the extreme values of n, as in Figure 3-3b, the same optimal lot is obtained, provided the other parameters of the system are the same. The minimum cost, however, will depend on the index n, which appears in the term $c_1(W/2)(1 - n)/(1 + n)$ in equation (7). This term can be interpreted as representing the resulting additional cost in a system with a power demand pattern as compared to the lot-size system in which demand is uniform. This additional cost ranges between $c_1 W/2$ (when $n = 0$) and $-c_1 W/2$ (when $n = \infty$).

UNIFORM REPLENISHING RATE

3-4 In this section we shall analyze a lot-size system in which the replenishment rate is not necessarily infinite as has been assumed in Sections 3-1, 3-2, and 3-3. Specifically, the system to be considered has a uniform replenishment rate p. (This rate must obviously be larger than, or at least equal to, the rate of demand r.) The inventory fluctuations can then be described graphically as in Figure 3-4.

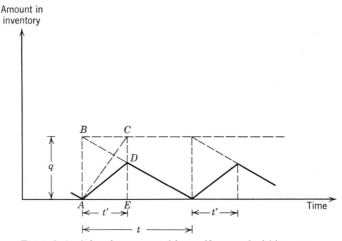

Figure 3-4 A lot-size system with a uniform replenishing rate.

For any lot size q the number of replenishments I_3 per unit time is r/q, as in the lot-size system. However, the average amount carried in inventory I_1 will not be $q/2$, as in the lot-size system, but somewhat less. The exact amount can be determined as follows.

Consider the first scheduling period in Figure 3-4. If there were no demand during the period t', inventories would have risen along the line AC at a rate p. Hence

$$t' = q/p \tag{1}$$

Since, however, there is a demand at a rate r, inventories will increase along the line AD at a rate $p - r$. Hence the maximum amount in inventory will be, using equation (1),

$$\overline{ED} = t'(p - r) = q(1 - r/p) \tag{2}$$

Therefore the average amount in inventory is $I_1 = q(1 - r/p)/2$. The total cost of the system is then

$$C(q) = \frac{c_1 q(1 - r/p)}{2} + \frac{c_3 r}{q} \tag{3}$$

Using the results of equations 3–1(7) to 3–1(10), we thus obtain the solution

$$q_o = \frac{\sqrt{2rc_3/c_1}}{\sqrt{1 - r/p}} \tag{4}$$

and the minimum cost

$$C_o = \sqrt{2rc_1c_3}\sqrt{1 - r/p} \tag{5}$$

When $p = \infty$ the present system reduces to the lot-size system. And indeed, in that case, equations (4) and (5) reduce to equations 3–1(5) and 3–1(6), as we would expect.

The special case $p = r$ should also be noted. Here the rate of replenishments equals the rate of demand. Obviously, then, replenishments will have to take place continuously (i.e., $t' = t$ in Figure 3–4) and there will be neither carrying costs nor replenishing costs. These conclusions also agree with equations (4) and (5). That is, if $p = r$, then by equation (4), $q = \infty$, which means that replenishments are continued indefinitely. In addition if $p = r$, then by equation (5) $C_o = 0$, as expected.

SEVERAL ITEMS

3–5 In many inventory systems one replenishment cost may apply to many different items. For example, when a truck is dispatched to bring a load containing different items, the replenishment cost may sometimes be just the cost of the trip. This cost may not depend on the number of different items in the shipment or on the specific amounts of each item.

Let us then consider a system in which there are N different items. The replenishment cost is c_3; this cost depends neither on the number of items nor on the lot sizes q_i of the items $i = 1, 2, \ldots, N$. Let r_i be the uniform constant rate of demand of item i, and let c_{1i} be its unit carrying cost.

Let t_i be the scheduling period of item i. Then

$$q_i = r_i t_i \tag{1}$$

In general, the inventory system will be as shown in Figure 3–5.

Before proceeding with the development of the general total cost equation for this system, we propose to show that for an optimal policy all scheduling periods ought to be of equal length. Suppose they are not. Let t designate the least scheduling period, say that of item k, that is, $t = t_k \leq t_i$, $i = 1, 2, \ldots, N$. Consider now an item j, for which $t_j > t$. Let the average inventory carried of this item be I_{1j}. Now suppose we decrease its scheduling period to $t_j' = t$. Obviously the average inventory will also decrease $I_{1j}' < I_{1j}$, and hence the carrying cost will decrease.

But what about the replenishing costs? Item k is replenished every $t_k = t$ units of time. And since the replenishing cost is independent of the number of items ordered, no additional replenishing costs are incurred for also replenishing item j every $t_j' = t$ units of time. Hence the total cost associated with item j is decreased if we order it as frequently as item k. In other words, for an optimal policy we cannot have $t_j > t$. Thus for all items we should have the same scheduling period t.

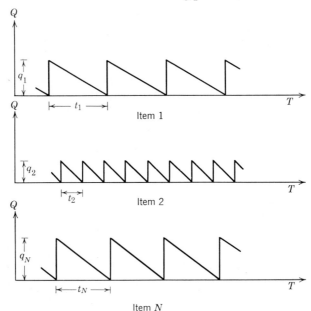

Figure 3–5   A lot-size system with several items.

The replenishment cost per unit time for all items is therefore only c_3/t. The lot size for each item is then $q_i = r_i t$. Thus the total-cost equation becomes

$$C(t) = \sum_{i=1}^{N} \frac{c_{1i} r_i t}{2} + \frac{c_3}{t} \tag{2}$$

Using the results of equations 3–1(7) to 3–1(10) we then have

$$t_o = \sqrt{2c_3 \Big/ \sum_{i=1}^{N} c_{1i} r_i} \tag{3}$$

and

$$C_o = \sqrt{2c_3 \sum_{i=1}^{N} c_{1i} r_i} \tag{4}$$

Therefore, by equation (1), the optimal lot sizes are

$$q_{io} = r_i \sqrt{2c_3 \Big/ \sum_{i=1}^{N} c_{1i} r_i} \tag{5}$$

The reader should note that when $N = 1$ this system reduces to the lot-size system and that equations (5) and (4) reduce to equations 3–1(5) and 3–1(6).

3–6 PROBLEMS

1. From first principles analyze the lot-size system (Section 3–1) using the scheduling period t as the controllable variable.
2. The lot-size system of Section 3–1 has an analogue in a type (2, 3) system in which no inventory is carried. Let the cost of shortage be c_2 per unit short per unit of time. Let the other parameters of the system be r and c_3 as in Section 3–1. Analyze the system.
3. In the system of problem 2 the yearly requirements are 320 units; $c_2 = \$0.10$ per unit short per week, $c_3 = \$52.00$ per setup.
   (a) Find q_o, t_o, and C_o.
   (b) The decision maker is unaware of the true parameters just given and assumes that $c_2' = \$0.05$ per unit short per week and $c_3' = \$58.50$ per setup. He therefore uses q' as a lot size. What is the true total cost of the system in this case?
4. The usuage of a certain item in a plant is at the rate of 600 parts per 6 months. The cost of carrying it in inventory is \$0.50 per part per month. The cost of a setup is \$100.00 per production run. At present the lot size used is 100 parts per production run. What would be the potential yearly saving if an optimal lot size were used?
5. For the lot-size system of Section 3–1, develop a decision rule for N, the optimal number of replenishments per unit time. Give a numerical example for which $N = 8$ setups per year.
6. Two definitions for inventory turnover are used in practice:
   (a) The ratio of the yearly demand to the average inventory during the year.
   (b) The ratio of the yearly sales (in dollars) to the dollar value of the average inventory during the year.
   Use the lot-size system to develop formulas for the optimal inventory turnover for (a) and (b). Give numerical examples. (For the numerical example in case (b) assume that the selling price is 40% higher than the value of the item in inventory.)
7. You have to supply your customers with 100 units of a certain product every Monday (and only then). You obtain the product from a local supplier at \$60 per unit. The costs of ordering and transportation from the supplier are \$150 per order. The cost of carrying inventory is estimated at 15% per year of the cost of the products carried.
   (a) Describe graphically the inventory system.
   (b) Find q_o and C_o.

8. The usage of a certain item in a refinery is constant and uniform at a rate of 2400 parts per year. When a part is needed and is not replaced, leakages occur which cost about $9 per month for each damaged part. The cost of setting up special equipment to manufacture the parts is $350. No inventory is carried. Replenishments are used only to make up shortages.

    (a) Find the yearly costs if setups are made every $\frac{1}{2}$ month, 1 month, $1\frac{1}{2}$ months.

    (b) What is the optimal lot size?

9. Compare the decision rule for the lot size in equation 3–1(16) with the rule

$$q_o' - u/2 \leq \sqrt{2rc_3/c_1} \leq q_o' + u/2 \tag{1}$$

    (a) Interpret this result.

    (b) Give a numerical example for the parameters r, c_1, c_3, and u for which equation (1) does not give the optimal lot size.

10. Derive equation 3–1(15).

11. Show that in the lot-size system

$$C_o = c_1 q_o \tag{2}$$

$$C_o = 2rc_3/q_o \tag{3}$$

12. In the system of Section 3–4 assume that the rate of replenishment can be controlled and that there is an additional cost associated with the replenishment process. That is, assume that it costs c_4 per time unit whenever replenishment is in progress.

Show that for the optimal solution either $p_o = \infty$ or $p_o = r$.

13. Compare the solution of the system of Section 3–5 with the solution of N lot-size systems in which we do not take advantage of the fact that the replenishment cost may apply to several items. Show algebraically that the minimum costs in the latter case are larger than or at least equal to the minimum cost given by equation 3–5(4).

14. Show that equation 3–1(16) always has one or at most two solutions. Hence conclude that it gives necessary and sufficient conditions for solving the lot-size system with discrete units.

15. In the system of Section 3–4 a decision regarding the lot size assumes that $p = \infty$ when in fact it is not. Let the corresponding cost be C'. Determine C'/C_o and discuss the sensitivity of the system.

16. The production department has to supply annually 3744 parts of a certain item at a constant and uniform rate. It can produce this part at a rate of 200 parts per week. The inventory carrying costs are $13 per part per year. The cost of setting up production runs is $144 per run.

    (a) Determine the optimal number of parts per run and the corresponding total annual cost.

    (b) Determine the total annual cost if the formula $q = \sqrt{2rc_3/c_1}$ is used to find the number of parts per run. (Assume 52 weeks in the year.)

17. The model of a system is $C(t) = At + B/t$, where C is the total cost and A and B are parameters. A decision rule for t is obtained assuming that $A = x$ and $B = y$. However, the true values are $A = p$ and $B = q$. Find the additional costs incurred by using x and y instead of p and q.

18. In the lot-size system $r = 3000$ parts per year, $c_1 = \$3$ per part per year, and $c_3 = \$125$. The decision maker assumes that the corresponding parameters are 2400 parts, $2, and $150.

   (a) What lot size does he choose? In his opinion, what is the minimum cost of the system?

   (b) What is the true cost of the system for the lot size selected by the decision maker? What is the minimum cost of the system?

Chapter 4

Order-Level Systems

4-0 Order-level systems are deterministic systems with a (t_p, S) policy. Since the scheduling period is prescribed, the replenishing costs are not subject to control. Hence these systems are type $(1, 2)$ systems, that is, only carrying costs are balanced against shortage costs.

All cost equations in the order-level systems are therefore of the form

$$C(S) = C_1(S) + C_2(S) \tag{1}$$

with the order level S the only variable subject to control.

Just as with the lot-size systems, there are numerous order-level systems. We shall reserve the designation "*the* order-level system" for the system described in Section 4-1. The properties of this system are similar to those of the lot-size system of Section 3-1. These two systems differ only in the constraints applied to them. In the lot-size system no shortages are allowed and the system is a type $(1, 3)$ system. In the order-level system the scheduling period is prescribed and the system is a type $(1, 2)$ system. Otherwise all other properties of the two systems are identical.

In Section 4-2 we analyze the sensitivity of the order-level system. The analysis is similar to the sensitivity analysis of the lot-size system given in Section 3-2. We note, though, that the results are not similar. The analysis of an order-level system with a power demand pattern is given in Section 4-3. Here, again, the results are somewhat different from those for a lot-size system with a power demand pattern of Section 3-3.

The analysis of an order-level system with a finite replenishment rate is not considered in this chapter. It is similar to the analysis in Section 3-4 and is left as an exercise [see problem 4-6(6)].

In Section 4-4 we analyze an order-level system in which the unit shortage cost is of dimension $[\$]/[Q]$. This is the case of lost sales. We shall see that the results are quite different from those for the order-level system of Section 4-1 in which the unit cost of shortage has the dimension $[\$]/[Q][T]$. Section 4-5 gives the analysis of an order-level system which has several items and in which there is a storage constraint. We use the Lagrangian multiplier technique to solve this system.

THE ORDER-LEVEL SYSTEM

4-1   *The* order-level system has the following properties:
1. Demand is deterministic at a constant rate of r quantity units per unit time.
2. The scheduling period is a prescribed constant t_p.
3. The replenishment size raises the inventory at the beginning of each scheduling period to the order level S. Shortages, if any, are made up. The order level S has to be determined.
4. The replenishment rate is infinite.
5. Leadtime is zero.*
6. The unit carrying cost is a constant c_1 whose dimension is $[\$]/[Q][T]$.
7. The unit shortage cost is a constant c_2 whose dimension is $[\$]/[Q][T]$.

From these properties we can conclude as follows:
(a) The number of replenishments per unit time will be $I_3 = 1/t_p$, a constant. Hence the third type of cost in this system, C_3, will be a constant and will not effect the decision about the optimal level S_o.
(b) The first three properties immediately imply that the lot size q is essentially also a prescribed constant

$$q_p = rt_p \tag{1}$$

(c) The inventory fluctuation of the system will depend on the relative values of S and q_p. This is illustrated in Figure 4-1a.

In case (i) of the figure there are only shortages; in case (ii) some inventories are carried and some shortages occur; in case (iii) there are no shortages and only inventories are carried.

The average amount in inventory in the system can therefore be given by

$$I_1(S) = \begin{cases} 0 & S \leq 0 \\ S^2/2q_p & 0 \leq S \leq q_p \\ S - q_p/2 & S \geq q_p \end{cases} \tag{2}$$

The derivation of the amount $S^2/2q_p$ for case (ii) ought to be explained, perhaps, in more detail. Consider the amounts in inventory during a

---
* However, see the pertinent comments in Section 2-2 for extending the results to systems with significant leadtime.

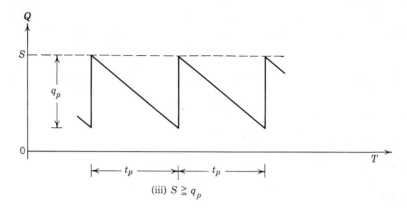

(iii) $S \geq q_p$

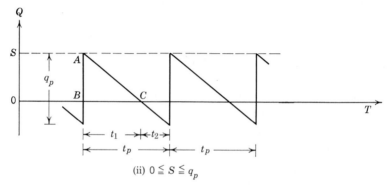

(ii) $0 \leqq S \leqq q_p$

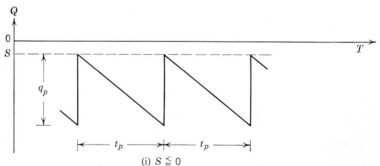

(i) $S \leqq 0$

Figure 4–1a   The order-level system.

typical scheduling period as in Figure 4–1a(ii). During the period t_1 the average amount carried is $S/2$, and during the period t_2 the amount carried is zero. Hence the average over the period $t_p = t_1 + t_2$ is

$$I_1(S) = \frac{S \, t_1}{2 \, t_p} \tag{3}$$

But, by similar triangles

$$\frac{t_1}{t_p} = \frac{S}{q_p} \tag{4}$$

Hence, from equations (3) and (4) we have $I_1(S) = S^2/2q_p$ as in the second line of equation (2).

[This result can also be derived by dividing the area of the triangle ABC by t_p. The area is $St_1/2$ and when dividing by t_p we obtain equation (3).]

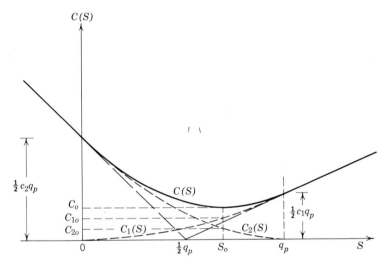

Figure 4–1b   Costs in the order-level system.

In a similar way the average shortage $I_2(S)$ can be seen to be

$$I_2(S) = \begin{cases} q_p/2 - S & S \leq 0 \\ (q_p - S)^2/2q_p & 0 \leq S \leq q_p \\ 0 & S \leq q_p \end{cases} \tag{5}$$

Hence the total cost of the order-level system is

$$C(S) = \begin{cases} c_2(q_p/2 - S) & S \leq 0 \\ c_1 S^2/2q_p + c_2(q_p - S)^2/2q_p & 0 \leq S \leq q_p \\ c_1(S - q_p/2) & S \geq q_p \end{cases} \tag{6}$$

The graphical representation of equation (6) is given in Figure 4–1b.

The function $C(S)$ is linear when $S \leq 0$ and when $S \geq q_p$, and it is quadratic when $0 \leq S \leq q_p$. We now show that its minimum must be in the interval $0 \leq S \leq q_p$. The minimum cannot be at $S' < 0$ since the cost $C(S = 0)$ is always smaller than the cost $C(S' < 0)$. Similarly, the minimum cannot be at $S'' > q_p$. Thus, to find the solution of the order-level system, we have to find the minimum of the function $C(S)$ in equation (7) for the indicated range:

$$C(S) = \frac{c_1 S^2}{2q_p} + \frac{c_2(q_p - S)^2}{2q_p} \qquad 0 \leq S \leq q_p \qquad (7)$$

Differentiating with respect to S, we have

$$\frac{dC(S)}{dS} = \frac{c_1 S}{q_p} - \frac{c_2(q_p - S)}{q_p} \qquad (8)$$

To find S_o we solve

$$\frac{c_1 S_o}{q_p} - \frac{c_2(q_p - S_o)}{q_p} = 0 \qquad (9)$$

which leads to

$$S_o = q_p \frac{c_2}{c_1 + c_2} \qquad (10)$$

Differentiating equation (8) we have

$$\frac{d^2 C}{dS^2} = \frac{c_1}{q_p} + \frac{c_2}{q_p} > 0 \qquad (11)$$

Hence S_o in equation (10) gives a minimum. It also satisfies the range in equation (7) (since $0 \leq c_2/(c_1 + c_2) \leq 1$). Therefore S_o in equation (10) gives the optimal order level. Substituting S_o in equation (7) gives the minimum cost

$$C_o = \frac{c_1[q_p c_2/(c_1 + c_2)]^2}{2q_p} + \frac{c_2[q_p - q_p c_2/(c_1 + c_2)]^2}{2q_p} \qquad (12)$$

$$= \frac{\tfrac{1}{2} q_p c_1 c_2}{c_1 + c_2} \frac{c_2}{c + c_2} + \frac{\tfrac{1}{2} q_p c_1 c_2}{c_1 + c_2} \frac{c_1}{c_1 + c_2} = \tfrac{1}{2} q_p \frac{c_1 c_2}{c_1 + c_2}$$

Marginal Analysis

The result in equation (10) can also be obtained by using a somewhat different approach, one called *marginal analysis*. We shall have occasion to use this approach in the analysis of several inventory systems with deterministic or probabilistic demand. We shall see that margin analysis is somewhat simpler to use than differentiation.

Let us refer back to Figure 4–1a(ii). Consider an arbitrary order level S'. Let the corresponding cost be $C(S')$. Suppose we now increase S' by a small amount h. This will cause the total carrying cost to increase for the period t_1, and the shortage cost to decrease for the period t_2. The change in the total cost is

$$C(S' + h) - C(S') = \frac{c_1 h t_1 - c_2 h t_2}{t_p} \tag{13}$$

Equation (13) also holds when S' is decreased in which case h is negative.

What can be said about this change in the total cost? If S' is not the optimal order level S_o, the change will be either negative or positive. However, when $S' = S_o$ it should be zero. That is, if we let t_{1o}, t_{2o} designate the t_1 and t_2 corresponding to the optimal solution, we should have

$$c_1 h t_{1o} = c_2 h t_{2o} \tag{14}$$

or

$$\frac{t_{1o}}{t_{2o}} = \frac{c_2}{c_1} \tag{15}$$

But, from Figure 4-1a(ii), in general

$$\frac{t_1}{t_2} = \frac{S}{q_p - S} \tag{16}$$

Hence, by equation (15),

$$\frac{S_o}{q_p - S_o} = \frac{c_2}{c_1} \tag{17}$$

from which we can immediately obtain the result in equation (10).

Before leaving this subject we draw the reader's attention again to equation (15). We shall see that this result applies to a large number of systems with a (t_p, S) policy.

Discrete Units

When the order level S is constrained to discrete units, we can use the methods described in Section 3-1 to find S_o. Let S be constrained to $\ldots -2u, -u, 0, u, 2u, \ldots$; then for S_o we should have

$$C(S_o) \leqq C(S_o + u) \tag{18}$$

$$C(S_o) \leqq C(S_o - u) \tag{19}$$

where $C(S)$ is as given in equation (6). Again, we can readily show that S_o should be in the range $0 \leqq S_o \leqq m_p u$ where m_p is an integer such that $(m_p - 1)u < q_p \leqq m_p u$.

Substituting the values of $C(S_o)$ of equation (7) in equations (18) and (19), and rearranging, we obtain

$$S_o - \frac{u}{2} \leqq q_p \frac{c_2}{c_1 + c_2} \leqq S_o + \frac{u}{2} \tag{20}$$

This is the desired solution for the discrete case. The result of equation (20) can be interpreted as follows. First compute the quantity

$$S_o' = \frac{q_p c_2}{c_1 + c_2}$$

as in the continuous case of equation (10). Then find the discrete S which is numerically closest to S_o'. This gives the desired S_o.

SENSITIVITY OF THE ORDER-LEVEL SYSTEM

4–2   In discussing the sensitivity of the order-level system we shall confine the analysis to non-negative order levels. In that case the total cost of the order-level system, by equation 4–1(6), is given by

$$C(S) = \begin{cases} c_1 S^2/2q_p + c_2(q_p - S)^2/2q_p & 0 \leqq S \leqq q_p \\ c_1(S - q_p/2) & S \geqq q_p \end{cases} \tag{1}$$

The optimal solution of the system as in equation 4–1(10) is

$$S_o = q_p \frac{c_2}{c_1 + c_2} \tag{2}$$

and the corresponding minimum cost of the system, by 4–1(12), is

$$C_o = \tfrac{1}{2} q_p \frac{c_1 c_2}{c_1 + c_2} \tag{3}$$

Suppose, now, that instead of the optimal S_o in equation (2), the decision maker uses another order level S', which is related to S_o by

$$S' = aS_o \qquad a \geqq 0 \tag{4}$$

Let C' designate the total cost of the system when S' is used. The ratio C'/C_o can then be used as a measure of the sensitivity of the system to deviations from the optimal S_o.

Substituting S' given by equation (4) in equation (1) and dividing by equation (3) eventually gives

$$C'/C_o = \begin{cases} 1 + (1 - a)^2(c_2/c_1) & 0 \leqq a \leqq 1 + c_1/c_2 \\ 2a - (1 + c_1/c_2) & a \geqq 1 + c_1/c_2 \end{cases} \tag{5}$$

[Thus, for the order-level system, C'/C_o depends both on the factor a and on the ratio c_2/c_1. In contrast, when finding the sensitivity of the lot-size system we saw that C'/C_o depended only on the factor b which is similar to a here (see Section 3–2 and equation 3–2(5)).]

Some numerical values of C'/C_o for various values of c_2/c_1 and a are given in Table 4–2a. According to this table, for example, if $c_2/c_1 = \frac{1}{2}$, and if $S_o = 100$ lb—but the order level chosen is $S' = 120$ lb, that is, $a = 1.2$—the additional cost as a result of deviating from the optimal solution is 2% of the minimum cost. But if $c_2/c_1 = 10$, the additional cost is 30% of the minimum cost.

TABLE 4–2a

Sensitivity of the Order-Level System:
Values of C'/C_o for Various c_2/c_1
When $S' = aS_o$

a / c_2/c_1	0.5	0.8	0.9	1.0	1.1	1.2	1.5	2.0	3.0
0.1	1.025	1.004	1.001	1.000	1.001	1.004	1.025	1.100	1.400
0.5	1.125	1.020	1.005	1.000	1.005	1.020	1.125	1.500	3.000
1.0	1.250	1.040	1.010	1.000	1.010	1.040	1.250	2.000	4.000
2.0	1.500	1.080	1.020	1.000	1.020	1.080	1.500	2.500	4.500
3.0	1.750	1.120	1.030	1.000	1.030	1.120	1.700	2.700	4.700
5.0	2.250	1.200	1.050	1.000	1.050	1.200	1.800	2.800	4.800
10.0	3.500	1.400	1.100	1.000	1.100	1.300	1.900	2.900	4.900
20.0	6.000	1.800	1.200	1.000	1.150	1.350	1.950	2.950	4.950

Effects of Estimates

Let the estimated values of the parameters in the order-level system be r', c_1', c_2' and let the true values be r, c_1, c_2. The order level chosen by equations (2) and 4–1(1) will be

$$S' = r't_p \frac{c_2'}{c_1' + c_2'} \qquad (6)$$

Hence the value of a, by equations (4), (6), and (2), will be

$$a = \frac{r't_p c_2'/(c_1' + c_2')}{rt_p c_2/(c_1 + c_2)}$$

$$= \frac{(r'/r)(c_2'/c_2)}{(c_1' + c_2')/(c_1 + c_2)} \qquad (7)$$

$$= \frac{(r'/r)(c_2'/c_2)}{\dfrac{c_1'/c_1 + (c_2'/c_2)(c_2/c_1)}{1 + c_2/c_1}}$$

Thus the factor a depends on the ratios of the estimates and the corresponding true values $(r'/r, c_1'/c_1, c_2'/c_2)$, and on the ratio c_2/c_1.

Let C' designate the total cost of the system when the estimates r', c_1', c_2' [and hence equation (6)] are used. Let C_o be the minimum cost based on the true parameters r, c_1, and c_2. Then equation (5) gives the ratio C'/C_o. Several values of this ratio are given in Table 4–2b to indicate the effects of estimates on the sensitivity of the order-level system.

TABLE 4–2b

Sensitivity of the Order-Level System
Values of C'/C_o for Various Estimates

c_2/c_1	2.0	10.0	2.0	10.0	2.0	10.0	2.0	10.0
r'/r	1.20	1.20	0.80	0.80	1.20	1.20	1.20	1.20
c_1'/c_1	1.20	1.20	1.20	1.20	0.80	0.80	1.20	1.20
c_2'/c_2	1.20	1.20	1.20	1.20	1.20	1.20	0.80	0.80
S'/S_o	1.20	1.20	0.80	0.80	1.35	1.24	1.03	1.15
C'/C_o	1.080	1.300	1.080	1.400	1.245	1.576	1.002	1.205

If we compare the results in Table 4–2b with those in Table 3–2b, it is not difficult to conclude that the order-level system is considerably more sensitive than the lot-size system.

POWER DEMAND PATTERN

4–3 In the system to be discussed in this section all the properties of the order-level system are unchanged with the exception of the demand pattern. In the order-level system the demand pattern is uniform; here the demand has the power demand pattern defined in Section 2–1. The inventory fluctuations of the system can be described graphically as in Figure 4–3.

The average amount carried in inventory $I_1(S)$ will be shown to be

$$I_1 = \begin{cases} 0 & S \leq 0 \\ \dfrac{S(S/q_p)^n}{n+1} & 0 \leq S \leq q_p \\ S - q_p \dfrac{n}{n+1} & S \geq q_p \end{cases} \tag{1}$$

The results for cases (ii) and (iii) of Figure 4–3 can be derived as follows.

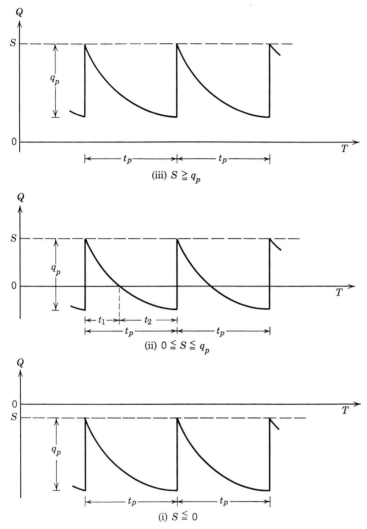

Figure 4-3 An order-level system with a power demand pattern.

When $0 \leqq S \leqq q_p$, then

$$I_1(S) = \frac{1}{t_p} \int_0^{t_1} Q(T) \, dT = \frac{1}{t_p} \int_0^{t_1} (S - q_p \sqrt[n]{T/t_p}) \, dT \qquad (2)$$

The length of time t_1 over which inventory is carried can be found from

$$Q(t_1) = S - q_p \sqrt[n]{t_1/t_p} = 0 \qquad (3)$$

Hence

$$t_1 = t_p(S/q_p)^n \tag{4}$$

Substituting this value of t_1 in equation (2) and evaluating the definite integral leads to appropriate result of equation (1). When $S \geqq q_p$, then

$$I_1(S) = \frac{1}{t_p} \int_0^{t_p} Q(T)\, dT = \frac{1}{t_p} \int_0^{t_p} (S - q_p \sqrt[n]{T/t_p})\, dT = S - q_p \frac{n}{n+1} \tag{5}$$

Similarly, the average shortage $I_2(S)$ will be shown to be

$$I_2(S) = \begin{cases} q_p n/(n+1) - S & S \leqq 0 \\[2mm] \dfrac{nq_p + S(S/q_p)^n}{n+1} - S & 0 \leqq S \leqq q_p \\[2mm] 0 & S \geqq q_p \end{cases} \tag{6}$$

The results for cases (i) and (ii) of Figure 4–3 can be derived as follows. When $S \leqq 0$, then, as in equation (5),

$$I_2 = \frac{1}{t_p} \int_0^{t_p} - Q(T)\, dT = -\left(S - q_p \frac{n}{n+1}\right) \tag{7}$$

When $0 \leqq S \leqq q_p$, then

$$I_2(S) = \frac{1}{t_1} \int_{t_1}^{t_p} - Q(T)\, dT = \frac{1}{t_p} \int_{t_p(S/q_p)^n}^{t_p} - (S - q_p \sqrt[n]{T/t_p})\, dT$$

$$= \cdots = \frac{nq_p + S(S/q_p)^n}{n+1} - S \tag{8}$$

The total cost equation of the system is therefore given by

$$C(S) = c_1 I_1(S) + c_2 I_2(S) \tag{9}$$

where $I_1(S)$ and $I_2(S)$ are as in equations (1) and (6).

By inspection we immediately note that when $S < 0$ then $C(S) < C(0)$, and when $S > q_p$ then $C(S) > C(q_p)$. Hence the optimal level S must lie in the range $0 \leqq S \leqq q_p$. Thus the pertinent total-cost equation becomes

$$C(S) = \frac{c_1 S(S/q_p)^n}{n+1} + c_2 \left[\frac{nq_p + S(S/q_p)^n}{n+1} - S\right]$$

$$= (c_1 + c_2) \frac{S(S/q_p)^n}{n+1} - c_2 S + \frac{c_2 q_p n}{n+1} \tag{10}$$

By differentiation, etc., we find that the optimal level S is given by

$$S_o = q_p \sqrt[n]{c_2/(c_1 + c_2)} \tag{11}$$

Substituting this value in equation (10) and rearranging, we obtain the minimum total cost of the system:

$$C_o = c_2 q_p [1 - \sqrt[n]{c_2/(c_1 + c_2)}] \frac{n}{n+1} \tag{12}$$

These results are, of course, more general than the results for the order-level system of Section 4–1 in which the power index is $n = 1$. And indeed, if we substitute this value of n in equations (11) and (12), we obtain the solution of the order-level system as in equations 4–1(10) and 4–1(12).

When demand occurs entirely at the beginning of the scheduling period, the optimal order level should equal the demand size and there should then be no costs since no inventory would be carried and no shortages would occur. This result can also be obtained from equations (11) and (12) for $n = \infty$. Similarly, when all demand occurs at the end of the scheduling period, the order level should be zero and again there should be no costs. This result corresponds to the index pattern $n = 0$.

Before leaving this system let us show how the optimal order level S_o in equation (11) can be obtained by marginal analysis, without having to derive the total-cost equation (10). Consider Figure 4–3(ii) and let S_o, t_{1o}, and t_{2o} be quantities corresponding to an optimal solution. In analogy with the analysis exemplified by equations 4–1(13) and 4–1(14), here too we have

$$c_1 h t_{1o} = c_2 h t_{2o} \tag{13}$$

or

$$\frac{t_{1o}}{t_{2o}} = \frac{c_2}{c_1} \tag{14}$$

Equation (14) also gives

$$\frac{t_{1o}}{t_{1o} + t_{2o}} = \frac{c_2}{c_1 + c_2} \tag{15}$$

or

$$t_{1o} = t_p \frac{c_2}{c_1 + c_2}$$

But t_1, in general, is given by equation (4); hence

$$t_p \left(\frac{S_o}{q_p}\right)^n = t_p \frac{c_2}{c_1 + c_2} \tag{16}$$

From this equation we can immediately obtain the result of equation (11).

LOST SALES

4-4 The system to be considered here is an extension of the order-level system when the cost of shortage depends only on the quantity short and not on the duration of shortages. That is, if there are y quantity units short at the end of the prescribed scheduling period, this costs an amount $c_2 y$. Here, then, the dimension of the unit shortage cost is

$$[c_2] = [\$]/[Q] \tag{1}$$

Applying this cost measure to the results obtained in Section 4-1 [as per equation 4-1(6)], and noting that the shortage at the end of the scheduling period is $q_p - S$, we obtain the total cost of the system

$$C(S) = \begin{cases} c_2(q_p - S)/t_p & S \leq 0 \\ c_1 S^2/2q_p + c_2(q_p - S)/t_p & 0 \leq S \leq q_p \\ c_1(S - q_p/2) & S \geq q_p \end{cases} \tag{2}$$

As in previous similar cases it is evident that the optimal level S_o should be in the range 0 to q_p; hence the pertinent total cost equation to be considered now is

$$C(S) = \frac{c_1 S^2}{2q_p} + \frac{c_2(q_p - S)}{t_p} \qquad 0 \leq S \leq rt_p \tag{3}$$

Differentiating, etc., we obtain

$$S_o = \frac{rc_2}{c_1} \tag{4}$$

But equation (4) holds only if $S_o \leq q_p$, that is, if $rc_2/c_1 \leq q_p$ or if $c_2 \leq c_1 t_p$. Otherwise, the optimal level should be q_p.

The solution of the system can therefore be summarized as follows:

$$S_o = \begin{cases} c_2 r/c_1 & c_2 \leq c_1 t_p \\ q_p & c_2 \geq c_1 t_p \end{cases} \tag{5}$$

Substituting now in equation (3) we also have

$$C_o = \begin{cases} c_2 r - c_2^2 r/2c_1 t_p & c_2 \leq c_1 t_p \\ c_1 q_p/2 & c_2 \geq c_1 t_p \end{cases} \tag{6}$$

It is interesting to compare equations (5) and (6) with the corresponding solution of the order-level system given by equations 4-1(10) and 4-1(12) which are reproduced below for easier reference.

$$S_o = \frac{q_p c_2}{c_1 + c_2} \tag{7}$$

$$C_o = \frac{\frac{1}{2} q_p c_1 c_2}{c_1 + c_2} \tag{8}$$

It should be recalled that in the order-level system the unit cost of shortage had the dimension $[\$]/[Q][T]$, whereas in the present system its dimension is $[\$]/[Q]$. Not only does this change in the property of the unit cost of shortage lead to different results for S_o and C_o, but the entire structure of the solution is changed. We shall see that this phenomenon will be repeated in other systems.

SEVERAL ITEMS AND LIMITED STORAGE

4–5   In this section we shall analyze an extension of the order-level system when N different items are involved and when the total storage space available at the beginning of the prescribed scheduling period is restricted to some given quantity.

Let q_{pn}, c_{1n}, c_{2n}, S_n, and b_n designate respectively the prescribed lot size, unit carrying cost, unit shortage cost, order level, and unit space of item n. In addition, let the total available space for all N items be B. The total-cost equation, by an extension of equation 4–1(7), is then

$$C(S_1, S_2, \ldots, S_N) = \sum_{n=1}^{N} \frac{c_{1n} S_n{}^2 + c_{2n}(q_{pn} - S_n)^2}{2q_{pn}} \tag{1}$$

where the S_n are constrained by

$$\sum_{n=1}^{N} b_n S_n \leqq B \tag{2}$$

The following method of solution may be applied here.

For each item let $S_n{}^*$ indicate the order level satisfying the following equation [which corresponds to equations 4–1(10) without the space constraint]:

$$S_n{}^* = q_{pn} \frac{c_{2n}}{c_{1n} + c_{2n}} \tag{3}$$

If these $S_n{}^*$ satisfy equation (2), they obviously constitute the solution looked for. If they do not satisfy equation (2), it is clear that for the optimal order levels S_{on} the equality must hold in equation (2), that is,

$$\sum_{n=1}^{N} b_n S_{on} = B \tag{4}$$

We can now use the Lagrangian multipliers technique to find the optimal order levels. The function F is formed:

$$F(S_1, S_2, \ldots, S_N, g) = C(S_1, S_2, \ldots, S_N) + g\left(\sum_{n=1}^{N} b_n S_n - B\right) \quad (5)$$

Hence, for an optimal solution $\partial F/\partial S_n = 0$ for $S_n = S_{no}$ and $g = g_o$. This leads to

$$S_{no} = q_{pn} \frac{c_{2n} - g_o b_n}{c_{1n} + c_{2n}} \quad (6)$$

Substituting these values of S_{no} in equation (4) leads to

$$g_o = \left(\sum_{n=1}^{N} \frac{c_{2n} b_n q_{pn}}{c_{1n} + c_{2n}} - B\right) \Big/ \sum_{n=1}^{N} \frac{b_n q_{pn}}{c_{1n} + c_{2n}} \quad (7)$$

The optimal order levels S_{no} can now be obtained from equations (6) and (7).

4-6   PROBLEMS

1. From first principles analyze the order-level system of Section 4-1 using the reorder point s as the controllable variable.

2. A refinery uniformly uses 2400 parts of a certain item during the year. The item is a component of many of the pumps in operation. It deteriorates frequently. Whenever a replacement is not available, leakages occur which cost \$9 per month for each part. Every month 200 parts of the item are manufactured. Manufacturing time is less than 1 day. The cost of each part is \$80. The percentage of inventory carrying cost is 15% per year.

   What should be the optimal inventory level of the item at the beginning of each month after all shortages have been made up?

3. In the order-level system show that $C_{1o}/C_{2o} = c_2/c_1$. Interpret the result and compare it with the lot-size system in which $C_{1o}/C_{3o} = 1$.

4. Sketch graphically the amounts in inventory for the optimal solutions of the system of Section 4-3 for $r = 200$ units per month, $t_p = 1$ month, $c_1 = \$7.6$ per unit per month, $c_2 = \$32.4$ per unit per month—when $n = 2, 1, \frac{1}{2}, \frac{1}{4}, \frac{1}{8}$, and $\frac{1}{16}$.
   (a) Show that $t_{1o} = c_2/(c_1 + c_2)$ for all n.
   (b) Find the corresponding minimum total cost per month for each n.

5. Prepare numerical examples (i.e., give numerical values for the parameters) for the system of Section 4-4, and find S_o and C_o for (a) $c_2/c_1 < t_p$ and (b) $c_2/c_1 > t_p$.

6. Describe and solve an order-level system similar to the order-level system of Section 4-1 with the exception that the replenishment rate p is not necessarily infinite. (Be sure to identify correctly the order level.)

7. Describe and solve an order-level system similar to the order-level systems of Sections 4–1 and 4–4 when the total shortage cost during the period t_p is c_2. This cost does not depend on the amount short or on the duration of shortage.

   Show that the structure of the solution is similar to that of the system of Section 4–4.

8. In the system of Section 4–5 there are five items and the total space available is 3000 ft³. The pertinent data are given in Table 4–6.

TABLE 4–6

Item	n	1	2	3	4	5
Lot size	q_{pn}	200	100	500	80	1000
Carrying cost	c_{1n}	2.0	1.0	4.0	5.0	1.0
Shortage cost	c_{2n}	50.0	40.0	20.0	30.0	10.0
Unit space	b_n	5.0	3.0	9.0	12.0	0.2

Solve the system.

9. The uniform annual demands for two bulky items are 90 tons and 160 tons respectively. The carrying costs are $250 and $200 per ton per year and the setup costs are $50 and $40 per production run respectively. No shortages are allowed. Space considerations restrict the average amount in inventory of both items to 4000 ft³. A ton of the first item occupies 1000 ft³ and a ton of the second item 500 ft³.

   Use Lagrangian multipliers to find the optimal lot size of each item. Show that the space restriction increases costs by about $75 per year.

10. In the order-level system $r = 13$ lb per week, $t = 9$ weeks, $c_1 = \$3.20$ per pound per week, and $c_2 = \$8.50$ per pound per week.

    A decision maker assumes that the corresponding parameters are 15 lb, $3.00, and $12.00. He then makes a decision accordingly.

    (a) What order level does he choose? What, in his opinion, is the minimum cost of the system?

    (b) What is the true cost of the system? What is the minimum cost of the system?

Chapter 5

Order-Level–Lot-Size Systems

5–0 Order-level–lot-size systems are deterministic systems with constant demand and an (S, q) policy.* These are $(1, 2, 3)$-type systems in which carrying, shortage, and replenishment costs are balanced. The total-cost equation of these systems can therefore be given by

$$C(S, q) = C_1(S, q) + C_2(S, q) + C_3(S, q) \tag{1}$$

The controllable variables S and q are related to the reorder point s and the scheduling period t by

$$s = S - q \tag{2}$$

and

$$t = q/r \tag{3}$$

where r is the constant rate of demand. Hence these systems may also be viewed as having a (t, S) policy, an (s, q) policy, or an (s, S) policy. To be specific we shall refer to the systems as having an (S, q) policy. (In passing it should be noted that when demand is probabilistic the three policies (t, S), (s, q), and (s, S) are not necessarily identical policies and they have then to be analyzed separately as in Chapters 8, 13, and 15.)

In this chapter we first discuss the order-level–lot-size system (Section 5–1). It will be seen that this system can be considered an extension either of the lot-size system of Section 3–1 or of the order-level system of Section 4–1. We shall also see that the lot-size system is a special case of the order-level–lot-size system, but the order-level system is not.

---

* Such a policy is meaningless in probabilistic systems. The reason for its use here will be given presently.

In Section 5-2 we examine the sensitivity of the order-level–lot-size system. We discuss the effect of deviations from optimal decisions and the effect of using estimates. The analysis is similar to those in Sections 3-2 and 4-2. In Section 5-3 we study an extension of a lot-size system with a uniform replenishment rate [Section 3-4—a type (1, 3) system] to a type (1, 2, 3) system. We obtain a general solution from which the solution of other systems can be obtained as special cases. In particular, the systems of Sections 3-1, 3-4, 3-5(2), and 5-1 turn out to be special cases of the system of Section 5-3.

The study of an extension of the lost-sales system of Section 4-4, a type (1, 2) system, is carried out in Section 5-4. A surprising but very important result is obtained, namely, for an optimal solution either all losses of sales are avoided or no inventory is replenished.

THE ORDER-LEVEL–LOT-SIZE SYSTEM

5-1 The order-level–lot-size system may be viewed as an extension of either the lot-size system of Section 3-1 or the order-level system of Section 4-1. If, in the lot-size system, we remove the constraint that $s_p = 0$ and allow shortages to occur, we obtain the present system. Similarly, if, in the order-level system, we remove the constraint that the scheduling period is prescribed, we also obtain the present system. The inventory fluctuations of the order-level–lot-size system can be described graphically as in Figure 5-1.

The properties of this system are as follows:

1. Demand is deterministic at a constant rate of r quantity units per time unit.
2. The replenishment size is constant; the lot size is q; shortages are made up.
3. The scheduling period t is constant; the order level is S.
4. The replenishment rate is infinite.
5. Leadtime is zero.*
6. The unit carrying cost c_1 is a constant whose dimension is $[\$]/[Q][T]$.
7. The unit shortage cost c_2 is constant whose dimension is** $[\$]/[Q][T]$.
8. The unit replenishing cost c_3 is a constant whose dimension is $[\$]$.

In order to find the total cost of the system, it is possible to use the results of the order-level system given by equation 4-1(6). We now replace

* However, see the pertinent comments in Section 2-2 for extending the results to systems with significant leadtime.

** For the analysis of a system in which the dimension of c_2 is $[\$]/[Q]$ (the lost-sales case), see Section 5-4.

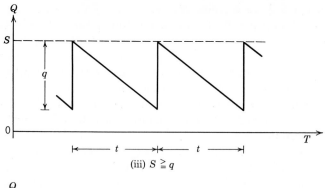

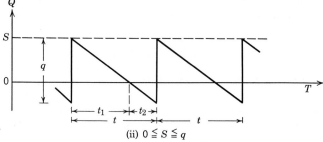

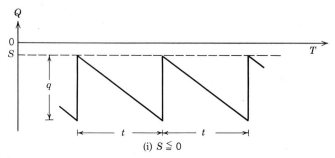

Figure 5-1   The order-level–lot-size system.

q_p with q and add the replenishment cost per time unit $c_3 r/q$, as in the lot-size system [equation 4–1(2)]. Hence the cost of the order-level–lot-size system is

$$C(S, q) = \begin{cases} c_2(q/2 - S) + c_3 r/q & S \leq 0 \\ c_1 S^2/2q + c_2(q - S)^2/2q + c_3 r/q & 0 \leq S \leq q \\ c_1(S - q/2) + c_3 r/q & S \geq q \end{cases} \quad (1)$$

Just as in Section 4–1 we can again conclude that for the optimal solution of the system S_o should not be smaller than zero [case (i) in Figure 5–1], nor should it be larger than q [case (iii) in Figure 5–1]. Hence the pertinent total-cost equation for finding optimal S and q is

$$C(S, q) = \frac{c_1 S^2}{2q} + \frac{c_2(q - S)^2}{2q} + \frac{c_3 r}{q} \tag{2}$$

This equation corresponds to case (ii) in Figure 5–1.

Taking partial derivatives with respect to S and q leads to

$$\frac{\partial C}{\partial S} = \frac{c_1 S}{q} - \frac{c_2(q - S)}{q} \tag{3}$$

$$\frac{\partial C}{\partial q} = \frac{c_2(q - S)}{q} - \frac{c_1 S^2 + c_2(q - S)^2 + 2c_3 r}{2q^2} \tag{4}$$

To find S_o and q_o we set equations (3) and (4) equal to zero and solve the resulting simultaneous equations. We eventually have

$$q_o = \sqrt{2rc_3}\sqrt{(c_1 + c_2)/(c_1 c_2)} \tag{5}$$

$$S_o = \frac{q_o c_2}{c_1 + c_2} = \sqrt{2rc_3/c_1}\sqrt{c_2/(c_1 + c_2)} \tag{6}$$

Taking the partial derivations of equations (3) and (4) with respect to S and q, we obtain

$$\frac{\partial^2 C}{\partial S^2} = \frac{c_1}{q} + \frac{c_2}{q} = \frac{c_1 + c_2}{q} \tag{7}$$

$$\frac{\partial^2 C}{\partial S \, \partial q} = -\frac{c_2}{q} - \frac{c_1 S - c_2(q - S)}{q^2} = -\frac{(c_1 + c_2)S}{q^2} \tag{8}$$

$$\frac{\partial^2 C}{\partial q^2} = \frac{c_2 S}{q^2} - \frac{c_2(q - S)}{q^2} + \frac{c_1 S^2 + c_2(q - S)^2 + 2c_3 r}{q^3} \tag{9}$$

$$= \frac{(c_1 + c_2)S^2 + 2c_3 r}{q^3}$$

For the values of q_o and S_o in equations (5) and (6), $\partial^2 C/\partial S^2$, $\partial^2 C/\partial q^2$, and $[\partial^2 C/\partial S^2][\partial^2 C/\partial q^2] - [\partial^2 C/(\partial S \, \partial q)]^2$ are all positive. Hence q_o and S_o indeed give a minimum cost, and equations (5) and (6) thus give the solution of the system.

The corresponding minimum total cost, by substitution in equation (2), is

$$C_o = \sqrt{2rc_3}\sqrt{c_1 c_2/(c_1 + c_2)} \tag{10}$$

Analysis of Solution

The following observations can be made with respect to the solution just derived.

1. The lot-size system of Section 3-1 is a special case of the present system. If we put $c_2 = \infty$ in all the results of the present system, the results of lot-size system are obtained.

2. The system described in problem 3-5(2) is a special case of the present system (when $c_1 = \infty$).

3. The order-level system of Section 4-1 is *not* a special case of the present system. (In the order-level system the scheduling period is prescribed; in the present system it is not.)

4. Let $\bar{c}$ be defined by

$$\bar{c} = \frac{1}{1/c_1 + 1/c_2} \tag{11}$$

Then the following results can be derived from equations (5), (6), (10), and (11):

$$C_o = \sqrt{2r\bar{c}\, c_3} \tag{12}$$

$$q_o = \frac{C_o}{\bar{c}} \tag{13}$$

$$S_o = \frac{C_o}{c_1} \tag{14}$$

5. The following relations also hold for the system

$$s_o = -\frac{C_o}{c_2} \tag{15}$$

$$t_o = \frac{q_o}{r} = \frac{C_o}{\bar{c}r} = \sqrt{2c_3/\bar{c}r} \tag{16}$$

$$C_{1o} = \frac{C_o}{2}\, \frac{c_2}{c_1 + c_2} \tag{17}$$

$$C_{2o} = \frac{C_o}{2}\, \frac{c_1}{c_1 + c_2} \tag{18}$$

$$C_{3o} = \frac{C_o}{2} \tag{19}$$

$$t_{1o} = t_o\, \frac{c_2}{c_1 + c_2} \tag{20}$$

$$t_{2o} = t_o\, \frac{c_1}{c_1 + c_2} \tag{21}$$

6. From equations (17), (18), (19), (20), and (21) we also obtain

$$\frac{C_{10}}{C_{20}} = \frac{c_2}{c_1} \tag{22}$$

$$C_{10} + C_{20} = C_{30} \tag{23}$$

$$\frac{t_{10}}{t_{20}} = \frac{c_2}{c_1} \tag{24}$$

Some of the results that we have derived may be obtained in an alternate way. For example, consider equation (2). If q is fixed for a moment, then by Section 4–1 the optimal S_o will be, by equation 4–1(10),

$$S_o = q \frac{c_2}{c_1 + c_2} \tag{25}$$

Hence by equation 4–1(12), equation (2) becomes

$$C(S_o, q) = \frac{\frac{1}{2}qc_1c_2}{c_1 + c_2} + \frac{c_3 r}{q} \tag{26}$$

Therefore, by equations 3–1(7), 3–1(8), 3–1(9), and 3–1(10) we can immediately obtain the results of equations (5), (6), (10), and (23). In addition, the results in equations (24), (20), and (21) may be obtained by marginal analysis.

Discrete Units

When the order level S and the lot size q are both restricted to discrete units, we can attempt to use the methods of Sections 3–1 and 4–1 to find the optimal S_o and q_o. It turns out, however, that whereas in the previous sections the conditions for optimality [equations 3–1(11), 3–1(12) and 4–1(18), 4–1(19)] were necessary and sufficient, similar conditions for the present system are *not* sufficient. Let us illustrate this by an example.

For the order-level–lot-size system let $r = 6$ lb per month, $c_1 = \$0.75$ per pound per month, $c_2 = \$1.50$ per pound per month, $c_3 = \$54.00$ per replenishment. Let the order level S be restricted to the amounts . . . $-2u$, $-u$, 0, u, $2u$, . . . , where $u = 1$ lb. Let the lot size be restricted to v, $2v$, $3v$, . . . , where $v = 6$ lb.

The following conditions are then necessary for the optimal solution:

$$C(S_o, q_o) \leqq C(S_o \pm u, q_o) \tag{27}$$

$$C(S_o, q_o) \leqq C(S_o, q_o \pm v) \tag{28}$$

Equation (27) corresponds to equations 4–1(18) and 4–1(19) and equation (28) to equations 3–1(11) and 3–1(12). We can also add a third requirement,

$$C(S_o, q_o) \leqq C(S_o \pm u, q_o \pm v) \tag{29}$$

In Table 5–1 the total cost of the system [as per equation (2)] is listed for various values of S and q for the numerical data just given. From the table we can see that for $S = 28$ lb and $q = 42$ lb all the conditions of equations (27), (28), and (29) are satisfied. Yet they do not constitute an optimal solution. Here the optimal solution can be derived directly from equations (5) and (6), namely, $q_o = 36$ lb, $S_o = 24$ lb, and by equation (12), $C_o = \$18.00$ per month.

TABLE 5–1

Some Costs in the Order-Level–Lot-Size System with Discrete Units

Order level S	Lot size q		
	36	42	48
27	18.37	18.25	19.53
28	18.67	18.21	19.25
29	19.04	18.25	19.03

This example illustrates the fact that equations (27), (28), and (29) need not give a unique solution. We shall, therefore, not attempt to reduce these equations to obtain results similar to equations 3–1(16) and 4–1(20). Furthermore, the topic of finding a minimum of a function of two variables that are restricted to discrete units is rather special and will not be covered here.*

SENSITIVITY OF THE ORDER-LEVEL–LOT-SIZE SYSTEM

5-2   Before considering the effect of deviating from optimal solutions in the order-level–lot-size system, let us repeat some of the relevant results of the previous section. The total-cost equation of the system is, by equation 5–1(1),

$$C(S, q) = \begin{cases} c_2(q/2 - S) + c_3r/q & S \leq 0 \\ c_1S^2/2q + c_2(q - S)^2/2q + c_3r/q & 0 \leq S \leq q \\ c_1(S - q/2) + c_3r/q & S \geq q \end{cases} \quad (1)$$

And the solution of the system is, by equations 5–1(5), 5–1(6), 5–1(10),

$$q_o = \sqrt{2rc_3(c_1 + c_2)/(c_1c_2)} \quad (2)$$

$$S_o = \sqrt{2rc_3c_2/[c_1(c_1 + c_2)]} \quad (3)$$

$$C_o = \sqrt{2rc_3c_1c_2/(c_1 + c_2)} \quad (4)$$

* For another illustration see Example 13–3a.

Suppose, now, that instead of the optimal values S_o and q_o given in equations (2) and (3) we use the values S' and q'. Let

$$S' = aS_o \qquad a \geqq 0 \tag{5}$$

and let

$$q' = bq_o \qquad b > 0 \tag{6}$$

Let C' designate the total cost of the system when S' and q' are used. Then equations (1) to (6) eventually lead to

$$\frac{C'}{C_o} = \begin{cases} \dfrac{1 + b^2 + (b - a)^2(c_2/c_1)}{2b} & 0 \leqq a \leqq \left(1 + \dfrac{c_1}{c_2}\right) b \\[3mm] a + \dfrac{1}{2b} - \dfrac{b(1 + c_1/c_2)}{2} & a \geqq \left(1 + \dfrac{c_1}{c_2}\right) b \end{cases} \tag{7}$$

In Table 5-2a we give some numerical values of C'/C_o for various values of a and b when $c_2/c_1 = 0.5$. In Table 5-2b similar values are given for $c_2/c_1 = 10.0$. To assess the sensitivity of the system, we may compare Tables 5-2a and 5-2b with similar tables for the lot-size system and the order-level system (Tables 3-2a and 4-2a). It is not difficult to conclude that the lot-size system is less sensitive than the order-level–lot-size system; the values of C'/C_o in Table 3-2a are always less than, or at most equal to, the corresponding values in Tables 5-2a and 5-2b. However, no similar conclusion can be drawn regarding the order-level system. As a matter of fact, it appears that sometimes (say, when $b = 1.0$ in Tables 5-2a and

TABLE 5-2a

Sensitivity of the Order-Level–Lot-Size System
Values of C'/C_o When $S' = aS_o$, $q' = bq_o$, and $c_2/c_1 = 0.5$

a \ b	0.5	0.8	0.9	1.0	1.1	1.2	1.5	2.0	3.0
0.5	1.250	1.053	1.051	1.063	1.088	1.120	1.249	1.531	2.188
0.8	1.295	1.025	1.009	1.010	1.026	1.051	1.164	1.430	2.070
0.9	1.330	1.028	1.006	1.003	1.015	1.036	1.142	1.401	2.034
1.0	1.375	1.038	1.009	1.000	1.008	1.026	1.124	1.375	2.000
1.1	1.430	1.053	1.017	1.003	1.006	1.020	1.109	1.351	1.968
1.2	1.495	1.075	1.031	1.010	1.008	1.017	1.097	1.330	1.937
1.5	1.750	1.178	1.106	1.063	1.042	1.036	1.082	1.281	1.854
2.0	2.750	1.475	1.343	1.250	1.190	1.151	1.124	1.250	1.750
3.0	3.250	2.425	2.206	2.000	1.827	1.693	1.457	1.375	1.667

TABLE 5-2b

Sensitivity of the Order-Level–Lot-Size System
Values of C'/C_o When $S' = aS_o$, $q' = bq_o'$, and $c_2/c_1 = 10.0$

a \\ b	0.5	0.8	0.9	1.0	1.1	1.2	1.5	2.0	3.0
0.5	1.250	1.588	1.896	2.250	2.644	3.561	4.412	9.375	12.083
0.8	1.525	1.025	1.062	1.200	1.415	2.060	2.714	4.850	9.734
0.9	1.625	1.085	1.006	1.050	1.188	1.393	2.281	4.275	9.017
1.0	1.725	1.185	1.061	1.000	1.051	1.184	1.915	2.750	8.333
1.1	1.825	1.285	1.161	1.050	1.006	1.059	1.615	3.275	7.683
1.2	1.925	1.385	1.261	1.150	1.051	1.077	1.382	2.850	7.067
1.5	2.225	1.685	1.561	1.450	1.350	1.257	1.083	1.875	5.417
2.0	2.725	2.185	2.061	1.950	1.850	1.757	1.508	1.250	3.333
3.0	3.725	3.185	3.061	2.950	2.850	2.757	2.508	2.150	1.667

5-2b) the order-level system is more sensitive than the order-level–lot-size system. However, at other times (when, for example, $b = 3.0$), it is the other way around.

Effects of Estimates

Let the estimated values of the parameters in the order-level–lot-size system be r', c_1', c_2', and c_3', and let the true values be r, c_1, c_2, and c_3. By equations (2) and (3) the decisions will be

$$q' = \sqrt{2r'c_3'(c_1' + c_2')/(c_1'c_2')} \tag{8}$$

$$S' = \sqrt{2r'c_3'c_2'/[c_1'(c_1' + c_2')]} \tag{9}$$

Hence the values of a and b, from equation (5), (6), (2), (3), (8), and (9), are

$$a = \sqrt{\frac{r'}{r} \frac{c_3'}{c_3} \frac{c_2'}{c_2} \frac{1 + c_2/c_1}{c_1'/c_1 + (c_2'/c_2)(c_2/c_1)}} \Big/ \frac{c_1'}{c_1} \tag{10}$$

$$b = \frac{a[c_1'/c_1 + (c_2'/c_2)(c_2/c_1)]}{(1 + c_2/c_1)(c_2'/c_2)} \tag{11}$$

Let the cost of the system, based on q' and S' (and hence on a and b), be C'. Then the measure of sensitivity is given by equation (7) where a and b are as in equations (10) and (11). As in the order-level system, the ratio C'/C_o now depends not only on the ratios of the estimated parameters to the true parameters but also on the ratio c_2/c_1.

Several values of C'/C_o, for some specific ratios of estimated parameters, are given in Table 5–2c.

TABLE 5–2c

Sensitivity of the Order-Level–Lot-Size System
Values of C'/C_o for Various Estimates

c_2/c_1	0.5	0.5	0.5	0.5	0.5	10.0	10.0	10.0	10.0	10.0
r'/r	1.20	0.80	1.20	1.20	1.20	1.20	0.80	1.20	1.20	1.20
c_1'/c_1	1.20	1.20	0.80	1.20	1.20	1.20	1.20	0.80	1.20	1.20
c_2'/c_2	1.20	1.20	1.20	0.80	1.20	1.20	1.20	1.20	0.80	1.20
c_3'/c_3	1.20	1.20	1.20	1.20	0.80	1.20	1.20	1.20	1.20	0.80
S'/S_o	1.095	0.894	1.521	0.947	0.894	1.095	0.894	1.362	1.071	0.894
q'/q_o	1.095	0.894	1.193	1.263	0.894	1.095	0.894	1.321	1.120	0.894
C'/C_o	1.004	1.006	1.038	1.039	1.006	1.004	1.006	1.047	1.017	1.006

The table uses estimates of the parameters which are $\pm 20\%$ of the true values for $c_2/c_1 = 0.5$ and for $c_2/c_1 = 10.0$. Somewhat comparable estimates have been used in Table 3–2b. The results for C'/C_o in the two tables seem to indicate that the sensitivity of the respective systems is about the same.

If we now compare the results of Table 5–2c for $c_2/c_1 = 10.0$ with the corresponding results in Table 4–2b, it is evident that the order-level system is indeed more sensitive to estimates of parameters than the order-level–lot-size system.

UNIFORM REPLENISHING RATE

5–3 In Section 3–4 we analyzed an inventory system with a uniform replenishing rate. In that system the reorder point s was prescribed (it was equal to zero) and the system was a type (1, 3) system. We now analyze an extension of that system with no restriction on the reorder point. We thus have a type (1, 2, 3) system. The inventory fluctuations of the system (when both inventory is carried and shortages exist) are described graphically in Figure 5–3.

We shall only investigate the case represented by this figure, since by previous arguments we have seen that the optimal solution will be in an appropriate range of S.

Let t' be the length of time over which replenishment takes place at the rate p. By the end of this period the lot size q will have been added to stock. Hence

$$t' = q/p \tag{1}$$

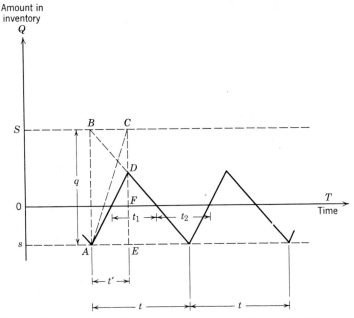

Figure 5-3 An order-level–lot-size system with a uniform replenishing rate.

Since inventory rises along the line AD at a rate of $p - r$, we have

$$\overline{ED} = t'(p - r) = q(1 - r/p) \tag{2}$$

From Figure 5-3 we also have

$$\overline{EF} = q - S \tag{3}$$

and from equations (2) and (3)

$$\overline{FD} = \overline{ED} - \overline{EF} = q(1 - r/p) - (q - S) = S - qr/p \tag{4}$$

From equation (4) we can conclude that for the optimal solution it is impossible to have $S - qr/p < 0$. Nor can we have $S > q$. Hence the relevant range for the optimal S should be

$$qr/p \leqq S \leqq q \tag{5}$$

From Figure 5-3 we also have

$$I_1 = \tfrac{1}{2}\overline{FD}\, t_1/t \tag{6}$$

But, by similar triangles,

$$\frac{t_1}{t} = \frac{\overline{FD}}{\overline{ED}} \tag{7}$$

Hence, by equations (4), (6), and (7) we have

$$I_1 = \frac{\frac{1}{2}(S - qr/p)^2}{q(1 - r/p)} \tag{8}$$

Similarly,

$$I_2 = \frac{\frac{1}{2}(q - S)^2}{q(1 - r/p)} \tag{9}$$

The number of replenishments per unit time, I_3, is $1/t$, or

$$I_3 = \frac{r}{q} \tag{10}$$

The total cost of the system, by equations (8), (9), and (10), and recalling equation (5), is

$$C(S, q) = \frac{c_1(S - qr/p)^2}{2q(1 - r/p)} + \frac{c_2(q - S)^2}{2q(1 - r/p)} + \frac{c_3 r}{q} \qquad \frac{qr}{p} \leqq S \leqq q \tag{11}$$

Let $\bar{c}$ be defined by

$$\bar{c} = \frac{1 - r/p}{1/c_1 + 1/c_2} \tag{12}$$

The minimum cost of the system can readily be shown to be

$$C_o = \sqrt{2r\bar{c}c_3} \tag{13}$$

The optimal order level and lot size are

$$S_o = \frac{C_o}{c_1} \tag{14}$$

and

$$q_o = \frac{C_o}{\bar{c}} \tag{15}$$

Similarly, results identical with those given by equations 5–1(15) to 5–1(24) hold here, remembering, though, that $\bar{c}$ is given by equation 5–3(12).

The present system is more general than several systems which we have analyzed before. In particular we can note the following.

1. The lot-size system of Section 3–1 can be obtained from the present system by taking $c_2 = \infty$ and $p = \infty$.

3. The system of Section 3–4 can be obtained by taking $c_2 = \infty$ in the present system.

3. The system of problem 3–5(2) can be obtained by taking $c_1 = \infty$ and $p = \infty$ in the present system.

4. The order-level–lot-size system of Section 5–1 can be obtained by taking $p = \infty$ in the present system.

(In passing, we should note, however, that the system of problem 4–6(6) *cannot* be obtained from the present system!)

LOST SALES

5–4 In all the previous sections of this chapter the unit shortage costs had the dimension $[\$]/[Q][T]$. In the present section we shall discuss a system for which the unit shortage cost has the dimension $[\$]/[Q]$. This is the lost-sales case discussed in Section 4–4. However, there we had a $(1, 2)$-type system. Here we shall extend the results to a $(1, 2, 3)$-type system.

The total cost of the system can be obtained immediately and directly from equation 4–4(2). It is only necessary to add to the equation the replenishment cost per unit time, $C_3 = c_3 r/q$, and to remove the constraint on t_p. Recalling also that $t = q/r$ and that for an optimal solution it will suffice to consider the costs for $0 \leqq S \leqq q$, we then have the pertinent total cost of the system as

$$C(S, q) = \frac{c_1 S^2}{2q} + \frac{c_2(q - S)r}{q} + \frac{c_3 r}{q} \qquad 0 \leqq S \leqq q \qquad (1)$$

If we attempt to find the optimal S_o and q_o by partial differentiation, etc., it turns out that this leads to a blind alley [see problem 5–5(7)]. The following approach leads to the correct solution with a minimum of effort. Let

$$k = \frac{S}{q} \qquad (2)$$

Since $0 \leqq S \leqq q$ then $0 \leqq k \leqq 1$. Equation (1) can then be given by

$$C(k, q) = \frac{c_1 k^2 q}{2} + c_2(1 - k)r + \frac{c_3 r}{q} \qquad 0 \leqq k \leqq 1 \qquad (3)$$

For a fixed k, using the methods leading to equations 3–1(8) and 3–1(10), we have

$$q_o = \sqrt{\frac{c_3 r}{c_1 k^2/2}} = \frac{1}{k}\sqrt{\frac{2r c_3}{c_1}} \qquad (4)$$

and

$$C(k, q_o) = \sqrt{4(c_1 k^2/2)(c_3 r)} + c_2(1 - k)r \qquad 0 \leqq k \leqq 1 \qquad (5)$$
$$= k(\sqrt{2r c_1 c_3} - c_2 r) + c_2 r$$

Equation (5) immediately implies that either $k_o = 0$ or $k_o = 1$: if $\sqrt{2rc_1c_3} - c_2r \geq 0$, then $k_o = 0$, and if $\sqrt{2rc_1c_3} - c_2r \leq 0$, then $k_o = 1$. That is,

$$k_o = \begin{cases} 0 & \sqrt{2rc_1c_3} - c_2r \geq 0 \\ 1 & \sqrt{2rc_1c_3} - c_2r \leq 0 \end{cases} \tag{6}$$

Using equations (2), (4), (5), and (6) we then have the solution for $c_2 \leq \sqrt{2c_1c_3/r}$

$$q_o = \infty$$
$$S_o = 0 \tag{7}$$
$$C_o = c_2r$$

and for $c_2 \geq \sqrt{2c_1c_3/r}$

$$q_o = \sqrt{2rc_3/c_1}$$
$$S_o = \sqrt{2rc_3/c_1} \tag{8}$$
$$C_o = \sqrt{2rc_1c_3}$$

The results in equations (7) and (8) can also be obtained directly by using the following argument. Consider the reorder point $s = S - q$. We know from previous work that the optimal reorder point s_o will not be a positive quantity, that is, $s_o \leq 0$. We now propose to show that either $s_o = 0$ or $s_o = -\infty$. Suppose this assertion is wrong. That is, suppose s_o has some finite negative value $s_o = v$. We can then ask why is $s = v$ better than, say, $s = v - e$ where e is a small positive or negative quantity. By ordering at $s = v$ instead of at $s = v - e$, we presumably have some advantage. For the latter case there is a change in the shortage cost of only c_2e. If such an advantage exists, then it should also apply for $s = v - e$ as compared to $s = v$, etc. Hence $s_o = v$ cannot be the optimal reorder point, so that indeed either $s_o = 0$ or $s_o = -\infty$. Once this is established the results of equations (7) and (8) follow immediately. (This argument, incidentally, does not hold for the order-level–lot-size system of Section 5-1. There the change in the shortage cost is not c_2e but $c_2(-s + e/2)$, a function of s.) Problem 5-5 (8) further illustrates the point.

The results in equations (7) and (8) indicate that the structure of the solution is an "either-or" affair. *Either* no inventory is carried ($S_o = 0$) and no replenishments are made ($q_o = \infty$) (this occurs when the unit cost of shortage is relatively small), *or* no shortages are allowed ($S_o = q_o$) and the system reduces to the lot-size system of Section 3-1 (this occurs when the unit shortage cost is relatively large, but not necessarily infinite).

The system of this section can be considered an extension of either the system of Section 4–4 or of the order-level–lot-size system of Section 5–1. However, the structure of its solution is quite different from the structures of the other two systems. This, we believe, is an interesting result.

5–5   PROBLEMS

1. Solve the order-level–lot-size system for $r = 25$ lb per month, $c_1 = \$9$ per pound per month, $c_2 = \$16$ per pound per month, and $c_3 = \$288$ per replenishment. For the optimal solution find I_1, I_2, I_3, t_1, and t_2.

2. Solve the previous problem if the order level S and the lot size q are both restricted to multiples of 20 lb.

3. In Section 5–1 derive the results given by equations (12) to (24).

4. Derive equation 5–2(7) from equations 5–2(1) to 5–2(6).

5. Prepare a table similar to Table 5–2c for $c_2/c_1 = 2.0$. Compare the results with Tables 3–2b and 4–2b.

6. In an order-level–lot-size system similar to that of Section 5–3, $r = 1200$ units per year, $p = 6000$ units per year, $c_1 = \$8$ per unit per year, $c_2 = \$24$ per unit per year, and $c_3 = \$180$ per setup.
   Solve the system and describe graphically the inventory fluctuations for the optimal solution.

7. Attempt to solve equation 5–4(1) using (a) partial differentiation, etc., and (b) Lagrangian multipliers.

8. In the system of Section 5–4, let $r = 4$ units per week, $c_1 = \$3$ per unit per week, and $c_3 = \$150$ per replenishment. Let the non-positive reorder point s be fixed. Let $C_o(s)$ be the minimum cost of the system for the optimal lot size q_o.
   Find $C_o(s)$ for $s = 0$, -1, and -2 when (a) $c_2 = \$10$ per unit, (b) $c_2 = \$20$ per unit.

9. In the system of Section 5–1 a decision maker assumes that $c_2 = \infty$ when in fact it is not. What additional costs are incurred?

10. Formulate and analyze order-level–lot-size systems that are extensions of the system of (a) Section 3–5, (b) Section 4–5, and (c) problem 4–6(7).

11. Demand for an item is at a uniform rate of r units per unit of time. The carrying cost is c_1 per unit per unit of time. The shortage cost is c_2 per unit of time over which the shortage exists. The replenishment cost is c_3. Solve the system and interpret the results. Compare the system with that of Section 5–4.

Chapter 6

Lot-Size Systems
with Various Cost Properties

6–0   In all the systems that have been analyzed so far, the unit cost of carrying inventory, c_1, was a constant with dimension $[\$]/[Q][T]$, and the unit cost of replenishments, c_3, was a constant with dimension $[\$]$. We shall now examine several systems in which the cost structure of these units has different properites.

In Section 6–1 we shall deal with inventory systems with quantity discounts. In these systems the price of the item dealt with depends on the lot size. This in turn affects both the unit carrying cost and the unit replenishing cost, which now become functions of the lot size. In the system of Section 6–2 we are also concerned with the price of the item. We are also interested in the kind of decisions that have to be made when a price change is anticipated. We shall see that the type of analysis needed here is somewhat different from the analysis of all other systems dealt with thus far in this book.

The system of Section 6–3 is an extension of that of Section 3–5. Both systems deal with several items in a lot-size system. In the system of Section 6–3 the unit cost of ordering, c_3, is not a constant as in Section 3–5 but depends on the number of items being ordered. In Section 6–4 we examine inventory systems in which the dimension of the unit carrying cost is $[\$]/[Q]^m[T]^n$. When $m = 1$ and $n = 1$, these systems reduce to the lot-size system of Section 3–1. When $m = 1$ and $n > 1$, we have the perishable-goods system. When $m > 1$ and $n = 1$, we have the expensive-storage system.

Additional systems with other special cost properties are covered in the problems, Section 6–5.

QUANTITY DISCOUNTS

6–1 Inventory systems in which the purchasing price per unit quantity depends on the quantity purchased are generally referred to as systems with *quantity discounts*. Such systems are frequently encountered in practice. Usually the unit purchasing price decreases as the quantity purchased increases. However, situations can arise when other relations may hold.

Let us consider an extension of the lot-size system of Section 3–1 when there is a quantity discount. Let $b(q)$ be the purchasing price per unit quantity whenever a lot size q is purchased. Let the carrying-cost fraction be f per unit time. Then the unit carrying cost will be, by equation 2–3(14),

$$c_1 = fb(q) \tag{1}$$

Let there be a fixed cost of e_3 whenever an order is placed and received. The unit cost of replenishment is then

$$c_3 = e_3 + qb(q) \tag{2}$$

Since replenishments will be made every q/r units of time, the total cost of the system is then

$$C(q) = fb(q)\frac{q}{2} + \frac{e_3 + qb(q)}{q/r} \tag{3}$$

$$= \tfrac{1}{2}fqb(q) + \frac{e_3 r}{q} + rb(q)$$

The solution of the system will now depend on the explicit form of the function $b(q)$.

Example 6–1a

Let $b(q) = b_0 - b_1 q$ where $b_0 \gg b_1$. Equation 3 then becomes

$$C(q) = \tfrac{1}{2}fq(b_0 - cb_1 q) + e_3 r/q + r(b_0 - b_1 q) \tag{4}$$

In this case the optimal lot size can be found by solving the cubic equation

$$fb_1 q_0{}^3 - (fb_0/2 - rb_1)q_0{}^2 + re_3 = 0 \tag{5}$$

This equation may also be written as

$$q_0 = \sqrt{(2re_3 + 2fb_1 q_0{}^3)/(fb_0 - 2rb_1)}$$

from which q_0 can be obtained by successive iterations. As we might expect, this result reduces to the classical lot-size formula of equation 3–1(5) for the case $b_1 = 0$, since $c_1 = fb_0$ and $c_3 = e_3$.

Discrete Quantity Discounts

In systems with discrete quantity discounts the function $b(q)$ will in general be given in the form

$$b(q) = \begin{cases} b_1 & q_1 \leq q < q_2 \\ b_2 & q_2 \leq q < q_3 \\ \cdot & \cdot \\ \cdot & \cdot \\ \cdot & \cdot \\ b_{n-1} & q_{n-1} \leq q < q_n \\ b_n & q \geq q_n \end{cases} \tag{6}$$

Here, then, n prices are specified. Lot sizes smaller than q_1 are not allowed. For lot sizes in the range q_1 to q_2 the price is b_1. In the range q_2 to q_3 the price is b_2, etc. For quantities equal to or larger than q_n the price is b_n. The quantities $q_1, q_2, \ldots$, are increasing. The prices $b_1, b_2, \ldots, b_n$, will, in general, be decreasing.

The total cost of the system, by equations (3) and (6), can thus be given by

$$C(q) = \tfrac{1}{2}fqb_i + e_3 r/q + rb_i \qquad q_i \leq q < q_{i+1} \tag{7}$$

A method of solving this system for decreasing prices is illustrated in the following example.

Example 6-1b

The purchasing price of a commodity depends on the quantity purchased as in Table 6-1.

TABLE 6-1
Quantity Discount Prices

Lot size	Between	100	500	2250	3200	5250
	And	499	2249	3199	5249	over
Price per unit		$2.55	$2.50	$2.45	$2.40	$2.35

The demand for the commodity is constant and uniform at a rate of 4000 per year. The carrying-cost fraction is 20% per year. The cost of ordering and handling is $40 per order. What is the optimal lot size?

Let $C(q')$ be the cost of the system for lot sizes $q' = q_i = 100, 500,$ 2250, 3200, and 5250. Let q_o' be a specific q' for which

$$C(q_o') \leq C(q') \tag{8}$$

Starting with $q' = 100$, we obtain $C(100) = \$11,826$ per year, $C(500) = \$10,445$, $C(2250) = \$10,422$, $C(3200) = \$10,418$, and $C(5250) = \$10,664$. Hence $q_o' = 3200$ and the corresponding total cost is $10,418 per year.

Let q_o'' be the largest lot size for which

$$q_i = q_o'' \leqq \sqrt{2re_3/fb_i} < q_{i+1} \tag{9}$$

In our example $q_o'' = 800$ and the corresponding total cost is \$10,400 per year. Since $C(q_o'') < C(q_o')$, the optimal lot size of the system is $q_o'' = 800$. Otherwise, q_o' would have been the optimal lot size. Figure 6–1 illustrates these results.

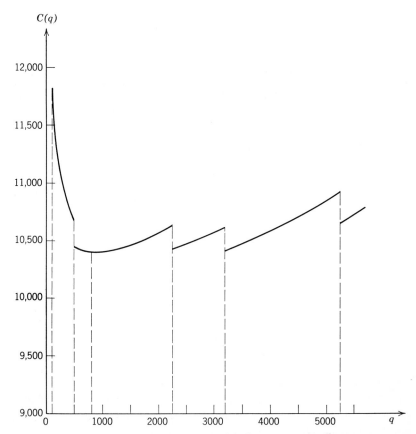

Figure 6–1   Total cost of a system with discrete quantity discounts.

PRICE CHANGE ANTICIPATION

6-2 In this section we analyze inventory systems in which the price of the commodity being replenished is expected to change. We first discuss a system in which a known increase of price is anticipated. We intuitively feel that a "large" amount should be purchased just before the new price goes into effect. The purchase of too large an amount, however, will considerably increase the carrying costs. We therefore have a problem of deciding what the optimum amount should be. After examining this system we discuss a more general one in which the anticipated change of price is not known precisely, but the probability density of the price change is known.

The type of decision made in both systems differs somewhat from the decisions discussed so far. Up to now most optimal decisions were of a repetitive type. That is, whenever we determined an optimal lot size q_o, it was assumed that this lot size would be ordered again and again, as long as the properties of the system remained the same. Therefore the measure of effectiveness used in these systems was the *total cost per unit time*. In the present systems, however, we do not have a repetitive decision. In each system a price change is anticipated and only one decision is made. Hence the measure of effectiveness to be used will be total cost ([$]) rather than total cost per unit time ([$]/[$T$]).

The general approach to the development of the appropriate models will be to compare the cost of not taking advantage of the anticipated price change with the cost of purchasing an amount q' just before the price change. The amount q_o' which will maximize the difference between these costs will thus give the required solution.

Known Price Increase

In an inventory system identical with the lot-size system of Section 3–1 let the cost of purchasing the commodity be d per unit quantity and let the carrying-cost fraction per unit time be p. The unit carrying cost will then be

$$c_1 = p\,d \tag{1}$$

Assume now that the vender announces that the price of the commodity will be increased by an amount k as of some date T_0. That is, purchases before time T_0 will cost d per quantity unit but purchases after time T_0 will cost $d + k$. In this system we must decide what amount should be purchased just before time T_0. Let the optimal amount be designated by q_o'.

In order to develop the appropriate model, we can reason as follows: if an amount q' is purchased just before time T_0, the next purchase will occur at time T_1 after an elapse q'/r units of time. This next purchase will be made at the new price of $d + k$ and the optimal lot size will then be, by equation 3–1(5),

$$q_o = \sqrt{2rc_3/[(d + k)p]} \tag{2}$$

After time T_1, purchases of q_o will continue to be made every q_o/r units of time, and the total cost of the system will then be, by equation 3–1(6), $\sqrt{2rc_3(d + k)p}$ per unit time. When $q' = 0$, that is, no purchase at all is made just before time T_0, T_1 and T_0 coincide and the cost of the system is again $\sqrt{2rc_3(d + k)p}$ per unit time but as of time T_0. The inventory situation is described graphically in Figure 6–2. The dotted lines represents what happens when $q' = 0$.

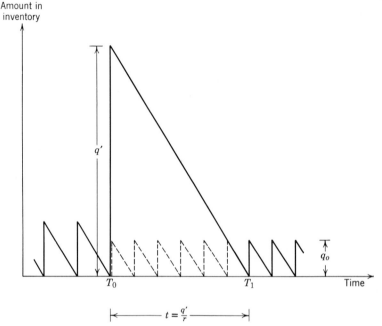

$$t = \frac{q'}{r}$$

Figure 6–2 Known price increase. Comparison of amounts in inventory for $q' > 0$ and for $q' = 0$.

Let K' designate the total cost of the system during the period T_0 to T_1 when an amount $q' > 0$ is purchased at the cost d per quantity unit. The total cost will comprise the purchasing cost dq', the carrying cost $(q'/2)(dp)t$, and the ordering cost c_3. That is,

$$K' = dq' + \frac{q'}{2} dp\frac{q'}{r} + c_3 \tag{3}$$

Let K designate the total cost of the system during the period T_0 to T_1 when no purchase is made just before T_0, but when several* purchases of

* On the average there will be q'/q_o such purchases during T_0 to T_1.

q_o are made at the new price $d + k$. This total cost will comprise the purchasing cost $(d + k)q'$, the carrying cost $(q_o/2)[(d + k)p]t$, and the ordering cost $(q'/q_o)c_3$. That is,

$$K = (d + k)q' + \frac{q_o}{2}(d + k)p\frac{q'}{r} + \frac{q'}{q_o}c_3$$

$$= (d + k)q' + \sqrt{2rc_3(d + k)p}\,\frac{q'}{r} \tag{4}$$

To find the optimal q_o' we must maximize the difference between K and K'. Let this difference be G. Then

$$G = K - K' = q'[k + \sqrt{2c_3(d + k)p/r}] - \frac{dp}{2r}q'^2 - c_3 \tag{5}$$

From equation (5) we can obtain the results

$$q_o' = \sqrt{2c_3r/[(d + k)p]}\,\frac{d + k}{d} + \frac{kr}{pd}$$

$$= q_o\left(1 + \frac{k}{d}\right) + \frac{r}{p}\frac{k}{d}$$

$$= q_o + \frac{k}{d}\left(q_o + \frac{r}{p}\right) \tag{6}$$

and

$$G_o = \frac{k}{d}\left[\frac{k}{2}\frac{r}{p} + q_o(d + k) + c_3\right] \tag{7}$$

Example 6–2

The purchasing price of a commodity, until December 31, 1968, will be $0.31 per pound. As of January 1, 1969, the price will be increased to $0.34 per pound. The commodity is being used at a uniform rate of 450 lb per month. The annual carrying cost is 20% of the cost of commodity carried in inventory. The cost of ordering and handling an order is $5.10. What amount should be purchased on December 31, 1968?

Here, then, $d = 0.31 per pound, $k = 0.03 per pound, $r = 450$ lb per month $= 5400$ lb per year, $p = 0.20$ per year, and $c_3 = 5.10. Hence, by equations (6) and (7), $q_o' = 3600$ lb and $G_o = 69.30. That is, we ought to purchase 3600 lb on December 31, 1968. This amount will last for 8 months; thereafter, $q_o = 900$ lb ought to be purchased every 2 months.

In Table 6–2 the total costs of the inventory system for the period December 31, 1968 to December 31, 1969 are given for various values of q'. For each value of q' we derive the corresponding total cost K' of equation (3). We then compute the remaining costs in 1969 for consecutive orders of 900, every 2 months. The last row in the table thus gives the values of G of equation (5). As expected, the computations confirm the results $q_o' = 3600$ lb and $G_o = \$69.30$.

TABLE 6-2

Total-Cost Comparisons: December 31, 1968 *to December* 31, 1969

Purchase q' on Dec. 31, 1968	0	900	1800	2700	3600	4500	5400
Period t covered (in months)	0	2	4	6	8	10	12
Purchases at $0.34 in 1969	5400	4500	3600	2700	1800	900	0
Number of purchases in 1969	6	5	4	3	2	1	0
Cost of purchase on Dec. 31, 1968	0	279.00	558.00	837.00	1116.00	1395.00	1674.00
Carrying cost during t	0	4.65	18.60	41.85	74.40	116.25	167.40
Ordering cost on Dec. 31, 1968	0	5.10	5.10	5.10	5.10	5.10	5.10
Total cost K' during t	0	288.75	581.70	883.95	1195.50	1516.35	1846.50
Cost of purchases in 1969	1836.00	1530.00	1224.00	918.00	612.00	306.00	0
Carrying costs of 1969 purchases	30.60	25.50	20.40	15.30	10.20	5.10	0
Ordering costs of 1969 purchases	30.60	25.50	20.40	15.30	10.20	5.10	0
Total cost of system	1897.20	1869.75	1846.50	1832.55	1827.90	1832.55	1846.50
Gain G bases on total cost for $q' = 0$	0	27.45	50.70	64.65	69.30	64.65	50.70

Variable Price Change

Before considering a general anticipated price change, a few observations must be made about price *decrease*. Most of the analysis which has just been developed also applies to a *price decrease* of an amount k' when $0 < k' < d$. We need only substitute $-k'$ for k and equations (2), (4), and (5) hold for a price decrease. The gain when purchasing q' will then be

$$G = q'[-k' + \sqrt{2c_3(d - k')p/r}] - \frac{dp}{2r} q'^2 - c_3 \qquad (8)$$

It is obvious that when a price decrease is anticipated, no quantity should be purchased at all, that is, $q_o' = 0$. Hence we would expect that whenever $k' > 0$ and $q' > 0$, then $G < 0$, that is, a loss will be incurred. To prove this statement we must show, by equation (8), that

$$\sqrt{2c_3(d - k')p/r} < \frac{c_3}{q'} + \frac{q'dp}{2r} + k'.$$

And indeed, for $k' > 0$ and $q' > 0$, we have*

$$\sqrt{2c_3(d - k')p/r} < \sqrt{2c_3\,dp/r} = 2\sqrt{(c_3/q')(q'\,dp/2r)}$$

$$\leqq \frac{c_3}{q'} + \frac{q'\,dp}{2r} < \frac{c_3}{q'} + \frac{q'\,dp}{2r} + k'.$$

Thus, whenever $k' > 0$, then $q_o' = 0$. (The corresponding optimal gain in this case is zero and not that obtained from either equation (8) or (5). These equations hold only for $q' > 0$.)

We now turn to the more general case of anticipated price change. Let k be the price change and let $f(k)$ be the probability density of k. The expected gain, for a purchase of quantity $q' > 0$, just before T_0 (when the price change is anticipated), will be

$$G(q') = \int_{-d}^{\infty} q'[k + \sqrt{2c_3(d + k)p/r}]f(k)\,dk - \frac{dp}{2r}q'^2 - c_3$$

$$= q'\left[\bar{k} + \int_{-d}^{\infty} \sqrt{2c_3(d + k)(p/r)}f(k)\,dk\right] - \frac{dp}{2r}q'^2 - c_3 \qquad (9)$$

where $\bar{k}$ is the expected value of k. In general the value of k will be relatively smaller than d, so that $\sqrt{d + k}$ can be approximated by $\sqrt{d}(\sqrt{1 + k/d} \approx \sqrt{d}(1 + k/2d)$. In that case equation (9) becomes

$$G(q') = q'\left[\bar{k} + \sqrt{2c_3\,dp/r}\left(1 + \frac{\bar{k}}{2d}\right)\right] - \frac{dp}{2r}q'^2 - c_3 \qquad (10)$$

Here again we can immediately see that when $\bar{k} < 0$, then $q_o' = 0$, since otherwise there will be a loss. To show this we have to demonstrate that

$$\sqrt{2c_3\,dp/r}\left(1 + \frac{\bar{k}}{2d}\right) < \frac{c_3}{q'} + \frac{q'\,dp}{2r} - \bar{k}.$$

* The relation between the second and third terms is based on the identity $2\sqrt{ab} \leqq a + b$, which in turn is based on $(\sqrt{a} - \sqrt{b})^2 \geqq 0$.

And indeed, for $k < 0$ and $q' > 0$, we have

$$\sqrt{2c_3\,dp/r}\left(1 + \frac{k}{2d}\right) < \sqrt{2c_3\,dp/r} = 2\sqrt{(c_3/q')q'\,dp/2r}$$

$$\trianglelefteq \frac{c_3}{q'} + \frac{q'\,dp}{2r} < \frac{c_3}{q'} + \frac{q'\,dp}{2r} - k$$

Now, when $\bar{k} > 0$, equation (10) leads to

$$q_o{}' = \bar{q}_o + \frac{\bar{k}}{d}\left(\bar{q}_o + \frac{r}{p}\right) \tag{11}$$

where $\bar{q}_o$ is an optimal lot size based on an expected price change of $\bar{k} > 0$. That is,

$$\bar{q}_o = \sqrt{2rc_3/[(d + \bar{k})p]} \tag{12}$$

The corresponding maximum gain will then be

$$G_o = \frac{\bar{k}}{d}\left[\frac{\bar{k}}{2}\frac{r}{p} + \bar{q}_o(d + \bar{k}) + c_3\right] \tag{13}$$

HANDLING ITEMS ON ORDERS

6-3 The system considered in this section is an extension of the system of Section 3–5 which is a lot-size system with an ordering cost pertaining to several items. In the system of Section 3–5, whenever an order is placed a fixed cost c_3 is incurred. This cost is independent of the number of items on the order (nor does it depend on the amount of each item ordered).

We now consider a system in which the ordering cost depends on the number of different items on the order. That is,

$$c_3 = c_{31} + c_{32}n \tag{1}$$

where c_{31} and c_{32} are constants and where n is the number of different items on the order.

There are N different items in our system. The constant rate of demand for item j is r_j, and its carrying cost is c_{1j} per quantity unit per time unit. Let t be the length of time between consecutive orders and let t_j be the length of time between the orders that include item j. Obviously the ratio t_j/t must be a positive integer. Let this ratio be designated by k_j:

$$k_j = t_j/t \qquad k_j = 1, 2, \ldots \tag{2}$$

If item j is ordered every $t_j = tk_j$ units of time, its lot size will be

$$q_j = t_j r_j = tk_j r_j \tag{3}$$

Therefore the carrying cost per time unit of item j will be

$$\tfrac{1}{2}q_j c_{1j} = \tfrac{1}{2}tk_j r_j c_{1j} \tag{4}$$

The carrying cost of all N items is therefore

$$C_1 = \sum_{j=1}^{N} \tfrac{1}{2}tk_j r_j c_{1j} = \tfrac{1}{2}t \sum_{j=1}^{N} k_j r_j c_{1j} \tag{5}$$

If an order is placed every t units of time, there will be $1/t$ orders per time unit. Item j will be ordered $1/t_j$ times per unit time. Therefore, on the average, item j will appear $(1/t_j)/(1/t) = t/t_j$ times on every order. Thus the average number of items per order $\bar{n}$ will be

$$\bar{n} = \sum_{j=1}^{N} \frac{t}{t_j} = \sum_{j=1}^{N} \frac{1}{k_j} \tag{6}$$

The cost of each order, by equation (1), will be $c_{31} + \bar{n}c_{32}$. The ordering cost per unit time is then

$$C_3 = \left(c_{31} + c_{32} \sum_{j=1}^{N} \frac{1}{k_j}\right)\Big/ t \tag{7}$$

The total cost of this system is therefore a function of t and the positive integers k_j, and is given by

$$C(t, k_j) = \tfrac{1}{2}t \sum_{j=1}^{N} k_j r_j c_{1j} + \left(c_{31} + c_{32} \sum_{j=1}^{N} \frac{1}{k_j}\right)\Big/ t \tag{8}$$

Prescribed Scheduling Period

When the scheduling period t is prescribed, the total cost of the system becomes

$$C(k_j) = \tfrac{1}{2}t_p \sum_{j=1}^{N} k_j r_j c_{1j} + \left(c_{31} + c_{32} \sum_{j=1}^{N} \frac{1}{k_j}\right)\Big/ t_p \qquad k_j = 1, 2, \ldots \tag{9}$$

There are no general methods for solving this equation. One approach is to treat the function $C(k_j)$ as if the k_j are continuous variables not restricted to discrete values. This then gives the approximate solution

$$k_{jo} \approx \frac{\sqrt{2c_{32}/t_p}}{\sqrt{r_j c_{1j}}} \qquad k_{jo} = 1, 2, \ldots \tag{10}$$

The corresponding minimum cost is then approximately

$$C_o \approx \sqrt{2c_{32}} \sum_{j=1}^{N} \sqrt{r_j c_{1j}} + \frac{c_{31}}{t_p} \tag{11}$$

The minimum cost in equation (11) will in general not be realized since for any item j the right-hand side of equation (10) will usually not be an integer and will have to be rounded off to the nearest integer.

Example 6–3a

A store uses four items for which the demand rates r_j in pounds per year and the inventory carrying costs c_{1j} per pound per year are

Item	j	1	2	3	4
Demand rate	r_j	180	100	320	36
Carrying cost	c_{1j}	$0.20	1.00	1.25	0.25

The cost of ordering is $5.00 per order and $1.00 for each item on the order. The prescribed scheduling period is 1 month. When should each item be ordered?

Here we have $c_{31} = \$5.00$, $c_{32} = \$1.00$, and $t_p = \frac{1}{12}$ years. Equation (10) gives

$$k_{jo} \approx \frac{16.96}{\sqrt{r_j c_{1j}}} \tag{12}$$

Hence, after rounding off, $k_{1o} = 3$, $k_{2o} = 2$, $k_{3o} = 1$, and $k_{4o} = 6$. Applying these results in equation (9) gives $C_o = \$115.76$ per year. (Note that equation (11) gives the somewhat lower value of $115.15, the difference resulting from the roundoffs of the k_{jo}.) In this example, then, item 1 ought to be ordered every 3 months, item 2 every 2 months, item 3 every month, and item 4 every 6 months.

Optimal Scheduling Period

When the scheduling period t is not prescribed, the optimal scheduling period t_o can be obtained from equation (8),

$$t_o = \sqrt{2\left(c_{31} + c_{32}\sum_{j=1}^{N}\frac{1}{k_j}\right)\bigg/\sum_{j=1}^{N}r_j c_{1j}k_j} \tag{13}$$

and the corresponding minimum cost is

$$C_o = \sqrt{2\left(c_{31} + c_{32}\sum_{j=1}^{N}\frac{1}{k_j}\right)\sum_{j=1}^{N}r_j c_{1j}k_j} \tag{14}$$

When the k_j are prescribed, equations (13) and (14) constitute the solution of the system. However, if their optimal values have to be determined, further analysis is necessary. The problem now is to find the k_{jo} which minimize C_o in equation (14).

There is no explicit method for finding the k_{jo}. One possible approach is as follows. Partial differentiation of C_o in equation (14) with respect to k_j, etc., gives equation (15) in which the k_{jo} are on both sides of the equation:

$$k_{jo} \approx \frac{\sqrt{c_{32}\sum_{j=1}^{N}r_j c_{1j}k_{jo}\bigg/\left(c_{31} + c_{32}\sum_{j=1}^{N}\frac{1}{k_{jo}}\right)}}{\sqrt{r_j c_{1j}}} \tag{15}$$

This equation can now be used to find the k_{jo} by an interative process. Estimates of k_{jo} are substituted on the right-hand side of equation (15) to give new estimates on the left. The process terminates when the new estimates are equal to the previous estimates. There is only the question of getting the first estimates. They can be obtained from

$$k_{jo} \approx \frac{\sqrt{c_{32} \sum_{i=1}^{N} \dfrac{r_i c_{1i}}{c_{31} + c_{32}N}}}{\sqrt{r_j c_{1j}}} \tag{16}$$

Example 6-3b

Using the data of Example 6-3a, find (1) the optimal scheduling period if $k_1 = 3$, $k_2 = 2$, $k_3 = 1$, and $k_4 = 6$, (2) the optimal scheduling period if the k_j are not prescribed.

To obtain the first solution we use equation (13). This gives $t_o = 1.43$ months and $C_o = \$103.8$ per year. In this case orders will be placed about every $1\frac{1}{2}$ months. Item 1 will be ordered every $4\frac{1}{2}$ months, item 2 every 3 months, item 3 every $1\frac{1}{2}$ months, and item 4 every 9 months. The cost of the system for this solution will be about $103.80 per year, an amount less than the cost of the system of Example 6-3a in which the scheduling period was prescribed.

To obtain the second solution we use equation (16) to obtain the first estimates: $k_{jo} \approx 7.8/\sqrt{r_j c_{1j}}$. Hence, after roundoffs, $k'_{1o} = 1$, $k'_{2o} = 1$, $k'_{3o} = 1$, and $k'_{4o} = 3$. Substituting these values on the right side of equation (15) gives $k_{jo} = 8.2/\sqrt{r_j c_{1j}}$. After roundoffs we again obtain $k_{1o} = k_{2o} = k_{3o} = 1$ and $k_{4o} = 3$. These indeed are the optimal values. Substituting them in equations (13) and (14), we eventually find $t_o = 2.06$ months and $C_o = \$96.85$ per year. Thus, orders will be placed every 2 months. Items 1, 2, and 3 will be ordered every 2 months and item 4 every 6 months.

VARIOUS CARRYING-COST PROPERTIES

6-4 The amounts in inventory during a typical scheduling period t in a lot-size system with a constant demand rate r are as shown in Figure 6-4. In all systems that have been studied until now, the total cost K of carrying inventory during the scheduling period t has been assumed to be

$$K = \tfrac{1}{2}c_1 qt \tag{1}$$

where c_1 had the dimension $[\$]/[Q][T]$. In these systems the total cost K can be said to change linearly with changes in the lot size q or with changes in the scheduling period t.

We will now study more general systems in which the total cost K is given by

$$K = ac_1 q^m t^n \tag{2}$$

where a is a dimensionless constant and where the unit carrying cost has the dimension

$$[c_1] = [\$]/[Q]^m[T]^n \tag{3}$$

Such systems may sometimes be encountered in practice.

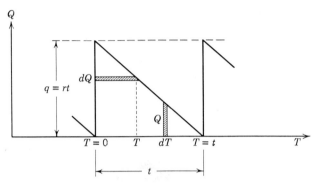

Figure 6–4   The amount in inventory in a lot-size system during a typical scheduling period.

The Perishable-Goods System

When perishable goods are carried in inventory the relevant total cost during the scheduling period will not be as in equation (1). That is, the cost of carrying an amount dQ for a period T (see Figure 6–4) will *not* be $c_1 T\, dQ$. Instead we can expect a cost of the form

$$dK = c_1 T^n\, dQ \tag{4}$$

where n is a parameter larger than 1 and c_1 has the dimension of $[\$]/[Q][T]^n$. To find the total cost K during the scheduling period we should first note that the amount in inventory Q at any time T is

$$Q(T) = q - rT \tag{5}$$

Hence, by equation (4),

$$K = \int_0^q c_1 T^n\, dQ = \int_0^q c_1 \left(\frac{q - Q}{r}\right)^n dQ = \frac{c_1 q^{n+1}}{r^n(n + 1)} \tag{6}$$

[Equation (6) can be compared with equation (2). If in equation (6) we put $q = rt$, we then have $K = [1/(n + 1)]c_1 qt^n$ so that the perishable goods system becomes a special case of equation (2) for $a = 1/(n + 1)$ and $m = 1$.]

The total cost of the system per unit time is therefore

$$C(q) = \frac{K + c_3}{t} = \frac{r(K + c_3)}{q} = \frac{c_1 q^n}{r^{n-1}(n + 1)} + \frac{rc_3}{q} \tag{7}$$

By differentiation, etc., we obtain the solution (for $n \geq 1$)

$$q_o = \sqrt[n+1]{\frac{n + 1}{n} \frac{c_3 r^n}{c_1}} \tag{8}$$

and

$$C_o = \sqrt[n+1]{[c_3(n + 1)/n]^n c_1 r} \tag{9}$$

The Expensive-Storage System

In analogy with the perishable-goods system there are systems in which the cost to carry Q quantity units in storage for a small period of time dT is

$$dK = c_1 Q^m \, dT \tag{10}$$

where $[c_1] = [\$]/[Q]^m[T]$. For a system with such a cost property we have, by equation (5),

$$K = \int_0^t c_1 Q^m \, dT = \int_0^t c_1(q - rT)^m \, dT = \frac{c_1 q^{m+1}}{r(m + 1)} \tag{11}$$

(This is a special case of equation (2) when $a = 1/(m + 1)$ and $n = 1$.)

The total cost of the system per unit time is thus

$$C(q) = \frac{K + c_3}{t} = \frac{c_1 q^m}{m + 1} + \frac{rc_3}{q} \tag{12}$$

Hence the solution of the system is (for $m \geq 1$)

$$q_o = \sqrt[m+1]{\frac{m + 1}{m} \frac{c_3 r}{c_1}} \tag{13}$$

and

$$C_o = \sqrt[m+1]{\left[\frac{c_3 r(m + 1)}{m}\right]^m c_1} \tag{14}$$

The General System

We have seen that the carrying-cost property of equation (4) led to the cost of equation (6) which was a special case of equation (2). Similarly, the carrying-cost property in equation (10) led to equation (11) which was also a special case of equation (2).

If we use equation (2) to obtain the total cost per unit time, we obtain

$$C(q) = \frac{K + c_3}{t} = ac_1 q^m t^{n-1} + \frac{c_3}{t} = \frac{ac_1 q^{m+n-1}}{r^{n-1}} + \frac{c_3 r}{q} \qquad (15)$$

from which we find the solution (for $m + n - 1 \geqq 0$)

$$q_o = {}^{m+n}\sqrt{c_3 r^n / [ac_1(m + n - 1)]} \qquad (16)$$

and

$$C_o = (m + n) \, {}^{m+n}\sqrt{ac_1 r^m c_3^{m+n-1} / (m + n - 1)^{m+n-1}} \qquad (17)$$

6-5   PROBLEMS

1. Curves A_1, A_2, and A_3 in Figure 6–5 represent the total costs of the quantity-discounts system of Section 6–1. The unit purchasing prices b_1, b_2, and b_3

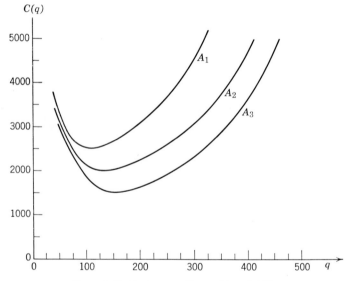

Figure 6–5   Cost curves for problem 6–5(1).

are respectively $0.10, $0.09, and $0.08. Find the optimal purchase quantity q_o and the corresponding purchasing price and minimum total cost when
    (a) b_1 = $0.10 for $1 \leqq q < 200$, b_2 = $0.09 for $200 \leqq q < 350$, b_3 = $0.08 for $q \geqq 350$.
    (b) b_1 = $0.10 for $1 \leqq q < 300$, b_2 = $0.09 for $300 \leqq q < 400$, b_3 = $0.08 for $q \geqq 400$.
2. In Section 6–2 on price-change anticipation assume that $r = 100$ parts per year, d(the old price) = $2.00 per part, x (the fraction increase of

price) $= 0.316$, p (the annual cost of carrying inventory as a fraction of the cost of a part) $= 0.10$, $c_3 = \$25.60$ per order, and q_o has the same value as in equation 6–2(2).

(a) Find the purchase quantity of q_o' using Whitin's ([55], pp. 38–41) solution.*

$$q' = \frac{r}{p}\frac{x}{1+x} + q_o\sqrt{1+x} \tag{1}$$

(b) Find the optimal purchase quantity q_o' using equation 6–2(6)

$$q_o' = \frac{r}{p}x + q_o(1+x) \tag{2}$$

(c) Find the difference in the total cost for these solutions for a comparable period of time (say 5 years).
(For ease in computations use the numerical values $x/(1+x) = 0.24$ and $\sqrt{1+x} = 1.15$, and roundoff the value of q' and q_o' to multiples of 10.)

3. The optimal purchase quantity has been 10,000 parts as long as the price was \$0.099 per part. A price change to \$0.101 per part suggested the purchasing of 20,000 parts just before the change.
Prepare a numerical example which could justify these statements.

4. Four items have constant and uniform usage. Their yearly requirements and their unit costs of carrying inventory per year are respectively 125 units, 64 units, 180 units, 16 units, \$0.20, \$1.00, \$1.25, and \$0.25. The cost of handling is \$5.00 per order. Find the minimum yearly costs if (a) each item is ordered separately and (b) all four items are placed on every order.

5. The data are as in problem 4, but in addition there is a cost of \$1.00 for each item on an order. Find the minimum yearly cost if (a) all four items are placed on every order, and (b) orders are handled at equal intervals, but not all four items are placed on every order.

6. A central warehouse handles orders from three districts.** The constant and uniform usage r_{ij} at each district i for item j and the unit costs of carrying inventory per year a_j are

j $\diagdown$ i	1	2	3	4
1	16	49	100	0
2	36	100	400	9
3	25	64	225	4
a_j	\$0.20	\$1.00	\$1.25	\$0.25

* This solution is based on somewhat different properties from the ones assumed in Section 6–2. It is the optimal solution for those properties.
** For a detailed treatment of problems of this kind see Naddor and Saltzman [40].

The cost of handling an order (at a district and at the warehouse) is $5.00 per order. The cost associated with each item placed on an order is $1.00 per item. All districts send their orders at the same equal intervals. Not all items, however, appear on each order.

   (a) Find the optimal interval of ordering.

   (b) Find the optimal frequency of placing each item on the orders.

   (c) Find the minimum cost of the system.

7. Interpret the system of Section 6–4 for the following special cases:

$$
\begin{array}{ll}
\text{(a) } m = 0,\, n = 0 & \text{(d) } m = 1,\, n = 1 \\
\text{(b) } m = 0,\, n = 1 & \text{(e) } m = 1,\, n = 0 \\
\text{(c) } m > 0,\, n = 1 & \text{(f) } m = 1,\, n > 0
\end{array}
$$

8. Consider an extension of the lot-size system of Section 3–1, in which there is an additional storage cost of a_1 per unit time for each unit storage required. Develop the model and give its solution.

9. In the order-level system of Section 4–1 the total cost per unit time of carrying inventories or for incurring shortages can be expressed as

$$
C_k = \frac{1}{2}\frac{c_k M_k t_k}{t_p} \tag{3}
$$

where $k = 1$ refers to carrying costs, $k = 2$ refers to shortage costs, and where $M_1 = S$ and $M_2 = rt_p - S$. Consider an extension of this system in which the corresponding costs are given by

$$
C_k = a\,\frac{c_k M_k{}^m t_k{}^n}{t_p} \tag{4}
$$

where a is some constant and where the dimension of c_k is $[\$]/[Q]^m[T]^n$. Solve the system and interpret the results for

$$
\begin{array}{ll}
\text{(a) } m = 0,\, n = 0 & \text{(d) } m = 1,\, n = 1 \\
\text{(b) } m = 0,\, n = 1 & \text{(e) } m = 1,\, n = 0 \\
\text{(c) } m > 0,\, n = 1 & \text{(f) } m = 1,\, n > 0
\end{array}
$$

10. Solve the system of Section 6–2 when an amount Q' is expected to be in inventory at time T_0. (Note that in the system of Section 6–2 $Q' = 0$.)

11. In an inventory system the cost of having Q units in inventory for T units of time is bQT^3. Demand is uniform at a constant rate of r units per unit time. No shortages are allowed. The replenishing cost is c_3. Solve the system.

Chapter 7

Deterministic Systems
with Non-constant Demand

7-0 Our definition of deterministic systems included systems in which demand is not necessarily constant. Whereas all systems discussed until now were deterministic systems with constant demand, we shall now deal with systems in which demand varies and the variability is known.

In the system of Section 7–1 the demand rate r changes continuously. At any point of time T the corresponding rate is aT where a is a known constant. We shall analyze a type (1, 3) system with such a property.

In the system of Section 7–2 the prescribed planning period H is divided into N equal subperiods. At the beginning of each subperiod i there is a demand x_i. The x_i are not necessarily equal. However, their magnitude is assumed to be known. A type (1, 2) system with this property will be analyzed.

The systems of Sections 7–1 and 7–2 should be considered only as examples of deterministic inventory systems with non-constant demands. The reader should have no difficulty in recognizing many other systems with deterministic but non-constant demands. The methods of this chapter may illustrate approaches to the solution of such systems.

INCREASING DEMAND

7-1 A type (1, 3) system with increasing demand may be operated under one of several policies. We shall first examine the system with a (s, q) policy where $s_o = 0$ and where q_o has to be determined. Then a (t, S_i) policy will be explored. We shall see that under this policy several order levels of S_i, which, in turn, depend on the optimal t_o, must be considered. Finally, a third policy will be proposed which is "better" than the previous two policies.

Under all policies the inventory system will be assumed to have the following properties.

1. The system operates only during a prescribed period which is H units of time long.

2. During the period H there exists a total demand for D quantity units.

3. The rate of demand r changes linearly with time T. That is,

$$r = aT \tag{1}$$

The constant a can be determined from

$$D = \int_0^H r \, dT = \int_0^H aT \, dT = \frac{aH^2}{2} \tag{2}$$

Hence

$$r = \frac{2D}{H^2} T \tag{3}$$

4. The relevant unit costs are c_1, the unit carrying cost in $[\$]/[Q][T]$, and c_3, the unit replenishing cost in $[\$]$.

Increasing Demand and a (s, q) Policy

For this policy it is obvious that $s_o = 0$. Hence the inventory fluctuations can be described graphically as in Figure 7–1a.

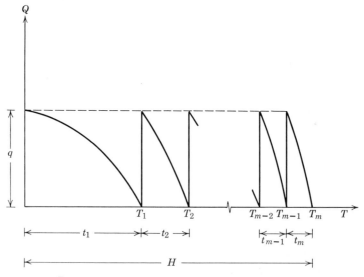

Figure 7–1a Increasing demand and an (s, q) policy.

Let m be the number of replenishments to be made during the period H. Then

$$q = \frac{D}{m} \qquad m = 1, 2, 3, \ldots \qquad (4)$$

To find the average amount carried in inventory during the period H, it is best to consider the amounts in inventory shown in Figure 7–1b. The total amount in inventory J_1 during the period H is the shaded portion

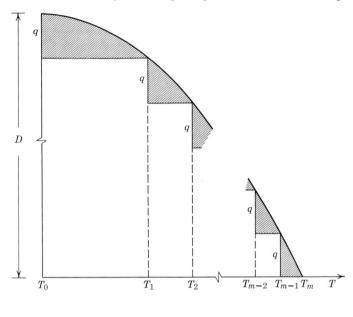

Figure 7–1b   Increasing demand and an (s, q) policy—alternate view.

in the figure and corresponds to the amount in Figure 7–1a. It can be computed as the difference between the area under the parabola and $m - 1$ rectangles:

$$J_1 = \tfrac{2}{3}DH - \sum_{i=1}^{m-1} (m - i)q(T_i - T_{i-1}) \qquad (5)$$

An expression for the T_i of Figure 7–1a (or of Figure 7–1b) can be obtained as follows. During any scheduling period t_i the total demand is $\int_{T_{i-1}}^{T_i} r\,dT$ and this equals the lot size q. Hence from equations (3) and (4) we obtain

$$\frac{D}{m} = \int_{T_{i-1}}^{T_i} r\,dT = \frac{D}{H^2}(T_i^2 - T_{i-1}^2) \qquad (6)$$

Therefore

$$T_i^2 - T_{i-1}^2 = \frac{H^2}{m} \qquad (7)$$

Since $T_0 = 0$, we may now derive a general expression for T_i from equation (7):

$$T_i = H\sqrt{i/m} \qquad (8)$$

The average amount in inventory is $I_1 = J_1/H$. Hence by equations (2), (4), (5), and (8),

$$I_1 = \frac{1}{H}\left[\frac{2}{3}DH - \sum_{1}^{m-1}(m-i)\frac{D}{m}H(\sqrt{i/m} - \sqrt{(i-1)/m})\right]$$

$$= D\left[\frac{2}{3} - \frac{1}{m\sqrt{m}}\sum_{1}^{m-1}(m-i)(\sqrt{i} - \sqrt{i-1})\right]$$

$$= \frac{D}{m}\left(\frac{2m}{3} - \frac{\sqrt{1} + \sqrt{2} + \cdots + \sqrt{m-1}}{\sqrt{m}}\right)$$

$$= \frac{D}{m}h(m) \qquad (9)$$

where

$$h(m) = \frac{2m}{3} - \frac{\sqrt{1} + \sqrt{2} + \cdots + \sqrt{m-1}}{\sqrt{m}} \qquad (10)$$

Several values of the function $h(m)$ are given in Table 7-1a.

TABLE 7-1a

Values of the Function

$$h(m) = 2m/3 - (\sqrt{1} + \sqrt{2} + \cdots + \sqrt{m-1})/\sqrt{m}$$

m	1	2	3	4	5	6	7	8	9	10
$h(m)$	0.667	0.626	0.606	0.594	0.585	0.578	0.573	0.568	0.565	0.562

The total-cost equation of the system becomes

$$C(m) = c_1 I_1 + c_3 I_3 = \frac{c_1 D h(m)}{m} + \frac{c_3 m}{H} \qquad (11)$$

Since m is discrete we can use the methods of Section 3-1 to find the optical value m_o. We readily obtain

$$F(m_o - 1) \leqq \frac{c_1 DH}{c_3} \leqq F(m_o). \qquad (12)$$

where

$$F(m) = \frac{m(m+1)}{(m+1)h(m) - mh(m+1)} \tag{13}$$

and where $h(m)$ is given by equation (10).

By relating the cost equation (11) to the cost equation of the lot-size system of Section 3–1, we can infer that the minimum cost of the present system will generally be within the range

$$2\sqrt{\tfrac{1}{2}c_1 c_3 D/H} < C_o < 2\sqrt{\tfrac{2}{3}c_1 c_3 D/H} \tag{14}$$

Increasing Demand and a (t, S_i) Policy

The inventory fluctuations for this policy may be described graphically as in Figure 7–1c. In this system the scheduling period t is constant. Hence

$$t = \frac{H}{m} \tag{15}$$

and

$$T_i = \frac{Hi}{m} \tag{16}$$

The order levels S_i at points of time T_{i-1} change from point to point. Hence by equations (3) and (2)

$$S(T_i) = S_{i+1} = \int_{T_i}^{T_{i+1}} r \, dT = \frac{D}{H^2}(T_{i+1}^2 - T_i^2) = \frac{D}{m^2}(2i + 1) \tag{17}$$

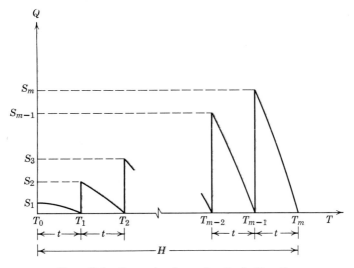

Figure 7–1c   Increasing demand and a (t, S) policy.

We can find the average inventory I_1 in a manner similar to that used for the (s, q) policy. The total amount in inventory J_1 during H may be found from Figure 7–1d. The amount J_1 is the shaded area. It is given by

$$J_1 = \tfrac{2}{3}DH - \sum_{1}^{m-1} itS(T_i) \tag{18}$$

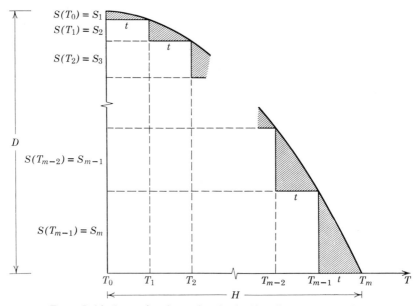

Figure 7–1d   Increasing demand and a (t, S_i) policy—alternate view.

Hence the average amount in inventory I_1, by equations (1), (3), and (4), is

$$
\begin{aligned}
I_1 &= \frac{1}{H}\left[\tfrac{2}{3}DH - \sum_{1}^{m-1} i\,\frac{H}{m}\frac{D}{m^2}(2i+1)\right]\\[4pt]
&= D\left[\frac{2}{3} - \frac{1}{m^3}\sum_{1}^{m-1} i(2i+1)\right]\\[4pt]
&= D\left[\frac{2}{3} - \frac{1}{m^3}\left(\sum_{1}^{m-1} 2i^2 + \sum_{1}^{m-1} i\right)\right]\\[4pt]
&= D\left\{\frac{2}{3} - \frac{1}{m^3}\left[\frac{2(m-1)m(2m-1)}{6} + \frac{(m-1)m}{2}\right]\right\}\\[4pt]
&= D\left[\frac{2}{3} - \frac{(1/m^2)(m-1)(4m+1)}{6}\right]\\[4pt]
&= \frac{D}{m}\left(\frac{1}{2} + \frac{1}{6m}\right) \tag{19}
\end{aligned}
$$

The average inventory can thus be expressed as

$$I_1 = \frac{D}{m} k(m) \qquad (20)$$

where

$$k(m) = \frac{1}{2} + \frac{1}{6m} \qquad (21)$$

Several values of $k(m)$ are given in Table 7-1b

TABLE 7-1b

Values of the Function $k(m) = \frac{1}{2} + 1/6m$

m	1	2	3	4	5	6	7	8	9	10
$k(m)$	0.667	0.583	0.556	0.542	0.533	0.528	0.524	0.521	0.519	0.517

The total-cost equation of the system becomes

$$C(m) = \frac{c_1 D k(m)}{m} + \frac{c_3 m}{H} \qquad (22)$$

where $k(m)$ is given by equation (21). The solution given by equations (12) to (14) applies here with the exception that the $h(m)$ should be replaced by $k(m)$.

Comparison of the (s, q) and (t, S_i) Policies

The total cost of the system under consideration for the (s, q) policy is given by equation (11) where $h(m)$ is as in equation (10) and for the (t, S_i) policy it is given by equation (22) where $k(m)$ is as in equation (21). Let the first total cost be designated by C_q and let the second cost be C_t. We will now show that

$$C_q \geqq C_t \qquad (23)$$

That is, the policy with equal scheduling periods is better than the policy with equal lot sizes. To show that the relation in equation (23) holds, it will be sufficient to show that for every m

$$\frac{2m}{3} - \frac{\sqrt{1} + \sqrt{2} + \cdots + \sqrt{m-1})}{\sqrt{m}} \geqq \frac{1}{2} + \frac{1}{6m} \qquad (24)$$

This result is illustrated for $m = 1, 2, \ldots, 10$ in Tables 7-1a and 7-1b. To prove it in general equation (24) can be rearranged so that we have only to show that

$$\sqrt{1} + \sqrt{2} + \cdots + \sqrt{m} \leqq \frac{(4m-1)(m+1)}{6\sqrt{m}} \qquad (25)$$

Let the left side of equation (25) be defined by

$$f(m) = \sqrt{1} + \sqrt{2} + \cdots + \sqrt{m} \qquad (26)$$

Thus we have to show that for all m

$$f(m) \leqq \frac{(4m - 1)(m + 1)}{6\sqrt{m}} \qquad (27)$$

We shall prove this by induction.

First note that equation (27) holds for $m = 1$ (both sides equal 1) and for $m = 2$ (2.414 < 2.475). Suppose now that equation (27) holds for $m = k$. That is, suppose

$$f(k) \leqq \frac{(4k - 1)(k + 1)}{6\sqrt{k}} \qquad (28)$$

For it to hold for $m = k + 1$ we must show that

$$f(k + 1) = f(k) + \sqrt{k + 1} \leqq \frac{[4(k + 1) - 1][(k + 1) + 1]}{6\sqrt{k + 1}} \qquad (29)$$

or that

$$f(k) \leqq \frac{(4k + 3)(k + 2)}{6\sqrt{k + 1}} - \sqrt{k + 1} \qquad (30)$$

But*

$$\frac{(4k - 1)(k + 1)}{6\sqrt{k}} < \frac{(4k + 3)(k + 2)}{6\sqrt{k + 1}} - \sqrt{k + 1} \qquad (31)$$

Hence if equation (28) holds so does equation (30). This completes the proof, and thus indeed the assertion of equation (23) is correct.

Increasing Demand and a (t_i, S_i) Policy

Both the (s, q) policy and the (t, S_i) policy, which were studied earlier, are restrictive in some sense. In the (s, q) policy all lot sizes are of the same magnitude q. Similarly, in the (t, S_i) policy all the scheduling periods are of the same length t. We have already seen that the (t, S_i) policy is better than the (s, q) policy. We can now ask whether there exists a policy in which the lot sizes and the scheduling periods are not constrained and which would be better than the (t, S_i) policy. There is, indeed, such a policy. We shall call it a (t_i, S_i) policy. The inventory fluctuations under such a policy are described graphically in Figure 7–1e.

Both the scheduling periods t_i and the order levels S_i depend on the number of replenishments m and on the scheduling points T_i.

---

* To show that equation (31) holds we must show that $(4k - 1)^2(k + 1)^3 < k^3(4k + 5)^2$. This result is immediate upon expanding both sides and comparing the corresponding fifth-degree polynomials.

From Figure 7–1e we have

$$t_i = T_i - T_{i-1} \tag{32}$$

And by equation (6) we have

$$S_i = \frac{D}{H^2}(T_i^{\,2} - T_{i-1}^2) \tag{33}$$

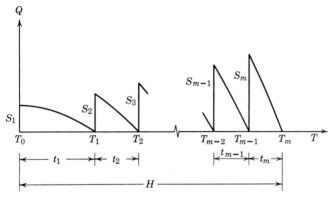

Figure 7–1e Increasing demand and a (t_i, S_i) policy.

To find J_1, the total amount in inventory during H, consider Figure 7–1d when the scheduling periods do not have the same length. By analogy with equation (18) we have, by equation (33),

$$J_1 = \tfrac{2}{3}DH - \sum_{i=2}^{m} S_i T_{i-1}$$

$$= \tfrac{2}{3}DH - \frac{D}{H^2}\sum_{i=2}^{m}(T_i^2 - T_{i-1}^2)T_{i-1} \tag{34}$$

The total cost of the system is then

$$C(m, T_i) = \frac{c_1 J_1}{H} + \frac{c_3 m}{H} \tag{35}$$

Equation (35) is rather difficult to solve, for we must find a positive integer m and continuous variables $T_1, \ldots, T_{m-1}$ which minimize the total cost in equation (35). The following method gives satisfactory results. The optimal number of replenishments m_o is found from equation (12) when $h(m)$ is replaced by $k(m)$ of equation (21). Then the optimal values of T_{io} are found from*

$$T_{io} = \tfrac{1}{2}H(i/m_o + \sqrt{i/m_o}) \tag{36}$$

* This is the mean of the results of equations (8) and (16). See also problem 7–3(11).

Example 7–1

A contract calls for the delivery of 7200 parts over a period of 3 years at a linearly increasing rate. The carrying cost is $0.56 per part per year and the setup cost is $42.00 per setup.

Under a (s, q) policy we find that for equations (12), (13), and (10):

$$c_1 DH/c_3 = 0.56 \times 7200 \times 3/42000 = 288, \quad F(12) = 268.5 \quad \text{and} \quad F(13) = 313.2.$$

Hence $m_o = 13$ setups in 3 years. By equation (4), $q_o = 7200/13 \approx 554$ parts. The corresponding cost, by equation (11), is $354 per year.

Under a (t, S_i) policy we find, by equations (12), (13), and (21), that $c_1 DH/c_3 = 288$ as before, $F(11) = 249.3$, and $F(12) = 296.0$. Hence $m_o = 12$ setups in 3 years. The optimal scheduling period, by equation (15), is then $\frac{1}{4}$ year = 3 months. The corresponding cost, by equation (22), is $341 per year.

Under the (t_i, S_i) policy m_o is again 12 setups in 3 years. The values for the T_{io}, by equation (36), can be found from $T_{io} = 1.5(i/12 + \sqrt{i/12})$. Substituting these values in equations (34) and (35) gives $327 per year.

VARIABLE KNOWN DEMAND

7–2   In the inventory system of this section there are N equal and pre-scribed scheduling periods t_p in every planning period H. The demand x_i occurs at the beginning of each scheduling period i. The x_i are not neces-sarily equal.

A constant and prescribed lot size q_p is added to inventory at the begin-ning of each scheduling period. This lot size is the average demand

$$q_p = \sum_{i=1}^{N} \frac{x_i}{N} \tag{1}$$

The only variable subject to control in the system is the inventory level S at the beginning of each planning period H. This is then a type $(1, 2r$ system in which the carrying costs have to be balanced against the shortage costs. We shall assume that the unit carrying cost is c_1 in $[\$]/[Q][T]$ and the unit shortage cost is c_2 in $[\$]/[Q][T]$. The inventory fluctuations of the system are represented graphically in Figure 7–2.

Let Q_i indicate the amount in inventory during the ith scheduling period. Then

$$Q_i = S + iq_p - \sum_{j=1}^{i} x_j \tag{2}$$

Let R_j' be defined by

$$R_i' = \sum_{j=1}^{i} x_j - iq_p \tag{3}$$

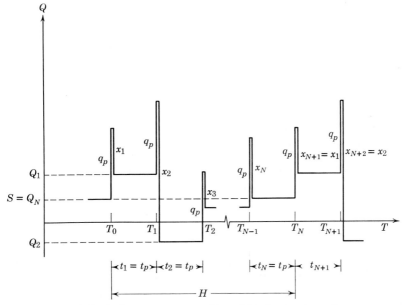

Figure 7–2   An inventory system with variable known demand.

(Note that $R_N' = 0$.) By equations (2) and (3) we thus have

$$Q_i \begin{cases} \geqq 0 & S \geqq R_i' \\ < 0 & S < R_i' \end{cases} \tag{4}$$

The R_i' of equation (3) form a sequence of N numbers. Let us rearrange these numbers into a sequence of N non-decreasing numbers and let us designate them by R_i. Thus

$$R_i \leqq R_{i+1} \qquad i = 1, \ldots, N - 1 \tag{5}$$

Suppose now that we consider a level S which lies in the interval $R_m \leqq S < R_{m+1}$ where m is some specific integer. The total cost of the system is then given by

$$C(S) = c_1 \sum_{i=1}^{m}(S - R_i) + c_2 \sum_{i=m+1}^{N}(R_i - S) \qquad R_m \leqq S < R_{m+1} \tag{6}$$

This equation can be rearranged to give

$$\begin{aligned}
C(S) &= c_1 \sum_{i=1}^{m} S - c_1 \sum_{i=1}^{m} R_i + c_2 \sum_{i=m+1}^{N} R_i - c_2 \sum_{i=m+1}^{N} S \\
&= c_1 m S - c_1 \sum_{i=1}^{m} R_i + c_2 \sum_{i=1}^{N} R_i - c_2 \sum_{i=1}^{m} R_i - c_2(N - m)S \\
&= (c_1 + c_2)\left(m S - \sum_{i=1}^{m} R_i \right) - c_2 N S + c_2 \sum_{i=1}^{N} R_i \tag{7}
\end{aligned}$$

Let F_m be defined by

$$F_m = \sum_{i=1}^{m} R_i \qquad (8)$$

Then the total cost of the system can be expressed as

$$C(S) = (c_1 + c_2)(mS - F_m) - c_2 NS + c_2 F_N \qquad R_m \leq S < R_{m+1} \qquad (9)$$

To find the optimal level S_o we first consider values of S which are equal exactly to some R_i. From equation (9) we have for $m = 1, \ldots, N - 1$

$$
\begin{aligned}
C(R_{m+1}) - C(R_m) &= (c_1 + c_2)[(m + 1)R_{m+1} - mR_m - (F_{m+1} - F_m)] \\
&\quad - c_2 N(R_{m+1} - R_m) \\
&= (c_1 + c_2)[m(R_{m+1} - R_m) + R_{m+1} - R_{m+1}] \\
&\quad - c_2 N(R_{m+1} - R_m) \\
&= [(c_1 + c_2)m - c_2 N](R_{m+1} - R_m) \qquad (10)
\end{aligned}
$$

Similarly, by equation (10), we have for $m = 2, \ldots, N$

$$C(R_{m-1}) - C(R_m) = [c_2 N - (c_1 + c_2)(m - 1)](R_m - R_{m-1}) \qquad (11)$$

Since the sequence R_i is non-decreasing, we conclude that for $S = R_m$ to be the best level (compared to any $S = R_i$) we should have both

$$(c_1 + c_2)m_o - c_2 N \geq 0$$

$$c_2 N - (c_1 + c_2)(m_o - 1) \geq 0 \qquad (12)$$

or

$$m_o - 1 \leq N \frac{c_2}{c_1 + c_2} \leq m_o \qquad (13)$$

We now consider values of S not exactly equal to R_i. Let us compare the total cost for $S = R_m + e$, where e is some positive amount less than $(R_{m+1} - R_m)$, with the cost for $S = R_m$. From equation (9) we have

$$
\begin{aligned}
C(R_m + e) - C(R_m) &= (c_1 + c_2)[m(R_m + e) - mR_m - (F_m - F_m)] \\
&\quad - c_2 N(R_m + e - R_m) \\
&= (c_1 + c_2)(me) - c_2 Ne = [(c_1 + c_2)m - c_2 N]e
\end{aligned}
$$
$$(14)$$

For the specific value $m = m_o$ of equation (13), we always have

$$C(R_{mo} + e) - C(R_{mo}) \geq 0.$$

The solution of the system can therefore be stated as follows: If $m_o - 1 \leq Nc_2/(c_1 + c_2) \leq m_o$, then

$$S_o = R_{mo} \tag{15}$$

and if $Nc_2/(c_1 + c_2) = m_o$, then

$$R_{mo} \leq S_o \leq R_{mo+1} \tag{16}$$

Example 7-2

The weekly demands are known to be: Monday 14 lb, Tuesday 9 lb, Wednesday 17 lb, Thursday 2 lb, Friday 0 lb, Saturday 19 lb, and Sunday 9 lb. The carrying cost is \$0.20 per pound per day, and the shortage cost is \$0.50 per pound per day. Find the optimal level S_o at the beginning of each week.

Here $N = 7$ and by equation (1) we obtain $q_p = (14 + \cdots + 9)/7 = 10$ lb. The sequence R_i' is

$R_1' = 14 - 10 = 4$ lb, $R_2' = 14 + 9 - 20 = 3$ lb, $R_3' = 14 + 9 + 17 - 30 = 10$ lb, $R_4' = 14 + \cdots + 2 - 40 = 2$ lb, $R_5' = 14 + \cdots + 0 - 50 = -8$ lb, $R_6' = 14 + \cdots + 19 - 60 = 1$ lb, and $R_7' = 14 + \cdots + 9 - 70 = 0$ lb

The rearranged non-decreasing sequence R_i is thus

$R_1 = -8$ lb, $R_2 = 0$ lb, $R_3 = 1$ lb, $R_4 = 2$ lb, $R_5 = 3$ lb, $R_6 = 4$ lb, and $R_7 = 10$ lb.

The value of $Nc_2/(c_1 + c_2)$ is $7 \times 0.50/(0.20 + 0.50) = 5$. Hence, by equation (16), $m_o = 5$, and 3 lb $\leq S_o \leq 4$ lb. That is, the optimal level is any quantity between 3 and 4 lb.

7-3 PROBLEMS

1. In the inventory system of Section 7-1 show that the general total cost of the system can be given by

$$C(m) = mc_3 + c_1 \sum_{i=1}^{m} h_i q_i t_i = mc_3 + c_1 h \sum_{i=1}^{m} q_i t_i \tag{1}$$

where

$$h_i = \frac{1}{3}\left(1 + \frac{T_i}{T_i + T_{i-1}}\right) \tag{2}$$

and where

$$h = \frac{1}{3}\left\{1 + \left[\sum_{i=1}^{m}(T_i - T_{i-1})^2 T_i\right] \Big/ \left[\sum_{i=1}^{m}(T_i - T_{i-1})^2(T_i + T_{i+1})\right]\right\} \tag{3}$$

2. Prepare a numerical example for which the system of Section 7–1 will give $m_o = 2$ as the optimal number of replenishments. Compute the exact value of T_{io} and compare it with the approximate solution given by equation 7–1(36).

3. A manufacturing concern has fixed known demands during any week. The following demands occur at the end of the day: Monday, 9: Tuesday, 17; Wednesday, 2; Thursday, 0; Friday, 19; Saturday, 9; and Sunday, 14. Daily production must be constant and is available at the end of each day. The unit cost of shortage is four times the unit carrying cost. Find the optimal inventory at the beginning of each week.

4. Demand is known to cycle over a 14-day period: it is 10 on days 1, 2, and 3; 15 on days 4 to 7; 5 on days 8, 9, and 10; and 7 on days 11 to 14. The unit carrying cost is \$1.00 and the unit shortage cost is \$1.00. There are daily constant replenishments of inventory. Find the optimal level at the beginning of each cycle.

5. Solve the system of Section 7–1 when the rate of demand is given by

$$r = r_0 + aT \qquad (4)$$

6. Discuss the solution of the system of Section 7–2 for very small scheduling periods t_p. Assume that production is at a constant rate and that demands occur continuously with varying rates.

7. Define and solve an extension of the system of Section 7–2 in which the scheduling period is not prescribed and in which there is also a replenishing cost c_3.

8. Check the expansion of the summation in equation 7–1(9).

9. Compare the result given by equation 7–1(12) with the solution of the lot-size system of Section 3–1.

10. Compare the solutions of Examples 1–1 and 7–1.

11. Find the necessary conditions for the optimal T_i of equation 7–1(35) for a given m. Compare the results with the approximate solution given by equation 7–1(36).

Part 3

PROBABILISTIC
SCHEDULING-PERIOD
SYSTEMS

In the chapters of this part we begin to study inventory systems in which demand is not known with certainty. The scheduling period in all the systems is constant. Sometimes the scheduling period is prescribed (e.g., Sections 8–2, 8–3, 9–2, and 9–3). Other times we have to determine the optimal scheduling period (e.g., Sections 8–1, 8–4, 9–1, and 9–4).

In Chapter 8 the inventory systems have zero leadtime, whereas in Chapter 9 leadtime is non-zero. For the first time we shall be able to see the significant effect of leadtime on the analysis of inventory systems. This effect was negligible in deterministic systems.

In Chapter 10 we show how the analysis of several inventory systems can be simplified by using the notion of equivalence of inventory systems. For example, we see how a system with non-zero leadtime can be solved by using the solution of another system in which leadtime is zero.

Chapter 11 is devoted to the study of the effects of probabilistic demand and of leadtime on the cost of inventory systems. As we might expect intuitively, the minimum cost of a probabilistic system is larger than, or at least equal to the minimum cost of a similar but deterministic system. Similarly, a probabilistic system with non-zero leadtime is more costly than, or as costly as, a similar system with zero leadtime.

Chapter 12 deals with a specific probabilistic scheduling-period system in which the forecast of future demands is a part of the system itself. The system is analyzed using first a Markov-chain approach and then a simulation approach.

Chapter 8

Scheduling-Period–Order-Level Systems
without Leadtime

8–0 All the systems of this chapter deal with probabilistic inventory systems with a (t, S) policy. In all the systems leadtime is zero.

In the system of Section 8–1 the order level is prescribed so that no shortages occur. It is a type (1, 3) system in which the optimal scheduling period has to be determined. In the systems of Sections 8–2 and 8–3 the scheduling period is prescribed and we have to determine the optimal order level. Both systems are type (1, 2) systems. In the system of Section 8–2 the demand pattern is uniform; but in the system of Section 8–3 it is instantaneous. (In Chapter 10 we show that the systems are equivalent.) In Section 8–4 we discuss an extension of the systems of Sections 8–1, 8–2, and 8–3 when no constraints are placed on either the scheduling period or the order level.

THE PROBABILISTIC SCHEDULING-PERIOD SYSTEM

8–1 The inventory fluctuations in the probabilistic scheduling-period system are described in Figure 8–1a. In this system no shortages are allowed. Hence the order level must be large enough so that the maximum demand $x_{max}(t)$ during the period t will not cause shortages. That is,

$$S_p = x_{max}(t) \tag{1}$$

[Obviously, to minimize costs, we would never want to consider $S_p > x_{max}(t)$.]

This is then a type (1, 3) system. Let the unit costs of carrying and replenishing be respectively c_1 in [$]/[Q][T] and c_3 in [$]. Let $f(x)$ be the probability density of demand x during the scheduling period t, let $\bar{x}(t)$ be its mean, and let the average rate of demand be $r = \bar{x}(t)/t$, a known constant.

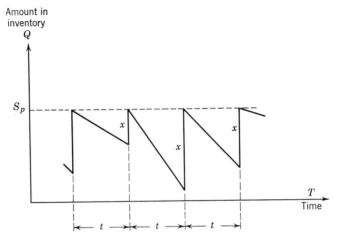

Figure 8–1a   The probabilistic scheduling-period system.

The average amount in inventory in any scheduling period during which there is a demand x is $S_p - x/2$. Hence the expected average amount in inventory is

$$I_1 = \int_{x_{\min}}^{x_{\max}} \left(S_p - \frac{x}{2} \right) f(x)\, dx = S_p - \frac{\bar{x}(t)}{2} = S_p - \frac{rt}{2} \qquad (2)$$

The number of replenishments per unit time is $1/t$. Hence, by equations (1) and (2), the expected total-cost equation of the system is

$$C(t) = c_1 \left(S_p - \frac{rt}{2} \right) + \frac{c_3}{t} = c_1 \left[x_{\max}(t) - \frac{rt}{2} \right] + \frac{c_3}{t} \qquad (3)$$

To find the optimal scheduling period it is now necessary to know only the function $x_{\max}(t)$. Let

$$x_{\max}(t) = \bar{x}(t)A(t) = rtA(t) \qquad (4)$$

where $A(t)$ is some function relating the maximum demand during any period t to the average demand during that period. Obviously,

$$A(t) \geq 1 \qquad (5)$$

Substituting the value of x_{max} of equation (4) into equation (3) gives

$$C(t) = c_1[A(t) - \tfrac{1}{2}]rt + \frac{c_3}{t} \qquad (6)$$

We now consider two special cases for the function $A(t)$. Other cases are given in the problems, Section 8–5.

Case 8–1a $A(t) = k$

When the ratio of maximum demand to the average demand during any period t is assumed to be a constant k, equation (6) becomes

$$C(t) = c_1(k - \tfrac{1}{2})rt + \frac{c_3}{t} \qquad (7)$$

Hence the solution of the system is

$$t_o = \sqrt{2c_3/[c_1 r(2k - 1)]} \qquad (8)$$
$$S_p = k\sqrt{2rc_3/[c_1(2k - 1)]} \qquad (9)$$
$$C_o = \sqrt{2c_1 c_3 r(2k - 1)} \qquad (10)$$

When demand is deterministic, then $k = 1$ and the system reduces to the lot-size system of Section 3–1. [In this connection compare equations (9) and (10) with equations 3–1(5) and 3–1(6).]

Case 8–1b $A(t) = 1 + b/t$

In realistic applications the ratio of the maximum demand to average demand during the period t would generally depend on t. We would expect that the larger t, the smaller the ratio. Suppose, then, that

$$A(t) = 1 + \frac{b}{t} \qquad (11)$$

where $[b] = [T]$. The cost equation of the system, by equation (6), becomes

$$C(t) = c_1\left(1 + \frac{b}{t} - \frac{1}{2}\right)rt + \frac{c_3}{t}$$
$$= \frac{c_1 rt}{2} + c_1 br + \frac{c_3}{t} \qquad (12)$$

Hence the solution

$$t_o = \sqrt{2c_3/(rc_1)} \qquad (13)$$
$$S_p = \sqrt{2rc_3/c_1} + br \qquad (14)$$
$$C_o = \sqrt{2rc_1 c_3} + c_1 br \qquad (15)$$

It is interesting to compare this system with the lot-size system of Section 3–1. If, in equation 3–1(2), we substitute rt for q we obtain

$$C(t) = \frac{c_1 rt}{2} + \frac{c_3}{t} \qquad (16)$$

Comparing this equation with equation (12), we immediately note that they differ only with respect to the term $c_1 br$ in equation (12). The amount br may thus be regarded as a buffer stock, as indicated in Figure 8–1b.

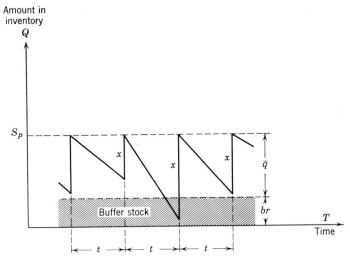

Figure 8–1b The probabilistic scheduling-period system when $x_{max}/\bar{x} = A(t) = 1 + b/t$.

THE PROBABILISTIC ORDER-LEVEL SYSTEM

8–2 The inventory fluctuations of the probabilistic order-level system are described in Figure 8–2a.

This is a type (1, 2) system in which the scheduling period t_p is pre-scribed and in which the optimal order level S_o must be determined. Let $f(x)$ be the probability density of demand x during t_p. This demand is assumed to occur with a uniform pattern. Let the unit carrying cost be c_1 in [\$]/[Q][T] and let the unit shortage cost be c_2 in [\$]/[Q][T].

Two typical situations arise in this system, depending on the relative values of S and x. They are described in Figure 8–2b. From the figure we see that the average amount in inventory $I_1(x)$ for a given demand x is

$$I_1(x) = \begin{cases} S - x/2 & x \leq S \\ S^2/2x & x \geq S \end{cases} \qquad (1)$$

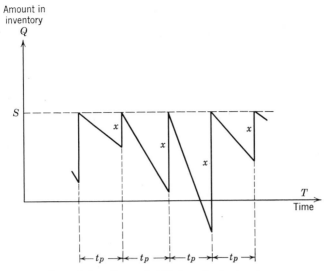

Figure 8–2a   The probabilistic order-level system.

Similarly, the average shortage is

$$I_2(x) = \begin{cases} 0 & x \leqq S \\ (x - S)^2/2x & x \geqq S \end{cases} \tag{2}$$

The expected average amount in inventory and the expected average shortage are therefore

$$I_1 = \int_0^S \left(S - \frac{x}{2}\right) f(x)\, dx + \int_S^\infty \frac{S^2}{2x} f(x)\, dx \tag{3}$$

and

$$I_2 = \int_S^\infty \frac{(x - S)^2}{2x} f(x)\, dx \tag{4}$$

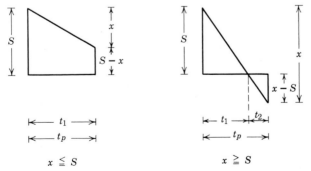

Figure 8–2b   Two typical situations in the probabilistic order-level system.

Hence the expected total cost of the system is

$$C(S) = c_1 \int_0^S \left(S - \frac{x}{2}\right) f(x)\, dx + c_1 \int_S^\infty \frac{S^2}{2x} f(x)\, dx$$

$$+ c_2 \int_S^\infty \frac{(x - S)^2}{2x} f(x)\, dx \quad (5)$$

To find the optimal level S_o, we have to differentiate $C(S)$ with respect to S and set the result equal to zero. This involves differentiation of an integral. It can be shown* that if

$$F(t) = \int_{A(t)}^{B(t)} G(t, x)\, dx \quad (6)$$

then

$$\frac{dF(t)}{dt} = \int_{A(t)}^{B(t)} \frac{\partial G(t, x)}{\partial t}\, dx + G[t, B(t)] \frac{dB(t)}{dt} - G[t, A(t)] \frac{dA(t)}{dt} \quad (7)$$

Applying this result to equation (5) we have

$$\frac{dC}{dS} = c_1 \left[\int_0^S f(x)\, dx + \frac{S}{2} f(S) \right] + c_1 \left[\int_S^\infty \frac{S}{x} f(x)\, dx - \frac{S}{2} f(S) \right]$$

$$+ c_2 \int_S^\infty \frac{-(x - S)}{x} f(x)\, dx \quad (8)$$

$$= (c_1 + c_2) \left[\int_0^S f(x)\, dx + \int_S^\infty \frac{S}{x} (fx)\, dx \right] - c_2$$

To find S_o we set $dC/dS = 0$. This leads to

$$\int_0^{S_o} f(x)\, dx + \int_{S_o}^\infty \frac{S_o}{x} f(x)\, dx = \frac{c_2}{c_1 + c_2} \quad (9)$$

To check whether S_o satisfying equation (9) gives a minimum we examine d^2C/dS^2. From equation (8) we obtain

$$\frac{d^2C}{dS^2} = (c_1 + c_2) \left[f(S) + \int_S^\infty \frac{f(x)}{x}\, dx - f(S) \right]$$

$$= (c_1 + c_2) \int_S^\infty \frac{f(x)}{x}\, dx \quad (10)$$

* See, for example, Sasieni, Yaspan, and Friedman [51], pp. 354–356.

Since $f(x)$ is a probability density, the value of d^2C/dS^2 is thus always positive; hence S_o satisfying equation (9) does indeed give the optimal solution.

Equation (9) is not in a form that permits the explicit evaluation of S_o. It is also impossible to evaluate the explicit minimum cost C_o. Only for some specific functions $f(x)$ is it possible to obtain S_o and C_o in explicit form. This is illustrated in Example 8-2a.

Example 8-2a

Let the demand density be

$$f(x) = \frac{1}{b^2} xe^{-x/b} \qquad x \geq 0 \tag{11}$$

This is a special case of the gamma distribution when the mean is $2b$ and the variance is $2b^2$. Substituting $f(x)$ in equation (9) gives

$$\int_0^{S_o} \frac{1}{b^2} xe^{-x/b}\, dx + \int_{S_o}^{\infty} S_o \frac{1}{b^2} e^{-x/b}\, dx = \frac{c_2}{c_1 + c_2} \tag{12}$$

The integrals can readily be evaluated so that we eventually obtain

$$S_o = b \ln \frac{c_1 + c_2}{c_1} \tag{13}$$

Substituting this value of S_o in equation (5) gives the minimum cost

$$C_o = bc_1 \ln \frac{c_1 + c_2}{c_1} \tag{14}$$

Discrete Units

When the demand x and the order level S are constrained to discrete units $0, u, 2u$, etc., let $P(x)$ be the probability distribution of the demand x. Then the integrals in equations (3) and (4) have to be replaced by summations so that the expected total cost of the system for discrete units, by equation (5), becomes

$$C(S) = c_1 \sum_{x=0}^{S} \left(S - \frac{x}{2} \right) P(x) + c_1 \sum_{x=S+u}^{\infty} \frac{S^2}{2x} P(x) + c_2 \sum_{x=S+u}^{\infty} \frac{(x-S)^2}{2x} P(x) \tag{15}$$

The necessary conditions for S_o to be the optimal order level are

$$C(S_o) \leq C(S_o + u) \tag{16}$$

$$C(S_o) \leq C(S_o - u) \tag{17}$$

To find the conditions for our system let us first evaluate in general the difference $C(S + u) - C(S)$:

$$C(S + u) - C(S) = c_1 \sum_{x=0}^{S+u} \left(S + u - \frac{x}{2}\right) P(x) + c_1 \sum_{x=S+2u}^{\infty} \frac{(S + u)^2}{2x} P(x)$$

$$+ c_2 \sum_{x=S+2u}^{\infty} \frac{(x - S - u)^2}{2x} P(x) - c_1 \sum_{x=0}^{S} \left(S - \frac{x}{2}\right) P(x)$$

$$+ c_1 \sum_{x=S+u}^{\infty} \frac{S^2}{2x} P(x) + c_2 \sum_{x=S+u}^{\infty} \frac{(x - S)^2}{2x} P(x) \qquad (18)$$

$$= \cdots$$

$$= u(c_1 + c_2)\left[\sum_{x=0}^{S} P(x) + \left(S + \frac{u}{2}\right) \sum_{x=S+u}^{\infty} \frac{P(x)}{x}\right] - uc_2$$

$$= u[(c_1 + c_2)M(S) - c_2]$$

where

$$M(S) = \sum_{x=0}^{S} P(x) + \left(S + \frac{u}{2}\right) \sum_{x=S+u}^{\infty} \frac{P(x)}{x} \qquad (19)$$

Applying this result in equations (16) and (17) we obtain the necessary conditions for finding S_o:

$$M(S_o - u) \leqq \frac{c_2}{c_1 + c_2} \leqq M(S_o) \qquad (20)$$

It can be shown [see problem 8–5(14)] that these are also sufficient conditions.

Example 8–2b

An item is ordered every week. The demand for the item during the week is uniform and with the probabilities $P(0) = 0.04$, $P(5) = 0.20$, $P(10) = 0.37$, $P(15) = 0.30$, and $P(20) = 0.09$. The carrying cost is $2 per unit per week. The shortage cost is $24 per unit per week. What should the optimal order level be at the beginning of each week?

In this example $u = 5$, $c_1 = 2, and $c_2 = 24. To find the values of $M(S)$ of equation (19) it is best to proceed as in Table 8–2. But $c_2/(c_1 + c_2) = 24/(2 + 24) = 0.923$. Hence, by equation (20) and Table 8–2, $S_o = 15$, since $0.91625 = M(10) < 0.923 < M(15) = 0.98875$.

As a check on this result we can calculate $C(S)$ of equation (15) for all values of S. This is done in the last column of Table 8–2. As expected, the least cost of the system occurs when $S = 15$.

TABLE 8-2

$$\text{Tabulation of } M(S) = \sum_{x=0}^{S} P(x) + \left(S + \frac{u}{2}\right) \sum_{x=S+u}^{\infty} \frac{P(x)}{x}.$$

x, S	$P(x)$	$\sum_{0}^{S} P(x)$	$\frac{P(x)}{x}$	$\sum_{S+u}^{\infty} \frac{(Px)}{x}$	$\left(S + \frac{u}{2}\right) \sum_{S+u}^{\infty} \frac{P(x)}{x}$	$M(S)$	$C(S)$
0	0.04	0.04		0.1015	0.25375	0.29375	132.00
5	0.20	0.24	0.0400	0.0615	0.46125	0.70125	50.19
10	0.37	0.61	0.0370	0.0245	0.30625	0.91625	21.35
15	0.30	0.91	0.0200	0.0045	0.07875	0.98875	20.46
20	0.09	1.00	0.0045	0	0	1.00000	29.00

THE PROBABILISTIC ORDER-LEVEL SYSTEM WITH INSTANTANEOUS DEMAND

8-3 In the previous section the inventory system had a uniform demand pattern. In the present section we shall deal with an instantaneous demand pattern. The inventory fluctuations of the system are described in Figure 8-3. This, too, is a type $(1, 2)$ system with a prescribed scheduling period t_p in which we want to determine the optimal order level S_o.

Let $f(x)$ be the probability density of demand x during t_p. This demand is now assumed to occur at the beginning of each scheduling period

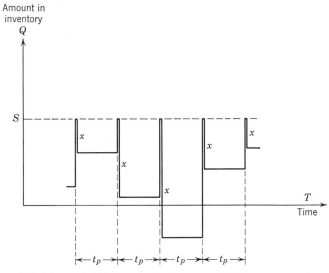

Figure 8-3 The probabilistic order-level system with instantaneous demand.

immediately after the inventory has been raised to the level S. Let the units of carrying cost and shortage cost be respectively c_1 and c_2 in $[\$]/[Q][T]$.

From Figure 8–3 we can immediately determine the amount in inventory $I_1(x)$ and the amount of shortage $I_2(x)$ for any demand x. Namely,

$$I_1(x) = \begin{cases} S - x & x \leq S \\ 0 & x \geq S \end{cases} \tag{1}$$

and

$$I_2(x) = \begin{cases} 0 & x \leq S \\ x - S & x \geq S \end{cases} \tag{2}$$

The expected amount in inventory and the expected shortage are now

$$I_1 = \int_0^S (S - x)f(x)\,dx \tag{3}$$

and

$$I_2 = \int_S^\infty (x - S)f(x)\,dx \tag{4}$$

Hence the expected total cost of the system is

$$C(S) = c_1 \int_0^S (S - x)f(x)\,dx + c_2 \int_S^\infty (x - S)f(x)\,dx \tag{5}$$

To differentiate $C(S)$ we again use equation 8–2(7). We find that

$$\frac{dC(S)}{dS} = c_1 \int_0^S f(x)\,dx - c_2 \int_S^\infty f(x)\,dx = (c_1 + c_2) \int_0^S f(x)\,dx - c_2 \tag{6}$$

Hence the optimal order level S_o can be obtained from

$$\int_0^{S_o} f(x)\,dx = \frac{c_2}{c_1 + c_2} \tag{7}$$

Example 8–3a

Let the demand density be

$$f(x) = (1/b)e^{-x/b} \qquad x \geq 0 \tag{8}$$

This is a negative exponential distribution with mean b and variance b^2. Substituting $f(x)$ in equation (7) gives

$$\int_0^{S_o} \frac{1}{b} e^{-x/b}\,dx = \frac{c_2}{c_1 + c_2} \tag{9}$$

from which we get immediately

$$S_o = b \ln \frac{c_1 + c_2}{c_1} \tag{10}$$

Substituting this value of S_o in the cost equation (5) gives the minimum cost

$$C_o = bc_1 \ln \frac{c_1 + c_2}{c_1} \tag{11}$$

The attentive reader will no doubt notice that the solution of this example is identical with the solution of Example 8–2a. This is not a coincidence. The relation will be explained in Chapter 10, which deals with the equivalence of probabilistic scheduling-period systems.

Discrete Units

Suppose now that demand x and the order level S are constrained to discrete units 0, u, $2u$, etc. Let $P(x)$ be the probability distribution of demand x. The expected total-cost equation, by analogy with equation (5), becomes

$$C(S) = c_1 \sum_{x=0}^{S} (S - x)P(x) + c_2 \sum_{x=S+u}^{\infty} (x - S)P(x) \tag{12}$$

Using the methods exemplified by equations 8–2(16), 8–2(17), etc., we find that

$$C(S + u) - C(S) = u[(c_1 + c_2)F(S) - c_2] \tag{13}$$

where

$$F(S) = \sum_{x=0}^{S} P(x) \tag{14}$$

The necessary conditions for the optimal S_o are then

$$F(S_o - u) \leqq \frac{c_2}{c_1 + c_2} \leqq F(S_o) \tag{15}$$

It can be shown [see problem 8–5(19)] that these are also sufficient conditions for S_o.

Example 8–3b*

"There are certain rather expensive items (some costing over $100,000 each) known as 'insurance spares' which are generally procured at the time a new class of ships is under construction. These spares are bought even though it is known that it is very unlikely that any of them will ever be needed and that they cannot be used on any ship except of that particular class. They are procured in order to provide insurance against the rather serious loss which would be suffered if one of these spares were not available when needed. Also the initial procurement of these spares is intended

* This example is taken from Laderman, Littauer, and Weiss, "The Inventory Problem" [30]. The solution, though, is based on the methods of this section.

to be the only procurement during the lifetime of the ships of that class, because it is extremely difficult and costly to procure these spares at a later date. Suppose, for example, that spares cost $100,000 each and that a loss of $10,000,000 is suffered for each spare that is needed when there is none available in stock. Further suppose that the probabilities that spares will be needed as replacements during the life term of the class of ships discussed are

Spares Required	Probability
1	0.0400
2	0.0100
3	0.0010
4	0.0002
5 or more	0.0000

How many spare parts should be procured?"

This system is indeed the system being considered in this section. Here $u = 1$ and $P(0) = 0.9488$, $P(1) = 0.0400$, $P(2) = 0.0100$, $P(3) = 0.0010$, and $P(4) = 0.0002$. In addition,* $c_1 = \$100,000$ and $c_2 = \$10,000,000 - \$100,000 = \$9,900,000$.

Now, by equation (14), $F(0) = 0.9488$, $F(1) = 0.9888$, $F(2) = 0.9988$, etc. But $c_2/(c_1 + c_2) = 0.9900$. Therefore, by equation (15), $S_o = 2$; that is, two spare parts should be procured.

THE PROBABILISTIC SCHEDULING-PERIOD–ORDER-LEVEL SYSTEM

8–4   The systems to be considered now are type $(1, 2, 3)$ systems. They may be considered extensions of the systems of either Section 8–1 or Section 8–2. No constraints are placed now on S or on t, and the optimal order level S_o and the optimal scheduling period t_o must be determined. We shall assume, as in Sections 8–1 and 8–2, that the demand pattern is uniform.

Convolutions

In type $(1, 2, 3)$ systems with a (t, S) policy we generally have to deal with convolutions of probability distributions. Some of the ideas involved may be illustrated as follows.

Consider a discrete probability distribution $P(x)$, where x is the demand size during some time period one unit of time long. Suppose we want to

---

* The reason for using these unit costs may not be immediately obvious. The reader may want to set up the total-cost model and check that its solution is given by equation 8–5(4) where $a = 0$, $b = \$100,000$, and $d = \$10,000,000$.

find the discrete distribution for the demand size during a time period which is two units long, assuming that demand in each time period is $P(x)$ and that the demands are independent. Let $P(x, 2)$ designate this new distribution. For consistency of notation let $P(x)$ be denoted as $P(x, 1)$.

Symbolically, the relation of $P(x, 2)$ and $P(x, 1)$ can be written as follows:

$$P(x, 2) = P(x, 1) * P(x, 1) \tag{1}$$

And in words, "The probability distribution $P(x, 2)$ is the convolution of $P(x, 1)$ and $P(x, 1)$." Similarly, to find the probability distribution for a period of three time units we write

$$P(x, 3) = P(x, 2) * P(x, 1) \tag{2}$$

And in general, for a period of t time units,

$$P(x, t) = P(x, t - 1) * P(x, 1) \tag{3}$$

From first principles $P(x, 2)$ may be computed from*

$$P(x, 2) = \sum_{y=y_{\min}}^{x} P(x - y, 1)P(y, 1) \qquad x = 2y_{\min}, \ldots, 2y_{\max} \tag{4}$$

where y refers to the values of x in $P(x, 1)$. And similarly for $P(x, t)$,

$$P(x, t) = \sum_{y=y_{\min}}^{x} P(x - y, t - 1)P(y, 1) \qquad x = ty_{\min}, \ldots, ty_{\max} \tag{5}$$

For example, let $P(0, 1) = 0.4$, $P(1, 1) = 0.6$. Then $P(0, 2) = P(0, 1) \times P(0, 1) = 0.4 \times 0.4 = 0.16$, $P(1, 2) = P(1, 1) \times P(0, 1) + P(0, 1) \times P(1, 1) = 0.6 \times 0.4 + 0.4 \times 0.6 = 0.48$, and $P(2, 2) = P(2, 1) \times P(0, 1) + P(1, 1) \times P(1, 1) + P(0, 1) \times P(2, 1) = 0 \times 0.4 + 0.6 \times 0.6 + 0.4 \times 0 = 0.36$.

Similarly $P(0, 3) = 0.16 \times 0.04 = 0.064$, $P(1, 3) = 0.48 \times 0.4 + 0.16 \times 0.6 = 0.288$, $P(2, 3) = 0.36 \times 0.4 + 0.48 \times 0.6 = 0.432$, and $P(3, 3) = 0.36 \times 0.6 = 0.216$.

To find convolutions of continuous probability densities $f(x)$ let us use the notations of the discrete case for the corresponding densities $f(x, 1)$, $f(x, 2), \ldots, f(x, t)$. Again, in a manner analogous to the discrete case, we may write in general

$$f(x, t) = f(x, t - 1) * f(x, 1) \tag{6}$$

and

$$f(x, t) = \int_0^x f(x - y, t - 1)f(y, 1) \, dy \tag{7}$$

For example, let $f(x, 1) = e^{-x}$. Then

$$f(x, 2) = \int_0^x e^{-(x-y)}e^{-y} \, dy = e^{-x} \int_0^x dy = xe^{-x}$$

* Note that for all t, however, $P(x < x_{\min}, t) = 0$ and $P(x > x_{\max}, t) = 0$.

Similarly,

$$f(x, 3) = \int_0^x (x - y)e^{-(x-y)}e^{-y}\, dy = e^{-x} \int_0^x (x - y)\, dy = \frac{x^2}{2}\, e^{-x}.$$

And by induction it is not difficult to show that

$$f(x, t) = \frac{x^{t-1}}{(t - 1)!}\, e^{-x}.$$

The (t, S) System with Continuous Units

We now consider an extension of the system of Section 8–2 for continuous units when t_p is not prescribed. The expected total cost, by equation 8–2 (5), now becomes

$$C(t, S) = c_1 \int_0^S \left(S - \frac{x}{2}\right) f(x, t)\, dx + c_1 \int_S^\infty \frac{S^2}{2x} f(x, t)\, dx$$

$$+ c_2 \int_S^\infty \frac{(x - S)^2}{2x} f(x, t)\, dx + \frac{c_3}{t} \quad (8)$$

where $f(x, t)$ is the continuous probability density of x for the scheduling period t.

For any given scheduling period t^* the corresponding optimal level $S_o(t^*)$ can be found as in Section 8–2 [equation 8–2(9)]. That is, it is the solution of the equation

$$\int_0^{S_o(t^*)} f(x, t^*)\, dx + \int_{S_o(t^*)}^\infty \frac{S_o(t^*)}{x} f(x, t^*)\, dx = \frac{c_2}{c_1 + c_2} \quad (9)$$

The corresponding minimum cost for t^* is then the value of $C(t^*, S_o(t^*))$ in equation (8). Let it be designated by $C_o(t^*)$. The optimal scheduling period t_o is then the value of t^* that minimized $C_o(t^*)$.

No general explicit solution, however, can be derived for t_o. We must resort to numerical computations to find t_o. The methodology is illustrated in Example 8–4.

The (t, S) System with Discrete Units

When all units are constrained to discrete quantities, the expected total cost equation, by analogy with equation (8), becomes*

$$C(t, S) = c_1 \sum_{x=0}^S \left(S - \frac{x}{2}\right) P(x, t) + c_1 \sum_{x=S+u}^\infty \frac{S^2}{2x} P(x, t)$$

$$+ c_2 \sum_{x=S+u}^\infty \frac{(x - S)^2}{2x} P(x, t) + \frac{c_3}{t} \quad (10)$$

* In this formulation we assume that a cost of c_3 is incurred every t units of time, even if no replenishments are made. Otherwise the last term in equation (10) would be $[1 - P(0, t)]c_3/t$.

where $P(x, t)$ is the probability that the demand will be x units in a scheduling period of t time units.

Using the methods of Section 8-2 for discrete units, we find that for a given scheduling period t^* the corresponding optimal level $S_o(t^*)$ can be determined from

$$M[S_o(t^*) - u] \leqq \frac{c_2}{c_1 + c_2} \leqq M[S_o(t)^*] \tag{11}$$

where

$$M(S, t) = \sum_{x=0}^{S} P(x, t) + \left(S + \frac{u}{2}\right) \sum_{x=S+u}^{\infty} \frac{P(x, t)}{x} \tag{12}$$

Here, as for continuous units, no general explicit solution can be obtained for the optimal scheduling period t_o. However, we shall illustrate by an example a useful procedure for solving the system.

Example 8-4

The demand for an item during a week varies from week to week. Past data indicates that during any week there may be demand for 0, 1, or 2 units with probabilities 0.2, 0.5, and 0.3 respectively. The carrying cost is $5 per unit per week; the shortage cost is $60 per unit per week. The cost of preparing an order and replenishing stocks is $18.

Assuming that demand may occur on any day of the week, that lead-time is zero, and that a (t, S) policy is used, what are the optimal values of the scheduling period and the order level? Here, then, $u = 1$, $P(0, 1) = 0.2$, $P(1, 1) = 0.5$, $P(2, 1) = 0.3$, $c_1 = $5 per unit per week, $c_2 = $60 per unit per week, and $c_3 = $18 per replenishment.

Let $t^* = 1$ week. Using the methods illustrated in Section 8-2 and in Table 8-2, we can prepare Table 8-4a. From the table and by equation (11) we find that $S_o(1) = 1$ since $0.525 < c_2/(c_1 + c_2) = 0.923 < 0.925$. Hence, by substitution in equation (10), we obtain $C_o(t^* = 1) = $25.125 per week.

Next, let $t^* = 2$ weeks. Before proceeding to prepare a table similar to Table 8-4a we first have to find $P(x, 2)$—the probability that demand is x during the scheduling period 2 weeks long. Using the method described

TABLE 8-4a

Tabulation of $M(S)$ When t^* Is One Week

x, S	$P(x, 1)$	$\sum_{0}^{S} P(x, 1)$	$\dfrac{P(x, 1)}{x}$	$\sum_{S+1}^{2} \dfrac{P(x, 1)}{x}$	$\left(S + \dfrac{1}{2}\right)\sum_{S+1}^{2} \dfrac{P(x, 1)}{x}$	$M(S)$
0	0.2	0.2		0.65	0.325	0.525
1	0.5	0.7	0.50	0.15	0.225	0.925
2	0.3	1.0	0.15	0	0	1.000

at the beginning of this section, we readily find that $P(0, 2) = 0.04$, $P(1, 2) = 0.20$, $P(2, 2) = 0.37$, $P(3, 2) = 0.30$, and $P(4, 2) = 0.09$. Now Table 8–4b can be prepared.

TABLE 8–4b

Tabulation of M(S) When t* Is Two Weeks

x, S	$P(x, 2)$	$\sum_{0}^{S} P(x, 2)$	$\dfrac{P(x, 2)}{x}$	$\sum_{S+1}^{4} \dfrac{P(x, 2)}{x}$	$\left(S + \dfrac{1}{2}\right) \sum_{S+1}^{4} \dfrac{P(x, 2)}{x}$	$M(S)$
0	0.04	0.04		0.5075	0.25375	0.29375
1	0.20	0.24	0.2000	0.3075	0.46125	0.70125
2	0.37	0.61	0.1850	0.1225	0.30625	0.91625
3	0.30	0.91	0.1000	0.0225	0.07875	0.98875
4	0.09	1.00	0.0225	0	0	1.00000

From the table and by equation (11) we find that $S_o(2) = 3$. By substitution in equation (10) we obtain $C_o(t^* = 2) = \$19.231$ per week. In a similar manner other values of $C_o(t^*)$ can be obtained. The results are summarized in Table 8–4c. From this table we immediately obtain the

TABLE 8–4c

Values of S_o(t*) and C_o(t*) for Various t*

t^*	1	2	3	4	5	6
$S_o(t^*)$	1	3	4	5	6	7
$C_o(t^*)$	25.125	19.231	19.212	20.647	22.636	24.885

solution of the system.* The optimal scheduling period is 3 weeks and the optimal order level is 4 units. That is, every 3 weeks an order is to be placed and inventory raised to 4 units.

The computations leading to Table 8–4c have been carried out on a digital computer. For details and some computational shortcuts in solving systems similar to the one given in this example see Section 11–2.

8-5   PROBLEMS

1. Suggest a method for solving the system of Section 8–1 for

$$A(t) = 1 + b/\sqrt{t} \qquad (1)$$

2. Use the data of problem 2–5(3) to estimate the function $A(t)$ of Section 8–1. Fit a curve of the form $1 + b/t$ and determine the value of b.

---

* We are thus assuming that $C_o(t^*)$ is a convex function. This seems to be an intuitively reasonable assumption. However, a general proof is not available at this time [see problem 8–5(25)].

3. Use the data and costs of problem 2–5(3) to solve the system of Section 8–1 for (a) $A = 2$, (b) $A = 1 + 4.5/t$. Compare the results with those of problem 2–5(3). Explain the differences.

4. For the system of Section 8–2 find S_o if $c_1 = \$1.00$ per pound per week, $c_2 = \$10.00$ per pound per week, $t = 2$ weeks, and the probability functions of demand over the 2-week periods are respectively

$$\text{(a) } f(x) = \begin{cases} 0.2 & 0.5 \leq x \leq 5.5 \\ 0 & \text{otherwise} \end{cases}$$

$$\text{(b) } P(x) = \begin{cases} 0.2 & x = 1, 2, 3, 4, 5 \\ 0 & \text{otherwise} \end{cases}$$

5. In the system of Section 8–3 demand follows a normal distribution with a a mean of 100 lb. The unit costs are $c_1 = \$2.00$ per pound per week, $c_2 = \$10.00$ per pound per week. Find the minimum cost of the system for standard deviations of 20 lb, 10 lb, 5 lb, and 0 lb.

6. In an inventory system a (t, S) policy is used. The index of the demand pattern is ∞ (i.e., all demands occur at the beginning if each t_p). The discrete probability distribution of demand is $P(x)$. The cost of starting each period t_p with S quantity units is bS. The revenue for each item in inventory, for which there is a demand during t_p, is d units per quantity unit. Items remaining in inventory at the end of the scheduling period t_p are junked, and the revenue is only a units per quantity unit. (Note that $a < b < d$.)

(a) Show that the profit equation can be given as

$$G(S) = d \sum_{x=x_{\min}}^{S} xP(x) + d \sum_{x=S+1}^{x_{\max}} SP(x) + a \sum_{x=x_{\min}}^{S-1} (S - x)P(x) - bS \qquad (2)$$

(b) Show that equation (2) can be rearranged and written as

$$G(S) = (d - b)\bar{x} - \left[(b - a) \sum_{x=x_{\min}}^{S} (S - x)P(x) \right.$$

$$\left. + (d - b) \sum_{x=S+1}^{x_{\max}} (x - S) P(x) \right] \qquad (3)$$

where $\bar{x}$ is the average demand.

(c) Relate this system to that of Section 8–3 and hence show that S_o can be obtained from

$$F(S_o - 1) \leq \frac{d - b}{d - a} \leq F(S_o) \qquad (4)$$

where $F(S) = \sum_{x=x_{\min}}^{S} P(x)$.

7. *The Newspaper Boy Problem.** A newspaper boy is required to buy his papers at $\$0.07$ each, he sells them for $\$0.10$, and he receives $\$0.01$ for each

* For the origin of this problem see Morse and Kimball [36], p. 31.

unsold paper. He has found by experience that on the average three customers want to buy papers and that they appear at random. How many papers should he buy? (The distribution of demand may be assumed to be the Poisson distribution; that is, $P(x) = e^{-3}3^x/x!$)

8. Solve the "newspaper boy" problem and the "spare-parts" problem of Example 8–3b, assuming that the corresponding potential demands are distributed as the data of problem 2–5(3) (The costs are as in the original problems.)

9. Use the methods of Section 8–4 to solve the system of problem 2–5(3) for a (t, S) policy.

10. Show that the expected total-cost equation of a probabilistic order-level inventory system with a power-demand pattern with index n is

$$C(S) = c_1 \int_0^S \left(S - \frac{n}{n+1} x \right) f(x)\, dx + c_1 \int_S^\infty \frac{S(S/x)^n}{n+1} f(x)\, dx$$

$$+ c_2 \int_S^\infty \left[\frac{nx + S(S/x)^n}{n+1} - S \right] f(x)\, dx \tag{5}$$

(This result can be obtained as an immediate extension of the results of Sections 4–3 and 8–2.) Also show that S_o can be obtained from

$$M_n(S_o) = \frac{c_2}{c_1 + c_2} \tag{6}$$

where

$$M_n(S) = \int_0^S f(x)\, dx + \int_S^\infty \left(\frac{S}{x} \right)^n f(x)\, dx \tag{7}$$

11. Show that the extension of the results of problem 10 to discrete units leads to

$$C(S) = c_1 \sum_0^S \left(S - \frac{n}{n+1} x \right) P(x) + c_1 \sum_{S+u}^\infty \frac{S(S/x)^n}{n+1} \tag{8}$$

$$+ c_2 \sum_{S+u}^\infty \left[\frac{nx + S(S/x)^n}{n+1} - S \right] P(x)$$

and

$$M_n(S_o - u) \leqq \frac{c_2}{c_1 + c_2} \leqq M_n(S_o) \tag{9}$$

where

$$M_n(S) = \sum_0^S P(x) + \sum_{S+u}^\infty \frac{(S+u)^{n+1} - S^{n+1}}{u(n+1)x^n} P(x) \tag{10}$$

12. Use the methods of marginal analysis introduced in Section 4–1 to solve the systems of Sections 8–2 and 8–3 and problem 10.

13. *Two-Scheduling-Period System.* Consider an inventory system in which only two decisions have to be made, one at the beginning of the first scheduling period and the other at the beginning of the second period. The variable

demand y in the first period occurs at the beginning of the period after the first decision has been made; it has the probability density $g(y)$. Similarly, the demand x in the second period has the probability density $f(x)$. Leadtime is zero. The scheduling periods are equal and of length t_p. The unit carrying cost and unit shortage cost are c_1 and c_2 per quantity unit per time unit respectively. Graphically, the inventory system may be described as in Figure 8–5. The system starts at T_0 and terminates at T_2. Let the inventory level at time T_0 be designated by S' and let the level at time T_1 be designated

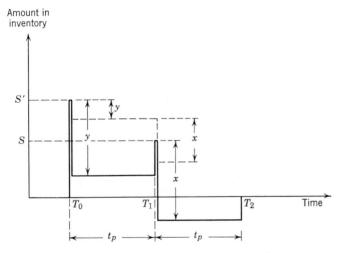

Figure 8–5   The amounts in inventory in the two-scheduling-period system.

by S. The problem is to find the optimal S_0' and S_0. When returns are allowed at time T_1, each scheduling period can be studied independently as in the system of Section 8–3. However, when returns are not allowed, and when y is such that $S' - y > S$, the amount in inventory at T_1 will be $S' - y$ (and *not* S).

Show that the expected total cost of the system will then be

$$C(S', S) = c_1 \int_0^{S'} (S' - y)g(y)\,dy + c_2 \int_{S'}^{\infty} (y - S')g(y)\,dy \tag{11}$$

$$+ \int_0^{S'-S} \left[c_1 \int_0^{S'-y} (S' - y - x)f(x)\,dx + c_2 \int_{S'-y}^{\infty} (x - S' + y) \right.$$

$$\left. \times f(x) \right] g(y)\,dy + \int_{S'-S}^{\infty} \left[c_1 \int_0^{S} (S - x)f(x)\,dx \right.$$

$$\left. + c_2 \int_{S}^{\infty} (x - S)f(x)\,dx \right] g(y)\,dy$$

Hence determine the solutions

$$\int_0^{S_0} f(x)\, dx = \frac{c_2}{c_1 + c_2} \tag{12}$$

and

$$\frac{\displaystyle\int_0^{S_0'} g(y)\, dy + \int_0^{S_0'-S_0} \int_0^{S_0'-y} f(x)\, dx\, g(y)\, dy}{\displaystyle 1 + \int_0^{S_0'-S_0} g(y)\, dy} = \frac{c_2}{c_1 + c_2} \tag{13}$$

14. Analyze the systems of Sections 8–2 and 8–3 when demand may also be negative. Be sure to consider the expected total costs of the systems when the order levels are negative.

15. Solve the two-scheduling-period system of problem 13 when the probability density of demand during the second period depends on the demand in the first period, that is, $f(x) = f(x \mid y)$.*

16. Study the sensitivity of the system of Section 8–3 when $f(x) = (1/b)e^{-x/b}$.

17. Solve Example 8–4 assuming that a cost of $18 is incurred only when a replenishment is scheduled. (Also see the footnote on page 140.)

18. Solve Example 8–4 for two items having a common replenishing cost every scheduling period. For the second item assume the probabilities of demand during a week to be $P(0, 1) = 0.4, P(1, 1) = 0.3, P(2, 1) = 0.2$, and $P(3, 1) = 0.1$. Also assume that the unit carrying and shortage costs are $2 and $130 respectively.**

19. Show that the results given by equations 8–2(20) and 8–3(15) indeed give necessary and sufficient conditions.

20. Formulate and solve the two-scheduling period system of problem 13 as a dynamic programming problem.

21. Demand during a week has the probability density $xe^{-x}, x \geqq 0$. The carrying cost is c_1 per unit per week, the shortage cost is c_2 per unit per week, and the setup cost is c_3. A (t, S) policy is used where t is in discrete units of weeks and S is in continuous quantity units. Attempt to find a general solution for t_0, S_0, and C_0.

22. The uniform and constant demand for an item during the prescribed scheduling period is 4 lb. The carrying and shortage costs are $2 and $6 per pound. per scheduling period.

    Find the optimal order level S_0 using equation 8–2(20). Compare the solution with that given by equation 4–1(10).

23. Show that for both continuous and discrete units

    (a) in the system of Section 8–2

$$I_1 - I_2 = S - \frac{\bar{x}}{2} \tag{14}$$

---

* H. Donald Messer [32] has solved the n scheduling-period system.
** This problem has been solved in detail by Naddor [39].

(b) in the system of Section 8–3

$$I_1 - I_2 = S - \bar{x} \tag{15}$$

Interpret the significance of these results.

24. Each week N perishable items are bought. A quantity of S_j is bought of the jth item at a unit cost of b_j. Demands during the week are uniform with the discrete distributions $P_j(x)$. The unit selling price is d_j. The annual cost of carrying inventory as a percentage of the unit purchasing cost of an item is p for all items. Leftovers at the end of the week are destroyed.

(a) Determine the total cost equation of ths system.

(b) State how you would go about finding the optimal S_j's.

25. Prove or disprove that $C_o(t^*)$ of Section 8–4 is convex.

26. Solve part (a) of problem 14–4(7). How does the result affect the analysis of the system in Section 8–4 in general and that in Example 8–4 in particular?

27. In the inventory system of Section 8–3 with discrete units the optimal order level S_o can be found from equation 8–3(15). Assume that $u = 1$

(a) What is S_o if $F(x) = x/10$, $c_1 = 1$, and $c_2 = 2$?

(b) Show that

$$\frac{c_1 F(S_o - 1)}{1 - F(S_o - 1)} \leqq c_2 \leqq \frac{c_1 F(S_o)}{1 - F(S_o)} \tag{16}$$

(c) Suppose $F(x) = x/10$ and $c_1 = 1$. The decision maker uses a level $S = 9$. He says that this is the optimal level. What can we therefore say about c_2?

Chapter 9

Scheduling-Period–Order-Level Systems
with Leadtime

9-0 The systems of this chapter are identical with those of Chapter 8, with the one exception that leadtime is now significant. Before proceeding, the reader may want to review several comments on leadtime in Sections 1–2 and 2–2.

The inventory systems of Sections 9–1 to 9–4 are immediate extensions of the corresponding systems of Sections 8–1 to 8–4. We shall later show (Section 10–2) that the corresponding systems are equivalent in a certain sense. However, in this chapter we emphasize the effect of leadtime on the analysis.

In Sections 9–2, 9–3, and 9–4 the demand size during the leadtime period will be designated by v. When v refers to a continuous quantity we denote by $h(v)$ the probability density of demand, and when it refers to a discrete quantity we denote by $H(v)$ the probability distribution of demand. In either case we shall assume that $h(v)$ or $H(v)$ are known.

THE PROBABILISTIC SCHEDULING-PERIOD
SYSTEM WITH LEADTIME

9-1 In the inventory system of this section, replenishments are scheduled every t units of time. The quantity ordered brings the amount on hand and on order to a level Z. The quantity arrives after the passage of a leadtime of L time units. Graphically the system may be represented as shown in Figure 9–1.

In this system no shortages are allowed. The order level Z must therefore be large enough so that the maximum demand during the period $L + t$ will not cause shortages. In a certain sense, then, the level Z is thus prescribed. For an optimal solution, then,

$$Z_p = x_{\max}(L + t) \tag{1}$$

where $x(T)$ designates the demand size during some period T. (For comparable notation see Sections 2–2 and 8–1.)

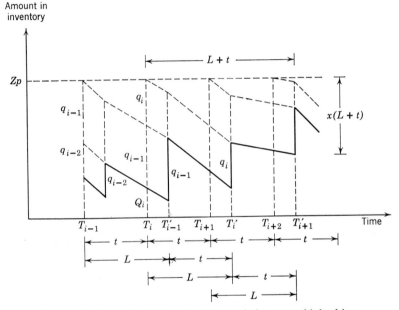

Figure 9–1   The probabilistic scheduling-period system with leadtime.

As in Section 8–1 we can derive an expression for the average amount in inventory I_1. This will be

$$I_1 = Z_p - rL - \frac{rt}{2} \tag{2}$$

If we assume the unit costs to be c_1 in [\$]/[Q][T] and c_3 in [\$], then, by analogy with equation 8–1(3), the expected total-cost equation of the system becomes

$$C(t) = c_1\left(Z_p - rL - \frac{rt}{2}\right) + \frac{c_3}{t} \tag{3}$$

Let the function $A(T)$ be defined as in Section 8–1. That is, let

$$A(T) = \frac{x_{max}}{\bar{x}(T)} = \frac{x_{max}}{rT} \tag{4}$$

Then, by equation (1),

$$Z_p = r(L + t)A(L + t) \tag{5}$$

Hence equation (3) becomes

$$C(t) = c_1\left[(L + t)A(L + t) - \left(L + \frac{t}{2}\right)\right]r + \frac{c_3}{t} \tag{6}$$

The solution of the system now depends only on the function $A(T)$. As in Section 8–1, we shall consider two special cases.

Case 9–1a $A(T) = k$

When $A(T)$ is a constant k independent of T, equation (6) becomes

$$C(t) = c_1 L(k - 1)r + c_1 t(k - \tfrac{1}{2})r + \frac{c_3}{t} \tag{7}$$

Hence the solutions

$$t_o = \sqrt{2c_3/[c_1 r(2k - 1)]} \tag{8}$$

$$Z_p = rLk + k\sqrt{2rc_3/[c_1(2k - 1)]} \tag{9}$$

$$C_o = c_1 L(k - 1)r + \sqrt{2c_1 c_3 r(2k - 1)} \tag{10}$$

When $L = 0$ these results reduce to those given by equations 8–1(7) to 8–1(10).

When $k = 1$ (i.e., demand is constant), we have the lot-size system with leadtime. Its minimum cost and the optimal lot size and scheduling period are the same as those in the lot-size system of Section 3–1. The order level is then $Z_p = rL + \sqrt{2rc_3/c_1} = rL + q_o$, where q_o is the optimal lot size. (In this case the remarks on leadtime in Section 2–2 apply. The present system with $k = 1$ may be considered system B and the lot-size system of Section 3–1 may be considered system A.)

Case 9–1b $A(T) = 1 + b/T$

When $A(T)$ is such that it decreases as T increases (as we might expect in realistic applications), we can consider the relation

$$A(T) = 1 + \frac{b}{T} \tag{11}$$

The cost equation of the system, by equation (6), is then

$$C(t) = c_1 br + \frac{c_1 rt}{2} + \frac{c_3}{t} \tag{12}$$

This equation is independent of leadtime L and is identical with equation 8–1(12). The solution of the system is then

$$t_o = \sqrt{2c_3/(rc_1)} \tag{13}$$

$$Z_p = (b + L)r + \sqrt{2rc_3/c_1} \tag{14}$$

$$C_o = \sqrt{2c_1c_3r} + c_1br \tag{15}$$

Here, then, the cost of the system does not depend on leadtime. Other characteristics of the system can be observed as in Case 8–1b.

THE PROBABILISTIC ORDER-LEVEL SYSTEM WITH LEADTIME

9–2 The inventory fluctuations in an inventory system with a (t_p, Z) policy, a uniform demand pattern, and significant leadtime may be described graphically as in Figure 9–2a.* In this system the amount in inventory at the end of each prescribed scheduling period t_p is reviewed. Let the

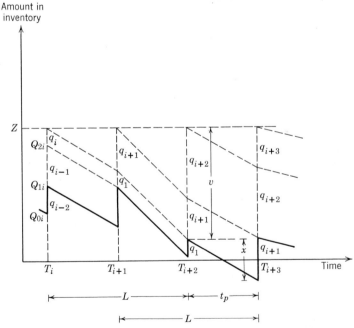

Figure 9–2a   The probabilistic order-level system with leadtime.

* In this figure it is assumed, for illustrative purposes, that leadtime equals in length two scheduling periods. In the general system to be analyzed leadtime may be of any length.

amount on hand at time T_i be designated by Q_{0i}. At that time, by Figure 9-2a, there are two outstanding orders; one for the amount q_{i-2}, which is presently due, and another, q_{i-1}, due at time T_{i+1}. Let Q_{1i} and Q_{2i} be defined by the relations

$$Q_{1i} = Q_{0i} + q_{i-2} \tag{1}$$

$$Q_{2i} = Q_{1i} + q_{i-1} \tag{2}$$

And, in general, for any leadtime period of length $L = mt_p$, we may write

$$Q_{j,i} = Q_{j-1,i} + q_{i+j-m+1} \qquad j = 1, 2, \ldots, m \tag{3}$$

Or, in general,*

$$Q_{j,i} = Q_{0,i} + \sum_{k=i-m}^{i+j-(m+1)} q_k \qquad j = 1, 2, \ldots, m \tag{4}$$

The lot size q_i which is ordered at time T_i is then

$$q_i = Z - Q_{m,i} = Z - \left(Q_{0,i} + \sum_{k=i-m}^{i-1} q_k \right) \tag{5}$$

where Z is the order level. This quantity q_i will be added to inventory at time T_{i+m}.

To develop the expected total-cost equation of the system for any lead-time,** the following observations must first be made.

1. The amount in inventory during any specific scheduling period depends only on the order level Z, the demand size during the leadtime preceding the period, and the demand size during the period.

2. Let v and x denote the demand sizes during leadtime and the scheduling period respectively. The amounts in inventory during any scheduling period will thus be one of the three cases shown in Figure 9-2b. Case (i) occurs when $v \leq Z$ and when $x \leq Z - v$. Case (ii) occurs when $v \leq Z$ and when $x \geq Z - v$. Case (iii) occurs when $v \geq Z$.

The expected total-cost equation of the system is therefore

$$C(Z) = \int_0^Z \int_0^{Z-v} c_1 \left(Z - v - \frac{x}{2} \right) f(x) h(v) \, dx \, dv$$

$$+ \int_0^Z \int_{Z-v}^\infty \left[c_1 \frac{(Z-v)^2}{2x} + c_2 \frac{(x-Z+v)^2}{2x} \right] f(x) h(v) \, dx \, dv$$

$$+ \int_Z^\infty \int_0^\infty c_2 \left(v - Z + \frac{x}{2} \right) f(x) h(v) \, dx \, dv \tag{6}$$

* By these definitions it is thus assumed that shortages in inventory are made up when replenishments arrive.

** The derivations to follow allow leadtime to be an arbitrary constant not necessarily an integer multiple of the scheduling period.

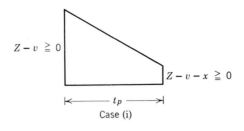

$Z - v \geqq 0$

$Z - v - x \geqq 0$

t_p

Case (i)

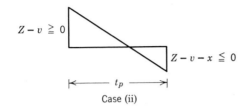

$Z - v \geqq 0$

$Z - v - x \leqq 0$

t_p

Case (ii)

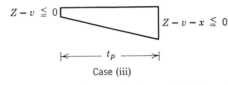

$Z - v \leqq 0$

$Z - v - x \leqq 0$

t_p

Case (iii)

Figure 9–2b Typical amounts in inventory in the probabilistic order-level system with leadtime.

where $h(v)$ is the probability density of demand during leadtime, and $f(x)$ is the probability density of demand during the scheduling period. Using the methods of differentiating under the integral sign given in Section 8–2, and after rearranging terms, we obtain the following result from which the optimal order level Z can be determined:

$$\int_0^{Z_0} \left[\int_0^{Z_0-v} f(x) \, dx + \int_{Z_0-v}^{\infty} \frac{Z-v}{x} f(x) \, dx \right] h(v) \, dv = \frac{c_2}{c_1 + c_2} \quad (7)$$

Example 9–2a

In an inventory system with a (t_p, Z) policy the prescribed scheduling period is 1 week and demand during the week has the probability density $f(x) = xe^{-x}$. Leadtime is 2 weeks. The unit shortage cost is 19 times that of the unit carrying cost. What is the optimal level Z_o?

We must first determine $h(v)$, the probability density of demand during leadtime. Using the methods of Section 8–4 and noting that $h(v) = f(x) * f(x)$, we can readily find that $h(v) = (v^3/6)e^{-v}$. Substitutions in equation (7) now lead to

$$1 - e^{-Z_o}\left(\frac{Z_o^{\,4}}{24} + \frac{Z_o^{\,3}}{6} + \frac{Z_o^{\,2}}{2} + Z_o + 1\right) = 0.95 \qquad (8)$$

To find Z_o we note that the left side of equation (8) can also be expressed as $\int_0^{2Z_o} [u^4/(4!\,2^5)]e^{-u/2}\,du$, which is the cumulative function of the chi-square distribution with 10 degrees of freedom. Using chi-square tables we readily find that $Z_o = 9.15$. Substitution of this value in equation (6) gives the minimum cost of $C_o = 5.65c_1$. [Other values of $C(Z)$ are $C(8) = 6.18c_1$, $C(9) = 5.68c_1$, and $C(10) = 5.84c_1$.]

Discrete Units

The extension of the results given by equations (6) and (7) can be carried out for discrete units as in Section 8-2. Let $H(v)$ be the probability distribution of demand during leadtime and let $P(x)$ be the probability distribution of demand during the scheduling period. For discrete units 0, u, $2u$, etc., equation (6) becomes

$$C(Z) = \sum_{v=0}^{Z} \sum_{x=0}^{Z-v} c_1\left(Z - v - \frac{x}{2}\right)P(x)\,H(v)$$

$$+ \sum_{v=0}^{Z} \sum_{x=Z-v+u}^{\infty} \left[c_1\frac{(Z-v)^2}{2x} + c_2\frac{(x-Z+v)^2}{2x}\right]P(x)\,H(v)$$

$$+ \sum_{v=Z+u}^{\infty} \sum_{x=0}^{\infty} c_2\left(v - Z + \frac{x}{2}\right)P(x)\,H(v) \qquad (9)$$

The solution can be shown to be

$$K(Z_0 - u) \leqq \frac{c_2}{c_1 + c_2} \leqq K(Z_0) \qquad (10)$$

where

$$K(Z) = \sum_{v=0}^{Z}\left[\sum_{x=0}^{Z-v} P(x) + \left(Z - v + \frac{u}{2}\right)\sum_{x=Z-v+u}^{\infty}\frac{P(x)}{x}\right]H(v) \qquad (11)$$

Example 9-2b

In an inventory system with a (t_p, Z) policy, the prescribed scheduling period is 1 week and demand during the week has the distribution $P(x)$ given by $P(0) = 0.2$, $P(1) = 0.5$, and $P(2) = 0.3$. Leadtime is 2 weeks. The unit shortage cost is 19 times that of the unit carrying cost. What is the optimal level Z_o?

Using the methods of Section 8-4, we find that the probability distribution during the leadtime period is given by $H(0) = 0.04$, $H(1) = 0.20$,

$H(2) = 0.37$, $H(3) = 0.30$, and $H(4) = 0.09$. $K(Z)$ of equation (11) can now be computed. Table 9-2 gives the numerical values for $K(Z)$.

Since $c_2/(c_1 + c_2) = 0.95$, then by equation (10) the optimal order level is $Z_o = 5$. The corresponding minimum cost, by using equation (9), is $C_o = 2.385c_1$. Some other values of $C(Z)$ are $C(4) = 2.690c_1$ and $C(6) = 3.250c_1$.

TABLE 9-2

Numerical Values of $K(Z)$ for Example 9-2b

Z	0	1	2	3	4	5	6
$K(Z)$	0.02100	0.14200	0.41925	0.73975	0.93475	0.99325	1.00000

THE PROBABILISTIC ORDER-LEVEL SYSTEM WITH INSTANTANEOUS DEMAND AND WITH LEADTIME

9-3 The system of this section can be considered an extension of those described in Sections 8-3 and 9-2. The inventory fluctuations of the system, for a leadtime period equal in length to two scheduling periods, are illustrated by Figure 9-3.

Let the probability density of demand during leadtime be $h(v)$, and during the scheduling period let it be $f(x)$. Let the pertinent unit costs be c_1 and c_2 in $[\$]/[Q][T]$.

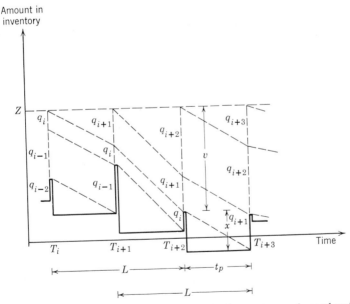

Figure 9-3 The probabilistic order-level system with instantaneous demand and with leadtime.

In contrast with the system of Section 9–2, only two typical cases arise. Either $Z - v - x \geqq 0$, in which case no shortages occur, or $Z - v - x \leqq 0$ and no inventory is carried. The expected total-cost equation of the system, by analogy with equations 8–3(5) and 9–2(6), becomes

$$C(Z) = \int_0^Z \int_0^{Z-v} c_1(Z - v - x)f(x)h(v)\, dx\, dv$$

$$+ \int_0^Z \int_{Z-v}^\infty c_2(v - Z + x)f(x)h(v)\, dx\, dv$$

$$+ \int_Z^\infty \int_0^\infty c_2(v - Z + x)f(x)h(v)\, dx\, dv \quad (1)$$

By differentiation, etc., we obtain the solution

$$\int_0^{Z_0} \int_0^{Z_0-v} f(x)h(v)\, dx\, dv = \frac{c_2}{c_1 + c_2} \quad (2)$$

Discrete Units

The extension of results to discrete units is similar to the analysis in Sections 8–3 and 9–2.

For the probability distributions $H(v)$ and $P(x)$, the expected total-cost equation is

$$C(Z) = \sum_{v=0}^Z \sum_{x=0}^{Z-v} c_1(Z - v - x)P(x)H(v)$$

$$+ \sum_{v=0}^Z \sum_{x=Z-v+u}^\infty c_2(v - Z + x)P(x)H(v)$$

$$+ \sum_{v=Z+u}^\infty \sum_{x=0}^\infty c_2(v - Z + x)P(x)H(v) \quad (3)$$

The solution is then given by

$$K(Z_o - u) \leqq \frac{c_2}{c_1 + c_2} \leqq K(Z_0) \quad (4)$$

where

$$K(Z) = \sum_{v=0}^Z \sum_{x=0}^{Z-v} P(x)H(v) \quad (5)$$

THE PROBABILISTIC SCHEDULING-PERIOD–ORDER-LEVEL SYSTEM WITH LEADTIME

9–4 The system to be discussed in this section can be considered an extension of that of Section 8–4 when leadtime is significant. Another way to look at the system of this section is to consider it an extension of that of Section 9–2 and to allow the scheduling period to be subject to control.

In a certain sense the system in this section is the most general probabilistic scheduling-period system with uniform demand. It is a type (1, 2, 3) system with variable demand and significant leadtime. The systems of Sections 8-4 and 9-2 are special cases of the system of this section.

Let $f(x, t)$ be the probability density of demand x during a scheduling period of length t. Let $h(v)$ be the probability density of demand v during leadtime. As an immediate extension of equations 8-4(8) and 9-2(6) the expected total-cost equation is

$$C(t, Z) = \int_0^Z \int_0^{Z-v} c_1 \left(Z - v - \frac{x}{2} \right) f(x, t) h(v) \, dx \, dv$$

$$+ \int_0^Z \int_{Z-v}^\infty \left[c_1 \frac{(Z - v)^2}{2x} + c_2 \frac{(x - Z + v)^2}{2x} \right] f(x, t) h(v) \, dx \, dv$$

$$+ c_2 \int_Z^\infty \int_0^\infty \left(v - Z + \frac{x}{2} \right) f(x, t) h(v) \, dx \, dv + \frac{c_3}{t} \quad (1)$$

It will be shown in Chapter 10 that equation (1) can be rewritten to give

$$C(t, Z) = c_1 \int_0^Z (Z - w) k(w, t) \, dw + c_2 \int_Z^\infty (w - Z) k(w, t) \, dw + \frac{c_3}{t} \quad (2)$$

where

$$k(w, t) = \int_0^w \int_{w-v}^\infty \frac{f(x, t)}{x} h(v) \, dx \, dv \quad (3)$$

We shall also show in Chapter 10 that, for any given scheduling period t^*, the corresponding optimal order-level $Z_0(t^*)$ can be found from

$$K(Z_0(t^*)) = \frac{c_2}{c_1 + c_2} \quad (4)$$

where

$$K(Z, t) = \int_0^Z k(w, t) \, dw \quad (5)$$

The corresponding minimum cost can then be shown to be

$$C_0(t^*) = \frac{c_2 r t^*}{2} + (c_1 + c_2) \int_0^{Z_0(t^*)} w k(w, t^*) \, dw + \frac{c_3}{t^*} \quad (6)$$

where r is the mean rate of demand per time unit. Equation (6) can now be used to find the optimal scheduling period t_0, by finding the value of t^* which minimizes $C_0(t^*)$. No general explicit solution, however, can be obtained for t_0 and we must resort to numerical computations to solve the system.

The following procedure may be helpful for solving the system. A first estimate for an integer t^* is obtained from

$$t^* \approx \sqrt{2c_3/(c_1 r)}\sqrt{(c_1 + c_2)/c_2} \tag{7}$$

About this value of t^*, several scheduling periods are selected. For each t^* the corresponding $Z_o(t^*)$ is found from equation (4). The values of t^* and $Z_o(t^*)$ are substituted in equation (6) to obtain values of $C_o(t^*)$. Since the function $C_o(t^*)$ may be expected to be convex, a condition for the optimal solution is

$$C_o(t_o) \leq C_o(t_o \pm 1) \tag{8}$$

Example 9-4 illustrates the use of this procedure.

Discrete Units

Let $P(x, t)$ be the probability distribution of demand x during a scheduling period t. Let $H(v)$ be the probability distribution of demand v during leadtime. Extension of equation 9-2(9) gives the expected total-cost equation

$$
\begin{aligned}
C(t, Z) = {} & \sum_{v=0}^{Z} \sum_{x=0}^{Z-v} c_1 \left(Z - v - \frac{x}{2} \right) P(x, t) H(v) \\
& + \sum_{v=0}^{Z} \sum_{x=Z-v+u}^{\infty} \left[c_1 \frac{(Z-v)^2}{2x} + c_2 \frac{(x-Z+v)^2}{2x} \right] P(x, t) H(v) \\
& + \sum_{v=Z+u}^{\infty} \sum_{x=0}^{\infty} c_2 \left(v - Z + \frac{x}{2} \right) P(x, t) H(v) + \frac{c_3}{t} \tag{9}
\end{aligned}
$$

Using the results of Chapter 10, equation (9) can be rearranged to give

$$C(t, Z) = c_1 \sum_{w=0}^{Z} (Z - w) R(w, t) + c_2 \sum_{w=Z+u}^{\infty} (w - Z) R(w, t) + \frac{c_3}{t} \tag{10}$$

where $R(w, t)$ is a discrete probability distribution whose cumulative probability distribution $K(w, t) = \sum_{i=0}^{w} R(i, t)$ is given by

$$K(w, t) = \sum_{v=0}^{w} \left[\sum_{x=0}^{w-v} P(x, t) + \left(w - v + \frac{u}{2} \right) \sum_{x=w-v+u}^{\infty} \frac{P(x, t)}{x} \right] H(v) \tag{11}$$

For any given scheduling period t^*, the corresponding order level $Z_o(t^*)$ can be found from

$$K[Z_o(t^*) - u] \leq \frac{c_2}{c_1 + c_2} = K[Z_o(t^*)] \tag{12}$$

The corresponding minimum total cost, for the given t^*, can be shown to be

$$C_o(t^*) = \sum_{w=0}^{\infty} c[Z_o(t^*) - w]R(w, t^*) + \frac{c_3}{t^*} \tag{13}$$

where $c(i)$ is defined by

$$c(i) = \begin{cases} c_1 i & i \geq 0 \\ -c_2 i & i \leq 0 \end{cases} \tag{14}$$

Equation (13) can be used to find the optimal scheduling period t_o.

The procedure suggested earlier for solving the system is applied in the following example.

Example 9-4

The demand during any week is either 0 or 1 with probabilities 0.4 and 0.6 respectively. Leadtime is 3 weeks. The carrying cost and the shortage cost are \$1 per unit per week and \$5 per unit per week respectively. The replenishing cost is \$2. A (t, Z) policy is used. Find the optimal scheduling period, the optimal order level, and the corresponding expected minimum total cost of the system.

In this example the discrete probability distribution for $t = 1$ week is given by $P(0, 1) = 0.4$ and $P(1, 1) = 0.6$. The average demand is $r = 0.6$ per week. Since leadtime is 3 weeks, the probability distribution of demand during leadtime, $H(v)$, is equal to $P(x, 3)$ and can be easily computed to give $H(0) = P(0, 3) = 0.064$, $H(1) = P(1, 3) = 0.288$, $H(2) = P(2, 3) = 0.432$, and $H(3) = P(3, 3) = 0.216$. The unit-cost parameters are $c_1 = \$1$ per unit per week, $c_2 = \$5$ per unit per week, and $c_3 = \$2$.

Applying the procedure outlined earlier in the section, we compute $\sqrt{(2c_3/c_1 r)(c_1 + c_2)/c_2}$, by equation (7), which gives 2.8 weeks. We therefore start with $t^* = 2$ weeks.

For $t^* = 2$ weeks, $P(x, t^*)$ can be computed from $P(x, 1)$ and is found to be given by $P(0, 2) = 0.16$, $P(1, 2) = 0.48$, and $P(2, 2) = 0.36$. Using this result and the values of $H(v)$ (which have been obtained previously) in equation (11) leads to the results for $K(w, 2)$ and $R(w, 2)$ in Table 9–4a. Since $c_2/(c_2 + c_2) = 0.833$, equation (12) and Table 9–4a lead to the solution $Z_o(2) = 3$. And by equation (13) we have $C_o(2) = \$2.61$ per week.

TABLE 9-4a

Values of $K(w, 2)$ and $R(w, 2)$ in Example 9-4

w	0	1	2	3	4	5
$K(w, 2)$	0.03136	0.19936	0.53776	0.85096	0.98056	1.00000
$R(w, 2)$	0.03136	0.16800	0.33840	0.31320	0.12960	0.01944

We next examine the case $t^* = 3$ weeks. $P(x, 3)$ has already been computed [for $H(v)$]. Equation (11) now leads to Table 9–4b. By equation (12) and Table 9–4b we now obtain the solution $Z_o(3) = 4$, and using this result in equation (13) we find $C_o(3) = \$2.39$ per week. Since this cost for $t^* = 3$ weeks is smaller than the cost for $t^* = 2$ weeks, we continue the computations.

TABLE 9–4b

Values of $K(w, 3)$ and $R(w, 3)$ in Example 9–4

w	0	1	2	3	4	5	6
$K(w, 3)$	0.022528	0.151552	0.439552	0.756352	0.937792	0.992224	1.000000
$R(w, 3)$	0.022528	0.129624	0.288000	0.316800	0.181400	0.054432	0.007776

TABLE 9–4c

Values of $K(w, 4)$ and $R(w, 4)$ in Example 9–4

w	0	1	2	3	4	5	6	7
$K(w, 4)$	0.0168064	0.1178560	0.3606688	0.6612328	0.8759728	0.9700624	0.9965008	1.0000000
$R(w, 4)$	0.0168064	0.1010496	0.2428128	0.3014640	0.2138400	0.0940896	0.0264384	0.0034992

For $t^* = 4$ weeks, $P(x, 4)$ is computed and is given by $P(0, 4) = 0.0256$, $P(1, 4) = 0.1536, P(2, 4) = 0.3456, P(3, 4) = 0.3456,$ and $P(4, 4) = 0.1296$. Table 9–4c can now be obtained from equation (11). By equation (12) and Table 9–4c we find that $Z_o(4) = 4$. Using this result in equation (13) we obtain $C_o(4) = \$2.44$ per week. Since $C_o(3) < C_o(4)$, no further computations are necessary. The complete solution is therefore: The optimal scheduling period is 3 weeks, the optimal order level is 4 units, and the expected minimum total cost of the system is \$2.39 per week.

9–5 PROBLEMS

1. In an inventory system indentical with the lot-size system (Section 3–1) but with leadtime we have $r = 3000$ parts per year, $c_1 = \$3$ per part per year, $c_3 = \$125$ per setup, $L = 3$ months. On January 1 there are 700 parts in stock and an outstanding order for 300 parts is due on February 1. What optimal policy can be recommended?

2. In an inventory system identical with the order-level system (Section 4–1) but with leadtime we have $r = 13$ lb per week, $t_p = 9$ weeks, $c_1 = \$3.20$ per pound per week, $c_2 = \$8.50$ per pound per week. Find Z_o when (a) $L = 4$ weeks, (b) $L = 2$ weeks, (c) $L = 10$ weeks. What will be the amount in inventory when the order is placed?

3. In the system of Section 9–1 assume that $r = 1.54$ lb per week, $c_1 = \$1$ per pound per week, $c_3 = \$30$ per setup, $A = 1.3, L = 8$ weeks.

(a) Find t_o in weeks, Z_o in pounds, C_o in dollars per year.

(b) At the beginning of the first week there are 9 lb in stock and a previously placed order for 8 lb is due at the beginning of the fourth week.

An order is placed at the beginning of the first week (which is due at the beginning of the ninth week). Subsequent orders are placed at t_o intervals.

(i) Prepare in tabular form the inventory fluctuations during the year using the data of Table 2-5.

(ii) Find the total yearly costs from the tabulation and compare them with C_o of part (a).

4. Explain why the results in Sections 9-2, 9-3, 9-4 do not hold when shortages cannot be made up.

5. Sketch the inventory fluctuations in an inventory system in which the scheduling period is 2 weeks and leadtime is 3 weeks.

6. Check the result given in equation 9-2(7). In addition, show that this result reduces to the result in equation 8-2(9) when leadtime is zero.

7. Check the numerical computations in Example 9-2a.

8. Interpret the meaning of the solution given by equation 9-3(2).

9. Derive the result in equation 9-2(7) by marginal analysis.

10. Compare the results given by Examples 8-2a and 9-2a.

11. Extend the results of problem 8-5(10) to a system with significant leadtime.

12. *Whitin's Multiperiod Example.** An inventory system comprises three scheduling periods each of length t_p. Leadtime is of length t_p. The carrying costs in the first two periods are zero. In the third period the carrying cost is \$1 per quantity unit left over. The shortage cost in any period is \$4 per shortage in that period. No returns are allowed. No shortages can be made up. Graphically the system can be described as in Figure 9-5.

The instantaneous demand in the first period is z and has the discrete probability $R(z)$. Similarly, for the second and third periods the probability distributions are $Q(y)$ and $P(x)$ respectively. The distributions $P(x)$, $Q(y)$, and $R(z)$ are independent. The numerical values of $P(x)$, $Q(y)$, and $R(z)$ are $P(0) = \frac{1}{4}$, $P(1) = \frac{2}{4}$, $P(2) = \frac{1}{4}$, $Q(0) = \frac{1}{8}$, $Q(1) = \frac{3}{8}$, $Q(2) = \frac{3}{8}$, $Q(3) = \frac{1}{8}$, $R(0) = \frac{1}{16}$, $R(1) = \frac{4}{16}$, $R(2) = \frac{6}{16}$, $R(3) = \frac{4}{16}$, and $R(4) = \frac{1}{6}$.

At time T_{-1} the first decision is made with respect to q'', the amount to be ordered which will be available at time T_0. Thus the inventory level at time T_0 is $S'' = q''$.

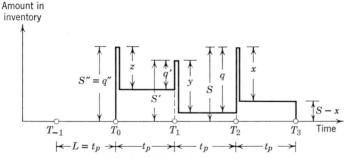

Figure 9-5   Whitin's multiperiod example.

* See Whitin [55], pp. 72-77. We present the system in our notation.

At time T_0 a decision is made about q' which will be available at T_1. The inventory level S' at time T_1 will be

$$S' = \begin{cases} q' + S'' - z & z \leq S'' \\ q' & z \geq S'' \end{cases} \tag{1}$$

At time T_1 a decision is made about q which will be available at time T_2. The inventory level at T_2 will be

$$S = \begin{cases} q + S' - y & y \leq S' \\ q & y \geq S' \end{cases} \tag{2}$$

Use dynamic programming to show that $q_o'' = 4$ or 5, that $q_o'' + q_o' = 5$, and that the corresponding minimum expected total cost is $\$1\frac{213}{256}$.

Chapter 10

Equivalence of Probabilistic Order-Level Systems

10-0 This chapter deals with the probabilistic order-level systems covered in Sections 8–2, 8–3, 9–2, and 9–3 and in problems 8–5(10) and 9–5(11). We shall show that for continuous units the expected total cost of all these systems can be given in the form

$$C(W) = c_1 \int_0^W (W - y)g(y)\, dy + c_2 \int_W^\infty (y - W)g(y)\, dy \qquad (1)$$

In this equation W is the order level S in systems with zero leadtime and Z in systems with non-zero leadtime. The probability density $g(y)$ will depend on the probability density of demand $f(x)$, on the probability density of demand during leadtime $h(v)$ (when leadtime is significant), and on the demand pattern index n.

Similarly, for discrete units, we shall show that the expected total cost of all the systems can be given in the form

$$C(W) = c_1 \sum_{y=0}^{W} (W - y)Q(y) + c_2 \sum_{y=W+u}^{\infty} (y - W)Q(y) \qquad (2)$$

where now the probability distribution $Q(y)$ depends on the probability distribution of demand $P(x)$, on the probability distribution of demand during leadtime $H(v)$, and on the demand pattern index n.

Equivalence of Systems

Let A and B designate two systems in each of which decisions have to be made with respect to the same m controllable variables, say, $x_1, \ldots, x_m$.

Let the set of the m variables be designated by X. For a given X let the corresponding measures of effectiveness of the systems be $M(X)_A$ and $M(X)_B$.

The two systems will be said to be *equivalent* if, for *every* X,

$$M(X)_A = M(X)_B \tag{3}$$

In other words, two systems that are affected identically by the same variables are said to be equivalent. By using the notion of equivalence, it is thus possible to find how system A behaves with respect to X by studying how an equivalent system B behaves with respect to X. In particular, if X_o is a value that optimizes system B, this value must also optimize system A.

The usefulness of equivalence will be demonstrated with respect to probabilistic order-level systems of Chapters 8 and 9. In these systems there is only one controllable variable, the order level. The measures of effectiveness in these systems are the expected total costs. It will be shown that the optimal order levels can be found by analyzing equivalent systems which are somewhat less complex than the original ones.

Three illustrations will now be given of equivalent inventory systems. The reason for choosing the specific expected total costs in these illustrations will become evident in later sections. As a first illustration, consider two inventory systems whose expected total costs are

$$C(S)_A = c_1 \int_0^S \left(S - \frac{x}{2}\right) xe^{-x}\, dx + c_1 \int_S^\infty \frac{S^2}{2x} xe^{-x}\, dx$$

$$+ c_2 \int_S^\infty \frac{(x - S)^2}{2x} xe^{-x}\, dx \tag{4}$$

and

$$C(S)_B = c_1 \int_0^S (S - y)e^{-y}\, dy + c_2 \int_S^\infty (y - S)e^{-y}\, dy \tag{5}$$

Direct evaluations of the definite integrals in these equations lead to the results

$$C(S)_A = C(S)_B = c_1 S + (c_1 + c_2)e^{-S} - c_1 \tag{6}$$

Hence, by our definition, the two systems are equivalent.

In the second illustration the demands and the order levels are discrete units 0, 1, 2, etc. The expected total costs of two inventory systems C and D are

$$C(S)_C = c_1 \sum_{x=0}^S \left(S - \frac{x}{2}\right) P(x) + c_1 \sum_{x=S+1}^4 \frac{S^2}{2x} P(x)$$

$$+ c_2 \sum_{x=S+1}^4 \frac{(x - S)^2}{2x} P(x) \tag{7}$$

and

$$C(S)_D = c_1 \sum_{y=0}^{S} (S - y)Q(y) + c_2 \sum_{y=S+1}^{4} (y - S)Q(y) \tag{8}$$

where $P(0) = 0.04$, $P(1) = 0.20$, $P(2) = 0.37$, $P(3) = 0.30$, and $P(4) = 0.09$, and where $Q(0) = 0.29375$, $Q(1) = 0.40750$, $Q(2) = 0.21500$, $Q(3) = 0.07250$, and $Q(4) = 0.01125$. Direct evaluations of the summations in equations (7) and (8) lead to the results

$$C(0)_C = C(0)_D = 1.10000c_2$$

$$C(1)_C = C(1)_D = 0.29375c_1 + 0.39375c_2$$

$$C(2)_C = C(2)_D = 1.00220c_1 + 0.09500c_2 \tag{9}$$

$$C(3)_C = C(3)_D = 1.91125c_1 + 0.01125c_2$$

$$C(S \geq 4)_C = C(S \geq 4)_D = (S - 1.10000)c_1$$

Hence, by the definition of equivalent systems, systems C and D are indeed equivalent.

In the third and final illustration, the total expected costs of systems E and F are

$$
\begin{aligned}
C(Z)_E = c_1 &\int_0^Z \int_0^{Z-v} \left(Z - v - \frac{x}{2} \right) xe^{-x} \frac{e^{-v}v^3}{6} \, dx \, dv \\
+ c_1 &\int_0^Z \int_{Z-v}^{\infty} \frac{(Z-v)^2}{2x} xe^{-x} \frac{e^{-v}v^3}{6} \, dx \, dv \\
+ c_2 &\int_0^Z \int_{Z-v}^{\infty} \frac{(x+v-Z)^2}{2x} xe^{-x} \frac{e^{-v}v^3}{6} \, dx \, dv \\
+ c_2 &\int_Z^{\infty} \int_0^{\infty} \left(v - Z + \frac{x}{2} \right) xe^{-x} \frac{e^{-v}v^3}{6} \, dx \, dv \tag{10}
\end{aligned}
$$

and

$$C(Z)_F = c_1 \int_0^Z (Z - y) \frac{e^{-4}y^4}{24} \, dy + c_2 \int_Z^{\infty} (y - Z) \frac{e^{-y}y^4}{24} \, dy \tag{11}$$

Direct evaluations of the definite integrals in these equations lead to the results

$$
\begin{aligned}
C(Z)_E &= C(Z)_F \\
&= c_1 Z + (c_1 + c_2)e^{-Z}\left(\frac{Z^4}{24} + \frac{2Z^3}{6} + \frac{3Z^2}{2} + 4Z + 5 \right) - 5c_1 \tag{12}
\end{aligned}
$$

Hence, as before, systems E and F are equivalent.

In each of these three illustrations the original cost equation of one of the systems is somewhat more complex than the original cost equation of its equivalent system. We shall show that it is possible to find the equivalent simpler systems by rather elementary operations.

EQUIVALENCE OF PROBABILISTIC ORDER-LEVEL SYSTEMS WITH UNIFORM AND INSTANTANEOUS DEMANDS

10–1   The expected total cost of the probabilistic order-level system of Section 8–3, by equation 8–3(5), is

$$C(S) = c_1 \int_0^S (S - x)f(x)\, dx + c_2 \int_S^\infty (x - S)f(x)\, dx \tag{1}$$

and by equation 8–3(7) the optimal order level S_o of this system can be obtained from

$$\int_0^{S_o} f(x)\, dx = \frac{c_2}{c_1 + c_2} \tag{2}$$

By equation 2–4(1), equation (2) can also be expressed as

$$F(S_o) = \frac{c_2}{c_1 + c_2} \tag{3}$$

Equation (1) is identical with equation 10–0(1) mentioned at the beginning of this chapter. Hence, we conclude that the optimal W_o of a system represented by equation 10–0(1) can be obtained from

$$G(W_o) = \frac{c_2}{c_1 + c_2} \tag{4}$$

where

$$G(W) = \int_0^W g(y)\, dy \tag{5}$$

Consider now the probabilistic order-level system of Section 8–2. In that system the expected total cost, by equation 8–2(5), is

$$C(S) = c_1 \int_0^S \left(S - \frac{x}{2}\right)f(x)\, dx + c_1 \int_S^\infty \frac{S^2}{2x} f(x)\, dx$$
$$+ c_2 \int_S^\infty \frac{(x - S)^2}{2x} f(x)\, dx \tag{6}$$

By equation 8–2(9) the optimal level S_o can be found from

$$\int_0^{S_o} f(x)\, dx + \int_{S_o}^\infty \frac{S_o}{x} f(x)\, dx = \frac{c_2}{c_1 + c_2} \tag{7}$$

This last equation can also be written as

$$M(S_o) = \frac{c_2}{c_1 + c_2} \tag{8}$$

where

$$M(S) = \int_0^S f(x)\, dx + \int_S^\infty \frac{S}{x} f(x)\, dx \tag{9}$$

An examination of the function $M(S)$ reveals the following properties: (1) $M(0) = 0$, (2) M is non-decreasing, and (3) $M(\infty) = 1$. Thus $M(S)$ satisfies all the properties of a cumulative distribution function. The similarity of equations (3) and (8), where both F and M are cumulative distribution functions, suggests that equation (6) can also be expressed in the form

$$C(S) = c_1 \int_0^S (S - y) m(y)\, dy + c_2 \int_S^\infty (y - S) m(y)\, dy \tag{10}$$

where

$$m(y) = \frac{dM(y)}{dy} \tag{11}$$

with $M(y)$ as given by equation (9). Differentiating equation (9) and using the result of equation 8–2(7) leads to

$$m(y) = \int_y^\infty \frac{f(x)}{x}\, dx \tag{12}$$

We are thus led to the conclusion that the probabilistic order-level systems of Sections 8–2 and 8–3 are equivalent since both can be expressed in the form of equation 10–0(1).

A Direct Proof of the Equivalence

The formal statement of the equivalence of the probabilistic order-level systems with uniform and instantaneous demands may be given as follows. An inventory system whose expected total cost is in the form of equation (6) can be given in the form of equation (10), if the function $m(y)$ is obtained from $f(x)$ according to equation (12). The direct proof of this statement follows.

We first show that $m(y)$ is indeed a probability density. Since $f(x)$ is a probability density and $x \geq 0$, then from equation (12) we find immediately that $m(y) \geq 0$. In addition,

$$\int_0^\infty m(y)\, dy = \int_0^\infty \left[\int_y^\infty \frac{f(x)}{x}\, dx \right] dy = \int_0^\infty \int_0^x \frac{f(x)}{x}\, dy\, dx$$

$$= \int_0^\infty \frac{f(x)}{x}\, x\, dx = \int_0^\infty f(x)\, dx = 1 \tag{13}$$

Therefore $m(y)$ is a probability density.

We next note that

$$\bar{y} = \int_0^\infty y m(y)\, dy = \int_0^\infty y \int_y^\infty \frac{f(x)}{x}\, dx\, dy = \int_0^\infty \frac{f(x)}{x} \int_0^x y\, dy\, dx$$

$$= \int_0^\infty \frac{f(x)}{x} \frac{x^2}{2}\, dx = \int_0^\infty \frac{x}{2} f(x)\, dx = \frac{\bar{x}}{2} \tag{14}$$

Equation (10) can now be rewritten to give

$$C(S) = (c_1 + c_2) \int_0^S (S - y) m(y)\, dy + c_2 \int_0^\infty (y - S) m(y)\, dy$$

$$= (c_1 + c_2) \int_0^S \int_0^v m(y)\, dy\, dv + c_2(\bar{y} - S) \tag{15}$$

since

$$\int_0^S \int_0^v m(y)\, dy\, dv = \int_0^S m(y) \int_y^S dv\, dy = \int_0^S m(y)(S - y)\, dy \tag{16}$$

Similarly, equation (6) can be rewritten to give

$$C(S) = (c_1 + c_2) \int_0^S \left(S - \frac{x}{2}\right) f(x)\, dx + \int_S^\infty \frac{S^2}{2x} f(x) + c_2\left(\frac{\bar{x}}{2} - S\right) \tag{17}$$

In comparing equations (15) and (17), we note, by equation (14), that the factors multiplying c_2 are the same. It therefore remains to be shown that the factors multiplying $c_1 + c_2$ are the same. And indeed, by equation (12),

$$\int_0^S \int_0^v m(y)\, dy\, dv = \int_0^S \int_0^v \int_y^\infty \frac{f(x)}{x}\, dx\, dy\, dv$$

$$= \int_0^S \int_0^v \frac{f(x)}{x} \int_0^x dy\, dx\, dv + \int_0^S \int_v^\infty \frac{f(x)}{x} \int_0^v dy\, dx\, dv$$

$$= \int_0^S \int_0^v f(x)\, dx\, dv + \int_0^S \int_v^\infty v \frac{f(x)}{x}\, dx\, dv \tag{18}$$

$$= \int_0^S f(x) \int_x^S dv\, dx + \int_0^S \frac{f(x)}{x} \int_0^x v\, dv\, dx$$

$$+ \int_S^\infty \frac{f(x)}{x} \int_0^S v\, dv\, dx$$

$$= \int_0^S (S - x) f(x)\, dx + \int_0^S \frac{x}{2} f(x)\, dx + \int_S^\infty \frac{S^2}{2x} f(x)\, dx$$

$$= \int_0^S \left(S - \frac{x}{2}\right) f(x)\, dx + \int_S^\infty \frac{S^2}{2x} f(x)\, dx$$

This completes the proof of the equivalence of the systems.

Example 10-1a

In a probabilistic order-level system with a uniform pattern of demand the probability density of demand is $f(x) = (1/b^2)xe^{-x/b}$, where $x \geq 0$. The unit cost of carrying inventory and of incurring shortages are c_1 and c_2 respectively. Find the optimal order level S_o. This is a restatement of Example 8-2a. We shall solve the system using the methods of this section.

By equation (12) we have $m(y) = \int_y^\infty (1/b^2)e^{-x/b}\,dx = (1/b)e^{-y/b}$. Hence, by equations (4) and (5), $\int_0^{S_o} (1/b)e^{-y/b} = c_2/(c_1 + c_2)$. Therefore $S_o = b \ln [(c_1 + c_2)/c_1]$. This result agrees, of course, with that in equation 8-2(13).

In passing, we note that the system of this example is system A in the first illustration in Section 10-0, for the case $b = 1$. The reason for the identical solution of Examples 8-2a and 8-3a is also now apparent.

Discrete Units

The expected total cost of the probabilistic order-level system of Section 8-3 for discrete units is, by equation 8-3(12),

$$C(S) = c_1 \sum_{x=0}^{S} (S - x)P(x) + c_2 \sum_{x=S+u}^{\infty} (x - S)P(x) \qquad (19)$$

And by equation 8-3(15) the optimal order level S_o can be obtained from

$$F(S_o - u) \leq \frac{c_2}{c_1 + c_2} \leq F(S_o) \qquad (20)$$

where $F(S)$ is the cumulative probability distribution of demand.

By comparing equations (19) and 10-0(2), we conclude immediately that the solution of a system represented by equation 10-0(2) can be obtained from

$$G(W_o - u) \leq \frac{c_2}{c_1 + c_2} \leq G(W_o) \qquad (21)$$

where

$$G(W) = \sum_{y=0}^{W} Q(y) \qquad (22)$$

The probabilistic order-level system of Section 8-2 with discrete units has, by equation 8-2(15), an expected total cost of

$$C(S) = c_1 \sum_{x=0}^{S} \left(S - \frac{x}{2}\right)P(x) + c_1 \sum_{x=S+u}^{\infty} \frac{S^2}{2x}P(x)$$
$$+ c_2 \sum_{x=S+u}^{\infty} \frac{(x - S)^2}{2x}P(x) \qquad (23)$$

The optimal order level of this system, by equations 8–2(19) and 8–2(20), can be found from

$$M(S_o - u) \leq \frac{c_2}{c_1 + c_2} \leq M(S_o) \tag{24}$$

where

$$M(S) = \sum_{x=0}^{S} P(x) + \left(S + \frac{u}{2} \right) \sum_{x=S+u}^{\infty} \frac{P(x)}{x} \tag{25}$$

Just as for continuous units, we can show that for discrete units the probabilistic order-level systems with uniform and instantaneous demands are also equivalent. That is, the inventory system whose expected total cost is in the form of equation (23) can be given in the form of equation 10–0(2), where W is replaced by S and where $Q(y)$ is a probability distribution given by

$$Q(y) = \begin{cases} P(0) + \dfrac{u}{2} \displaystyle\sum_{x=u}^{\infty} \dfrac{P(x)}{x} & y = 0 \\[2ex] \dfrac{u}{2} \dfrac{P(y)}{y} + u \displaystyle\sum_{x=y+u}^{\infty} \dfrac{P(x)}{x} & y = u, 2u, \ldots \end{cases} \tag{26}$$

The background of this statement and its proof follow the reasoning given earlier for continuous units. [See problems 10–4(4) and 10–5(5).]

Example 10–1b

To illustrate the advantage of using the notion of equivalent systems, consider the computations in Example 8–2b. We shall compute the minimum expected total cost $20.46 without using equation 8–2(15).

The pertinent system is the probabilistic order-level system with discrete units of 0, 5, 10, etc. The costs are $c_1 = \$2$ per unit per week, and $c_2 = \$24$ per unit per week. The distribution $P(x)$ and the method for computing the equivalent distribution $Q(y)$ of equation (26) are illustrated in Table 10–1.

Since $c_2/(c_1 + c_2) = 0.923$, then, by equation (14), $S_o = 15$. Hence, directly from equation 10–0(2),

$$C(15) = 2 \sum_{y=0}^{15} (15 - y)Q(y) + 24 \sum_{y=20}^{20} (y - 15)Q(y) = \$20.46.$$

The reader may note that Table 10–1 is somewhat simpler than the corresponding Table 8–2. He may also note the relation between this example and the second illustration in Section 10–0.

TABLE 10–1

Tabulation of the Equivalent Distribution $Q(y)$ of Equation 10–1(26)

x, y	$P(x)$	$\dfrac{P(x)}{x}$	$\displaystyle\sum_{y+u}^{\infty} \dfrac{P(x)}{x}$	$Q(y)$	$M(y)$
0	0.04		0.1015	0.29375	0.29375
5	0.20	0.0400	0.0615	0.40750	0.70125
10	0.37	0.0370	0.0245	0.21500	0.91625
15	0.30	0.0200	0.0045	0.07250	0.98875
20	0.09	0.0045	0	0.01125	1.00000

EQUIVALENCE OF PROBABILISTIC ORDER-LEVEL SYSTEMS WITH UNIFORM AND INSTANTANEOUS DEMANDS AND ANY LEADTIME

10–2   In this section we propose to show that the systems of Sections 9–2 and 9–3 are each equivalent to the system of Section 10–0. That is, we propose to show that equations 9–2(6) and 9–3(1) can be given in the form of equation 10–0(1), or that equations 9–2(9) and 9–3(3) can be given in the form of equation 10–0(2).

Instantaneous Demand

We first consider the system of Section 9–3 for continuous units. The expected total cost of the system is

$$C(Z) = \int_0^Z \int_0^{Z-v} c_1(Z - v - x) f(x) h(v) \, dx \, dv$$
$$+ \int_0^Z \int_{Z-v}^{\infty} c_2(v - Z + x) f(x) h(v) \, dx \, dv$$
$$+ \int_Z^{\infty} \int_0^{\infty} c_2(v - Z + x) f(x) h(v) \, dx \, dv \quad (1)$$

Let y be the demand during a period equal in length to the leadtime and one scheduling period. Then

$$y = v + x \quad (2)$$

The density of y is given by

$$g(y) = \int_0^y f(y - v) h(v) \, dv \quad (3)$$

If this value of $g(y)$ is substituted in equation 10–0(1) and W is replaced by Z, we then have

$$
\begin{aligned}
C(Z) &= c_1 \int_0^Z (Z - y)\left[\int_0^y f(y - v)h(v)\,dv\right]dy \\
&\quad + c_2 \int_Z^\infty (y - Z)\left[\int_0^y f(y - v)h(v)\,dv\right]dy \\
&= c_1 \int_0^Z \left[\int_v^Z (Z - y)f(y - v)h(v)\,dy\right]dv \\
&\quad + c_2 \int_0^Z \left[\int_Z^\infty (y - Z)f(y - v)h(v)\,dy\right]dv \\
&\quad + c_2 \int_Z^\infty \left[\int_v^\infty (y - Z)f(y - v)h(v)\,dy\right]dv \\
&= c_1 \int_0^Z \left[\int_0^{Z-v} (Z - v - x)f(x)h(v)\,dx\right]dv \\
&\quad + c_2 \int_0^Z \left[\int_{Z-v}^\infty (x + v - Z)f(x)h(v)\,dx\right]dv \\
&\quad + c_2 \int_Z^\infty \int_0^\infty (x + v - Z)f(x)h(v)\,dx\,dv
\end{aligned}
\tag{4}
$$

which is identical with equation (1). Hence the expected total cost given by equation 9–3(1) can also be expressed in the form of equation 10–0(1), provided the various densities are related as in equation (3).

A similar result pertains to systems with discrete units. The expected total cost of equation 9–3(3) can be given in the form of equation 10–0(2) provided the various distributions are related by

$$
Q(y) = \sum_{v=0}^y P(y - v)H(v)
\tag{5}
$$

[The reader should note that for continuous variables equation (3) gives the convolution of $f(x)$ and $h(v)$, and that for discrete variables equation (5) gives the convolution of $P(x)$ and $H(v)$.]

Uniform Demand

We now consider the system of Section 9–2 for continuous units. The expected total cost of the system is given by equation 9–2(6). The results which have just been derived and the results of Section 10–1 can immediately be extended as follows.

Using equations 10–1(12) and 10–2(3) as starting points, let the function $g(y)$ be defined by

$$
g(y) = \int_0^y m(y - v)h(v)\,dv = \int_0^y \left[\int_{y-v}^\infty \frac{f(x)}{x}\,dx\right]h(v)\,dv
\tag{6}
$$

This is a density with a mean of $\bar{y} = \bar{v} + \bar{x}/2$. We leave it to the reader to show that by using this density equation 9–2(6) can be written in the form of equation 10–0(1) [see Problem 10–4(6)].

Example 10–2a

In an inventory system the demand during any week is xe^{-x}. The demand occurs uniformly throughout the week. Inventories are replenished every week and leadtime is 2 weeks. The unit carrying cost and the unit shortage cost are \$5 and \$95 respectively. We want to find the optimal order level Z_o.

In this system $h(v) = \int_0^v [(v - x)e^{-(v-x)}][xe^{-x}] \, dx = e^{-v}v^3/6$. In addition, by equation 10–1(12), $m(y) = \int_y^\infty [(xe^{-x})/x] \, dx = e^{-y}$, and by equation (6), $g(y) = \int_0^y e^{-(y-v)}[e^{-v}v^3/6] \, dv = e^{-y}y^4/24$. Hence the expected total cost of the system is given by equation 10–0(1):

$$C(Z) = 5 \int_0^Z (Z - y) \frac{e^{-y}y^4}{24} \, dy + 95 \int_Z^\infty (y - Z) \frac{e^{-y}y^4}{24} \, dy.$$

By using equation 10–0(4) we obtain

$$\int_0^{Z_o} \frac{e^{-y}y^4}{24} \, dy = 0.95 \quad \text{or} \quad \int_0^{2Z_o} \frac{e^{-u/2}u^4}{2^5 \times 24} \, du = 0.95$$

The value of Z_o can now be found from χ^2 tables. It is $Z_o = 9.15$. (The reader may note that this is the third illustration of Section 10–0 and also a variation of Example 9–2a.)

The results that have been derived for continuous units can be readily extended to discrete units. We shall illustrate this with a numerical example.

Example 10–2b

In an inventory system the uniform demand during the scheduling period (a week) has the probabilities $P(2) = 0.4$, $P(3) = 0.6$. Leadtime is 3 weeks. The unit costs are $c_1 = 1$ and $c_2 = 4$. Find the optimal level Z_o.

Let $H(v)$ be the probability distribution of demand during leadtime. This distribution can be found from $P(x) * P(x) * P(x)$, that is, $H(6) = 0.064$, $H(7) = 0.288$, $H(8) = 0.432$, and $H(9) = 0.216$. Let $Q(y)$ be the distribution defined by equation 10–1(26). Then $Q(0) = 0.2$, $Q(1) = 0.4$, $Q(2) = 0.3$, and $Q(3) = 0.1$. Let $K(z)$ be the distribution resulting from convolving $Q(y)$ and $H(v)$ where $z = y + v$. We find that $K(6) = 0.0128$, $K(7) = 0.0832$, $K(8) = 0.2208$, $K(9) = 0.3088$, $K(10) = 0.2448$, $K(11) = 0.1080$, and $K(12) = 0.0216$.* Let $F(Z) = \sum_{z=6}^Z K(z)$. Then, by equation 10–1(20), $Z_o = 10$ since $F(9) = 0.6256$ and $F(10) = 0.8704$.

* A check on the arithmetic should give $\bar{z} = \bar{v} + \bar{y} = 3\bar{x} + \bar{x}/2 = 3.5\bar{x}$.

EQUIVALENCE OF PROBABILISTIC ORDER-LEVEL SYSTEMS
WITH ANY POWER PATTERN AND ANY LEADTIME

10-3   The expected total cost of a probabilistic order-level system with a
power demand pattern is given by equation 8–5(5). The solution of the
system is given by equation 8–5(6). Examination of the function $M_n(S)$ of
equation 8–5(7) in a manner similar to that of $M(S)$ of equation 10–1(9)
will reveal that (1) $M_n(0) = 0$, (2) $M(S)$ is non-decreasing, and (3)
$M_n(\infty) = 1$. This function is therefore a cumulative distribution. Just as
in Section 10–1, we can then define the probability density

$$m_n(y) = \frac{dM_n(y)}{dy} = ny^{n-1} \int_y^\infty \frac{f(x)}{x^n}\, dx \qquad (1)$$

The expected total cost of the probabilistic order-level system with a power
pattern can now be given in the form

$$C(S) = c_1 \int_0^S (S - y) m_n(y)\, dy + c_2 \int_S^\infty (y - S) m_n(y)\, dy \qquad (2)$$

The proof of this statement is left as an exercise [see problem 10–4(9)].

The result just obtained can be extended to a system for which leadtime
is not necessarily zero. Let $h(v)$ be the density of demand during leadtime
and let

$$s = v + y \qquad (3)$$

The density of s is then

$$g(s) = \int_0^s m_n(s - v) h(v)\, dv \qquad (4)$$

The expected total cost of a probabilistic order-level system with any power
demand pattern and any leadtime can then be expressed in the form of
equation 10–0(1) where W is replaced by Z and where the function g is
given by equation (4) [see problem 10–4(10)].

We shall now illustrate the extension of all our results by solving a
probabilistic order-level system with discrete units, a power demand
pattern, and significant leadtime.

Example 10–3

In an inventory system the power pattern of demand can be characterized
by the parameter $n = 2$ (i.e., demands toward the beginning of each
scheduling period are somewhat larger than demands at the end of the
scheduling period). Leadtime is 2 months, and the scheduling period is

1 month. The unit costs are $c_1 = 1$ and $c_2 = 20$. The probability distribution of demand during a month is $P(0) = 0.14$, $P(50) = 0.27$, $P(100) = 0.26$, $P(150) = 0.18$, $P(200) = 0.09$, $P(250) = 0.05$, and $P(300) = 0.01$. The problem is to find the optimal order level Z_o and the corresponding minimum expected cost of the system.

From equation 8–5(10) we derive a general expression for $Q_2(y)$ as a function of $P(x)$:

$$Q_2(y) = \begin{cases} P(0) + \dfrac{1}{3} \displaystyle\sum_{x=u}^{\infty} \dfrac{P(x)}{(x/u)^2} & y = 0 \\[2ex] \dfrac{(y/u - \frac{1}{3})P(y)}{(y/u)^2} + \dfrac{2y}{u} \displaystyle\sum_{x=y+u}^{\infty} \dfrac{P(x)}{(x/u)^2} & y = u,\, 2u,\, \ldots \end{cases} \tag{5}$$

In our example $u = 50$. Hence $Q_2(0) = 0.26$, $Q_2(50) = 0.37$, $Q_2(100) = 0.22$, $Q_2(150) = 0.10$, $Q_2(200) = 0.04$, $Q_2(250) = 0.01$, and $Q_2(300) = 0.00$. Since leadtime is 2 months, $H(v) = P(x) * P(x)$. Hence $H(0) = 0.0196$, $H(50) = 0.0756$, $H(100) = 0.1457$, $H(150) = 0.1908$, $H(200) = 0.1900$, $H(250) = 0.1562$, $H(300) = 0.1090$, $H(350) = 0.0638$, $H(400) = 0.0313$, $H(450) = 0.0126$, $H(500) = 0.0043$, $H(550) = 0.0010$, and $H(600) = 0.0001$.

We can now derive

$$K_2(s) = Q_2(y) * H(v) \tag{6}$$

Namely, $K_2(0) = 0.005$, $K_2(50) = 0.027$, $K_2(100) = 0.070$, $K_2(150) = 0.122$, $K_2(200) = 0.160$, $K_2(250) = 0.171$, $K_2(300) = 0.154$, $K_2(350) = 0.119$, $K_2(400) = 0.081$, $K_2(450) = 0.048$, $K_2(500) = 0.025$, $K_2(550) = 0.011$, $K_2(600) = 0.005$, and $K_2(650) = 0.0002$.

Now $c_2/(c_1 + c_2) = 20/21 = 0.952$. Hence $Z_o = 450$, since

$$\sum_{s=0}^{400} K_2(s) = 0.909 < 0.952 < 0.957 = \sum_{s=0}^{450} K_2(s).$$

To find the minimum expected total cost of the system, we use equation 10–0(2) with W replaced by Z_o and Q replaced by K_2. The minimum cost is 257.4 per month.

10–4   PROBLEMS

1. Find a probabilistic order-level system with an expected total cost as in equation 10–0(1) which is equivalent to the order-level system of Section 4–1.
2. Solve problem 1 for discrete units and equation 10–0(2).

3. In an order-level system the weekly demand with a uniform pattern has the probability density $\frac{1}{2}e^{-x/2}$, $x \geq 0$. The scheduling period is 2 weeks and the leadtime is 3 weeks. The carrying cost is \$3 per unit per week and the shortage cost is \$30 per unit per week. What is the optimal order level Z_o and what is the minimum expected total cost?

4. Show that $Q(y)$ of equation 10–1(26) is a probability distribution.

5. Show that the cumulative distribution of y of equation 10–1(26) is given by equation 10–1(25).

6. Prove the statement on the equivalence of the probabilistic order-level systems with uniform and instantaneous demands for any leadtime. (The statement follows equation 10–2(6).)

7. Show that the order-level system with leadtime of Section 9–3 is equivalent to a similar system without leadtime using only equation 10–0(2) and referring to Figure 9–3.

8. Show that $m_n(y)$ of equation 10–3(1) is a probability density and that $\bar{y} = [n/(n + 1)]\bar{x}$.

9. Prove the statement preceding equation 10–3(2) by using the results of problem 8.

10. Prove the statement following equation 10–3(4) by using the results of problem 9–5(11).

11. Check equation 10–3(5) by reference to the derivation of equations 8–4(10), 10–1(26), and 10–3(1).

12. Check the results given by equations 9–4(10) and 9–4(11).

13. Let $u_n{}^f$ designate the nth moment about the origin for any density $f(x)$. Let $u_n{}^m$ be the nth moment about the origin for the density $m(y)$ of equation 10–1(12). Show that

$$u_n{}^m = u_n{}^f/(n + 1) \qquad (1)$$

14. Discuss the possibility of the equivalence of the systems of Sections 8–2 and 9–2 when shortages cannot be made up. [See also problem 9–5(4).]

Chapter 11

Effects of Probabilistic Demand
and Leadtime on the Cost
of Scheduling-Period–Order-Level Systems

11–0 When two inventory systems are alike in all respects except that in one demand is deterministic and in the other it is probabilistic, it seems reasonable to expect that the total cost of the deterministic system is smaller than, or at most equal to, the expected total cost of the probabilistic system. In this chapter we shall show that this is indeed true for scheduling-period–order-level systems.

   In Section 11–1 only order-level systems will be dealt with, and a number of examples will be given to illustrate the effect of variability of demand on the cost of the systems. We shall also conjecture that the larger the standard deviation of demand, the larger the expected total cost of the order-level system. This conjecture will be shown to be incorrect.

   In Section 11–2 the results of the previous section will be extended to type (1, 2, 3) systems. The extensions are rather straightforward. But, in order to illustrate the results, rather lengthy computations are needed. For this reason flow charts are given from which computer programs can be written; the computer programs can in turn be used to provide the desired results.

   The remainder of the chapter deals with the effect of leadtime on the cost of the systems. We shall show that the cost of a system without lead-time is smaller than, or at most equal to, the cost of a system with leadtime. Furthermore, we shall show that the larger the leadtime, the larger (or at least the same) the cost.

   In Section 11–3 we deal with order-level systems and in Section 11–4 with scheduling-period–order-level systems. The main portion of Section

177

11–3 is devoted to formal proofs and the background for the proofs. Section 11–4 is an extension of the results of Sections 11–2 and 11–3.

EFFECTS OF PROBABILISTIC DEMAND ON THE COST OF ORDER-LEVEL SYSTEMS

11–1   The order-level system with probabilistic demand was studied in Section 8–2. For this system we have seen that the expected total cost is given by equation 8–2(5). For $S \geq 0$ this equation can be rearranged to give

$$
\begin{aligned}
C^P(S) &= c_1 \int_0^S \left(S - \frac{x}{2}\right) f(x)\, dx + c_1 \int_S^\infty \frac{S^2}{2x} f(x)\, dx \\
&\quad + c_2 \int_S^\infty \frac{(x - S)^2}{2x} f(x)\, dx \\
&= c_1 \left(S - \frac{\bar{x}}{2}\right) + (c_1 + c_2) \int_S^\infty \frac{(x - S)^2}{2x} f(x)\, dx
\end{aligned}
\tag{1}
$$

where $\bar{x}$ is the mean demand.

The expected total cost of this system has been designated by C^P to distinguish it from the cost of the order-level system of Section 4–1, which will be designated by C^D. We propose to compare C^P and C^D, assuming that the same unit costs c_1 and c_2 apply in both systems and that in the deterministic system the demand during t_p equals the average demand in the probabilistic system. That is,

$$
q_p = r t_p = \bar{x}
\tag{2}
$$

For $0 \leq S \leq \bar{x}$ equation 4–1(6) can be rewritten to give

$$
\begin{aligned}
C^D(S) &= \frac{c_1 S^2}{2\bar{x}} + \frac{c_2(\bar{x} - S)^2}{2x} \\
&= c_1 \left(S - \frac{\bar{x}}{2}\right) + \frac{(c_1 + c_2)(\bar{x} - S)^2}{2\bar{x}}
\end{aligned}
\tag{3}
$$

We shall now show that, for any order level S, the total cost of the deterministic system is always less than, or at most equal to, the expected total cost of the probabilistic system. In other words, we shall show that

$$
C^D(S) \leqq C^P(S)
\tag{4}
$$

Only the case $0 \leq S \leq \bar{x}$ will be discussed here. The proofs for the cases $S < 0$ and $S > \bar{x}$ are left as an exercise [see problem 11–5(1)].

In order to show that the inequality (4) holds, it will suffice to show, by equations (1) and (3), that

$$\frac{(\bar{x} - S)^2}{\bar{x}} \leqq \int_S^\infty \frac{(x - S)^2}{x} f(x)\, dx \tag{5}$$

or that

$$\bar{x} \int_S^\infty \frac{(x - S)^2}{x} f(x)\, dx \geqq (\bar{x} - S)^2 \tag{6}$$

And indeed

$$\bar{x} \int_S^\infty \frac{(x - S)^2}{x} f(x)\, dx = \left[\int_0^S xf(x)\, dx + \int_S^\infty xf(x)\, dx \right] \int_S^\infty (x - S)^2 f(x)\, dx$$

$$= \int_0^S xf(x)\, dx \int_S^\infty \frac{(x - S)^2}{x} f(x)\, dx + \int_S^\infty xf(x)\, dx \int_S^\infty \frac{(x - S)^2}{x} f(x)\, dx \tag{7}$$

The first term on the right-hand side of equation (7) is a positive quantity. Let it be designated by $A(S)$. For the second term we can use Schwarz's inequality.* This leads to

$$\bar{x} \int_S^\infty \frac{(x - S)^2}{x} f(x)\, dx \geqq A(S) + \left\{ \int_S^\infty \sqrt{xf(x)[(x - S)^2/x]f(x)}\, dx \right\}^2$$

$$= A(S) + \left[\int_S^\infty (x - S)f(x)\, dx \right]^2$$

$$= A(S) + \left[\int_0^\infty (x - S)f(x)\, dx \right.$$

$$\left. - \int_0^S (x - S)f(x)\, dx \right]^2 \tag{8}$$

$$= A(S) + \left[(\bar{x} - S) + \int_0^S (S - x)f(x)\, dx \right]^2$$

$$= A(S) + (\bar{x} - S)^2 + 2(\bar{x} - S) \int_0^S (S - x)f(x)\, dx$$

$$+ \left[\int_0^S (S - x)f(x)\, dx \right]^2$$

Since all terms on the right side of the last line of inequality (8) are positive, the assertion of inequality (6) has been proved and thus also the assertion of inequality (4). Hence, a deterministic order-level system is indeed less costly than, or as costly as, a similar probabilistic order-level system.

* $\int_a^b g^2(x)\, dx \int_a^b h^2(x)\, dx \geqq \left[\int_a^b g(x)h(x)\, dx \right]^2.$

Comparison of Minimum Costs

Consider now the minimum costs of the two order-level systems. Let the minimum total cost of the deterministic system be C_o^D and let the minimum expected total cost of the probabilistic system be C_o^P. Let the optimal order levels of the two systems be S_o^D and S_o^P respectively. Then

$$C_o^D = C^D(S_o^D) \leqq C^D(S_o^P) \leqq C^P(S_o^P) = C_o^P \tag{9}$$

The relations in inequality (9) can be explained as follows. The minimum cost of the deterministic system is smaller than, or at most equal to, the minimum cost of the probabilistic system for two reasons: first, because S_o^D is the optimal level in the deterministic system, and second, because inequality (4) holds for any S.

Example 11-1a

In a probabilistic order-level system the probability density of demand is given by $f(x) = (1/b^2)xe^{-x/b}$, $x \geq 0$. Using the results of Example 8–2a, we have, by equations 8–2(13) and 8–2(14), $S_o^P = b \ln [(c_1 + c_2)/c_1]$ and $C_o^P = bc_1 \ln [(c_1 + c_2)/c_1]$. A comparable deterministic system should then have $q_p = rt_p = \bar{x} = 2b$. For this reason, by equations 4–1(10) and 4–1(12), $S_o^D = 2bc_2/(c_1 + c_2)$ and $C_o^D = bc_1c_2/(c_1 + c_2)$.

To compare C^P and C^D we expand the term $\ln [(c_1 + c_2)/c_1]$ by infinite series.* This gives

$$C_o^P = bc_1 \ln \frac{c_1 + c_2}{c_1} \tag{11}$$

$$= \frac{bc_1c_2}{c_1 + c_2}\left[1 + \frac{1}{2}\frac{c_2}{c_1 + c_2} + \frac{1}{3}\left(\frac{c_2}{c_1 + c_2}\right)^2 + \cdots\right]$$

$$= C_o^D\left[1 + \frac{1}{2}\frac{c_2}{c_1 + c_2} + \frac{1}{3}\left(\frac{c_2}{c_1 + c_2}\right)^2 + \cdots\right]$$

Equation (11) thus illustrates inequality (4). The equality holds only when $c_1 = \infty$, in which case $S_o = 0$ and $C_o = bc_2$. In Table 11–1a values of C_o^P/C_o^D of equation (11) are given for various values of c_2/c_1.

TABLE 11–1a

The Ratio of Minimum Costs in Example 11–1a

c_2/c_1	0.0	0.1	0.5	1.0	2.0	3.0	4.0	5.0	10.0	20.0
C_o^P/C_o^D	1.00	1.04	1.22	1.39	1.63	1.85	2.01	2.14	2.63	3.20

* For $a > \frac{1}{2}$,

$$\ln a = \frac{a-1}{a} + \frac{1}{2}\left(\frac{a-1}{a}\right)^2 + \frac{1}{3}\left(\frac{a-1}{a}\right)^3 + \cdots$$

Here $a = (c_1 + c_2)/c_1 \geq 1$.

Example 11-1b

In a probabilistic order-level system the probability density of demand is the uniform density with a mean of $\bar{x}$ and a range of $\bar{x}(1 - a)$ to $\bar{x}(1 + a)$, where $0 \leqq a \leqq 1$. Thus

$$f(x) = \begin{cases} \dfrac{1}{2a\bar{x}} & \bar{x}(1 - a) \leqq x \leqq \bar{x}(1 + a) \\ 0 & \text{otherwise} \end{cases} \tag{12}$$

This density has been chosen in order to show how the minimum cost of the system changes with changes in a. When a approaches zero, the system becomes deterministic.

The following solution can be obtained for this system using the methods of Section 8-2. Let

$$b = \ln \frac{1 + a}{1 - a} \tag{13}$$

Then, if

$$0 \leqq \frac{c_2}{c_1 + c_2} \leqq \frac{b(1 - a)}{2a} \tag{14}$$

we find that

$$S_o = \frac{2a}{b} \bar{x} \frac{c_2}{c_1 + c_2} \tag{15}$$

and

$$C_o = \tfrac{1}{2} c_2 (\bar{x} - S_o) \tag{16}$$

And when

$$\frac{b(1 - a)}{2a} \leqq \frac{c_2}{c_1 + c_2} \leqq 1 \tag{17}$$

then S_o can be derived from

$$S_o \left[1 + \ln \frac{\bar{x}(1 + a)}{S_o} \right] = [(1 - a)c_1 + (1 + a)c_2] \frac{\bar{x}}{c_1 + c_2} \tag{18}$$

and the minimum expected total cost is

$$C_o = \frac{c_1 [S_o - \bar{x}(1 - a)]^2 + c_2 [\bar{x}(1 + a) - S_o]^2}{8a\bar{x}} \tag{19}$$

By using these results, Table 11-1b has been obtained for $\bar{x} = 1$ and $c_1 = 1$. [The costs above the broken line are based on equation (16) and those below on equation (19).] The entries in the last line of the table give the

TABLE 11–1b

The Minimum Expected Total Cost in Example 11–1b

c_2 \\ a	0.1	0.5	1.0	2.0	5.0	10.0	20.0	∞
0	0.045	0.167	0.250	0.333	0.417	0.455	0.480	0.500
0.1	0.045	0.167	0.251	0.336	0.424	0.470	0.505	0.600
0.2	0.046	0.168	0.253	0.342	0.444	0.509	0.567	0.700
0.3	0.046	0.169	0.258	0.354	0.477	0.558	0.623	0.800
0.4	0.046	0.171	0.264	0.370	0.516	0.612	0.689	0.900
0.5	0.046	0.174	0.272	0.392	0.557	0.667	0.756	1.000
0.6	0.046	0.178	0.284	0.416	0.601	0.725	0.825	1.100
0.7	0.046	0.183	0.297	0.442	0.647	0.783	0.894	1.200
0.8	0.047	0.189	0.313	0.471	0.693	0.842	0.963	1.300
0.9	0.047	0.197	0.330	0.499	0.740	0.902	1.034	1.400
1.0	0.048	0.207	0.348	0.530	0.788	0.963	1.105	1.500
	1.064	1.242	1.393	1.590	1.892	2.118	2.321	3.000

ratio of the minimum cost of the probabilistic order-level system when $a = 1$ and the minimum cost of the corresponding deterministic system ($a = 0$). They are therefore somewhat comparable to the entries of Table 11–1a.

The Effect of the Standard Deviation

We have shown that the minimum total cost of a deterministic order-level system is smaller than, or at most equal to, the minimum expected total cost of a similar probabilistic system. We may now ask whether this result can be generalized. That is, given two probabilistic order-level systems with standard deviations d^A and d^B and minimum expected total costs C^A and C^B, is it true that "if $d^A \leqq d^B$ then $C^A \leqq C^B$?" Let us call the statement in quotations a *conjecture*.

The results in Table 11–1b certainly seem to indicate that for the probability density of equation (12) the conjecture is true. Moreover, it appears that the minimum cost increases linearly with the standard deviation of demand. (See Figure 11–1. Note that here the standard deviation of demand is $d = a\bar{x}/\sqrt{3} = a\sqrt{3}/3 = 0.577a$.)

Unfortunately, however, the conjecture is not true in general. Example 11–1c illustrates the point. Although many such examples can be constructed, the reader will have no difficulty in recognizing that the systems

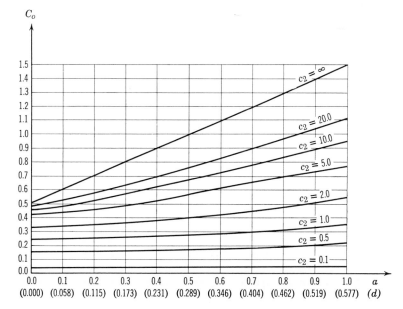

Figure 11-1 The minimum expected total cost of the probabilistic order-level system of Example 11-1b.

for which the conjecture is not true are rather special and have probability distributions with unusual special properties. One of the properties of these distributions is their not being unimodal.

Example 11-1c

In a probabilistic discrete order-level system the average demand during the scheduling period is 3.0 quantity units. The carrying cost is $2.00 per quantity unit per time unit and the shortage cost is $65.00 per quantity unit per time unit.

For the probability distribution of demand, $P^A(0) = 0.01$, $P^A(1) = 0.18$, $P^A(2) = 0.42$, $P^A(5) = 0.36$, and $P^A(6) = 0.03$, the average demand is 3.0 quantity units, the standard deviation is $d^A = 1.715$ quantity units, the optimal order level is $S_o^A = 5$ quantity units, and the corresponding minimum expected total cost is $C = \$7.17$ per time unit.

Now if demand has the probability distribution $P^B(1) = 0.5$ and $P^B(5) = 0.5$, the average demand is again 3.0 quantity units, the standard deviation is $d^B = 2.0$ quantity units, the optimal order level again happens to be $S_o^B = 5$ quantity units, and the corresponding minimum expected total cost is $C_o^B = \$7.00$ per time unit. Thus although $d^A < d^B$, we do have $C^A > C^B$.

The details of the computations leading to these results are given in Table 11–1c. The computations are based on the methods suggested in Section 10–1 and exemplified by Table 10–1. The value of $c_2/(c_1 + c_2)$ is $65.0/67.00 = 0.9701$, and $u = 1$. Hence, by equation 10–1(24), for both systems the optimal order level happens to be 5. The corresponding expected total cost can now be derived by applying equation 10–0(2). (It should be noted that for all values of the order level S, except $S = 5$, we indeed have $C^A(S) \leqq C^B(S)$. See Table 11–1d.)

TABLE 11–1c

Tabulation of $Q(y)$ and $M(y)$ of Example 11–1c

x, y	$P(x)$	$\dfrac{P(x)}{x}$	$\dfrac{\Sigma P(x)}{x}$	$Q(y)$	$M(y)$
0	0.01		0.467	0.2435	0.2435
1	0.18	0.180	0.287	0.3770	0.6205
2	0.42	0.210	0.077	0.1820	0.8025
3	0.00	0.000	0.077	0.0770	0.8795
4	0.00	0.000	0.077	0.0770	0.9565
5	0.36	0.072	0.005	0.0410	0.9975
6	0.03	0.005	0.000	0.0025	1.0000
0	0.0		0.6	0.30	0.30
1	0.5	0.5	0.1	0.35	0.65
2	0.0	0.0	0.1	0.10	0.75
3	0.0	0.0	0.1	0.10	0.85
4	0.0	0.0	0.1	0.10	0.95
5	0.5	0.1	0.0	0.05	1.00

TABLE 11–1d

The Expected Total Costs of the Two Systems of Example 11–1c

System	Standard deviation	S							
		0	1	2	3	4	5	6	7
A	1.715	97.50	48.81	25.39	14.16	8.08	7.17	9.00	11.00
B	2.000	97.50	52.62	31.15	16.40	8.35	7.00	9.00	11.00

EFFECTS OF PROBABILISTIC DEMAND ON THE COST OF SCHEDULING-PERIOD–ORDER-LEVEL SYSTEMS

11–2 The results of the previous section can readily be extended to systems for which both the scheduling period t and the order level S are subject to control.

We shall first show formally that the total cost of a deterministic scheduling-period–order-level system is smaller than, or at most equal to, the expected total cost of a similar probabilistic system.* As in the previous section, D will be used as a superscript denoting a deterministic system, and P will be used for a similar but probabilistic system. For the deterministic system we then have

$$C^D(t, S) = C_1^D(t, S) + C_2^D(t, S) + C_3^D(t, S) \tag{1}$$

where $C^D(t, S)$ is $C(q, S)$ of equation 5–1(1) and where $t = q/r$. The cost of the probabilistic system can be written as

$$C^P(t, S) = C_1^P(t, S) + C_2^P(t, S) + C_3^P(t, S) \tag{2}$$

where $C^P(t, S)$ is $C(t, S)$ of equation 8–4(8), $C_1^P(t, S)$ is the sum of the first two terms of that equation, $C_2^P(t, S)$ is the third term, and $C_3^P(t, S)$ is the last term (which is actually only a function of t).

Using this notation, we now show that

$$C^D(t, S) \leqq C^P(t, S) \tag{3}$$

for all t and all S. We first note that for all t

$$C_3^D(t, S) = C_3^P(t, S) = c_3/t \tag{4}$$

But by inequality 11–1(4) of the previous section, for any t and any S

$$C_1^D(t, S) + C_2^D(t, S) \leqq C_1^P(t, S) + C_2^P(t, S) \tag{5}$$

Hence the assertion of inequality (3) holds.

In a similar way it is possible to show that the minimum total cost of a deterministic system is smaller than, or at most equal to, the minimum expected total cost of a similar probabilistic system, namely

$$
\begin{aligned}
C_o^D = C^D(t_o^D, S_o^D) &= C_1^D(t_o^D, S_o^D) + C_2^D(t_o^D, S_o^D) + c_3/t_o^D \\
&\leqq C_1^D[t_o^P, S_o(t_o^P)] + C_2^D[t_o^P, S_o(t_o^P)] + c_3/t_o^P \\
&\leqq C_1^D(t_o^P, S_o^P) + C_2^D(t_o^P, S_o^P) + c_3/t_o^P \tag{6} \\
&\leqq C_1^P(t_o^P, S_o^P) + C_2^P(t_o^P, S_o^P) + c_3/t_o^P \\
&= C^P(t_o^P, S_o^P) = C_o^P
\end{aligned}
$$

In this inequality the notation $S_o(t_o^P)$ means that the order level S has been selected optimally on the basis of the specified scheduling period t_o^P.

---

* The deterministic system is the order-level–lot-size system of Section 5–1. The probabilistic system is that of Section 8–4.

The reason for the first inequality lies in the fact that the scheduling period t_o^P is not necessarily optimal for the deterministic system. The reason for the second inequality is that the order level S_o^P is not necessarily the optimal level for a scheduling period t_o^P in a deterministic system. Finally, the third inequality is a special case of inequality 11-1(4) for t_o^P and S_o^P.

Computer Flow Charts

To give some numerical results illustrating the effects of probabilistic demands on costs, we have to resort to rather laborious computations. These can best be performed on a digital computer. The methods of Sections 8-4 and 10-1 can be used for this purpose. A brief explanation of the pertinent flow charts from which a computer program can be prepared is in order here.

Figures 11-2a to 11-2e illustrate the main program and its subprograms. The main program (Figure 11-2a) follows the general methodology suggested in Section 10-1. First the unit costs, and the demand probabilities for $t = 1$ are read in. These are the necessary data. They are immediately printed out so that the results that follow will be known to be associated with the given data. Next the function $Q(y)$ of equation 10-1(26) is computed. The details are given in Figure 11-2b. Then the optimal order level S_o is obtained for $t = 1$. The details are given in Figure 11-2c. Then the expected costs C_1, C_2, and C_3 and the expected total cost C for $t = 1$ are found using equations 8-4(10) and 10-0(2) (Figure 11-2d). The results are then printed out. The computations that are based on $t = 1$ are concluded with a provisional assumption that the minimum expected cost occurs at $t = 1$, that is, $C_o = C$.

The next series of operations in the main program of Figure 11-2a are for any scheduling period t, starting with $t = 2$. First the probability distribution of demand $P(x, t)$ during the period t is computed, using the methods of Section 8-4 (see Figure 11-2e). The other computations are similar to those for $t = 1$. They lead to an optimal order level S_o (based on t) and the corresponding costs C_1, C_2, C_3, and C. The new expected total cost C is now compared with the previous expected total cost C_o. If the current cost C is smaller than, or at most equal to, the previous cost C_o, then C is assumed to be the minimum cost and the operation is repeated for the next scheduling period. When, however, C is larger than C_o, the computations stop and C_o is indeed the minimum expected total cost of the system.

The subprograms given in Figures 11-2b to 11-2d are self-explanatory and follow immediately from the equations on which they are based. The subprogram in Figure 11-2e requires some additional explanations. As equation 8-4(5) now stands it cannot be used for a computer program.

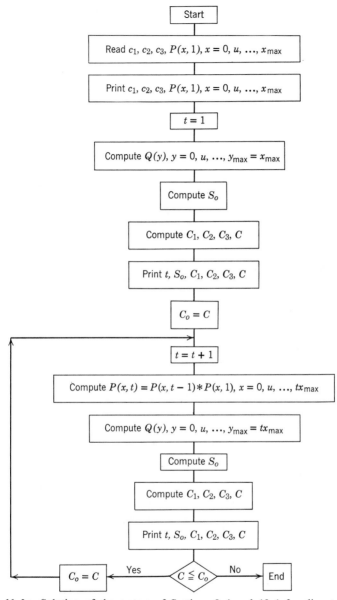

Figure 11–2a Solution of the system of Sections 8–4 and 10–1 for discrete units. Flow chart of the main program.

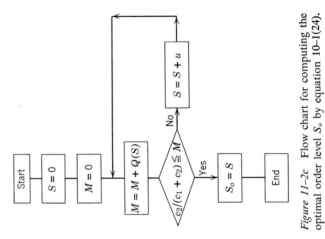

Figure 11-2c Flow chart for computing the optimal order level S_o by equation 10-1(24).

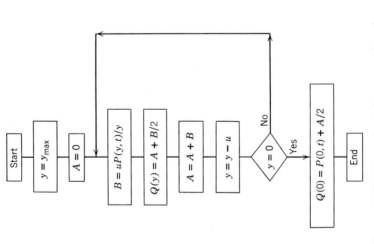

Figure 11-2b Flow chart for computing the equivalent distribution $Q(y)$ by equation 10-1(26).

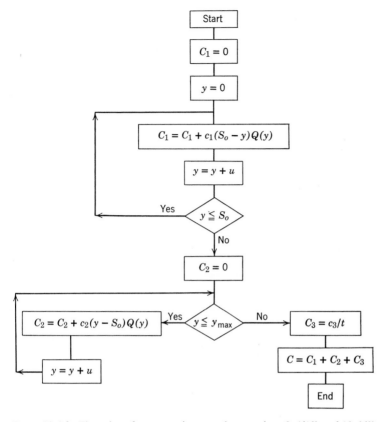

Figure 11–2d   Flow chart for computing costs by equations 8–4(10) and 10–0(2).

We must first make sure that the footnote relating to this equation is accounted for in the program. Or we can adopt the procedure used in Figure 11–2e, namely, that the pertinent equation is

$$P(x, t) = \sum_{y=y_1}^{y_2} P(z = x - y, t - 1)P(y, 1) \tag{7}$$

where

$$y_1 = \max [y_{\min}, x - z_{\max}] \tag{8}$$

and

$$y_2 = \min [x, y_{\max}] \tag{9}$$

Example 11–2

To illustrate a use of the program just described, consider a probabilistic scheduling-period–order-level system in which $c_1 = \$1.00$ per unit per

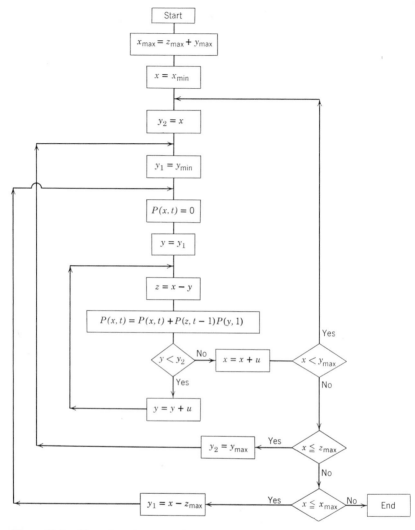

Figure 11–2e   Flow chart for computing the convolution $P(x, t) = P(x, t - 1) * P(x, 1)$ using the methods of Section 8–4 and equation 11–2(7).

week, $c_2 = \$9.00$ per unit per week, and $c_3 = \$20.00$ per replenishment. The probability distribution of demand during a period of 1 week is a Poisson distribution with a mean of 3.0. That is, $P(0, 1) = 0.050, P(1, 1) = 0.149, P(2, 1) = 0.224, P(3, 1) = 0.224, P(4, 1) = 0.168, P(5, 1) = 0.101, P(6, 1) = 0.051, P(7, 1) = 0.021, P(8, 1) = 0.008, P(9, 1) = 0.003,$ and $P(10, 1) = 0.001$.

$$C1 = 1.000$$

$$C2 = 9.000$$

$$C3 = 20.000$$

$$XBAR = 3.000$$
$$P(0) = 0.050$$
$$P(1) = 0.149$$
$$P(2) = 0.224$$
$$P(3) = 0.224$$
$$P(4) = 0.168$$
$$P(5) = 0.101$$
$$P(6) = 0.051$$
$$P(7) = 0.021$$
$$P(8) = 0.008$$
$$P(9) = 0.003$$
$$P(10) = 0.001$$

T	SO	C1	C2	C3	C
1	3	1.645	1.301	20.000	22.946
2	6	3.164	1.479	10.000	14.643
3	9	4.675	1.575	6.667	12.916
4	12	6.182	1.638	5.000	12.821
5	14	6.780	2.519	4.000	13.299

Figure 11–2f Computer printout of the results for Example 11–2a.

By using these data and a program written in Fortran for the IBM 7094, the results in Figure 11–2f were obtained. Neither subscripts nor lower-case letters can be obtained on the 7094. Hence the S_o is given as SO, the unit costs c_1, c_2, c_3 are given as C1, C2, C3, and the costs per unit time C_1, C_2, C_3 are also given by C1, C2, C3. It is clear from these results that for the optimal solution of the system $t_o = 4$ weeks, $S_o = 12$ units and the minimum expected total cost of the system is $C_o = \$12.82$ per week.

EFFECTS OF LEADTIME ON THE COST OF ORDER-LEVEL SYSTEMS

11–3 The inventory fluctuations of the order-level system without leadtime are illustrated by Figure 8–2a. The expected total cost of this system is given by equation 8–2(5). In the present section we shall refer to this cost as $C^{WL}(S)$. The inventory fluctuations of the order-level system with lead-time are illustrated by Figure 9–2. The expected total cost of that system is given by equation 9–2(6). In the present section we shall refer to this cost as $C^L(Z)$. Let the optimal order levels and the corresponding minimum costs in the two systems be designated respectively by S_o, Z_o and $C_o{}^{WL}, C_o{}^L$. That is, let

$$C_o{}^{WL} = C^{WL}(S_o) = \min_S C^{WL}(S) \tag{1}$$

$$C_o{}^L = C^L(Z_o) = \min_Z C^L(Z) \tag{2}$$

It seems intuitively reasonable to expect that the minimum cost of the system with leadtime should be greater than, or at least equal to, the minimum cost of the system without leadtime, namely,

$$C_o{}^L \geqq C_o{}^{WL} \tag{3}$$

This inequality can be proved as follows.*

Let $E[J(v)]$ designate the expected value of the function $J(v)$ where v is the demand during leadtime. That is,

$$E[J(v)] = \int_0^\infty J(v)h(v)\, dv \tag{4}$$

where $h(v)$ is the probability density of v. Using the notation of this section and comparing equations 8–2(5) and 9–2(6) leads us to the conclusion that they are related as follows:

$$C^L(Z) = E[C^{WL}(Z - v)] \tag{5}$$

Equation (5) really signifies that if we start the system with leadtime at a level Z and a demand of v occurs during leadtime, essentially we have a system without leadtime at a level $Z - v$. Hence the expected costs must be related as in equation (5). But, by definition, for any specific demand v^*

$$C^{WL}(Z - v^*) \geqq C_o{}^{WL} \tag{6}$$

Therefore

$$E[C^{WL}(Z - v)] \geqq E[C_o{}^{WL}] = C_o{}^{WL} \tag{7}$$

Inequality (3) can now be proved, using equations (1), (2), (5), and (7):

$$C_o{}^L = \min_Z C^L(Z) = \min_Z E[C^{WL}(Z - v)] \geqq \min_Z C_o{}^{WL} = C_o{}^{WL} \tag{8}$$

* Certain aspects of this proof have been suggested by John W. Pratt in a private communication.

The Cost Difference

The result represented by inequality (3) can also be obtained using a somewhat different approach. First we can show that

$$Z_o \geqq S_o \tag{9}$$

and then that

$$C_o^L - C_o^{WL} = (c_1 + c_2) \left\{ \int_0^{Z_o - S_o} N(v)[M(Z_o - v) - M(S_o)]\, dv \right.$$

$$\left. + \int_{Z_o - S_o}^\infty [1 - N(v)][M(S_o) - M(Z_o - v)]\, dv \right\} \tag{10}$$

where

$$N(v) = \int_0^v h(w)\, dw \tag{11}$$

and where

$$M(S) = \int_0^S f(x)\, dx + \int_S^\infty \frac{S}{x} f(x)\, dx \tag{12}$$

Equation (10) represents the cost difference between the system with leadtime and the one without leadtime. Since all terms on the right-hand side of the equation are non-negative, inequality (3) is proved. The proofs of equations (9) and (10) are left as exercises [see problems 11–5(10) and 11–5(11)]. An insight to the proofs can be gained by extending the following derivations.

Systems with Discrete Distributions

Some of the results that have been presented so far, and especially the relations in equation (10), were obtained by the author only *after* he had analyzed similar systems with discrete distributions. This analysis is of interest not only because it serves as a background for the previous results, but also because it contains various results that are more general in some respects.

In systems with discrete units let $P(x)$, $H(v)$, $Q(w)$, and $K(y)$ designate discrete distributions where the demands x, v, w, and y can have the discrete values 0, 1, 2, ... By using the methods of Sections 10–2 and 9–2, the cost of a system with leadtime can be given by*

$$C^L(Z) = c_1 \sum_{y=0}^{Z} (Z - y)K(y) + c_2 \sum_{Z+1}^{\infty} (y - Z)K(y)$$

$$= (c_1 + c_2) \sum_{y=0}^{Z} (Z - y)K(y) - c_2(Z - \bar{y}) \tag{13}$$

where $Q(w)$ is defined by equation 10–1(26) and where $K(y) = H(v) * Q(w)$.

* See also Example 10–2b.

Note that

$$\bar{y} = \bar{v} + \bar{w} = \bar{v} + \frac{\bar{x}}{2} \tag{14}$$

Let $G(Z)$ and $V(Z)$ be defined by

$$G(Z) = \sum_{y=0}^{Z} K(y) \tag{15}$$

and

$$V(Z) = \sum_{r=0}^{Z-1} G(r) = \sum_{r=0}^{Z-1} \sum_{y=0}^{r} K(y) = \sum_{y=0}^{Z-1} \sum_{r=y}^{Z-1} K(y) = \sum_{y=0}^{Z-1} K(y)(Z - y)$$

$$= \sum_{y=0}^{Z} (Z - y)K(y) \tag{16}$$

Hence the cost of a system with leadtime can be given by

$$C^L(Z) = (c_1 + c_2)V(Z) - c_2(Z - \bar{y}) \tag{17}$$

The optimal level Z_o can be found from

$$G(Z_o - 1) \leqq \frac{c_2}{c_1 + c_2} \leqq G(Z_o) \tag{18}$$

These inequalities imply that more than one optimal solution may thus exist. For definiteness we assume that if several values of Z lead to the minimum expected total cost, then Z_o will be the largest of these values. That is,

$$G(Z_o - 1) \leqq \frac{c_2}{c_1 + c_2} < G(Z_o) \tag{19}$$

In a similar manner the expected total cost of a system without leadtime can be obtained, namely,

$$C^{WL}(S) = (c_1 + c_2)W(S) - c_2(S - \bar{w}) \tag{20}$$

where

$$M(S) = \sum_{w=0}^{S} Q(w) \tag{21}$$

where

$$W(S) = \sum_{r=0}^{S-1} M(r) \tag{22}$$

and where $\bar{w} = \bar{x}/2$.

The optimal S_o, by analogy with equation (19), is now given by

$$M(S_o - 1) \leqq \frac{c_2}{c_1 + c_2} < M(S_o) \tag{23}$$

Consider now the probability distribution $H(v)$ with mean $\bar{v}$. The demand v during leadtime may have the values $0, 1, \ldots, v_{max}$, where $H(v > v_{max}) = 0$. When $v_{max} = 0$, a system with leadtime reduces to a system without leadtime. We shall review the principal results for the cases $v_{max} = 1$, $v_{max} = 2$, and $v_{max} = 3$ and then for the general case. No proofs are given. The reader should be able to obtain the results using equations (13) to (23).

The Results for $v_{max} = 1$

$$Z_o = S_o + k \qquad k = 0, 1 \tag{24}$$

For $Z_o = S_o$,

$$C^L(Z_o) - C^{WL}(S_o) = (c_1 + c_2)H(1)[c_2/(c_1 + c_2) - M(S_o - 1)] \geqq 0 \tag{25}$$

For $Z_o = S_o + 1$,

$$C^L(Z_o) - C^{WL}(S_o) = (c_1 + c_2)H(0)[M(S_o) - c_2/(c_1 + c_2)] \geqq 0 \tag{26}$$

The Results for $v_{max} = 2$

$$Z_o = S_o + k \qquad k = 0, 1, 2 \tag{27}$$

For $Z_o = S_o$,

$$C^L(Z_o) - C^{WL}(S_o)$$
$$= (c_1 + c_2) \{\bar{v}[c_2/(c_1 + c_2) - M(S_o - 1)] + H(2)Q(S_o - 1)\} \geqq 0 \tag{28}$$

For $Z_o = S_o + 1$ and $\bar{v} \leqq 1$,

$$C^L(Z_o) - C^{WL}(S_o)$$
$$= (c_1 + c_2) \{(1 - \bar{v})[M(S_o) - c_2/(c_1 + c_2)] + H(2)Q(S_o)\} \geqq 0 \tag{29}$$

For $Z_o = S_o + 1$ and $\bar{v} \geqq 1$,

$$C^L(Z_o) - C^{WL}(S_o)$$
$$= (c_1 + c_2) \{(\bar{v} - 1)[c_2/(c_1 + c_2) - M(S_o - 1)] + H(0)Q(S_o)\} \geqq 0 \tag{30}$$

For $Z_o = S_o + 2$,

$$C^L(Z_o) - C^{WL}(S_o)$$
$$= (c_1 + c_2) \{(2 - \bar{v})[M(S_o) - c_2/(c_1 + c_2)] + H(0)Q(S_o + 1)\} \geqq 0 \tag{31}$$

The Results for $v_{max} = 3$

$$Z_o = S_o + k \qquad k = 0, 1, 2, 3 \tag{32}$$

For $Z_o = S_o$,

$$C^L(Z_o) - C^{WL}(S_o)$$
$$= (c_1 + c_2) \{\bar{v}[c_2/(c_1 + c_2) - M(S_o - 1)] + [H(2) + H(3)]Q(S_o - 1)$$
$$+ H(3)[Q(S_o - 2) + Q(S_o - 1)]\} \tag{33}$$

For $Z_o = S_o + 1$ and $\bar{v} \leqq 1$,

$$C^L(Z_o) - C^{WL}(S_o) = (c_1 + c_2)\{(1 - \bar{v})[M(S_o) - c_2/(c_1 + c_2)]$$
$$+ [H(2) + H(3)]Q(S_o) + H(3)[Q(S_o - 1) + Q(S_o)]\} \quad (34)$$

For $Z_o = S_o + 1$ and $\bar{v} \geqq 1$,

$$C^L(Z_o) - C^{WL}(S_o) = (c_1 + c_2)\{(\bar{v} - 1)[c_2/(c_1 + c_2) - M(S_o - 1)]$$
$$+ H(0)Q(S_o) + H(3)Q(S_o - 1)\} \quad (35)$$

For $Z_o = S_o + 2$ and $\bar{v} \leqq 2$,

$$C^L(Z_o) - C^{WL}(S_o) = (c_1 + c_2)\{(2 - \bar{v})[M(S_o) - c_2/(c_1 + c_2)]$$
$$+ H(0)Q(S_o + 1) + H(3)Q(S_o)\} \quad (36)$$

For $Z_o = S_o + 2$ and $\bar{v} \geqq 2$,

$$C^L(Z_o) - C^{WL}(S_o) = (c_1 + c_2)\{(\bar{v} - 2)[c_2/(c_1 + c_2) - M(S_o - 1)]$$
$$+ [H(0) + H(1)]Q(S_o) + H(0)[Q(S_o) + Q(S_o + 1)]\} \quad (37)$$

For $Z_o = S_o + 3$,

$$C^L(Z_o) - C^{WL}(S_o) = (c_1 + c_2)\{(3 - \bar{v})[M(S_o) - c_2/(c_1 + c_2)]$$
$$+ [H(0) + H(1)]Q(S_o + 1) + H(0)[Q(S_o + 1) + Q(S_o + 2)]\} \quad (38)$$

The Results for the General Case

$$Z_o = S_o + k \qquad k = 0, 1, \ldots, v_{\max} \quad (39)$$

For $\bar{v} \leqq k$,

$$C^L(Z_o) - C^{WL}(S_o) = (c_1 + c_2)\Big\{(k - \bar{v})[M(S_o) - c_2/(c_1 + c_2)]$$

$$+ \sum_{v=1}^{k}[1 - E(v)][M(S_o + k - v) - M(S_o)]$$

$$+ \sum_{v=k+1}^{v_{\max}} E(v)[M(S_o) - M(S_o + k - v)]\Big\} \geqq 0 \quad (40)$$

where

$$E(Z) = \sum_{v=Z}^{v_{\max}} H(v) \quad (41)$$

For $\bar{v} \geqq k$,

$$C^L(Z_o) - C^{WL}(S_o) = (c_1 + c_2)\Big\{(\bar{v} - k)[c_2/(c_1 + c_2) - M(S_o - 1)]$$

$$+ \sum_{v=1}^{k}[1 - E(v)][M(S_o + k - v) - M(S_o - 1)]$$

$$+ \sum_{v=k+1}^{v_{\max}} E(v)[M(S_o - 1) - M(S_o + k - v)]\Big\} \geqq 0$$
$$\quad (42)$$

The reader may now wish to review the earlier portion of the section. In particular, he may wish to compare equation (10) with equations (40) and (42).

Example 11-3

In an order-level system the probability distribution of demand during a one-week scheduling period is $P(0) = 0.4$ and $P(1) = 0.6$. The unit carrying cost is $18 per unit per week. Analyze the system for $L = 0, 1,$ and 2 and for $c_2 = $2, 4.5, 12, 27, 42, 72, 82, 102,$ and 342.

$L = 0$

The values of the functions $Q(w)$, $M(S)$, and $W(S)$, by equations 10-1(26), (21), and (22), are computed in Table 11-3a. (Note that $\bar{w} = 0.3$.) We now use equations (23) and (20) to obtain the solutions given in Table 11-3b.

TABLE 11-3a

Values of the Functions P(x), Q(w), M(S), and W(S)

x, w, S	$P(x)$	$\dfrac{P(x)}{x}$	$\displaystyle\sum_{w+1}\dfrac{P(x)}{x}$	$Q(w)$	$M(S)$	$W(S)$
0	0.4		0.6	0.7	0.7	0.0
1	0.6	0.6	0.	0.3	1.0	0.7

TABLE 11-3b

Solution of Example 11-3a for L = 0

c_2	2	4.5	12	27	42	72	82	102	342
S_0	0	0	0	0	1	1	1	1	1
C_0^{WL}	0.60	1.35	3.60	8.10	12.60	12.60	12.60	12.60	12.60

$L = 1$

The distribution of demand during a leadtime of 1 week is $H(0) = 0.4$, $H(1) = 0.6$. Hence the function $K(y)$ of equation (13) is given by $K(0) = 0.28$, $K(1) = 0.54$, and $K(2) = 0.18$. Table 11-3c can now be obtained giving the values of the functions $G(Z)$ and $V(Z)$ of equations (15) and (16).

TABLE 11-3c

Value of the Functions K(y), G(Z), V(Z) for L = 1

y, Z	$K(y)$	$G(Z)$	$V(Z)$
0	0.28	0.28	0.00
1	0.54	0.82	0.28
2	0.18	1.00	1.10

Note that $\bar{y} = 0.90$. Equations (19) and (17) can now be used to obtain the solution in Table 11–3d.

The values of Tables 11–3b and 11–3d can now be compared. They provide illustrations for equations (24), (25), and (26). We can also see here the case when $C_o{}^L = C_o{}^{WL}$. This occurs when $c_2 = 42$.

TABLE 11–3d

Solution of Example 11–3a for $L = 1$

c_2	2	4.5	12	27	42	72	82	102	342
Z_0	0	0	1	1	1	1	2	2	2
$C_o{}^L$	1.80	4.05	7.30	9.90	12.60	18.00	19.80	19.80	19.80

$L = 2$

The distribution of demand during a leadtime of 2 weeks is obtained from $P(x) * P(x)$ and is readily found to be $H(0) = 0.16$, $H(1) = 0.48$, and $H(2) = 0.36$. Hence the function $K(y) = H(v) * Q(w)$ can be computed. We thus have Table 11–3e. Note that now $\bar{y} = 1.5$. Table 11–3f can now be prepared using equations (19) and (17).

Once again the inequality $C_o{}^L \geqq C_o{}^{WL}$ is illustrated and equations (27), (28), (30), and (31) are exemplified.

TABLE 11–3e

Value of the Functions $K(y)$, $G(2)$, and $V(2)$ for $L = 2$

y, Z	$K(y)$	$G(Z)$	$V(Z)$
0	0.112	0.112	0.000
1	0.384	0.496	0.112
2	0.396	0.892	0.608
3	0.108	1.000	1.500

TABLE 11–3f

Solutions of Example 11–3a for $L = 2$

c_2	2	4.5	12	27	42	72	82	102	342
Z_0	0	1	1	2	2	2	2	2	3
$C_o{}^L$	3.00	4.77	9.36	13.86	15.48	18.72	19.80	21.96	27.00

Effects of Various Leadtimes

Thus far we have been comparing order-level systems without leadtime with systems with leadtime. We now extend the results to systems with various leadtimes. Let L_1 be the leadtime of one system and let L_2 be the leadtime of another system. Let the corresponding minimum costs of the systems be $C_o{}^{L_1}$, $C_o{}^{L_2}$. We shall show that if $L_2 \geqq L_1$, then

$$C_o{}^{L_2} \geqq C_o{}^{L_1} \tag{43}$$

Let v_{21} designate the demand during the period $L_2 - L_1$ and let $E[J(v_{12})]$ designate the expected value of the function $J(v_{12})$. Then by analogy with equation (5) we have

$$C^{L_2}(Z) = E[C^{L_1}(Z - v_{12})] \qquad (44)$$

Following the reasoning leading to equations (6), (7), and (8), equation (43) can be proved with relative ease. Example 11–3 provides an illustration when we compare $L_2 = 2$ with $L_1 = 1$ in Tables 11–3f and 11–3d.

EFFECTS OF LEADTIME ON THE COST OF SCHEDULING–PERIOD–ORDER–LEVEL SYSTEMS

11–4 The results of the previous section can readily be extended to systems whose scheduling periods and order levels are both subject to control.

Let $C^{WL}(t^S, S)$ designate the cost of a system without leadtime when the scheduling period is t^S and the order level is S. Similarly, let $C^L(t^Z, Z)$ designate the cost of a system with leadtime when the scheduling period is t^Z and the order level is Z. Let $C_o{}^{WL}(t^S, S) = C^{WL}(t_o{}^S, S_o)$ and $C_o{}^L(t^Z, Z) = C^L(t_o{}^Z, Z_o)$ designate the corresponding minimum costs of the systems for the optimal values of the scheduling periods and order levels. We propose to show that

$$C_o{}^{WL}(t^S, S) \leqq C_o{}^L(t^Z, Z) \qquad (1)$$

To prove this inequality, we have only to use inequality 11–3(3), namely,

$$\begin{aligned}
C_o{}^{WL}(t^S, S) &= C^{WL}[S_o(t_o{}^S)] + c_3/t_o{}^S \\
&\leqq C^{WL}[S_o(t_o{}^Z)] + c_3/t_o{}^Z \\
&\leqq C^L[Z_o(t_o{}^Z)] + c_3/t_o{}^Z \\
&= C_o{}^L(t^Z, Z)
\end{aligned} \qquad (2)$$

In equation (2) the notations $S_o(t^*)$ and $Z_o(t^*)$ mean that the order levels S_o and Z_o have been chosen optimally on the basis of the specified scheduling period t^*. The first inequality holds since $t_o{}^Z$ is not necessarily the optimal scheduling period in the system without leadtime. The second inequality is an extension of inequality 11–3(3). Thus, inequality (1) is indeed true.

Computer Flow Charts for Systems with Leadtime

To illustrate the effects of leadtime on the costs of scheduling-period–order-level systems we can follow the procedures of Section 11–2. The modifications that have to be made in the main program of Figure 11–2a to account for leadtime are given in Figure 11–4a. The only two significant changes are the introduction of the functions $K(y)$ and $H(v, L)$.

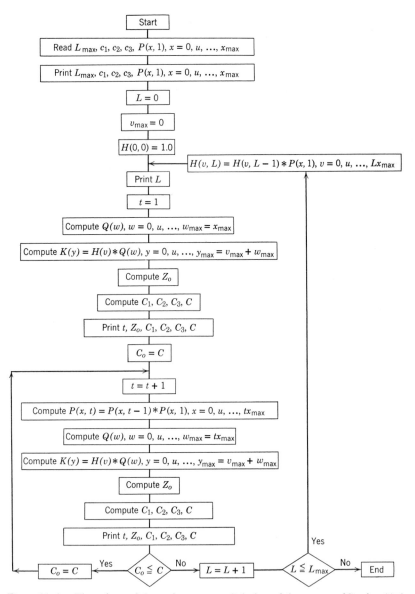

Figure 11–4a   Flow chart of the main program. Solution of the system of Section 11–2 with leadtime.

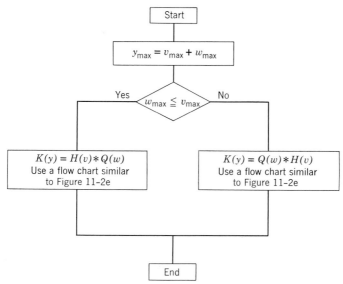

Figure 11–4b   Flow chart for the computation of the convolution $K(y) = H(v) * Q(W)$ using the methods of Section 8–4 and equation 11–2(7).

The function $K(y)$ has been used in Section 11–3 [for example, see equation 11–3(13)]. Its flow chart is given in Figure 11–4b, which in turn is based on the flow chart of Figure 11–2e. It should be noted that the computations of the convolutions in Figure 11–2e assume that $y_{max} \leqq z_{max}$. This should explain the pertinent ordering in Figure 11–4b.

The function $H(v, L)$ is an immediate extension of the function $H(v)$ of Chapter 9 and of Section 11–3. The flow chart of Figure 11–4c is self-explanatory.

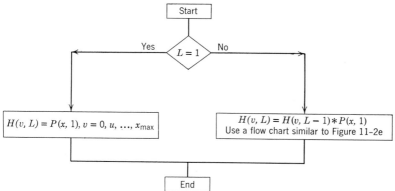

Figure 11–4c   Flow chart for the computation of the convolution $H(v, L) = H(v, L - 1) * P(x, 1)$ using the methods of Section 8–4 and equation 11–2(7).

```
C1 =   1.000

C2 =   9.000

C3 =  20.000


LMAX =  10

XBAR =    3.000
P( 0) = 0.050
P( 1) = 0.149
P( 2) = 0.224
P( 3) = 0.224
P( 4) = 0.168
P( 5) = 0.101
P( 6) = 0.051
P( 7) = 0.021
P( 8) = 0.008
P( 9) = 0.003
P(10) = 0.001

LEADTIME = 0
```

T	Z0	C1	C2	C3	C
1	3	1.645	1.301	20.000	22.946
2	6	3.164	1.479	10.000	14.643
3	9	4.675	1.575	6.667	12.916
4	12	6.182	1.638	5.000	12.821
5	14	6.780	2.519	4.000	13.299

```
LEADTIME = 1
```

T	Z0	C1	C2	C3	C
1	7	2.682	1.636	20.000	24.317
2	10	4.156	1.404	10.000	15.559
3	12	4.748	2.231	6.667	13.645
4	15	6.237	2.133	5.000	13.370
5	18	7.732	2.084	4.000	13.815

```
LEADTIME = 2
```

T	Z0	C1	C2	C3	C
1	11	3.680	1.616	20.000	25.296
2	13	4.239	2.147	10.000	16.386
3	16	5.710	1.887	6.667	14.264
4	18	6.293	2.639	5.000	13.933
5	21	7.777	2.489	4.000	14.265

```
LEADTIME = 3
```

T	Z0	C1	C2	C3	C
1	15	4.665	1.484	20.000	26.149
2	17	5.206	1.850	10.000	17.055
3	19	5.770	2.428	6.667	14.864
4	22	7.244	2.193	5.000	14.436
5	24	7.822	2.899	4.000	14.721

Figure 11-4d　Portion of the computer printout of the results for Example 11-4.

Example 11-4

The computer program which has just been described has been used with data similar to the data of Example 11-2, except that leadtime was added. Figure 11-4d provides an illustration of the output from an IBM 7094 computer, using the following data. The unit costs are $c_1 = \$1.00$ per unit

TABLE 11-4

The Optimal Order Level $Z_0(t)$ and the Expected Minimum Cost $C_0(t)$ for Various Scheduling Periods t in Example 11-4

L \ t	1	2	3	4	5
0	3	6	9	12	14
	22.946	14.643	12.916	12.821	13.299
1	7	10	12	15	18
	24.317	15.559	13.645	13.370	13.815
2	11	13	16	18	21
	25.296	16.386	14.264	13.933	14.265
3	15	17	19	22	24
	26.149	17.055	14.864	14.436	14.721
4	18	20	23	25	28
	26.914	17.735	15.423	14.908	15.175
5	22	24	26	28	31
	27.559	18.298	15.929	15.390	15.563
6	25	27	29	32	34
	28.184	18.863	16.450	15.822	15.959
7	29	31	33	35	37
	28.749	19.391	16.902	16.235	16.359
8	32	34	36	38	41
	29.270	19.867	17.346	16.657	16.733
9	35	37	39	42	44
	29.856	20.357	17.801	17.060	17.081
10	39	41	43	45	47
	30.253	20.799	18.204	17.425	17.435

per week, $c_2 = \$9.00$ per unit per week, $c_3 = \$20.00$ per replenishment. The probability distribution of demand is the Poisson distribution with a mean of 3.0. Leadtimes up to a maximum of 10 have been computed. The figure gives only a portion of the output and includes leadtimes up to 3.

A summary of all the results is given in Table 11-4.

11-5 PROBLEMS

1. Let $C^P(S)$ be the expected total cost of the probabilistic order-level system and let $C^D(S)$ be the total cost of the deterministic order-level system. Show that when $S < 0$, then $C^D(S) = C^P(S)$ and when $S > \bar{x}$, then $C^D(S) \leqq C^P(S)$.

2. (a) Prepare a table similar to Table 11-1b for the probability density

$$f(x) = \frac{(2n + 1)!}{(n!)^2} [x(1 - x)]^n \qquad n > -1, 0 \leqq x \leqq 1.$$

   (b) Compare the results for the pairs of parameters $a = 0$, $n = \infty$ and $a = 1$, $n = 0$.

   (c) Plot the minimum costs as a function of the standard deviation.

3. In a type $(1, 2)$ inventory system with a (t_p, S) policy the probability density of demand is $f(x) = 6x(1 - x)$, $0 \leqq x \leqq 1$. The unit carrying cost c_1 and the unit shortage cost c_2 are related by $\sqrt[3]{(c_1 + c_2)/c_1} = m$.

   (a) Show that $S_o = (m - 1)/m$ and that $C_o = 3(m - 1)c_1/4m$

   (b) Compare the results in (a) with the solution of a similar system in which demand is constant.

4. Check the results given by equations 11-1(13) to 11-1(19).

5. Prepare a non-trivial numerical example, similar to Example 11-1c, when $\bar{x} = 4.0$, which will demonstrate that a larger variance does not necessarily imply a larger minimum cost.

6. Prove inequality 11-1(4) for order-level systems with instantaneous demand. Can your proof be extended to systems with uniform demand?

7. In a probabilistic order-level system with instantaneous demand, the probability distribution of demand is given by $P_A(0) = 0.4$, $P_A(1) = 0.3$, $P_A(2) = 0.2$, $P_A(3) = 0.1$. Choose numerical values of c_1 and c_2 and construct a probability distribution $P_B(x)$ having the same mean as P_A but a smaller variance than that of P_A so that the minimum expected total cost of system B will be larger than that of system A.

8. Compare the solutions of Examples 1-1 and 7-1c, and note, in particular, the minimum total costs of these systems. Try to explain the difference.

9. What can be said about the effect of variability on other than inventory systems (e.g., queueing systems)?

10. Show that in the system of Section 11-3, for continuous units, $S_o \leqq Z_o \leqq S_o + v_{max}$.

11. Prove the statement given by equation 11-3(10).

12. Show that when demand during leadtime is constant, the minimum expected total costs of probabilistic order-level systems with and without leadtime are the same.

13. Show that $\bar{y} = y_{max} - V(y_{max})$ where $V(Z)$ is the function defined by equation 11-3(16).

14. Prove some of the results given by equations 11-3(27) to 11-3(42).

15. In an inventory system similar to that described in Section 8–3, let the discrete probability distribution of demand be $P(x_1) = p$ and $P(x_2 > x_1) = q$, where $p + q = 1$. Let d_x be the standard deviation of demand and let $d_C(S)$ be the standard deviation of the total cost of the system when the order level is S.

   (a) Show that $d_C(S) = |(x_2 - S)c_2 - (S - x_1)c_1| \sqrt{pq}$.

   (b) What must be the values of p, q, c_1, and c_2 so that for the optimal level S_o we would obtain $d_C(S_o) > d_C(S \neq S_o)$.

16. The results in Table 11–4 seem to indicate that the optimal scheduling period is not too sensitive to changes in leadtime. Explore this point further.

17. The uniform demand during any week has the probability distribution $P(0) = 0.2$, $P(1) = 0.5$, and $P(2) = 0.3$. The unit carrying cost and the unit shortage cost are $1.00 and $19.00 per unit per week respectively. A (t_p, Z) policy is used where t_p is 1 week. Leadtime is 2 weeks. It is possible to reduce this leadtime to 1 week, but at an additional cost of $0.60 per week.

   Should leadtime be reduced?

18. The flow chart for computing convolutions in Figure 11–2e can be simplified. Show how this can be done.

Chapter 12

The Inventory-Bank System

12–0   The problem of estimating demands in inventory systems is a very important one. As we have seen, in order to solve an inventory system we must know the probability distribution of demand. In most cases, however, the distribution of demand is not known precisely. It usually has to be derived from historical data. This topic is a special one and will not be covered in this book.*

This chapter deals with an inventory system in which the decision rules are in part associated with the problem of forecasting the average demand. In this way the forecast of the demand is part of the inventory system itself. The forecast is used for the establishment of what is called an inventory bank. Hence the name of the system. The details are given in Section 12–1.

Two new methods of analysis, Markov chains and simulation, are introduced in this chapter. The first is used in Section 12–2 and the second in Section 12–3. The results are compared in Section 12–4, and some conclusions on the system as a whole are stated.

DESCRIPTION OF THE INVENTORY-BANK SYSTEM

12–1   The policy used in replenishing inventories in the system of this chapter may be called a modified (t, S) policy. Every t units of time a decision with respect to a replenishment is made. The amount to be

---

* For some detailed treatments see Brown [11, 12]. You may also want to review Section 2–1.

206

replenished at time i raises the available inventories A_i to a *bank* B_i. No returns are allowed. Thus the quantity P_i ordered for replenishment of inventory may be formally given by

$$P_i = \max [B_i - A_i, 0] \tag{1}$$

Whether this is a good policy and how to evaluate other policies will not be discussed in this chapter. We will also not investigate the variable t in the given policy. We shall assume it is prescribed and is not subject to control. Furthermore, for ease of discussion, t will be assumed to be 1 week.

Our analysis will thus be concerned only with the bank B_i which is subject to control by a decision maker. The bank may be viewed as composed of several weeks of average demand,

$$B_i = N\bar{S}_i \tag{2}$$

where N is the number of weeks in the bank and $\bar{S}_i$ is the average demand as of week i.

Several methods may be used to determine the average demand $\bar{S}_i$. In this chapter only one such method* will be studied: the average demand at time i is determined by finding the mean demand over a period of M weeks immediately preceding time i:

$$\bar{S}_i = \frac{1}{M} \sum_{j=i-M+1}^{i} S_j \tag{3}$$

The parameters N and M thus completely specify how decisions may be reached in the inventory system. Table 12–1a illustrates the system when demand ranges from 0 to 300, leadtime is 2 weeks, M is 4, and N is 6. In the table we use the notation:

i = week number,
Q_i = the inventory on hand at the beginning of week i,
S_i = the demand during week i,
q_i = the inventory on hand at end of week i,
$\bar{S}_i$ = The average demand as of end of week i, based on equation (3),
B_i = the bank as of end of week i, based on equation (2),
A_i = The available inventory as of end of week i before ordering a replenishment (i.e., the amounts on hand and on order),
P_i = the replenishment quantity ordered at the end of week i, based on equation (1),
R_i = the replenishment added to inventory at end of week i, available at beginning of week $i + 1$.

---

* A variation of this method is being used by the General Motors Parts Division.

Let L designate leadtime in weeks. Then, in addition to equations (1), (2), and (3), we also have

$$q_i = Q_i - S_i \tag{4}$$

$$A_i = \begin{cases} q_i & L = 0 \\ q_i + \sum_{j=i-L}^{i-1} P_j & L > 0 \end{cases} \tag{5}$$

$$R_i = P_{i-L} \tag{6}$$

$$Q_{i+1} = q_i + R_i \tag{7}$$

Let I_1 designate the expected average amount in inventory, let I_2 designate the expected average shortage, and let I_3 designate the expected

TABLE 12–1a

The Inventory-Bank System When $L = 2$, $M = 4$, and $N = 6$

i	Q_i	S_i	q_i	$\bar{S}_i$	B_i	A_i	$B_i - A_i$	P_i	R_i
8	.	100	.	.	.	.	.	.	.
9	.	100	.	.	.	.	.	100	.
10	.	100	300	.	.	.	.	100	100
11	400	100	300	100	600	500	100	100	100
12	400	300	100	150	900	300	600	600	100
13	200	100	100	150	900	800	100	100	100
14	200	100	100	150	900	800	100	100	600
15	700	100	600	160	900	800	100	100	100
16	700	100	600	100	600	800	−200	0	100
17	700	200	500	125	750	600	150	150	100
18	600	0	600	100	.	.	.	.	0
19	600	100	500	100	.	.	.	.	150
20	650	100	550	100	.	.	.	.	.
.	.	.	.	.	.	.	.	.	.

number of replenishments per week. The quantities I_1, I_2, I_3 are each dependent on the controllable variables N and M. The main purpose of this chapter is to find the explicit relations $I_1 = I_1(M, N)$, $I_2 = I_2(M, N)$, and $I_3 = I_3(M, N)$. Once these relations are known, the expected total cost of the system is

$$C(M, N) = c_1 I_1(M, N) + c_2 I_2(M, N) + c_3 I_3(M, N) \tag{8}$$

Equation (8) can then be used to find the optimal M_o and N_o.

The Varying Demands S_i

The use of decision rules based on equations (1), (2), and (3) in inventory systems involving many items stems from practical considerations. In such systems it is impractical to find the probability distributions of demand for all items. Hence methods similar to those used in Chapters 8 and 9 may not be applicable. Furthermore, these decision rules can be integrated with relative ease into electronic data-processing systems.

The decision rule of equation (3) is also claimed to have another desirable feature. Presumably it can detect trends in demand, particularly if the parameter M is relatively small. On the other hand, however, a large random change in demand may unduly influence the average demand $\bar{S}_i$, and this may lead to excessive inventories or to excessive shortages.

We shall presently see that the analytical methods available to analyze the inventory system with the decision rules of equations (1), (2), and (3) are rather complex, even if we ignore trends in demand. We shall therefore consider only the system whose leadtime is zero and whose probability distribution of demand is assumed to be known. To fix ideas and to illustrate some of the complexity of the numerical calculations, a specific simple probability distribution of demand will be used extensively in this chapter: $P(0) = 0.2$, $P(100) = 0.7$, $P(200) = 0.0$, and $P(300) = 0.1$; the average demand is $\bar{S} = 100$.

The Case When M Is Very Large

For purposes of comparison it is worthwhile to examine equation (3) when the parameter M approaches infinity. This leads to the special case

$$\bar{S}_i = \bar{S} = \text{constant} \tag{9}$$

The bank B_i will also be a constant. For zero leadtime the system then becomes an extension of the probabilistic order-level system of Section 8-2 where now only the variable N is subject to control. Each scheduling period will start with an amount $N\bar{S}$ in inventory. Then

$$I_1(N) = \sum_{S=0}^{N\bar{S}} \left(N\bar{S} - \frac{S}{2}\right) P(S) + \sum_{S=N\bar{S}+u}^{\infty} \frac{(N\bar{S})^2}{2S} P(S) \tag{10}$$

$$I_2(N) = \sum_{S=N\bar{S}+u}^{\infty} \frac{(S - N\bar{S})^2}{2S} P(S) \tag{11}$$

$$I_3(N) = \sum_{S=u}^{\infty} P(S) = 1 - P(0) \tag{12}$$

Equations (10) and (11) are immediate extensions of equations 8-2(3) and 8-2(4) for discrete units using the special notation of this chapter. Equation (12), in which I_3 is really not a function of N, is self-explanatory. It has been added for comparison with cases in which M is not necessarily very large. We shall see that in those cases I_3 will be a function of N (and of M).

In Table 12–1b the numerical value of I_1, I_2, and I_3 of equations (10), (11), and (12) are given using the probability distribution of demand mentioned earlier. These values will later be compared with systems in which M is not infinite.

TABLE 12–1b

Values of I_1, I_2, and I_3 When $M = \infty$

N	1	2	3
I_1	56.667	151.667	250.000
I_2	6.667	1.667	0.
I_3	0.800	0.800	0.800

The General Case for Any M

When M is not infinite, the amount Q in inventory at the beginning of each scheduling period will not be a constant. Let $G(Q)$ be the probability distribution of the amount Q. This distribution will in general depend both on M and on N. We shall therefore designate it by $G(Q; M, N)$. The determination of this distribution will be discussed in detail in the next section. Here we only want to state how the expected values I_1, I_2, and I_3 can be determined if $G(Q; M, N)$ is known.

An immediate extension of equation (10) gives

$$I_1(M, N) = \sum_{Q=0}^{Q_{max}} \left[\sum_{S=0}^{Q} \left(Q - \frac{S}{2} \right) P(S) + \sum_{S=Q+u}^{\infty} \frac{Q^2}{2S} P(S) \right] G(Q; M, N) \quad (13)$$

Similarly, equation (11) leads to

$$I_2(M, N) = \sum_{Q=0}^{Q_{max}} \left[\sum_{S=Q+u}^{\infty} \frac{(S - Q)^2}{2S} P(S) \right] G(Q; M, N) \quad (14)$$

Note that these equations are related by

$$I_1(M, N) - I_2(M, N) = \bar{Q}(M, N) - \frac{\bar{S}}{2} \quad (15)$$

where $\bar{Q}(M, N)$ is the expected amount in inventory at the beginning of each scheduling period.

The determination of $I_3(M, N)$ cannot be stated as a simple extension of equation (12). At this stage we can say only that

$$I_3(M, N) = \sum_{Q=0}^{Q_{max}} \sum_{S=0}^{S_{max}} P(S)G(Q; M, N)B(Q, S) \quad (16)$$

where $B(Q, S) = 1$ whenever a replenishment is scheduled and $B(Q, S) = 0$ otherwise.

MARKOV CHAIN APPROACH

12–2   To find the values of I_1, I_2, and I_3 of equations (13), (14), and (16), we must be able to find the distribution $G(Q; M, N)$ and the function $B(Q, S)$. To do this it will be convenient to define certain states of the inventory system and treat them as states in a Markov chain.* We shall first consider the case $M = 1$ and then the case $M = 2$. The possibility of extending the analysis to other cases will be discussed.

The Case $M = 1$

Suppose we first consider a numerical illustration when $M = 1$ and when $N = 2$. The inventory system will operate as in Table 12–2a. Inspection of

TABLE 12–2a

The Inventory System When $L = 0$, $M = 1$, and $N = 2$

i	Q_i	S_i	q_i	$\bar{S}_i$	B_i	A_i	$B_i - A_i$	P_i	R_i
1	200	100	100	100	200	100	100	100	100
2	200	300	−100	300	600	−100	700	700	700
3	600	100	500	100	200	500	−300	0	0
4	500	100	400	100	200	400	−200	0	0
5	400	100	300	100	200	300	−100	0	0
6	300	0	300	0	0	300	−300	0	0
7	300	100	200	100	200	200	0	0	0
8	200	100	100	100	200	100	100	100	100
9	200	0	200	0	0	200	−200	0	0
10	200	100	100	100	200	100	100	100	100
.	.	.	.	.	.	.	.	.	.

the table leads us to the conclusion that

$$Q_{i+1} = \max [2S_i, Q_i - S_i] \tag{1}$$

This equation can also be established formally from equations 12–1(1) to 12–1(7) for $M = 1$, $N = 2$:

$$Q_{i+1} = q_i + R_i = q_i + P_i = q_i + \max [B_i - A_i, 0]$$
$$= q_i + \max [2\bar{S}_i - q_i, 0] = q_i + \max [2S_i - q_i, 0] \tag{2}$$
$$= \max [2S_i, q_i] = \max [2S_i, Q_i - S_i]$$

Thus the amount in inventory Q_{i+1} at the beginning of any period $i + 1$ depends only on the amount Q_i at the beginning of the previous period i

* Some references on Markov chains are Kemeny et al. [28], pp. 384–438; Feller [17], pp. 338–379; and Kemeny and Snell [29].

TABLE 12–2b

The Transition Probabilities p_{jk} When $M = 1$ and $N = 2$

Q	j \ k	1	2	3	4	5
200	1	0.9	0.	0.	0.	0.1
300	2	0.7	0.2	0.	0.	0.1
400	3	0.	0.7	0.2	0.	0.1
500	4	0.	0.	0.7	0.2	0.1
600	5	0.	0.	0.	0.7	0.3

and the demand S_i in that period. The amount Q_i can therefore be associated with a state j in a Markov chain. We can then speak of going from state j (with an amount Q_i) to a state k (with an amount Q_{i+1}), the transition probability being $p_{jk} = P(S_i)$. For the specific distribution $P(S)$ which we have been using for illustrative purposes, it is rather simple to verify (from Table 12–2a, etc.) that the only amounts Q_i that we can have in inventory are 200, 300, 400, 500, and 600. We thus have only five states and the transition probabilities are as given in Table 12–2b.

Let p_r be the steady-state probability of finding the system in state r. That is, essentially,

$$p_r = G[Q = 100(r + 1); M = 1, N = 2] \tag{3}$$

For the various p_r we must have*

$$p_1 = 0.9p_1 + 0.7p_2$$
$$p_2 = 0.2p_2 + 0.7p_3$$
$$p_3 = 0.2p_3 + 0.7p_4 \tag{4}$$
$$p_4 = 0.2p_4 + 0.7p_5$$
$$p_5 = 0.1p_1 + 0.1p_2 + 0.1p_3 + 0.1p_4 + 0.3p_5$$
$$p_1 + p_2 + p_3 + p_4 + p_5 = 1$$

The solution of these equations and the related results are given in Table 12–2c. Equations 12–1(13), and 12–1(14) [or 12–1(15)] can now be used to evaluate I_1 and I_2. They give $I_1(1, 2) = 261.277$ and $I_2(1, 2) = 0.977$.

TABLE 12–2c

The Steady-State Probabilities When $M = 1$ and $N = 2$

State r	1	2	3	4	5
Amount Q	200	300	400	500	600
$p_r = G(Q; M = 1, N = 2)$	0.586	0.084	0.096	0.109	0.125

* The first five equations are not independent.

We now turn to finding values of the function $B(Q, S)$ of equation 12–2(16). First we note that whenever $S = 0$ no replenishment is scheduled. Hence $B(Q, 0) = 0$. Now, if $Q = 200$, a replenishment is scheduled both when $S = 100$ and when $S = 300$. But if $Q = 300, 400, 500,$ or 600 a replenishment is scheduled only when $S = 300$. Thus the function $B(Q, S)$

TABLE 12–2d

The Function $B(Q, S)$ When $M = 1$ and $N = 2$

S \ Q	200	300	400	500	600
0	0	0	0	0	0
100	1	0	0	0	0
300	1	1	1	1	1

is as given in Table 12–2d. Using the values of Tables 12–2c and 12–2d in equation 12–1(16), we now find that $I_3(1, 2) = 0.510$.

In a similar manner we can analyze the system for other values of N. A summary of the results is given in Table 12–2e.

TABLE 12–2e

Values of I_1, I_2 and I_3 When $M = 1$

N	1	2	3
I_1	91.189	261.277	464.100
I_2	5.289	0.977	0.
I_3	0.636	0.510	0.414

The Case $M = 2$

Let us again start the analysis with an illustration. The pertinent details are given in Table 12–2f, the corresponding inventory fluctuations in Figure 12–2.

By analogy with equation (2), we now obtain for $M = 2$ and $N = 2$

$$Q_{i+1} = q_i + R_i = q_i + P_i = q_i + \max [B_i - A_i, 0]$$

$$= q_i + \max [2(S_{i-1} + S_i)/2 - q_i, 0] \tag{5}$$

$$= \max [S_{i-1} + S_i, q_i] = \max [S_{i-1} + S_i, Q_i - S_i]$$

Equation (5) implies that the transition from an amount Q_i to an amount Q_{i+1} depends both on S_{i-1} and on S_i. This result suggests defining a Markov chain state as the couple (S_{i-1}, Q_i) from which we can go to the

TABLE 12–2f

The Inventory-Bank System When $L = 0$, $M = 0$, *and* $N = 2$

i	Q_i	S_i	q_i	$\bar{S}_i$	B_i	A_i	$B_i - A_i$	P_i	R_i
0		100							
1	200	300	−100	200	400	−100	500	500	500
2	400	0	400	150	300	400	−100	0	0
3	400	100	300	50	100	300	−200	0	0
4	300	100	200	100	200	200	0	0	0
5	200	0	200	50	100	200	−100	0	0
6	200	300	−100	150	300	−100	400	400	400
7	300	100	200	200	400	200	200	200	200
8	400	100	300	100	200	300	−100	0	0
9	300	100	200	100	200	200	0	0	0
10	200	100	100	100	200	100	100	100	100
11	200	100	100	100	200	100	100	100	100
12	200	0	200	50	100	200	−100	0	0
13	200	100	100	50	100	100	0	0	0
14	100	100	0	100	200	0	200	200	100
15	200	100	100	100	200	100	100	100	100
16	200	100	100	100	200	100	100	100	100
17	200	100	100	100	200	100	100	100	100
18	200	0	200	50	100	200	−100	0	0
19	200	100	100	50	100	100	0	0	0
20	100	100	0	100	200	0	200	200	200
·	·	·	·	·	·	·	·	·	·

state (S_i, Q_{i+1}).* This transition now depends only on the occurrence of S_i, the probabilities of which are known. How many such states are there? In general, there will be very many, but in the present example, it is relatively simple to show that only the 14 states in Table 12–2g should be considered.** Using these definitions, Table 12–2h then gives the transition probabilities p_{jk} for going from state j to state k.

TABLE 12–2g

The States When $M = 2$

State	1	2	3	4	5	6	7	8	9	10	11	12	13	14
S_{i-1}	0	0	0	0	0	0	100	100	100	100	100	300	300	300
Q_i	100	200	300	400	500	600	100	200	300	400	500	300	400	600

* For another approach see problem 12–5(10).
** See also problem 12–5(4).

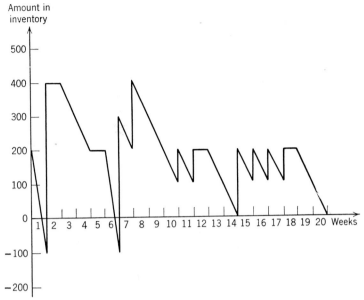

Figure 12–2 The inventory-bank system when $L = 0$, $M = 2$, $N = 2$, $P(0) = 0.2$, $P(100) = 0.7$, and $P(300) = 0.1$.

TABLE 12–2h

The Transition Probabilities p_{jk} When $M = 2$ and $N = 2$

j \ k	1	2	3	4	5	6	7	8	9	10	11	12	13	14
1	0.2	0.	0.	0.	0.	0.	0.7	0.	0.	0.	0.	0.1	0.	0.
2	0.	0.2	0.	0.	0.	0.	0.7	0.	0.	0.	0.	0.1	0.	0.
3	0.	0.	0.2	0.	0.	0.	0.	0.7	0.	0.	0.	0.1	0.	0.
4	0.	0.	0.	0.2	0.	0.	0.	0.	0.7	0.	0.	0.1	0.	0.
5	0.	0.	0.	0.	0.2	0.	0.	0.	0.	0.7	0.	0.1	0.	0.
6	0.	0.	0.	0.	0.	0.2	0.	0.	0.	0.	0.7	0.1	0.	0.
7	0.2	0.	0.	0.	0.	0.	0.	0.7	0.	0.	0.	0.	0.1	0.
8	0.	0.2	0.	0.	0.	0.	0.	0.7	0.	0.	0.	0.	0.1	0.
9	0.	0.	0.2	0.	0.	0.	0.	0.7	0.	0.	0.	0.	0.1	0.
10	0.	0.	0.	0.	0.	0.	0.	0.	0.7	0.	0.	0.	0.1	0.
11	0.	0.	0.	0.	0.2	0.	0.	0.	0.	0.7	0.	0.	0.1	0.
12	0.	0.	0.2	0.	0.	0.	0.	0.	0.	0.7	0.	0.	0.	0.1
13	0.	0.	0.	0.2	0.	0.	0.	0.	0.	0.7	0.	0.	0.	0.1
14	0.	0.	0.	0.	0.	0.2	0.	0.	0.	0.	0.7	0.	0.	0.1

TABLE 12–2i

The Steady-State Probabilities When $M = 2$ and $N = 2$

State r	1	2	3	4	5	6	7	8	9	10	11	12	13	14
S_{i-1}	0	0	0	0	0	0	100	100	100	100	100	300	300	300
Q_i	100	200	300	400	500	600	100	200	300	400	500	300	400	600
p_r	0.024	0.113	0.023	0.035	0.002	0.002	0.096	0.451	0.074	0.071	0.009	0.020	0.070	0.010

As in the case $M = 1$ the transition probabilities can now be used to find the steady-state probabilities p_r. The results are given in Table 12–2i. From these results we can immediately find the probability distribution $G(Q; M = 2, N = 2)$, given in Table 12–2j. The values of $I_1(2, 2)$ and $I_2(2, 2)$ of equations 12–1(13) and 12–1(14) [or equation 12–1(15)] can now be computed. They are $I_1(2, 2) = 194.838$, $I_2(2, 2) = 1.738$.

TABLE 12–2j

The Probability Distribution $G(Q; M = 2, N = 2)$

States r	1, 4	2, 8	3, 9, 12	4, 10, 13	5, 11	6, 14
Q	100	200	300	400	500	600
$G(Q; M = 2, N = 2)$	0.120	0.564	0.117	0.176	0.011	0.012

If we now attempt to find $B(Q, S)$ of equation 12–1(16), it immediately becomes evident that this cannot be done directly. A more appropriate method of calculation is to use the relation

$$I_3(M, N) = \sum_{r=1}^{r_{max}} \sum_{S=0}^{S_{max}} P(S)p_r B(r, S) \tag{6}$$

The function $B(r, S)$ can readily be found to be as shown in Table 12–2k. The average number of replenishments per week, by equation (6), and by Tables 12–2i and 12–2k, is thus $I_3(2, 2) = 0.562$. In a similar manner we can find the values of I_1, I_2, and I_3 for $N = 1$. A summary of the results is given in Table 12–2l.

TABLE 12–2k

The Function $B(r, S)$ When $M = 2$ and $N = 2$

S \ r	1	2	3	4	5	6	7	8	9	10	11	12	13	14
0	0	0	0	0	0	0	0	0	0	0	0	0	0	0
100	1	0	0	0	0	0	1	1	0	0	0	1	1	0
300	1	1	1	1	1	0	1	1	1	1	1	1	1	1

TABLE 12–21

Values of I_1, I_2, and I_3 When $M = 2$

N	1	2
I_1	76.093	194.838
I_2	7.293	1.738
I_3	0.691	0.562

The General Case

The use of the Markov chain approach for finding the values of I_1, I_2, and I_3 has so far been demonstrated through numerical illustrations. Of course, a formal presentation can be made by introducing suitable notation, but that will not be done here. Our main goal is only to introduce a new approach for the analysis of an inventory system.

It should be pointed out, however, that this kind of analysis is generally rather difficult to apply. Consider, for example, the maximum number of states r_{max} that have to be dealt with. We have seen that for our specific distribution when $M = 1$, $N = 2$, then $r_{max} = 5$, and when $M = 2$, $N = 2$, then $r_{max} = 14$. It can be shown that

$$r_{max} \approx \frac{MNn^M}{(M, N)} \tag{7}$$

where n is the number of different demands, and (M, N) is the largest common divisor of M and N. For our distribution $n = 3$, and hence, when $M = 3$, then for $N = 1$ we find that r_{max} is about 81, for $N = 2$ it is about 162, and for $N = 3$ it is about 81. [Somewhat better estimates are $r_{max}(N = 1) \approx 72$, $r_{max}(N = 2) \approx 135$.] To these rather large values of r_{max} correspond numerous transition probabilities p_{jk} which in turn make the analysis rather cumbersome from a computational point of view. These computations become even more involved if leadtime is significant.

An alternative approach for finding I_1, I_2, and I_3 is suggested in the following section. Later, in Section 12–4, the system as a whole is discussed and some comments are made on the behavior of I_1, I_2, and I_3 as functions of M and N.

SIMULATION APPROACH

12–3 The methodology of simulation can best be introduced by referring to Table 12–1a in which $L = 2$, $M = 4$, and $N = 6$. To be able to simulate the system given in the table we need means for (1) generating random demands S_i that follow the distribution $P(S)$, (2) establishing initial conditions. The other computations follow directly from equations 12–1(1) to 12–1(7).

Once the simulation has been carried out, it is relatively easy to estimate I_1, I_2, and I_3. Suppose m scheduling periods have been simulated starting with period a. (In Table 12–1a, $m = 10$ and $a = 11$.) The values of I_1, I_2, and I_3 can then be determined as follows:

$$I_j(M, N) = \frac{1}{m} \sum_{i=a}^{a+m-1} I_{ji}(M, N) \qquad j = 1, 2, 3 \tag{1}$$

where

$$I_{1i} = \begin{cases} (Q_i + q_i)/2 & q_i \geqq 0 \\ Q_i^2/2S_i & q_i \leqq 0 \text{ and } Q_i \geqq 0 \\ 0 & q_i \leqq 0 \text{ and } Q_i \leqq 0 \end{cases} \tag{2}$$

where

$$I_{2i} = \begin{cases} 0 & q_i \geqq 0 \\ q_i^2/2S_i & q_i \leqq 0 \text{ and } Q_i \geqq 0 \\ -(Q_i + q_i)/2 & q_i \leqq 0 \text{ and } Q_i \leqq 0 \end{cases} \tag{3}$$

and where

$$I_{3i} = \begin{cases} 0 & A_i \geqq B_i \\ 1 & A_i < B_i \end{cases} \tag{4}$$

Generating Random Demands

Let $F(S)$ be the cumulative distribution of demand. That is, let

$$F(S) = \sum_{x=0}^{S} P(x) \tag{5}$$

The flow chart of Figure 12–3a describes how random demands $S = 0$, u, $2u$, ..., which have the cumulative probability distribution $F(S)$, can be

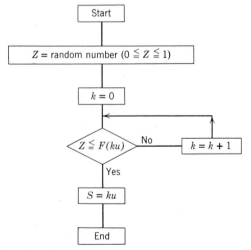

Figure 12–3a Flow chart for generation of random demands that have a cumulative probability distribution $F(S)$.

generated. In the flow chart it is assumed that a means is available for generating pseudo-random numbers* Z from a uniform distribution in the range from 0 to 1. For example, let $u = 100$, $F(0) = 0.2$, $F(100) = 0.9$, $F(200) = 0.9$, and $F(300) = 1.0$. If Z happens to be 0.563 ..., the corresponding demand is 100. Similarly, for values of Z of 0.431 ..., 0.213 ..., 0.109 ..., 0.897 ..., 0.952 ..., and 0.631 ..., the corresponding demands are 100, 100, 0, 100, 300, and 100.

Establishing Initial Conditions

Referring again to Table 12–1a, it will be noticed that in order to start the simulation with the period $a = 11$, certain values of S_i, q_i, P_i, and R_i had to be assumed for previous periods. In general, to use equation 12–1(3) we need $M - 1$ values of S_i; $S_{a-1}, \ldots, S_{a-M+1}$. And, to use equations 12–1(5) and 12–1(6) we need L values of P_i: $P_{a-1}, \ldots, P_{a-L}$. The only other values needed are q_{a-1} and R_{a-1}. When the number m of periods simulated is large, the initial conditions will in general have relatively little effect on the results. For smaller simulations it may be advisable to assume the following values:

$$S_i = \bar{S} \qquad\qquad i = a - M + 1, \ldots, a - 1 \qquad (6)$$

$$P_i = \bar{S} \qquad\qquad i = a - L, \ldots, a - 1 \qquad (7)$$

$$q_{a-1} = (N - L - 1)\bar{S} \qquad\qquad\qquad\qquad (8)$$

$$R_{a-1} = \bar{S} \qquad\qquad\qquad\qquad\qquad (9)$$

These are essentially the values that we obtain if demand is constant and $S_i = \bar{S}$. Replenishments are then ordered every period and each period starts with an amount $Q_i = (N - L)\bar{S}$ in inventory.

The Simulation Flow Chart and Some Results

In Figure 12–3b a flow chart is given for the simulation of the inventory-bank system. The upper part of the left side of the flow chart is devoted to the reading of the data and to setting up the initial conditions. The right side of the flow chart is devoted to the actual simulation of m weeks, starting with week a. The printing of the quantities i, Q_i, S_i etc., for each i has been included for checking and illustration purposes. In large runs this printing would be omitted, of course.

The computation of S_i is in accordance with the flow chart of Figure 12–3a. The computations of I_{1i} and I_{2i} are in accordance with the flow chart of Figure 12–3c.

---

* For more details on this topic see, for example, Galliher [20], or Meyer [33], pp. 15–28.

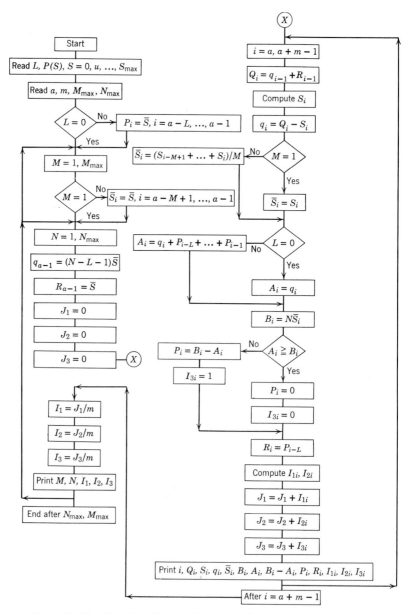

Figure 12–3b   Flow chart for the simulation of the inventory-bank system.

The author has programmed the simulation for an IBM 7094 using the flow chart of Figure 12–3b. The distribution discussed in Sections 12–1 and 12–2 was used to allow comparisons. Each simulation was over a 100-week period. For zero leadtime the simulation was run when $M = 1, 2, 3, 4$ and $N = 1, 2, 3, 4$; and for 1- and 2-week leadtime it was run when $M = 1, 2$ and $N = 1, 2, 3, 4$. A reprint of a portion of the computer output for $L = 2$, $M = 2$, and $N = 3$ is given in Figures 12–3d and 12–3e. In these

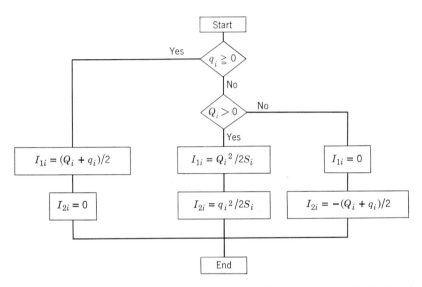

Figure 12–3c Flow chart for computing I_{1i} and I_{2i} by equations 12–3(2) and 12–3(3).

figures IU is the unit u, IA the first week a, IM the number of weeks m simulated, MMAX the maximum value of M, NMAX the maximum value of N, SBAR the mean demand $\bar{S}$, and SSIM the average of the simulated demands $S(I)$. The symbols on top of the columns correspond to the variables in the last "print" instruction in Figure 12–3b (i.e., i, Q_i, S_i, ..., I_{3i}). All the results in Figures 12–3d and 12–3e are self-explanatory. It should be noted that the average of the simulated demands SSIM only by chance equals the mean demand SBAR. The actual distribution of the simulated demands happened to be $P^*(0) = 0.24$, $P^*(100) = 0.64$, $P^*(300) = 0.12$.

To allow meaningful comparisons, the same demands were generated for all simulations. Table 12–3a gives a summary of the results for zero lead-time. Table 12–3b gives the results for a leadtime of 1 week and a leadtime of 2 weeks.

```
    L   IU  ISMAX  IA  IM  MMAX  NMAX  SBAR   SSIM
    2  100   300   11  100   2     4   100.0  100.0

         PI   01= 0.200
         PI 1001= 0.700
         PI 2001= 4.
         PI 3001= 0.100

              M = 2   N = 3
```

I	QB(I)	S(I)	QE(I)	SB(I)	B(I)	A(I)	BA(I)	PR(I)	R(I)	I1(I)	I2(I)	I3(I)
11	100.0	100.0	-0.0	100.0	300.0	200.0	100.0	100.0	100.0	50.0	0.0	1.0
12	100.0	100.0	-0.0	100.0	300.0	200.0	100.0	100.0	100.0	50.0	0.0	1.0
13	100.0	100.0	-0.0	100.0	300.0	200.0	100.0	100.0	100.0	50.0	0.0	1.0
14	100.0	100.0	-0.3	200.0	300.0	200.0	100.0	100.0	100.0	50.0	0.0	1.0
15	-100.0	300.0	-200.0	200.0	600.0	-0.	100.0	600.0	100.0	16.7	66.7	1.0
16	100.0	100.0	-200.0	200.0	600.0	500.0	-100.0	600.0	600.0	0.	150.0	0.
17	-500.0		-400.0	50.0	150.0	600.0	-450.0	0.	0.	450.0	100.0	0.
18	500.0	100.0	-200.0	100.0	300.0	500.0	-350.0	0.	0.	450.0	0.	0.
19	500.0		400.0	50.0	150.0	400.0	-100.0	0.	0.	400.0	0.	0.
20	400.0		400.0	50.0	150.0	400.0	-250.0	0.	0.	250.0	0.	1.0
21	400.0	300.0	0.	150.0	450.0	100.0	350.0	350.0	0.	50.0	0.	0.
22	100.0	100.0	0.	200.0	600.0	350.0	250.0	250.0	0.	0.	50.0	0.
23	0.	100.0	-100.0	100.0	300.0	400.0	-200.0	0.	350.0	200.0	0.	0.
24	250.0		400.0	50.0	150.0	400.0	-250.0	0.	250.0	400.0	0.	0.
25	400.0	100.0	150.0	50.0	150.0	300.0	-150.0	0.	0.	350.0	0.	1.0
26	400.0		300.0	50.0	150.0	400.0	-150.0	0.	0.	300.0	0.	0.
27	300.0	100.0	200.0	100.0	300.0	300.0	-50.0	0.	0.	250.0	0.	1.0
28	300.0	100.0	100.0	100.0	300.0	300.0	-50.0	0.	0.	150.0	0.	0.
29	200.0	100.0	0.	100.0	300.0	100.0	200.0	200.0	200.0	50.0	0.	0.
30	100.0			50.0	150.0	300.0	-100.0	100.0	100.0	0.	0.	1.0
31	200.0	100.0	100.0	50.0	150.0	200.0	-50.0	0.	0.	150.0	0.	0.
32	200.0	100.0	100.0	100.0	300.0	100.0	200.0	200.0	200.0	150.0	0.	1.0
33	200.0	100.0	0.	100.0	300.0	200.0	100.0	100.0	100.0	50.0	0.	0.
34	100.0	100.0	-100.0	50.0	150.0	200.0	-50.0	0.	0.	50.0	0.	1.0
35		100.0	200.0	50.0	150.0	200.0	-150.0	0.	0.	50.0	50.0	0.
36	100.0	100.0	0.	100.0	300.0	200.0	-100.0	200.0	200.0	50.0	0.	1.0
37		100.0	100.0	100.0	300.0	200.0	100.0	100.0	100.0	100.0	0.	1.0
38	100.0		200.0	50.0	150.0	300.0	-150.0	100.0	100.0	200.0	0.	0.
39	200.0	100.0	0.	0.	0.	300.0	-300.0	0.	100.0	150.0	0.	0.
40	300.0	300.0	0.	150.0	450.0	0.	450.0	450.0	0.	0.	50.0	1.0
41	0.	300.0	-100.0	200.0	600.0	350.0	250.0	250.0	450.0	0.	250.0	0.
42	-100.0	300.0	-400.0	200.0	600.0	300.0	300.0	300.0	250.0	12.5	12.5	1.0
43			-50.0	100.0	300.0	100.0	-50.0	100.0	250.0	200.0	0.	1.0
44	200.0	100.0	200.0	50.0	150.0	500.0	-450.0	0.	300.0	400.0	0.	1.0
45	500.0	100.0	400.0	100.0	300.0	500.0	-350.0	0.	100.0	450.0	0.	1.0
46	500.0		400.0	100.0	300.0	400.0	-100.0	0.	0.	450.0	0.	0.
47	400.0	100.0	300.0	100.0	300.0	300.0	0.	0.	0.	350.0	0.	1.0
48	300.0	100.0	200.0	100.0	300.0	200.0	100.0	100.0	100.0	250.0	0.	1.0
49	100.0	100.0	100.0	50.0	300.0	300.0	-150.0	100.0	100.0	100.0	0.	0.
50	100.0	100.0	0.	50.0	150.0	300.0	-150.0	0.	0.	66.7	16.7	1.0
51	200.0	300.0	-100.0	150.0	450.0	-0.	450.0	450.0	100.0	0.	0.	1.0
52	-0.	100.0	-100.0	200.0	600.0	350.0	250.0	250.0	0.	16.7	50.0	1.0
53	-100.0	100.0	-200.0	100.0	300.0	500.0	-200.0	0.	450.0	0.	150.0	1.0
54	-250.0	100.0	-50.0	100.0	600.0	100.0	400.0	400.0	250.0	104.2	4.2	1.0

Figure 12–3d Computer printout of a simulation of the inventory-bank system (first part).

55	200.0	0.	200.0	150.0	450.0	600.0	-150.0	0.	0.	200.0	0.	0.
56	200.0	100.0	100.0	50.0	150.0	500.0	-350.0	400.0	400.0	150.0	0.	0.
57	300.0	300.0	100.0	200.0	600.0	200.0	-400.0	100.0	100.0	350.0	0.	1.0
58	200.0	100.0	100.0	200.0	600.0	500.0	100.0	0.	0.	150.0	0.	1.0
59	100.0	100.0	300.0	100.0	300.0	400.0	-200.0	400.0	400.0	50.0	0.	1.0
60	400.0	100.0	100.0	100.0	300.0	300.0	-100.0	100.0	100.0	350.0	0.	0.
61	400.0	100.0	0.	100.0	300.0	200.0	100.0	0.	0.	250.0	0.	0.
62	200.0	100.0	0.	50.0	300.0	200.0	100.0	100.0	100.0	150.0	0.	1.0
63	100.0	100.0	100.0	100.0	300.0	200.0	100.0	100.0	100.0	50.0	0.	1.0
64	100.0	100.0	200.0	100.0	300.0	200.0	100.0	100.0	100.0	100.0	0.	0.
65	200.0	100.0	-200.0	100.0	150.0	300.0	-150.0	0.	0.	100.0	0.	0.
…												
110	50.0	100.0	50.0	50.0	150.0	150.0	100.0	100.0	50.0	50.0	0.	1.0
AVERAGES										172.500	172.500	15.500	0.440

Figure 12-3e Computer printout of a simulation of the inventory-bank system (second part).

TABLE 12–3a

Values of I_1, I_2, and I_3 in a 100-Week Simulation When $L = 0$

N \ M	1	2	3	4	
1	100.333	76.500	67.519	66.552	I_1
	6.333	8.000	8.852	8.552	I_2
	0.560	0.650	0.720	0.760	I_3
2	280.833	202.667	178.130	170.417	I_1
	0.833	1.667	1.796	1.917	I_2
	0.440	0.530	0.620	0.640	I_3
3	494.000	356.167	306.167	288.698	I_1
	0.	0.167	0.167	0.198	I_2
	0.340	0.480	0.530	0.620	I_3
4	733.000	520.000	446.333	410.000	I_1
	0.	0.	0.	0.	I_2
	0.260	0.430	0.500	0.520	I_3

TABLE 12–3b

Values of I_1, I_2, and I_3 in a 100-Week Simulation When $L = 1$ and $L = 2$

	L = 1		L = 2		
N \ M	1	2	1	2	
1	40.000	24.750	12.667	5.625	I_1
	47.000	57.250	120.667	138.625	I_2
	0.560	0.650	0.560	0.650	I_3
2	189.000	118.833	114.833	59.667	I_1
	10.000	17.833	36.833	58.667	I_2
	0.440	0.530	0.440	0.530	I_3
3	395.167	260.000	303.000	172.500	I_1
	2.167	3.500	11.000	15.500	I_2
	0.340	0.480	0.340	0.480	I_3
4	632.000	421.500	533.667	326.667	I_1
	0.	0.500	2.667	4.667	I_2
	0.260	0.430	0.260	0.430	I_3

SUMMARY OF RESULTS AND EXTENSIONS

12–4 We are now in position to compare the results of the two approaches to the analysis of the inventory-bank system. In Table 12–2e are given the results for $M = 1$ and in Table 12–2l those for $M = 2$. These results are based on the Markov chain approach and give precise values of I_1, I_2, and I_3. In Table 12–1b the results for $M = \infty$ are given. These results were obtained using the methods of Section 8–2. They, too, give precise values. In contrast, the values of I_1, I_2, and I_3 in Table 12–3a are only approximate values.

TABLE 12–4a

*Comparison of Results Using the Markov Chain Approach (Mar)
and the Simulation Approach (Sim)*

Method	Mar	Sim	Mar	Sim	Sim	Sim			
M / N	1		2		3	4	$\cdots$	∞	
1	91.19	100.33	76.09	76.50	67.52	66.55		56.67	I_1
	5.29	6.33	7.29	8.50	8.85	8.55		6.67	I_2
	0.64	0.56	0.69	0.65	0.72	0.76		0.80	I_3
2	261.28	280.83	194.84	202.67	178.13	170.42		151.67	I_1
	0.98	0.83	1.74	1.67	1.80	1.92		1.67	I_2
	0.51	0.44	0.56	0.53	0.62	0.64		0.80	I_3
3	464.10	494.00		356.17	306.17	288.70		250.00	I_1
	0.	0.		0.17	0.17	0.20		0.	I_2
	0.41	0.34		0.48	0.53	0.62		0.80	I_3

All the pertinent results are combined in Table 12–4a. Although only 100 weeks were simulated, the results based on the simulations seem to agree with the precise results. Even better results would have been obtained if the demands could have been simulated in such a way that their distribution matched exactly the given distribution.* In any case, larger runs would ensure more accurate results, if such accuracy were needed.

From Table 12–4a it seems that we can draw the following conclusions about the inventory-bank system.

1. The system is more sensitive to the number of weeks in the bank N than to the number of weeks M used to compute the average demand.

2. The choices of the optimal M and N depend entirely on the unit costs of the system.

3. As N increases then I_1 increases, and I_2 and I_3 decrease. This result seems to be self-evident.

* In this connection see Naddor [43], p. 96, and Brenner [10], p. 292.

TABLE 12–4b

Probability Distributions of Demand P(S) in Various Systems

S	0	100	200	300	400	500	600	Mean	Standard Deviation
System A		1.000						100.0	0.
System B	0.100	0.800	0.100					100.0	44.7
System C	0.200	0.600	0.200					100.0	63.2
System D	0.200	0.700	0.	0.100				100.0	77.5
System E	0.400	0.300	0.200	0.100				100.0	100.0
System F	0.368	0.368	0.184	0.061	0.015	0.003	0.001	100.0	100.2

TABLE 12–4c

The Effect of the Standard Deviation d on I_1, I_2, and I_3

System		A	B	C	D	E	F	
M	N	0.	44.7	63.2	77.5	100.0	100.2	d
1	1	50.000	65.750	86.250	100.333	135.250	141.958	I_1
		0.	2.750	3.750	6.333	4.750	6.458	I_2
		1.000	0.770	0.620	0.560	0.460	0.480	I_3
	2	150.000	189.000	231.500	280.833	338.833	351.792	I_1
		0.	0.	0.	0.833	0.333	1.292	I_2
		1.000	0.680	0.540	0.440	0.330	.340	I_3
	3	250.000	324.000	392.500	994.000	580.500	613.500	I_1
		0.	0.	0.	0.	0.	0.	I_2
		1.000	0.600	0.480	0.340	0.290	0.280	I_3
	4	350.000	468.000	561.500	733.000	830.500	912.500	I_1
		0.	0.	0.	0.	0.	0.	I_2
		1.000	0.550	0.430	0.260	0.260	0.200	I_3
2	1	50.000	61.500	72.500	76.500	102.917	103.294	I_1
		0.	4.000	5.500	8.500	9.917	11.294	I_2
		1.000	0.850	0.700	0.650	0.520	0.530	I_3
	2	150.000	168.250	193.500	202.667	263.250	259.092	I_1
		0.	0.250	0.	1.667	1.750	3.592	I_2
		1.000	0.710	0.560	0.530	0.370	0.340	I_3
	3	250.000	286.000	335.000	356.167	451.333	448.417	I_1
		0.	0.	0.	0.167	0.333	0.917	I_2
		1.000	0.700	0.530	0.480	0.320	0.310	I_3
	4	350.000	405.000	481.500	520.000	650.500	649.625	I_1
		0.	0.	0.	0.	0.	0.125	I_2
		1.000	0.620	0.470	0.430	0.280	0.270	I_3

4. As M increases then I_1 decreases and I_3 increases. This, too, seems self-evident. With increasing M, however, I_2 first increases and then decreases. This result is not self-evident.

The Effects of Probabilistic Demand and of Leadtime

Several inventory-bank systems were simulated, as in Section 12-3, in order to observe the effect of variability of demand on the average inventory carried, the average shortage, and the average number of replenishments per week. The probability distributions of demand in the systems

TABLE 12-4d

The Effect of Leadtime on the Inventory-Bank System

M	1			2		
L	0	1	2	0	1	2
N	1	2	3	1	2	3
I_1	100.333	189.000	303.000	76.500	118.833	172.500
I_2	6.333	10.000	11.000	8.500	17.833	15.500
I_3	0.560	0.440	0.340	0.650	0.530	0.480
N	2	3	4	2	3	4
I_1	280.833	395.167	533.667	202.667	260.000	326.667
I_2	0.833	2.167	2.667	1.667	3.500	4.667
I_3	0.440	0.340	0.260	0.530	0.480	0.430

are given in Table 12-4b. In this table system D is the one that has been used extensively in Sections 12-2 and 12-3. The results of the simulations are given in Table 12-4c.

As we might have expected, inventories and shortages increase with increasing variability and replenishments decrease. The effects of N and M on the various systems seem to be about the same in terms of direction of increases and decreases.

The effects of leadtime can be seen by examining Table 12-3a (in which leadtime is zero) and Table 12-3b (in which $L = 1$ and $L = 2$). In order to make meaningful comparisons it seems that the results for $L = 0$ and $N = J$ should be compared with those for $L = 1$, $N = J + 1$ and $L = 2$, $N = J + 2$. This is done in Table 12-4d. It appears from the table that leadtime tends to increase inventories and, to a lesser degree, shortages. Replenishments do not seem to be affected to any great extent.

All the preceding conclusions should be regarded as tentative, for they are based on the analysis of a limited number of systems. However, the method of analysis is general and could be readily adapted to any desired detailed studies.

12-5 PROBLEMS

1. Compare the method of finding an average demand by equation 12–1(3) with the exponential smoothing method in which

$$\bar{S}_i = aS_i + (1 - a)\bar{S}_{i-1} \qquad (1)$$

where a is a given constant between zero and one. Assume that S_i is a random variable whose probability distribution is $P(S)$ with mean $\bar{S}$ and variance V. Show that for both methods the expected value of S_i is $\bar{S}$. What must be the relation between M and a so that the variance of $\bar{S}_i$ will be the same for both methods?

2. Prepare a table similar to Table 12–2a, in which $M = 2$ and $N = 4$. By choosing appropriate values for S_i, show how (a) a series of large random demands causes excessive inventories, (b) a series of small random demands causes excessive shortages.

3. Prove the result given by equation 12–1(15).

4. Explain why the following states have not been considered in Section 12–2 for $M = 2$: (100, 600), (300, 100), (300, 200), and (300, 500).

5. Find I_1, I_2, and I_3 in an inventory-bank system in which $L = 1$, $N = 2$, and $M = 1$ when the probability distribution of weekly demand is given by $P(0) = 0.4$, $P(1) = 0.3$, $P(2) = 0.2$, $P(3) = 0.1$. (a) Use Markov chains. (b) Simulate over a 50-week period.

6. How can seasonal trends in demands be incorporated in the simulation of Section 12–3?

7. Compare the results in Table 12–3b for $N = 2$ with solutions based on the Markov chain approach for (a) $L = 1$, (b) $L = 2$.

8. Explain the basis of the comparisons in Table 12–4d by examining a deterministic inventory-bank system.

9. Simplify the flow chart of Figure 12–3a by eliminating the variable k. That is, instead of $k = 0$ put $S = 0$; instead of $k = k + 1$ put $S = S + u$; etc.

10. The results in Tables 12–2g to 12–2j were obtained from equation 12–2(5) by defining a Markov chain state as the couple (S_{i-1}, Q_i). Obtain the results in Table 12–2j by defining a Markov chain state as the amount Q_i.

11. Demand for a part on any day is either for two units or for four units with probabilities $\frac{1}{2}$ and $\frac{1}{2}$, respectively. Leadtime is 1 day. A (t, Z_i) policy is used, where $t = 1$ day, $Z_i = N\bar{x}_i$, $N = 3$, $\bar{x}_i = (x_i + x_{i-1})/2$, and where x_i is the demand on day i. No returns are allowed.

   Find the distribution of the amounts in inventory at the end of each day.

12. Over a period of N days a newspaper boy buys S papers every day. Each paper costs him a cents, he sells if for b cents, and he receives c cents if he does not sell it. The probability that on any day there are x customers is $P(x)$.

(a) Simulate the boy's operations and use the simulation to estimate his expected daily profit for the following numerical values: $N = 5$ days, $S = 65$ papers, $a = \$0.05\ b, = \$0.09$, $c = \$0.2$, $P(50) = 0.2$, $P(60) = 0.4$, $P(70) = 0.3$, and $P(80) = 0.1$.

(b) Prepare a detailed flow chart of this simulation for the given numerical values. The flow chart should enable us to compute the expected daily profit as a function of S.

(c) Use the flow chart, step by step, to estimate the expected daily profit for $S = 70$.

Part 4

PROBABILISTIC
REORDER-POINT SYSTEMS

In this part of the book we study probabilistic inventory systems in which inventories are replenished whenever the amounts on hand and on order are equal to or below the reorder point. Chapters 13 and 14 deal with lot-size systems whereas Chapters 15 and 16 deal with order-level systems. In Chapters 13 and 15 leadtime is zero, but in Chapter 14 and in Section 16–2 leadtime is significant. The inventory policies examined in the chapters are thus: (s, q), (z, q), (s, S), and (z, Z). In Chapters 13, 14, and 15 we first examine type $(1, 3)$ systems, then type $(1, 2)$ systems, and finally type $(1, 2, 3)$.

Chapter 17 is devoted to a comparison of (s, S), (s, q), and (t, s) policies. We show that for systems with one item the minimum cost for a (s, S) policy is smaller than, or at most equal to, the minimum cost for a (s, q) policy, which in turn is smaller than, or at most equal to, the minimum cost for a (t, S) policy.

Chapter 13

Probabilistic Reorder-Point–
Lot-Size Systems without Leadtime

13–0 The inventory fluctuations in the probabilistic reorder-point–lot-size systems without leadtime can be described graphically as shown in Figure 13–0. Whenever the amount on hand is equal to, or below, the reorder point s, a lot size q is scheduled for a replenishment. Since leadtime is zero, that lot size is immediately added to inventory.

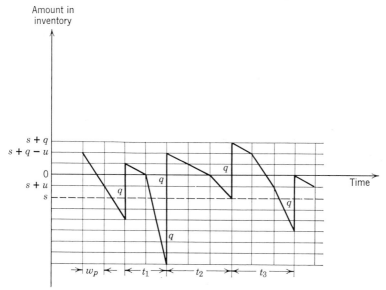

Figure 13–0 The probabilistic reorder-point–lot-size system.

The systems in this chapter may be regarded as extensions of the systems of Sections 3–1, 4–1, and 5–1. In Section 13–1 the reorder point is prescribed in such a manner that no shortages occur. The optimal lot size is then determined. In Section 13–2 the lot size is prescribed and the reorder point is determined. The system of Section 13–3 is an extension of the previous systems, and the optimal reorder point and the optimal lot size are determined.

The analysis of each section starts with the discrete case and proceeds to the continuous.

Multiple Lot Sizes

In the systems of this chapter more than one lot size may have to be scheduled at one time. Such a situation occurs whenever the addition of only one lot size will not raise the amount in inventory above the reorder point. As an illustration, consider the end of the scheduling period t_1 in Figure 13–0. At that time two lot sizes have to be scheduled in order to raise inventory above the reorder point s.

The replenishment cost c_3 will be assumed to be independent of the number of lot sizes scheduled at one time. This assumption makes the analysis somewhat more difficult. The reader will find it relatively simple to extend the results to systems in which the replenishment cost is proportional to the number of lot sizes [problem 13–4(16)].

Multiple lot sizes tend to occur whenever the lot size is relatively small. In particular, we must mention the lot size $q = u$ in the discrete case and $q = 0$ in the continuous case. In the former the amount in inventory at the beginning of every scheduling period is $s + u$, and in the latter it is s.

The Probability Distribution of Q

Let Q designate the amount in inventory at the beginning of each reviewing period.* We propose to show that the probability distribution of Q is the uniform distribution. That is, we will show that Q is equally likely to be any amount between $s + u$ and $s + q$. We shall only treat the case when all units are discrete and the basic unit is u. The continuous case then follows when u approaches zero.

Let $P(x)$ be the probability distribution of demand during the reviewing period, where $x = 0, u, 2u, \ldots, x_{\max}$. Let $H(Q)$ be the probability distribution of the amount in inventory at the beginning of each reviewing period. We thus want to show that

$$H(Q) = \frac{1}{q/u} = \frac{u}{q} \qquad Q = s + u, s + 2u, \ldots, s + q \qquad (1)$$

* The quantity Q refers to the amount in inventory after a replenishment, if any.

The amount Q may be regarded as a state in a Markov chain. The transition probabilities of going from one inventory state Q to another are given in Table 13-0. The transition matrix represented by the table is what is known as a doubly stochastic matrix, for the sum of the elements in each

TABLE 13-0

The Transition Probabilities of Going from One State of Inventory, at the Beginning of a Reviewing Period, to Another State, at the Beginning of the Next Period

From \ To	$s + q$	$s + q - u$	$\cdots$	$s + 2u$	$s + u$
$s + q$	$P(0) + P(q)$ $+ \cdots$	$P(u) + P(q + u)$ $+ \cdots$	$\cdots$	$P(q - 2u)$ $+ P(2q - 2u) + \cdots$	$P(q - u)$ $+ P(2q - u) + \cdots$
$s + q - u$	$P(q - u) + \cdots$	$P(0) + P(q)$ $+ \cdots$	$\cdots$	$P(q - 3u)$ $+ P(2q - 3u) + \cdots$	$P(q - 2u)$ $+ P(2q - 2u) + \cdots$
$\vdots$					
$s + 2u$	$P(2u) + \cdots$	$P(3u) + \cdots$	$\cdots$	$P(0) + P(q) + \cdots$	$P(u) + P(q + u) + \cdots$
$s + u$	$P(u) + \cdots$	$P(2u) + \cdots$	$\cdots$	$P(q - u) + \cdots$	$P(0) + P(q) + \cdots$

column is equal to 1. The steady-state probabilities of a doubly stochastic matrix are known to be equal.* This proves the result represented by equation (1).

THE PROBABILISTIC LOT-SIZE SYSTEM

13-1 The probabilistic lot size system is a type $(1, 3)$ system in which demand is probabilistic and the optimal lot size has to be determined.

Let x be the demand during the reviewing period w_p. Let $\bar{x}$ be the average demand and let x_{max} be the maximum demand. Let r be the average rate of demand. That is,

$$\bar{x} = w_p r \tag{1}$$

Let $P(x)$, $x = 0, u, \ldots, x_{max}$, be the probability distribution of demand. Since no shortages are allowed, the reorder point is essentially prescribed, namely,**

$$s_p = x_{max} - u \tag{2}$$

Let Q be the amount in inventory at the beginning of each reviewing period and let $H(Q)$ be its probability distribution. Using the results of

* See Feller [17], p. 358.
** For larger values of s unnecessary inventories will be carried.

the previous section we can now derive the expected average amount in inventory. From Figure 13-0 and equations (2) and 13-0(1) we have

$$I_1 = \sum_{Q=s_p+u}^{s_p+q} \sum_{x=0}^{x_{\max}} \left(Q - \frac{x}{2}\right) P(x)H(Q)$$

$$= \sum_{Q=s_p+u}^{s_p+q} \left(Q - \frac{\bar{x}}{2}\right)\frac{u}{q} = \frac{q}{u}\left(s_p + \frac{u+q}{2} - \frac{\bar{x}}{2}\right)\frac{u}{q} \tag{3}$$

$$= s_p + \frac{u+q}{2} - \frac{\bar{x}}{2} = \frac{q}{2} + x_{\max} - \frac{\bar{x}+u}{2}$$

In order to determine the expected number of replenishments per unit of time I_3, it will be convenient to ascertain the probability of the occurrence of a replenishment at the beginning of a reviewing period. Let this probability be designated by g. Then

$$I_3 = g/w_p \tag{4}$$

Consider any state $Q = s_p + y$. A replenishment will occur whenever the demand is equal to, or is larger than, y. Hence, by equation 13-0(1),

$$g = \sum_{Q=s_p+u}^{s_p+q} \sum_{x=Q-s_p}^{x_{\max}} P(x)H(Q)$$

$$= \sum_{Q=s_p+u}^{s_p+q} [1 - F(Q - s_p - u)]\frac{u}{q} = 1 - \frac{u}{q}\sum_{x=0}^{q-u} F(x) \tag{5}$$

$$= 1 - \frac{u}{q} V(q - u)$$

where

$$V(x) = \sum_{y=0}^{x} F(y) = \sum_{y=0}^{x} \sum_{z=0}^{y} P(z) \tag{6}$$

We can now state the expected total cost of the probabilistic reorder-point system. By equations (3), (4), and (5) we have

$$C(q) = c_1\left(\frac{q}{2} + x_{\max} - \frac{\bar{x}+u}{2}\right) + c_3\frac{1 - (u/q)V(q-u)}{w_p}$$

$$= \frac{c_1 q}{2} - \frac{c_3 u V(q-u)}{q w_p} + c_1\left(x_{\max} - \frac{\bar{x}+u}{2}\right) + \frac{c_3}{w_p} \tag{7}$$

To find the optimal lot size q_o, we compare $C(q_o + u)$ with $C(q_o)$, etc., which gives us the solution

$$R(q_o - u) \leqq \frac{2c_3}{c_1 w_p} \leqq R(q_o) \tag{8}$$

where

$$R(q) = q(q + u)\Big/ \sum_{x=0}^{q} xP(x) \qquad q = u, 2u, \ldots \tag{9}$$

It is important to note that the function $R(q)$ is not necessarily an increasing function. Hence equation (8) may have more than one solution. Whenever it does, we have to examine equation (7) to find the optimal lot size. The following example illustrates this point.

Example 13-1a

In an inventory system with an (s, q) policy, no shortages are allowed. The amounts in inventory are reviewed every 2 weeks. The probability distribution of demand during a 2-week period is given by $P(0) = 0.25$, $P(5) = 0.20$, $P(10) = 0.10$, $P(15) = 0.20$, and $P(20) = 0.25$. The carrying cost is \$3.20 per unit per week. The replenishing cost is \$180.00.

Assuming that the lot size must be a multiple of 5 units, we wish to find the optimal lot size and the corresponding expected minimum total cost of the system.

In this example we have $u = 5$ units, $w_p = 2$ weeks, $\bar{x} = 10$ units, $x_{max} = 20$ units, $r = 5$ units per week, $c_1 = \$3.20$ per unit per week, and $c_3 = \$180.00$. The function $V(x)$ of equation (6) is $V(0) = 0.25$, $V(5) = 0.70$, $V(10) = 1.25$, $V(15) = 2.00$, $V(20) = 3.00$, and $V(25) = 4.00$, etc. The function $R(q)$ of equation (10) is $R(5) = 50$, $R(10) = 75$, $R(15) \doteq 60$, $R(20) = 50$, $R(25) = 75$, and $R(30) = 105$, etc. The value of $2c_3/c_1 w_p$ is 56.25. Hence equation (8) gives two solutions, $q_1 = 10$ and $q_2 = 25$. Substituting these values in equation (7) gives $C(10) = \$114.50$ per week and $C(25) = \$116.00$ per week. Hence the solution: the optimal lot size is $q_o = 10$ units and the corresponding minimum expected total cost is $C_o = \$114.50$ per week. The expected total cost of the system for various lot sizes is given in Table 13-1a.

TABLE 13-1a

The Expected Total Costs of the Probabilistic Lot-Size System of Example 13-1a

q	5	10	15	20	25	30	35
$C(q)$	115.50	114.50	116.50	117.00	116.00	118.00	121.70

Continuous Units

The results which have been obtained for discrete units can be immediately extended to continuous units. Let $f(x)$ be the probability density of demand during the reviewing period. Let $\bar{x}$ be its mean and let x_{max} be the maximum demand.

The inventory fluctuations can again be described as in Figure 13-0, except that the amount Q at the beginning of a reviewing period can be any quantity between s and $s + q$. Equation (1) applies here too. But equations (2) and 13–0(1) should now read

$$s_p = x_{\max} \tag{10}$$

and

$$h(Q) = 1/q \qquad s_p \leq Q \leq s_p + q \tag{11}$$

where $h(Q)$ is the probability density of Q. In a similar way we obtain from equation (3)

$$I_1 = \int_{s_p}^{s_p+q} \left[\int_0^{x_{\max}} \left(Q - \frac{x}{2} \right) f(x) \, dx \right] h(Q) \, dQ$$

$$= s_p + \frac{q}{2} - \frac{\bar{x}}{2} = \frac{q}{2} + x_{\max} - \frac{\bar{x}}{2} \tag{12}$$

Equation (4) holds for the continuous case, but equation (5) now gives

$$g = \int_{s_p}^{s_p+q} \int_{Q-s_p}^{x_{\max}} f(x) h(Q) \, dx \, dQ$$

$$= \int_{s_p}^{s_p+q} \frac{1 - F(Q - s_p)}{q} \, dQ = 1 - \frac{V(q)}{q} \tag{13}$$

where

$$V(x) = \int_0^x F(y) \, dy = \int_0^x \left[\int_0^y f(z) \, dz \right] dy \tag{14}$$

Thus the expected total cost of the probabilistic reorder-point system for continuous units is

$$C(q) = \frac{c_1 q}{2} - \frac{c_3 V(q)}{q w_p} + c_1 \left(x_{\max} - \frac{\bar{x}}{2} \right) + \frac{c_3}{w_p} \tag{15}$$

The results given by equations (8) and (9) can be readily extended to continuous units by having $u = 0$. Alternatively the optimal q_o can be found directly from equation (15). Differentiating $C(q)$ twice with respect to q gives

$$\frac{dC}{dq} = \frac{c_1}{2} - \frac{c_3}{w_p} \left[\frac{F(q)}{q} - \frac{V(q)}{q^2} \right]$$

$$= \frac{c_1}{2} - \frac{c_3}{w_p q^2} \int_0^q x f(x) \, dx \tag{16}$$

and

$$\frac{d^2 C}{dq^2} = - \frac{c_3}{w_p} \left[\frac{f(q)}{q} - \frac{2}{q^3} \int_0^q x f(x) \, dx \right] \tag{17}$$

For the existence of a local minimum we must have the conditions $dC/dq = 0$ and $d^2C/dq^2 > 0$. The first condition and equation (16) give

$$q_o^2 \bigg/ \int_0^{q_o} x f(x) \, dx = \frac{2 c_3}{c_1 w_p} \tag{18}$$

The second condition and equation (18) give

$$f(q_o) < \frac{c_1 w_p}{c_3} \tag{19}$$

It is important to note that equations (18) and (19) may have more than one solution. Furthermore, we must also remember to check for a possible solution at the boundary when $q = 0$.

Example 13–1b

In a probabilistic lot-size system the probability density of demand during a reviewing period w_p is

$$f(x) = 6x(1 - x) \qquad 0 \leq x \leq 1 \tag{20}$$

What is the optimal lot size as a function of the parameter $A = c_3/c_1 w_p$, where c_1 is the unit carrying cost in $[\$]/[Q][T]$ and c_3 is the replenishing cost in $[\$]$?

For the probability density of equation (20) we have $\bar{x} = \frac{1}{2}$, $x_{\max} = 1$, and by equation (14)

$$V(q) = \begin{cases} q^3 - \frac{1}{2}q^4 & 0 \leq q \leq 1 \\ q - \frac{1}{2} & q \geq 1 \end{cases} \tag{21}$$

Hence, by equation (15), the expected total cost of the system is

$$C(q) = \begin{cases} \dfrac{c_1 q}{2} - \dfrac{c_3(q^2 - \frac{1}{2}q^3)}{w_p} + \dfrac{c_1}{2} + \dfrac{c_3}{w_p} & 0 \leq q \leq 1 \\[3mm] \dfrac{c_1 q}{2} - \dfrac{c_3(q - \frac{1}{2})}{q w_p} + \dfrac{c_1}{2} + \dfrac{c_3}{w_p} & q \geq 1 \end{cases} \tag{22}$$

or

$$C(q) = \begin{cases} (c_1/2)[q - A(2q^2 - q^3 - 2) + 1] & 0 \leq q \leq 1 \\ (c_1/2)[q + A/q + 1] & q \geq 1 \end{cases} \tag{23}$$

Differentiating twice with respect to q, we have

$$\frac{dC}{dq} = \begin{cases} (c_1/2)[1 - A(4q - 3q^2)] & 0 \leq q \leq 1 \\ (c_1/2)[1 - A/q^2] & q \geq 1 \end{cases} \tag{24}$$

and

$$\frac{d^2C}{dp^2} = \begin{cases} (c_1/2)[-A(4 - 6q)] & 0 \leq q \leq 1 \\ (c_1/2)[2A/q^3] & q \geq 1 \end{cases} \tag{25}$$

[As we might expect, the values of $C(q)$, dC/dq and d^2C/dq^2 for $q = 1$ can be obtained by either the upper or the lower form of equations (22), (23), (24), or (25)].

From equations (24) and (25) we have

$$q' = \begin{cases} (2 + \sqrt{4 - 3/A})/3 & \tfrac{3}{4} \leq A \leq 1 \\ \sqrt{A} & A \geq 1 \end{cases} \qquad (26)$$

But the corresponding costs for these values of the lot size, and for $q' = 0$ are

$$C(q') = \begin{cases} (c_1/2)[(2q'/3)(1 - Aq') + 2A + 1] & q' = (2 + \sqrt{4 - 3/A})/3, \tfrac{3}{4} \leq A \leq 1 \\ (c_1/2)(2\sqrt{A} + 1) & q' = \sqrt{A}, & A \geq 1 \\ (c_1/2)(2A + 1) & q' = 0, & A \geq 0 \end{cases} \qquad (27)$$

It is now obvious that when $A \leq 1$ the optimal lot size is $q' = 0$ and not $q' = (2 + \sqrt{4 - 3/A})/3$, for then $1 - Aq' > 0$. Hence the complete solution:

$$q_o = \begin{cases} 0 & 0 \leq A \leq 1 \\ \sqrt{A} & A \geq 1 \end{cases} \qquad (28)$$

and

$$C_o = \begin{cases} (c_1/2)(2A + 1) & 0 \leq A \leq 1 \\ (c_1/2)(2\sqrt{A} + 1) & A \geq 1 \end{cases} \qquad (29)$$

As another illustration of the results, the expected total cost of equation (23) is plotted in Figure 13–1.

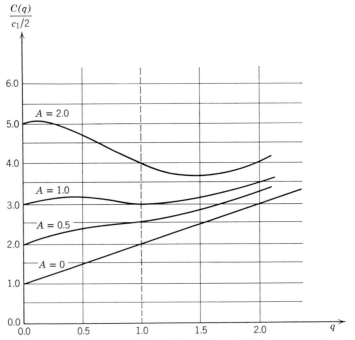

Figure 13–1   The expected total cost in the probabilistic lot-size system of Example 13–1b.

THE PROBABILISTIC REORDER-POINT SYSTEM

13-2 In the probabilistic reorder-point system, the lot size is prescribed. It is thus a type $(1, 2)$ system in which demand is probabilistic and the optimal reorder point has to be determined. The inventory fluctuations of the system are shown in Figure 13-0, with the exceptions that the lot size is q_p, a prescribed constant, and the reorder level may be positive, zero, or negative.

The Case When $s \geq 0$

Let Q be the amount in inventory at the beginning of each reviewing period. As in Section 13-0, we have

$$H(Q) = \frac{1}{q_p/u} = \frac{u}{q_p} \qquad Q = s + u, \ldots, s + q_p \qquad (1)$$

Let $I_1(Q)$ designate the expected average amount in inventory during a reviewing period, when an amount Q is in inventory at the beginning of the period. Then

$$I_1(Q) = \sum_{x=0}^{Q} \left(Q - \frac{x}{2}\right) P(x) + \sum_{x=Q+u}^{\infty} \frac{Q^2}{2x} P(x) \qquad (2)$$

where $P(x)$ is the probability distribution of demand during the reviewing period. If we use the notion of equivalence introduced in Chapter 10, equation (2) may be expressed as

$$I_1(Q) = \sum_{y=0}^{Q} (Q - y)R(y) \qquad (3)$$

where $R(y)$ is the function $Q(y)$ of equation 10-1(26). Equation (3) can be further simplified to the form

$$I_1(Q) = u \sum_{y=0}^{Q-u} G(y) = uW(Q - u) \qquad (4)$$

where

$$W(S) = \sum_{z=0}^{S} G(z) = \sum_{z=0}^{S} \sum_{y=0}^{z} R(y) \qquad (5)$$

Similarly, the expected average shortage during the reviewing period is

$$I_2(Q) = \sum_{y=Q+u}^{\infty} (y - Q)R(y) = uW(Q - u) + \bar{y} - Q \qquad (6)$$

where $\bar{y}$ is the mean of the equivalent demand y. The expected total cost of the system, by equations (1), (4), and (6), is thus

$$
\begin{aligned}
C(s) &= \sum_{Q=s+u}^{s+q_p} [c_1 I_1(Q) + c_2 I_2(Q)] H(Q) \\
&= \sum_{Q=s+u}^{s+q_p} [(c_1 + c_2) u W(Q - u) + c_2(\bar{y} - Q)] \frac{u}{q_p} \qquad (7) \\
&= (c_1 + c_2) \frac{u^2}{q_p} \sum_{Q=s+u}^{s+q_p} W(Q - u) + c_2(\bar{y} - \bar{Q})
\end{aligned}
$$

The value of $\bar{Q}$ by equation (1) is

$$
\bar{Q} = \frac{(s + u) + (s + q_p)}{2} = s + \frac{u + q_p}{2} \qquad (8)
$$

and we know (Section 10–1) that $\bar{y} = \bar{x}/2$, where $\bar{x}$ is the mean demand during the reviewing period. Let

$$
N(B) = \sum_{S=0}^{B} W(S) \qquad (9)
$$

Equation (7) can now be expressed as

$$
C(s) = (c_1 + c_2) \frac{u^2}{q_p} [N(s + q_p - u) - N(s - u)]
$$
$$
+ c_2 \left(\frac{\bar{x}}{2} - \frac{q_p + u}{2} - s \right) \qquad (10)
$$

To find the optimal s_o we compare the costs $C(s + u)$ with $C(s)$, etc., which eventually leads to

$$
g(s_o - u) \leqq \frac{c_2}{c_1 + c_2} \leqq g(s_o) \qquad (11)
$$

where

$$
g(s) = \frac{W(s + q_p) - W(s)}{q_p/u} \qquad (12)
$$

The General Case for Any s

The results that have just been obtained can readily be extended to the case for which the reorder point s is negative.

Let the definitions of the functions $W(S)$ of equation (5) and $N(B)$ of equation (9) be extended to negative values of their arguments. Namely, let

$$
W(S) = N(S) = 0 \qquad S < 0 \qquad (13)
$$

Equations (7) and (10) then also hold for negative s. Thus equation (10) gives the total cost of the system for any s and equation (11) gives the general condition for finding the optimal s.

Example 13–2a

In a reorder-point system the prescribed lot size is 6 units. The reviewing-period is 1 week. The probability distribution of demand during the reviewing period is $P(0) = 0.05$, $P(2) = 0.24$, $P(4) = 0.38$, $P(6) = 0.21$, and $P(8) = 0.12$. The unit carrying cost is $c_1 = \$5$ per week. We wish to find the optimal reorder point for three possible unit costs of shortage $c_2 = \$5$, $c_2 = \$50$, and $c_2 = \$100$.

To find s_o Table 13–2a is prepared. The pertinent values of $c_2/(c_1 + c_2)$ are $0.5, 0.909$, and 0.952. Hence by equation (11) the corresponding optimal reorder points are $-2, 2$, and 4.

TABLE 13–2a

Values of $W(s)$ and $g(s)$ of Equations (5) and (12) for Example 13–2a

x, s	$P(x)$	$\dfrac{P(x)}{x}$	$\displaystyle\sum_{s+u}^{\infty} \dfrac{P(x)}{x}$	$R(s)$	$G(s)$	$W(s)$	$g(s)$
-8	0.					0.	0.
-6	0.					0.	0.105
-4	0.					0.	0.347
-2	0.					0.	0.653
0	0.05		0.265	0.315	0.315	0.315	0.877
2	0.24	0.120	0.145	0.410	0.725	1.040	0.968
4	0.38	0.095	0.050	0.195	0.920	1.960	0.995
6	0.21	0.035	0.015	0.065	0.985	2.945	1.000
8	0.12	0.015	0.	0.015	1.000	3.945	1.000
10	0.	0.	0.	0.	1.000	4.945	1.000

Continuous Units

We shall now extend the results to systems with continuous units in which the density of demand is $f(x)$. As in Section 13–1 the probability density of Q (the amount in inventory at the beginning of each reviewing period) is

$$h(Q) = 1/q_p \qquad s \leq Q \leq s + q_p \qquad (14)$$

The expected average amount in inventory during a reviewing period can be found as an immediate extension of equations (2), (3), and (4), namely,

$$I_1(Q) = \int_0^Q \left(Q - \frac{x}{2}\right) f(x)\, dx + \int_Q^\infty \frac{Q^2}{2x} f(x)\, dx$$

$$= \int_0^Q (Q - y) m(y)\, dy = \int_0^Q \int_0^z m(y)\, dy\, dz = \int_0^Q M(z)\, dz = T(Q) \qquad (15)$$

where $m(y)$ is as in equation 10–1(12) and $M(z)$ is the cumulative distribution of y.

Similarly, by equation (6), and noting equation (15),

$$I_2(Q) = \int_Q^\infty (y - Q)m(y)\, dy = T(Q) + \bar{y} - Q \tag{16}$$

Hence, for $s \geqq 0$, in analogy with equations (7), (8), and (9), the expected total cost of the system is

$$
\begin{aligned}
C(s) &= \int_s^{s+q_p} [c_1 I_1(Q) + C_2 I_2(Q)] h(Q)\, dQ \\
&= \int_s^{s+q_p} [(c_1 + c_2)T(Q) + c_2(\bar{y} - Q)] \frac{1}{q_p}\, dQ \\
&= (c_1 + c_2) \frac{1}{q_p} \int_s^{s+q_p} T(Q)\, dQ + c_2(\bar{y} - \bar{Q}) \\
&= (c_1 + c_2) \frac{K(s + q_p) - K(s)}{q_p} + c_2 \left(\frac{\bar{x}}{2} - \frac{q_p}{2} - s \right)
\end{aligned}
\tag{17}
$$

where, by equation (15),

$$K(S) = \int_0^S T(Q)\, dQ = \int_0^S \int_0^Q \int_0^z m(y)\, dy\, dz\, dQ \tag{18}$$

But equation (17) also holds for $s \leqq 0$ if we define

$$T(S) = K(S) = 0 \qquad S \leqq 0 \tag{19}$$

Differentiation of equation (17), etc., leads to the solution

$$g(s_o) = \frac{c_2}{c_1 + c_2} \tag{20}$$

where

$$g(s) = \frac{T(s + q_p) - T(s)}{q_p} \tag{21}$$

Example 13–2b

The probability density of demand during the reviewing period is

$$f(x) = 6x(1 - x) \qquad 0 \leqq x \leqq 1 \tag{22}$$

An (s, q_p) policy is employed. The numerical values of the units of carrying cost and shortage cost are equal. What are the optimal reorder points for lot sizes of 0.1 and 2.0?

For the probability density of equation (22) the mean demand is $\bar{x} = 0.5$. The corresponding equivalent density is

$$m(y) = \int_y^1 \frac{6x(1-x)}{x} \, dx = 3(1-y)^2 \qquad 0 \le y \le 1 \qquad (23)$$

where, as expected, the mean equivalent demand is $\bar{y} = 0.25$. The functions $T(y)$ and $K(y)$ of equation (18) can readily be computed. They are

$$T(y) = \begin{cases} 0 & y \le 0 \\ 1.5y^2 - y^3 + 0.25y^4 & 0 \le y \le 1 \\ y - 0.25 & y \ge 1 \end{cases} \qquad (24)$$

and

$$K(y) = \begin{cases} 0 & y \le 0 \\ 0.5y^3 - 0.25y^4 + 0.05y^5 & 0 \le y \le 1 \\ 0.5y^2 - 0.25y + 0.05 & y \ge 1 \end{cases} \qquad (25)$$

We can now find the function $g(s)$ of equation (21) for any value of q_p. For $q_p = 0.1$ we have

$$g(s) = \begin{cases} 0 & s \le 0.1 \\ \begin{aligned} &15(s + 0.1)^2 - 10(s + 0.1)^3 \\ &\qquad + 2.5(s + 0.1)^4 \end{aligned} & -0.1 \le s \le 0 \\ \begin{aligned} &15(s + 0.1)^2 - 10(s + 0.1)^3 \\ &\qquad + 2.5(s + 0.1)^4 \\ &\qquad - (15s^2 - 10s^3 + 2.5s^4) \end{aligned} & 0 \le s \le 0.9 \\ \begin{aligned} &10(s + 0.1) \; - 2.5 \\ &\qquad - (15s^2 - 10s^3 + 2.5s^4) \end{aligned} & 0.9 \le s \le 1 \\ 1 & s \ge 1 \end{cases} \qquad (26)$$

It can be readily ascertained that $g(s)$ is an increasing function.* But $g(0) = 0.14025$, $g(0.9) = 0.99975$, and $c_2/(c_1 + c_2) = 0.5$. Hence to find s_o [using equation (20)] we have to solve

$$15[(s + 0.1)^2 - s_o^2] - 10[(s + 0.1)^3 - s_o^3] + 2.5[(s_o + 0.1)^4 - s_o^4]$$

$$= s_o^3 - 2.85s_o^2 + 2.71s_o + 0.14025 = 0.5 \quad (27)$$

This gives the solution $s_o = 0.155$. The corresponding minimum cost, by equations (17) and (25), is $C_o = 0.156c_1$.

* This can also be concluded from equation (20).

For $q_p = 2.0$ we have

$$g(s) = \begin{cases} 0 & s \leqq -2 \\ 0.75(s+2)^2 - 0.5(s+2)^3 + 0.125(s+2)^4 & -2 \leqq s \leqq -1 \\ 0.5(s+2) - 0.125 & 1 \leqq s \leqq 0 \\ 0.5(s+2) - 0.125 - (0.75s^2 - 0.5s^3 + 2.5s^4) & 0 \leqq s \leqq 1 \\ 1 & s \geqq 1 \end{cases} \quad (28)$$

Here $g(-1) = 0.375$ and $g(0) = 0.875$. Hence to find s_o we have to solve

$$0.5(s_o + 2) - 0.125 = 0.5 \quad (29)$$

This gives $s_o = -0.75$. The corresponding minimum cost is $C_o = 0.519c_1$.

THE PROBABILISTIC REORDER-POINT–LOT-SIZE SYSTEM

13-3   In the probabilistic reorder-point–lot-size system we have to determine both the optimal reorder point s_o and the optimal lot size q_o. This is a type $(1, 2, 3)$ system with unit costs c_1 and c_2 of dimensions $[\$]/[Q][T]$ and c_3 of dimension $[\$]$. As in Sections 13–1 and 13–2 we shall consider discrete units first and then continuous units.

An immediate extension of equations 13–1(4), 13–1(5), and 13–2(10) gives the expected total cost of the reorder-point–lot-size system:

$$C(s, q) = (c_1 + c_2) \frac{u^2}{q} [N(s + q - u) - N(s - u)]$$

$$+ c_2 \left(\frac{\bar{x}}{2} - \frac{q+u}{2} - s \right) + \frac{c_3[1 - (u/q)V(q - u)]}{w_p} \quad (1)$$

where

$$N(B) = \sum_{S=0}^{B} W(S) = \sum_{S=0}^{B} \sum_{z=0}^{S} G(z) = \sum_{S=0}^{B} \sum_{z=0}^{S} \sum_{y=0}^{z} K(y) \quad (2)$$

where $K(y)$ is a probability distribution equivalent to $P(x)$ [as in equation 10–1(26)], and where

$$V(S) = \sum_{z=0}^{S} F(z) = \sum_{z=0}^{S} \sum_{x=0}^{z} P(x) \quad (3)$$

By equations 13–2(11) and 13–2(12), for any lot size q the corresponding optimal reorder point $s_o{}^q$ can be determined from

$$g(s_o{}^q - u, q) \leqq \frac{c_2}{c_1 + c_2} \leqq g(s_o{}^q, q) \quad (4)$$

where

$$g(s, q) = \frac{W(s + q) - W(s)}{q/u} \quad (5)$$

and where the function W is as in equation (2).

We shall now develop a means for finding the optimal lot size $q_o{}^s$ which corresponds to a given reorder point s. From equation (1) for any q,

$$C(s, q + u) - C(s, q)$$

$$= (c_1 + c_2)u^2\left\{\left[\frac{N(s + q)}{q + u} - \frac{N(s + q - u)}{q}\right] - N(s - u)\left(\frac{1}{q + u} - \frac{1}{q}\right)\right\}$$

$$- c_2\left(\frac{q + u}{2} - \frac{q}{2}\right) - \frac{c_3 u}{w_p}\left[\frac{V(q)}{q + u} - \frac{V(q - u)}{q}\right]$$

$$= (c_1 + c_2)u^2\left[\frac{qW(s + q) - uN(s + q - u)}{q(q + u)} + \frac{N(s - u)u}{q(q + u)}\right]$$

$$- c_2\frac{u}{2} - \frac{c_3 u}{w_p}\frac{qF(q) - uV(q - u)}{q/(q - u)} \qquad (6)$$

$$= \frac{(c_1 + c_2)u^2[qW(s + q) - uN(s + q - u) + uN(s - u)]}{q(q + u)}$$
$$ \quad - (c_3 u/w_p)\sum xP(x)$$

$$- \frac{c_2 u}{2}$$

$$= u\left[\frac{(c_1 + c_2)uA(s, q) - (c_3/w_p)B(q)}{q(q + u)} - \frac{c_2}{2}\right]$$

$$= u\left[D(s, q) - \frac{c_2}{2}\right]$$

where

$$A(s, q) = qW(s + q) - uN(s + q - u) + uN(s - u)$$

$$= \sum_{y=0}^{s+q}(y - s)G(y) + \sum_{y=0}^{s}(s - y)G(y) = \sum_{y=\max(0, s+u)}^{s+q}(y - s)G(y) \quad (7)$$

where

$$B(q) = \sum_{x=0}^{q} xP(x) \qquad (8)$$

and where

$$D(s, q) = \frac{(c_1 + c_2)uA(s, q) - (c_3/w_p)B(q)}{q(q + u)} \qquad (9)$$

Similarly, by replacing q with $q - u$ in equation (6), we have

$$C(s, q) - C(s, q - u) = u[D(s, q - u) - c_2/2] \qquad (10)$$

Hence, for a given s, the optimal lot size $q_o{}^s$ can be derived from

$$D(s, q_o{}^s - u) \leqq c_2/2 \leqq D(s, q_o{}^s) \qquad (11)$$

This result can also be expressed in another form which is somewhat similar to equation 13–1(8):

$$J(s, q_o{}^s - u) \leqq 2c_3/c_1 w_p \leqq J(s, q_o{}^s) \tag{12}$$

where

$$J(s, q) = R(q)\left[1 - L(s, q)\frac{c_1 + c_2}{c_1}\right] \tag{13}$$

where $R(q)$ is as in equation 13–1(9), namely,

$$R(q) = q(q + u)\Big/ \sum_{x=0}^{q} xP(x) \tag{14}$$

and where

$$L(s, q) = 1 - \frac{2uA(s, q)}{q(q + u)} \tag{15}$$

We would expect equation (12) to reduce to equation 13–1(8) when $s = x_{\max} - u$. And indeed it will, for $A(x_{\max} - u, q) = (q/u)(q + u)/2$.

Let $s_o{}^*$ and $q_o{}^*$ designate values of the reorder point and the lot size satisfying the simultaneous equations (4) and (12). It is important to note that these values are not unique. Hence a pair of values satisfying equations (4) and (12) may not necessarily give the solution of the system. This is illustrated in Example 13–3a. Let us therefore refer to these values as locally optimal values.

The following search procedure is suggested for finding one pair of locally optimal values of $s_o{}^*$ and $q_o{}^*$. Let $q_1, s_2, q_3, s_4, \ldots$ designate successive values of lot sizes and reorder points. For any given lot size q_i the corresponding locally optimal order level s_{i+1} can be derived from equation (4). Similarly for any given s_j the corresponding locally optimal lot size q_{j+1} can be computed from equation (12). The search stops when $s_{i+1} = s_{i-1}$ or when $q_{j+1} = q_{j-1}$. For the initial lot size we can use, say, the solution of the system of Section 5–1:

$$q_1 \approx \sqrt{2\frac{\bar{x}}{w_p}\frac{c_3}{\bar{c}}} = \sqrt{2\frac{\bar{x}}{w_p}c_3\frac{c_1 + c_2}{c_1 c_2}} \tag{16}$$

Different initial lot sizes may lead to different locally optimal values of $s_o{}^*$ and $q_o{}^*$.

Example 13–3a

In a reorder-point–lot-size system the reviewing period is 1 week. The probability distribution of the weekly demand is $P(0) = 0.05$, $P(2) = 0.24$, $P(4) = 0.38$, $P(6) = 0.21$, and $P(8) = 0.12$. The carrying cost is \$5 per unit per week, the shortage cost is \$50 per unit per week, and the replenishing cost is \$40. We wish to find the optimal reorder point and the optimal lot size.

This example is an extension of Example 13–2a. (The replenishing cost has been chosen so that some of the results of Example 13–2a can be used here.) We have $\bar{x} = 4.22$, $w_p = 1$, $c_1 = \$5$, $c_2 = \$50$, $c_3 = \$40$, and $u = 2$. By equation (16), $q_1 \approx \sqrt{74.272} \approx 8$. The corresponding reorder point s_2 can now be found using equation (4). From Table 13–2a and equation (5) we find that $g(0, 8) = 0.9075$, $g(2, 8) = 0.9760$, and $g(4, 8) = 0.9962$. But $c_2/(c_1 + c_2) = 0.909$. Hence equation (4) gives the result $s_2 = 2$.

Equation (12) can now be used to find q_3. First the value of $2c_3/c_1 w_p$ is computed and found to be 16. Next, we find that $A(2, 8)$ of equation (7) is 19.78. Hence $L(2, 8)$ of equation (15) is 0.011. In addition, by equation (14),

TABLE 13–3

The Expected Total Cost in Example 13–3a

s \ q	2	4	6	8	10	12
-2	143.500	106.025	81.717	67.762	60.100	56.658
0	78.150	63.225	53.583	48.750	46.890	47.317
2	57.900	53.700	50.017	48.575	48.750	50.533
4	59.100	58.475	56.533	55.962	56.660	58.792
6	67.450	67.650	65.983	65.550	66.330	68.517

$R(8) = 80/4.22$. Therefore $J(2, 8)$ of equation (13) is 16.66, a quantity larger than $2c_3/c_1 w_p$. Hence, to satisfy equation (12), we try $q = 6$. We find that $A(2, 6) = 11.78$, $L(2, 6) = 0.11/6$, $R(6) = 48/3.26$, and $J(2, 6) = 11.75 < 16$. Hence $s_2 = 2$ implies $q_3 = 8$. Now, since $q_1 = 8$ and also $q_3 = 8$, our search is terminated. The locally optimal values are $s_o{}^* = 2$ and $q_o{}^* = 8$.

The expected total cost of the system, for various reorder points and lot sizes, is given in Table 13–3. We note that indeed for $s_o{}^* = 2$ and $q_o{}^* = 8$ equations (4) and (12) are satisfied. Yet this pair of values does not give the solution of the system. The optimal values are $s_o = 0$, $q_o = 10$.

The Continuous Case

An immediate extension of the results of Sections 13–1 and 13–2 leads to the cost equation of the probabilistic reorder-point–lot-size system for continuous units. Let $f(x)$ be the probability density of demand. Then from equations 13–2(17), 13–1(4), and 13–1(13) we obtain

$$C(s, q) = \frac{c_1 + c_2}{q} \int_s^{s+q} T(Q) \, dQ + c_2\left(\frac{\bar{x}}{2} - \frac{q}{2} - s\right) + \frac{c_3[1 - (1/q)V(q)]}{w_p}$$

$$(17)$$

where

$$T(Q) = \begin{cases} \displaystyle\int_0^Q M(z)\, dz = \int_0^Q \int_0^z m(y)\, dy\, dz \\[2mm] \qquad = \displaystyle\int_0^Q \int_0^z \int_y^\infty \frac{f(x)}{x}\, dx\, dy\, dz & Q \geqq 0 \quad (18) \\[4mm] 0 & Q \leqq 0 \end{cases}$$

and where

$$V(q) = \int_0^q F(y)\, dy = \int_0^q \int_0^y f(x)\, dx\, dy \tag{19}$$

Let $s_o{}^q$ designate an optimal reorder point corresponding to some given lot size q. Similarly, let $q_o{}^s$ designate an optimal lot size for some given reorder point s. The quantity $s_o{}^q$ can be determined as in Section 13-2, namely,

$$g(s_o{}^q, q) = \frac{c_2}{c_1 + c_2} \tag{20}$$

where

$$g(s, q) = \frac{T(s + q) - T(s)}{q} \tag{21}$$

To find $q_o{}^s$ we differentiate $C(s, q)$ of equation (17) with respect to q.

$$\begin{aligned}
\frac{\partial C(s, q)}{\partial q} &= (c_1 + c_2)\left[\frac{1}{q} T(s + q) - \frac{1}{q^2}\int_s^{s+q} T(Q)\, dQ\right] - \frac{c_2}{2} \\
&\qquad\qquad - \frac{c_3}{w_p}\left[\frac{1}{q} F(q) - \frac{1}{q^2} V(q)\right] \\
&= \frac{1}{q^2}(c_1 + c_2)\int_0^{s+q}(z - s)M(z)\, dz + \int_0^s (s - z)M(z)\, dz \\
&\qquad\qquad\qquad\qquad - \frac{c_2}{2} - \frac{c_3}{w_p q^2}\int_0^q xf(x)\, dx \\
&= \frac{1}{q^2}\left[(c_1 + c_2)\int_{\max(0,s)}^{s+q}(z - s)M(z)\, dz - \frac{c_3}{w_p}\int_0^q xf(x)\, dx\right] - \frac{c_2}{2} \\
&= \frac{1}{q^2}\left[(c_1 + c_2)A(s, q) - \frac{c_3}{w_p} B(q)\right] - \frac{c_2}{2} \tag{22}
\end{aligned}$$

where

$$A(s, q) = \int_{\max(0,s)}^{s+q}(z - s)M(z)\, dz \tag{23}$$

and where

$$B(q) = \int_0^q xf(x)\, dx \tag{24}$$

The quantity $q_o{}^s$ can be found by solving $\partial C/\partial q = 0$. This leads to

$$(q_o{}^s)^2 = 2\left[\frac{c_1 + c_2}{c_2} A(s, q_o{}^s) - \frac{c_3}{w_p c_2} B(q_o{}^s)\right] \tag{25}$$

or to

$$\frac{(q_o{}^s)^2}{B(q_o{}^s)} = \frac{2c_3}{c_1 w_p} \Bigg/ \left[2\left(1 + \frac{c_2}{c_1}\right)\frac{A(s, q_o{}^s)}{(q_o{}^s)^2} - \frac{c_2}{c_1}\right] \tag{26}$$

Note that when $s = x_{\max}$, then $A(s, q) = q^2/2$ and equation (26) reduces to equation 13–1(18), as we might have expected.

Equations (20) and (25) [or (26)] can be used to find the locally optimal $s_o{}^*$ and $q_o{}^*$ in a manner analogous to that for the discrete units. Once again, it is important to note that equation (25) [or (26)] may have more than one solution or that q_o may equal zero.

Example 13–3b

In a probabilistic reorder-point–lot-size system, the amounts in inventory are reviewed every 2 weeks. The probability density of demand during a 2-week period is given by

$$f(x) = 6x(1 - x) \qquad 0 \leq x \leq 1 \tag{27}$$

The carrying cost is \$5 per unit per week, the shortage cost is \$5 per unit per week, and the replenishing cost is \$20. We wish to determine the optimal lot size q_o and the optimal reorder point s_o.

Here $w_p = 2$, $\bar{x} = \frac{1}{2}$, $x_{\max} = 1$, $c_1 = \$5$, $c_2 = \$5$, and $c_3 = \$20$. This example is similar to Examples 13–1b and 13–2b. It is an extension of Example 13–2b for a type $(1, 2, 3)$ system. The numerical values of w_p and c_3 have been chosen so that some of the results of Example 13–2b could be used here.

We first compute the value of q_1 using equation (16). This gives $q_1 = \sqrt{2(0.5/2)20(5 + 5)/(5 \times 5)} = 2$. We next compute s_2 using equation (20). But this has already been done in Example 13–2b where, for $q = 2$, we found that $s_2 = -0.75$. Now q_3 is computed, using, say, equation (25). This equation reduces to

$$(q_o{}^s)^2 = 2\left[\frac{5 + 5}{5} A(s, q_o{}^s) - \frac{20}{2 \times 5} B(q_o{}^s)\right]$$

$$= 4[A(s, q_o{}^s) - B(q_o{}^s)] \tag{28}$$

The specific form of the function A of equation (23) now depends on whether $s + q$ is smaller or larger than 1. Similarly, the function B, of equation (24), depends on whether q is smaller or larger than 1. Since

$q_1 = 2$, we can first assume that $-0.75 + q_3 \geq 1$ or that $q_3 \geq 1.75$. From equations (23) and 13–2(23) for $s \leq 0$ and $s + q \geq 1$, we obtain

$$A(s, q) = \int_0^{s+q} (z - s) M(z) \, dz = \int_0^1 (z - s) \int_0^z m(y) \, dy \, dz + \int_1^{s+q} (z - s) \, dz$$

$$= \int_0^1 (z - s) \int_0^z 3(1 - y)^2 \, dy \, dz + \int_1^{s+q} (z - s) \, dz \qquad (29)$$

$$= \frac{q^2}{2} - \frac{s^2}{2} + \frac{s}{4} - \frac{1}{20}$$

And from equation (24), for $q = 1$, we obtain

$$B(q) = \int_0^q x f(x) \, dx = \int_0^1 x f(x) \, dx = \bar{x} = \tfrac{1}{2} \qquad (30)$$

Substitution of the results of equations (29) and (30) in equation (28) leads to the following relation for $s \leq 0$ and $s + q_o^s \geq 1$:

$$(q_o^s)^2 = 4 \left[\frac{(q_o^s)^2}{2} - \frac{s^2}{2} + \frac{s}{4} - \frac{1}{20} - \frac{1}{2} \right]$$

or

$$(q_o^s)^2 = 2s^2 - s + \tfrac{11}{5} \qquad (31)$$

Hence for $s_2 = -0.75$ we obtain $q_3 = \sqrt{163/40} = 2.0186$. To find s_4 we use equation (20). The function g depends on the function T of equation (18). For $s_o^q \leq 0$ and for $s_o^q + q \geq 1$ we can readily find [e.g., equation 13–2(24)] that $T(s_o^q) = 0$ and $T(s_o^q + q) = s_o^q + q - \tfrac{1}{4}$. Hence $g(s_o^q, q) = (s_o^q + q - \tfrac{1}{4})/q = c_2/(c_1 + c_2) = \tfrac{1}{2}$, or

$$s_o^q = \frac{1}{4} - \frac{q'}{2} \qquad (32)$$

so that if $q_3 = 2.0186$, then $s_4 = \tfrac{1}{4} - 1.0093 = -0.7593$. It is not really necessary to continue the computations for q_5, s_6, etc. In the present case we can rather easily solve the simultaneous equations (31) and (32). These lead immediately to the locally optimum values of $q_o^* = \sqrt{4.15} = 2.0374$ and $s_o^* = -0.7687$.

It should be recalled that our solution is based on the assumption that $s_o^* \leq 0$ and that $s_o^* + q_o^* \geq 1$. We leave it to the reader to show that the results obtained indeed give the optimal value of the lot size and the reorder point [problem 13–4(14)].

13-4   PROBLEMS

1. Examine the adequacy of equation 13–0(1) for deterministic systems.
2. Verify the result given by equation 13–1(8).

3. (a) Show that the function $R(q)$ of equation 13–1(9) is an increasing function when $q \geq x_{max}$

(b) Show that this function is not necessarily increasing when $q < x_{max}$.

4. Analyze Example 13–1b when the demand density is

$$f(x) = 12(x - \tfrac{1}{2})^2 \qquad 0 \leq x \leq 1 \qquad (1)$$

5. Analyze the probabilistic lot-size system of Section 13–1 when $w_p = 0$.

6. Equation 13–2(11) suggests that there exists a probability distribution whose cumulative distribution is the function g. Derive this probability distribution and use it to find an inventory system similar to that of Section 8–3 which is equivalent to the probabilistic reorder-point system.

7. Examine the system of Section 13–2 when $P(0) = q$, $P(u) = p = 1 - q$ and when u approaches zero.

8. Derive equation 13–3(12) from equation 13–3(11).

9. Compare the cost equation 13–3(1) with the cost equation 5–1(1) by assuming $P(0) = 0$, $P(u) = 1$, $r = u/w_p$, etc.

10. Solve the order-level–lot-size system of Section 5–1 for discrete units [e.g., problem 5–5(2)] by using the methods of Section 13–3.

11. Solve the system of Section 13–3 when c_1 is infinite.

12. Find the solution of the probabilistic reorder-point–lot-size system when $w_p = 1$, $P(0) = 0.08$, $P(10) = 0.10$, $P(20) = 0.20$, $P(30) = 0.30$, $P(40) = 0.16$, $P(50) = 0.10$, $P(60) = 0.06$, $c_1 = 1$, $c_2 = 10$, and $c_3 = 25$. Show that the minimum expected cost of the system is 49.35.

13. Solve an extension of Example 13.1a when the reorder point is not prescribed but has to be determined. Assume that the unit shortage cost is $50 per week.

14. In Example 13–3b show that $s_o = -0.7687$ and $q_o = 2.0374$ give the minimum expected total cost of the system.

15. In a probabilistic lot-size system demands may be assumed to be those in Table 1–5. The carrying cost is $1 per pound per week, the replenishing cost $30.

(a) Find the optimal lot size.

(b) Check your results by simulating the system for various lot sizes, using the data for Table 1–5.

16. Extend the results of this chapter to systems in which there is a replenishment cost of c_3 for every lot size scheduled.

Chapter 14

Probabilistic Reorder-Point–
Lot-Size Systems with Leadtime

14–0   The extension of the results of the previous chapter to systems with significant leadtime turns out to be a rather simple task. This extension will be carried out in this section and will cover all the systems of Chapter 13. In Sections 14–1, 14–2, and 14–3 we shall use these results and then also introduce an alternate approach to the analysis of certain (z, q) systems.

The Equivalence of Reorder-Point–Lot-Size Systems with and
*   without Leadtime*

Consider Figure 14–0 in which the inventory fluctuations of a reorder-point–lot-size system with leadtime are given. In this figure leadtime is equal in length to two reviewing periods, but the results that follow hold for any leadtime.

Let the demand during leadtime be v and let its probability distribution be $E(v)$. Let Q be the amount on hand and on order at the beginning of each reviewing period. The fluctuations of Q in this system are exactly the same as the fluctuations of Q in a similar system without leadtime (e.g., compare Figures 13–0 and 14–0). Thus the distribution $H(Q)$, by equation 13–0(1), is

$$H(Q) = \frac{1}{q/u} = \frac{u}{q} \qquad Q = z + u, z + 2u, \ldots, z + q \qquad (1)$$

For the continuous case, by equation 13–1(11), the probability density $h(Q)$ is

$$h(Q) = 1/q \qquad z \leqq Q \leqq z + q \qquad (2)$$

The expected number of replenishments per unit time, I_3, is therefore identical with this value in a similar system without leadtime. Thus such equations as 13–1(4), 13–1(5), 13–1(13), etc., apply both to systems without leadtime and with leadtime.

For the values of the expected average inventories and shortages, I_1 and I_2, we can also use the results of Chapter 13. This can be done rather simply

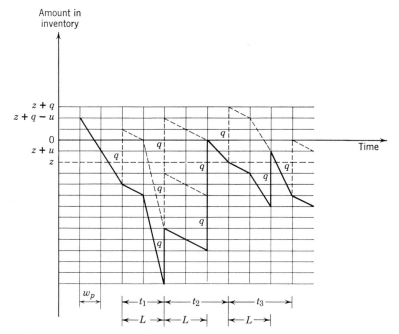

Figure 14–0   The probabilistic reorder-point–lot-size system with leadtime.

using equivalent relations. Let w be an instantaneous demand equivalent to the uniform demand x during the reviewing period. And let y be a demand equal to the sum of the demands of w and v:

$$y = w + v \tag{3}$$

We can then regard the system with leadtime as if leadtime were zero, but the demand during a reviewing period is y. This approach has been used in Section 10–2 and applies again here. Thus, to solve the reorder-point–lot-size systems with leadtime, we can use all the results of Chapter 13 for I_1 and I_2. We only have to replace s by z and the demand x by the demand y of equation (3). Of course, the appropriate distribution functions have to be used, and we must remember that $\bar{x}/2$ should be replaced by $\bar{x}/2 + \bar{v}$. Illustrative examples are given in the following sections.

THE PROBABILISTIC LOT-SIZE SYSTEM WITH LEADTIME

14–1 This system is an immediate extension of the system of Section 13–1. Drawing on the comments of Section 14–0 and using the results of Section 13–1, we readily reach the following conclusions.

For discrete units, extending equation 13–1(2), we have

$$z_p = x_{\max} + v_{\max} - u \tag{1}$$

Let $P_e(y)$ be the probability distribution of the equivalent demand y described in Section 14–0. Then

$$
\begin{aligned}
I_1 &= \sum_{Q=z_p+u}^{z_p+q} \sum_{y=0}^{y_{\max}} (Q - y)P_e(y)H(Q) \\
&= z_p + \frac{u+q}{2} - \bar{y} = x_{\max} + v_{\max} - u + \frac{u+q}{2} - \left(\frac{\bar{x}}{2} + \bar{v}\right) \tag{2} \\
&= \frac{q}{2} + x_{\max} + v_{\max} - \frac{\bar{x}+u}{2} - \bar{v}
\end{aligned}
$$

The expected total-cost equation, by analogy with equation 13–1(7), is therefore

$$C(q) = \frac{c_1 q}{2} - \frac{c_3 u V(q-u)}{qw_p} + c_1\left(x_{\max} + v_{\max} - \frac{\bar{x}+u}{2} - \bar{v}\right) + \frac{c_3}{w_p} \tag{3}$$

where the function V is as in equation 13–1(6). Since this cost differs from the cost equation 13–1(7) only by a constant, the solution given by equation 13–1(8) applies here too.

In a similar way we obtain the results for continuous units. Extending equation 13–1(10), we have

$$z_p = x_{\max} + v_{\max} \tag{4}$$

From equation 13–1(12) we obtain

$$I_1 = z_p + \frac{q}{2} - \left(\frac{\bar{x}}{2} + \bar{v}\right) = \frac{q}{2} + x_{\max} + v_{\max} - \frac{\bar{x}}{2} - \bar{v} \tag{5}$$

The expected total cost, by equation 13–1(15), is

$$C(q) = \frac{c_1 q}{2} - \frac{c_3 V(q)}{qw_p} + c_1\left(x_{\max} + v_{\max} - \frac{\bar{x}}{2} - \bar{v}\right) + \frac{c_3}{w_p} \tag{6}$$

where the function V is defined by equation 13–1(14). The optimal q_o can now be found from equations 13–1(18), 13–1(19), etc.

Continuous Reviewing

Let us now consider a special case of the system for continuous units when $w_p = 0$. In this system, whenever the amount on hand and on order is exactly z_p, an order is placed for q units. These units are added to stock after a leadtime of L.

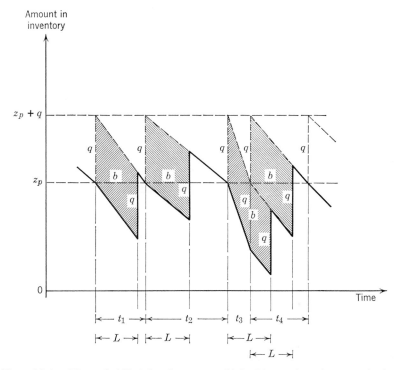

Figure 14–1a   The probabilistic lot-size system with leadtime and continuous reviewing.

The inventory fluctuations in this system can be approximated as in Figure 14–1a. During a typical scheduling period t (say, t_3) the amount on hand and on order will be $z_p + q$ at the beginning of the period and z_p at the end of the period, so that on the average the amount on hand and on order is $z_p + q/2$. The expected average amount in inventory can then be expressed as

$$I_1 = z_p + \frac{q}{2} - \frac{b}{\bar{t}} \tag{7}$$

where b is an area covered by the amounts on order and $\bar{t}$ is the average length of a scheduling period. The area b can be seen to be

$$b = Lq \tag{8}$$

Let r be the average rate of demand. Then

$$\bar{t} = q/r \tag{9}$$

And since $w_p = 0$, then

$$z_p = v_{max} \tag{10}$$

Hence equation (7) can be rewritten as

$$I_1 = v_{max} + \frac{q}{2} - \frac{Lq}{q/r} = v_{max} + \frac{q}{2} - \bar{v} \tag{11}$$

[As a check we note that equation (5) reduces to equation (11), since $x_{max} = 0$ and $\bar{x} = 0$ when $w_p = 0$.]

The expected number of replenishments per unit time is

$$I_3 = \frac{1}{\bar{t}} = \frac{r}{q} \tag{12}$$

[To check this result, consider the system of Section 13–1 with a very small reviewing period w_p. For such a system the function F of equation 13–1(14) is given by $F(y) = 1$ for $y \geqq rw_p$, and $F(y) = 0$ for $y < rw_p$. Hence, by equation 13–1(14), $V(q) = q - rw_p$, and by equation 13–1(13), $g = rw_p/q$, so that indeed, by equation 13–1(4), $I_3 = r/q$.]

The expected total cost of the probabilistic lot-size system with continuous reviewing is then

$$C(q) = c_1\left(v_{max} + \frac{q}{2} - \bar{v}\right) + \frac{c_3 r}{q} \tag{13}$$

The optimal lot size is then

$$q_o = \sqrt{2rc_3/c_1} \tag{14}$$

and the corresponding minimum expected total cost is

$$C_o = \sqrt{2rc_1c_3} + c_1(v_{max} - \bar{v}) \tag{15}$$

The Discrete Case and $x_{max} = u$

The continuous reviewing system, which has just been analyzed, has its analog in a discrete system with a reviewing period w_p in which $x_{max} = u$. The graphical representation of the system is given in Figure 14–1b.

The amounts on hand and on order at the beginning of each reviewing period fluctuate between $z_p + u$ and $z_p + q$. Hence the average amount on

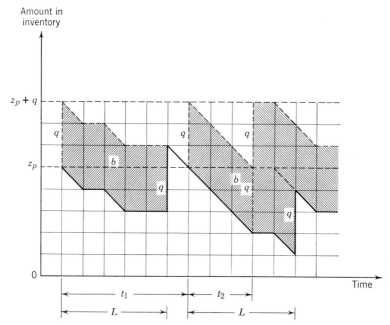

Amount in
inventory

Figure 14-1b   The probabilistic lot-size system with leadtime, discrete units, and
$x_{max} = u$.

hand and on order is $(z_p + u + z_p + q)/2 - \bar{x}/2$. From this we subtract
$b/\bar{t}$, the average amount on order. Hence

$$I_1 = \frac{z_p + u + z_p + q}{2} - \frac{\bar{x}}{2} - \frac{b}{\bar{t}}$$

$$= z_p + \frac{u + q}{2} - \frac{\bar{x}}{2} - \frac{qL}{q/r}$$

$$= z_p + \frac{u + q}{2} - \frac{\bar{x}}{2} - \bar{v} \tag{16}$$

$$= z_p + \frac{q}{2} - \bar{v} + \frac{u - \bar{x}}{2}$$

[This result is identical with that of equation (2) for $x_{max} = u$.]
   In this system

$$z_p = x_{max} + v_{max} - u \tag{17}$$

and

$$\bar{x} = rw_p \tag{18}$$

Hence

$$I_1 = v_{max} + \frac{q}{2} - \bar{v} + \frac{u - rw_p}{2} \tag{19}$$

The expected number of replenishments per unit of time is

$$I_3 = \frac{1}{\bar{t}} = \frac{r}{q} \tag{20}$$

Hence the expected total cost of the system is

$$C(q) = c_1\left(v_{max} + \frac{q}{2} - \bar{v} + \frac{u - rw_p}{2}\right) + \frac{c_3 r}{q} \tag{21}$$

[Note that this equation reduces to equation (13) when $u = 0$, since then w_p also equals zero.]

The optimal lot size can then be determined from

$$(q_o - u)q_o \leqq \frac{2rc_3}{c_1} \leqq q_o(q_o + u) \tag{22}$$

THE PROBABILISTIC REORDER-POINT SYSTEM WITH LEADTIME

14–2 The probabilistic reorder-point system without leadtime is described and analyzed in detail in Section 13–2. In particular, for discrete units, the expected total cost is given by equation 13–2(10). On the basis of the remarks of Section 14–0, we can immediately state the expected total cost of a similar system with leadtime. Let $P(x)$ be the probability distribution of demand during the reviewing period and let $E(v)$ be the probability distribution of demand during leadtime. Then

$$C(z) = (c_1 + c_2)\frac{u^2}{q_p}[N(z + q_p - u) - N(z - u)]$$

$$+ c_2\left(\frac{\bar{x}}{2} + \bar{v} - \frac{q_p + u}{2} - z\right) \tag{1}$$

where

$$N(B) = \begin{cases} \sum_{S=0}^{B} W(S) = \sum_{S=0}^{B}\sum_{j=0}^{S}G(j) = \sum_{S=0}^{B}\sum_{j=0}^{S}\sum_{y=0}^{j}R(y) & B = 0, u, 2u, \dots \\ 0 & B < 0 \end{cases} \tag{2}$$

but where now y is defined as in equation 14–0(3). That is, $D(w)$ is a probability distribution equivalent to the distribution $P(x)$, namely,

$$D(w) = \begin{cases} P(0) + \dfrac{u}{2} \displaystyle\sum_{x=u}^{\infty} \dfrac{P(x)}{x} & w = 0 \\[3mm] \dfrac{u}{2} \dfrac{P(w)}{w} + u \displaystyle\sum_{x=w+u}^{\infty} \dfrac{P(x)}{x} & w = u,\, 2u,\, \ldots \end{cases} \tag{3}$$

and

$$R(y) = D(w) * E(v) = \sum_{v=0}^{y} D(y - v)E(v) \tag{4}$$

The solution of the system, by equation 13–2(17), is then

$$g(z_o - u) \leq \frac{c_2}{c_1 + c_2} \leq g(z_o) \tag{5}$$

where

$$g(z) = \frac{W(z + q_p) - W(z)}{q_p} \tag{6}$$

where the function W is defined in equation (2) and where $W(S < 0) = 0$.

The analysis is quite similar for continuous units. Let $f(x)$ be the probability density of demand during the reviewing period, and let $e(v)$ be the probability density of demand during leadtime. Then, by equation 13–2(17), the expected total cost is

$$C(z) = (c_1 + c_2)\frac{[K(z + q_p) - K(z)]}{q_p} + c_2\left(\frac{\bar{x}}{2} + \bar{v} - \frac{q_p}{2} - z\right) \tag{7}$$

where

$$K(S) = \begin{cases} \displaystyle\int_0^{S} T(Q)\, dQ = \int_0^{S}\int_0^{Q}\int_0^{z} m(y)\, dy\, dz\, dQ & S \geq 0 \\[3mm] 0 & S \leq 0 \end{cases} \tag{8}$$

but where y is defined as in equation 14–0(3). That is,

$$d(w) = \int_w^{\infty} \frac{f(x)}{x}\, dx \tag{9}$$

and

$$m(y) = d(w) * e(v) = \int_0^{y} d(y - v)e(v)\, dv \tag{10}$$

Thus by equation 13–2(20) the solution for continuous units is

$$g(z_o) = \frac{c_2}{c_1 + c_2} \tag{11}$$

where

$$g(z) = \frac{T(z + q_p) - T(z)}{q_p} \tag{12}$$

where the function T is defined in equation (8), and where $T(Q \leq 0) = 0$.

Continuous Reviewing

Just as in Section 14–1, it is instructive to consider the special case with continuous units when $w_p = 0$. The inventory fluctuations are similar to those given by Figure 14–1a, but now shortages may occur. Four typical cases corresponding to Figure 14–1a are described in Figure 14–2.

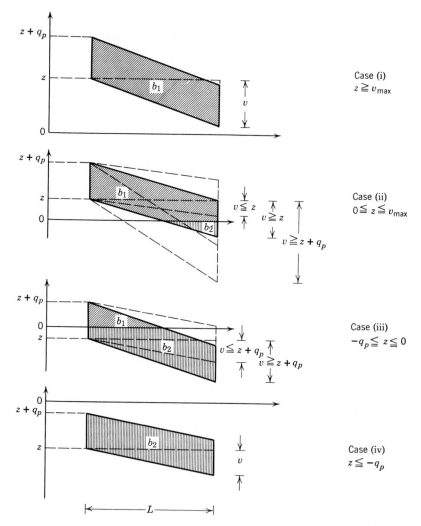

Figure 14–2 Typical cases in the probabilistic reorder-point system with leadtime and continuous reviewing.

In case (i), when $z \geqq v_{max}$, we have essentially the situation of Figure 14–1a and hence, by equations 14–1(7), 14–1(8), 14–1(9), we have

$$I_1 = z + \frac{q_p}{2} - \frac{\bar{b}_1}{\bar{t}} = z + \frac{q_p}{2} - \bar{v} \qquad z \geqq v_{max} \qquad (13)$$

and also

$$I_2 = 0 \qquad z \geqq v_{max} \qquad (14)$$

In case (ii), by analogy with case (i), we have

$$I_1 = z + \frac{q_p}{2} - \frac{\bar{b}_1}{\bar{t}} \qquad 0 \leqq z \leqq v_{max} \qquad (15)$$

and

$$I_2 = \frac{\bar{b}_2}{\bar{t}} \qquad 0 \leqq z \leqq v_{max} \qquad (16)$$

where

$$\bar{b}_1 + \bar{b}_2 = b = q_p L \qquad (17)$$

and where, from Figure 14–2 [case (ii)],

$$\bar{b}_2 = L \left\{ \int_z^{z+q_p} \frac{(v-z)^2}{2v} e(v) \, dv + \int_{z+q_p}^{v_{max}} \left[\frac{(v-z)^2}{2v} - \frac{(v-z-q_p)^2}{2v} \right] e(v) \, dv \right\}$$

$$= L \left\{ \int_z^{v_{max}} \frac{(v-z)^2}{2v} e(v) \, dv - \int_{z+q_p}^{v_{max}} \frac{(v-z-q_p)^2}{2v} e(v) \, dv \right\} \qquad (18)$$

so that

$$I_2 = \frac{\bar{v}}{q_p} \left[\int_z^{v_{max}} \frac{(v-z)^2}{2v} e(v) \, dv - \int_{z+q_p}^{v_{max}} \frac{(v-z-q_p)^2}{2v} e(v) \, dv \right]$$

$$0 \leqq z \leqq v_{max} \qquad (19)$$

In case (iii) the average amount on hand and on order, $I_1{}^*$, is not $z + \frac{1}{2}q_p$, as in cases (i) and (ii), but

$$I_1{}^* = \frac{(z+q_p)^2}{2q_p} \qquad -q_p \leqq z \leqq 0 \qquad (20)$$

Similarly the corresponding average shortage (which includes outstanding orders) is

$$I_2{}^* = \frac{z^2}{2q_p} \qquad -q_p \leqq z \leqq 0 \qquad (21)$$

Hence

$$I_1 = I_1{}^* - \frac{\bar{b}_1}{\bar{t}} = \frac{(z+q_p)^2}{2q_p} - \frac{\bar{b}_1}{\bar{t}} \qquad -q_p \leqq z \leqq 0 \qquad (22)$$

and

$$I_2 = I_2{}^* + \frac{\bar{b}_2}{\bar{t}} \qquad -q_p \leqq z \leqq 0 \qquad (23)$$

where $\bar{b}_1 + \bar{b}_2 = q_p L$ as in equation (17) and where, by Figure 14–2 [case (iii)],

$$\bar{b}_1 = L\left[\int_0^{z+q_p} \left(z + q_p - \frac{v}{2}\right) e(v)\, dv + \int_{z+q_p}^{v_{max}} \frac{(z + q_p)^2}{2v} e(v)\, dv\right]$$

$$-q_p \leqq z \leqq 0 \quad (24)$$

so that

$$I_1 = \frac{(z + q_p)^2}{2q_p} - \frac{\bar{v}}{q}\left[\int_0^{z+q_p} \left(z + q_p - \frac{v}{2}\right) e(v)\, dv + \int_{z+q_p}^{v_{max}} \frac{(z + q_p)^2}{2v} e(v)\, dv\right]$$

$$= \frac{(z + q_p - \bar{v})^2}{2q_p} - \frac{\bar{v}}{q}\int_{z+q_p}^{v_{max}} \frac{(v - z - q_p)^2}{2v} e(v)\, dv \quad (25)$$

Finally, in case (iv),

$$I_1 = 0 \qquad\qquad z \leqq -q_p \quad (26)$$

and, by analogy with equation (13),

$$I_2 = -z - \frac{q_p}{2} + \bar{v} \qquad z \leqq -q_p \quad (27)$$

It is relatively easy to ascertain that equation (17) holds for *all* cases, and that for *all* cases

$$I_1 - I_2 = z + \frac{q_p}{2} - \bar{v} \quad (28)$$

The expected total cost of the system can now be expressed as

$$C(z) = c_1 I_1 + c_2 I_2 = c_1\left(z + \frac{q_p}{2} - \bar{v}\right) + (c_1 + c_2) I_2 \quad (29)$$

Hence we eventually obtain

$$C(z) = c_1\left(z + \frac{q_p}{2} - \bar{v}\right) + (c_1 + c_2)\frac{A(z) - A(z + q_p)}{q_p} \quad (30)$$

where

$$A(p) = \begin{cases} 0 & p \geqq v_{max} \\[2mm] \dfrac{\bar{v}}{2}\displaystyle\int_p^{v_{max}} \frac{(v - p)^2}{v} e(v)\, dv & 0 \leqq p \leqq v_{max} \\[2mm] \dfrac{(\bar{v} - p)^2}{2} & p \leqq 0 \end{cases} \quad (31)$$

It is important to note that the expression for $C(z)$ in equation (30) will not always be identical with that in equation (7). The reason for this difference is discussed in problem 14–4(7). (See also Examples 14–2a and 14–2b.)

The optimal z_o can now be found from

$$D(z_o) = \frac{c_1}{c_1 + c_2} \tag{32}$$

where

$$D(z) = \frac{B(z + q_p) - B(z)}{q_p} \tag{33}$$

and where

$$B(p) = \frac{dA(p)}{dp} = \begin{cases} 0 & p \geq v_{max} \\ -v \int_p^{v_{max}} \frac{v - p}{v} e(v) \, dv & 0 \leq p \leq v_{max} \\ -(v - p) & p \leq 0 \end{cases} \tag{34}$$

When $q_p \geq v_{max}$, the function $D(z)$ is given by

$$D(z) = \begin{cases} 0 & z \geq v_{max} \\ \dfrac{\bar{v}}{q_p} \displaystyle\int_z^{v_{max}} \dfrac{v - z}{v} e(v) \, dv & 0 \leq z \leq v_{max} \\ \dfrac{\bar{v}}{q_p} \left(1 - \dfrac{z}{\bar{v}}\right) & -(q_p - v_{max}) \leq z \leq 0 \\ \dfrac{\bar{v}}{q_p} \left[1 - \dfrac{z}{\bar{v}} - \displaystyle\int_{z+q_p}^{v_{max}} \dfrac{v - z - q_p}{v} e(v) \, dv\right] & \\ & \begin{matrix} -q_p \leq z \leq -(q_p - v_{max}) \\ z \leq -q_p \end{matrix} \\ 1 & \end{cases} \tag{35}$$

But when $q_p \leq v_{max}$, it is given by

$$D(z) = \begin{cases} 0 & z \geq v_{max} \\ \dfrac{\bar{v}}{q_p} \displaystyle\int_z^{v_{max}} \dfrac{v - z}{v} e(v) \, dv & v_{max} - q_p \leq z \leq v_{max} \\ \dfrac{\bar{v}}{q_p} \left[\displaystyle\int_z^{v_{max}} \dfrac{v - z}{v} e(v) \, dv - \displaystyle\int_{z+q_p}^{v_{max}} \dfrac{(v - z - q_p)}{v} e(v) \, dv\right] & \\ & 0 \leq z \leq v_{max} - q_p \\ \dfrac{\bar{v}}{q_p} \left[1 - \dfrac{z}{\bar{v}} - \displaystyle\int_{z+q_p}^{v_{max}} \dfrac{v - z - q_p}{v} e(v) \, dv\right] & -q_p \leq z \leq 0 \\ 1 & z \leq -q_p \end{cases} \tag{36}$$

In either case the function $D(z)$ is an increasing function in z. Hence, for any given values c_1, c_2, q_p, and $\bar{v}$, it is relatively simple to establish the range within which z_o ought to be and then it can be computed from equation (32).

Example 14–2a

In a probabilistic reorder-point system with continuous reviewing, lead-time is 1 month. The density of demand during leadtime is

$$e(v) = 6v(1 - v) \qquad 0 \leq v \leq 1 \tag{37}$$

The prescribed lot size is two units. The carrying cost is $6 per unit per day. We want to find the optimal reorder point and the corresponding minimum expected total cost of the system for the following daily unit costs of shortage: ∞, $75, $18, and $12. In this system $c_1 = 6$, $q_p = 2$, $\bar{v} = \frac{1}{2}$, and $v_{max} = 1$. We shall therefore use the results of equation (35).

TABLE 14–2a

Solutions of Example 14–2a *Based on Equations* 14–2(7) *and* 14–2(30)

c_2	Equation 14–2(30)		Equation 14–2(7)			
	z_o	C_o	z_o	C_o	z	$C(z)$
∞	1	9.00	1	9.00		
75	$\frac{1}{3}$	6.00	0.405	6.40	$\frac{1}{3}$	6.47
18	0	4.50	0	4.80		
12	$-\frac{1}{6}$	4.00	$-\frac{1}{6}$	4.02		

For $c_2 = \infty$, $c_1/(c_1 + c_2) = 0$, hence $z_o = v_{max} = 1$. Equation (30) then gives $C_o = 6(1 + \frac{2}{1} - \frac{1}{2}) = \$9$ per day.

For $c_2 = \$75$, $c_1/(c_1 + c_2) = \frac{6}{81} = \frac{2}{27}$. Hence $0 \leq z_o \leq 1$ and we have to solve $[\frac{1}{2}/2] \int_{z_o}^{1} [(v - z_o)/v]6v(1 - v) \, dv = \frac{2}{27}$. This leads to $z_o = \frac{1}{3}$. The corresponding minimum cost, by equations (30) and (31), is $C_o = 6(\frac{1}{3} + \frac{2}{2} - \frac{1}{2}) + (6 + 75)A(\frac{1}{3}) = 5 + 81[\frac{1}{2}/(2 \times 2)] \int_{1/3}^{1} [(v - \frac{1}{3})^2/v]6v(1 - v) \, dv = 5 + 81[\frac{1}{8}](\frac{1}{2})(1 - \frac{1}{3})^4 = \$6$ per day.

For $c_2 = \$18$, $c_1/(c_1 + c_2) = \frac{6}{24} = \frac{1}{4}$. By inspection we find immediately that $z_o = 0$ and hence $C_o = 6(0 + \frac{2}{2} - \frac{1}{2}) + (6 + 18)A(0) = 3 + 24(\frac{1}{2})^2/ (2 \times 2) = \$4.5$ per day. Finally, for $c_2 = \$12$, $c_1/(c_1 + c_2) = \frac{6}{18} = \frac{1}{3}$. We now solve $[\frac{1}{2}/2][1 - z_o/\frac{1}{2}] = \frac{1}{3}$. Hence $z_o = -\frac{1}{6}$ and the corresponding minimum cost is $C_o = 6(-\frac{1}{6} + \frac{2}{2} - \frac{1}{2}) + 18A(-\frac{1}{6}) = 2 + 18(\frac{1}{2} + \frac{1}{6})^2/ (2 \times 2) = \$4$ per day.

This example could have been solved using equation (7). A comparison of the various results is given in Table 14–2a.

The Discrete Case and $x_{\max} = u$

By analogy with the results of Section 14–1, we can now give the solution of a system with discrete units in which $x_{\max} = u$. Let $E(v)$ be the probability distribution of demand during leadtime. Then, by equations (30) and (31), and noting equation 14–1(16), we have

$$C(z) = c_1\left(z + \frac{q_p}{2} - \bar{v} + \frac{u - \bar{x}}{2}\right) + (c_1 + c_2)\frac{A(z) - A(z + q_p)}{q_p} \tag{38}$$

where

$$A(p) = \begin{cases} 0 & p \geqq v_{\max} \\ \dfrac{\bar{v}}{2}\displaystyle\sum_{v=p+u}^{v_{\max}} \dfrac{(v - p)^2}{v} E(v) & 0 \leqq p \leqq v_{\max} \\ \dfrac{(\bar{v} - p)^2}{2} + p\,\dfrac{u - \bar{x}}{2} & p \leqq 0 \end{cases} \tag{39}$$

It should be noted that the main difference between this system and the continuous reviewing system is the term $(u - \bar{x})/2$ in equations (38) and (39). This term comes about because we have here a system with discrete units and $x_{\max} = u$. When $z \geqq v_{\max}$, equation (38) reduces to $C(z) = c_1 I_1$ where I_1 is essentially as in equation 14–1(16). Similarly, when $z \leqq -q_p$, then $C(z) = c_2 I_2$, where $I_2 = -[z + q_p/2 - \bar{v} + (u - \bar{x})/2]$, again a result related to equation 14–1(16). It is also important to note that $C(z)$ in equation (38) will not always be identical with $C(z)$ in equation (1). This is illustrated in Example 14–2b. [See also problem 14–4(7).]

Example 14–2b

In a probabilistic reorder-point system the reviewing period is 2 weeks and leadtime is 6 weeks. Demand during the reviewing period is for five units with a probability 0.3; otherwise there is no demand.

What are the expected average inventory carried and the expected shortage for reorder points of 10, 5, 0, −5, and −10 when the lot sizes are 10 and 20?

We shall obtain results based first on equation (1) and then on equation (38). In both cases we have $u = 5$, $P(0) = 0.7$, $P(5) = 0.3$, $\bar{x} = 1.5$, $L = 6$, $E(0) = 0.343$, $E(5) = 0.441$, $E(10) = 0.189$, $E(15) = 0.027$, $\bar{v} = 4.5$, and $v_{\max} = 15$. To find the function N of equations (1) and (2) we first need the function R of equation (4). The distribution $D(w)$, by equation (3), can readily be seen to be $D(0) = 0.85$, $D(5) = 0.15$. Hence by equation (4) we have the values of $R(y)$. These values as well as those of the functions $G(y)$, $W(y)$, and $N(y)$ are given in Table 14–2b.

TABLE 14–2b

Determination of the Function N of Equations (1)
and (2) *in Example* 14–2

y	$R(y)$	$G(y)$	$W(y)$	$N(y)$
0	0.29155	0.29155	0.29155	0.29155
5	0.42630	0.71785	1.00940	1.30095
10	0.22680	0.94465	1.95405	3.25500
15	0.05130	0.99595	2.95000	6.20500
20	0.00405	1.00000	3.95000	10.15500
25	0.	1.00000	4.95000	15.10500
30	0.	1.00000	5.95000	21.05500

From equation (1) we have

$$I_1(z, q) = \frac{u^2}{q} [N(z + q - u) - N(z - u)]$$

$$= \frac{25}{q} [N(z + q - 5) - N(z - 5)] \tag{40}$$

and

$$I_2(z, q) = I_1(z, q) + \frac{\bar{x}}{2} + \bar{v} - \frac{q + u}{2} - z$$

$$= I_1(z, q) + 2.75 - \frac{q}{2} - z \tag{41}$$

TABLE 14–2c

Values of I_1 and I_2 in Example 14–2b
Comparisons Based on Equations 14–2(1) *and* 14–2(38)

z	$q = 10$		$q = 20$		
	Eq. 14–2(1)	Eq. 14–2(38)	Eq. 14–2(1)	Eq. 14–2(38)	
10	12.260	12.260	17.255	17.255	I_1
	0.010	0.010	0.005	0.005	I_2
5	7.409	7.398	12.329	12.323	I_1
	0.159	0.148	0.079	0.073	I_2
0	3.252	3.252	7.756	7.756	I_1
	1.002	1.002	0.506	0.506	I_2
-5	0.729	0.741	4.069	4.069	I_1
	3.479	3.491	1.819	1.819	I_2
-10	0.	0.	1.626	1.626	I_1
	7.750	7.750	4.376	4.376	I_2

We can now obtain the values of I_1 and I_2 for various values of z and q. They are given in Table 14–2c in the column marked Eq. 14–2(1).

Now, from equation (38), we have

$$I_2(z, q) = \frac{A(z) - A(z + q)}{q} \tag{42}$$

and

$$I_1(z, q) = I_2(z, q) + z + \frac{q}{2} - \bar{v} + \frac{u - \bar{x}}{2}$$

$$= I_2(z, q) + z + \frac{q}{2} - 2.75 \tag{43}$$

The function $A(p)$, by equation (39), can be computed as in Table 14–2d. Using these values of $A(p)$ in equations (38) and (39) we obtain results for I_1 and I_2 which are based on equation (38). The numerical values are recorded in Table 14–2c.

As can be seen from the table, when we compare the use of the cost equation (1) with that of the cost equation (38), only sometimes are different results obtained.

TABLE 14–2d
The Function $A(p)$ of Equation (39) for Example 14–2b

p, v	$E(v)$	$vE(v)$	$\dfrac{E(v)}{v}$	$\displaystyle\sum_{p+5}^{15} vE(v)$	$\displaystyle\sum_{p+5}^{15} E(v)$	$\displaystyle\sum_{p+5}^{15} \dfrac{E(v)}{v}$	$A(p)$
-10							87.625
-5							36.375
0	0.343	0.		4.500	0.657	0.1089	10.125
5	0.441	2.205	0.0882	2.295	0.216	0.0207	1.468
10	0.189	1.890	0.0189	0.405	0.027	0.0018	0.101
15	0.027	0.405	0.0018	0.	0.	0.	0.
20	0.	0.		0.	0.	0.	0.

THE PROBABILISTIC REORDER-POINT–LOT-SIZE SYSTEM WITH LEADTIME

14-3 The results of the last two sections can readily be extended to reorder-point–lot-size systems. For discrete units, by equations 14–2(1) and 14–1(3), the expected total-cost equation is

$$C(z, q) = (c_1 + c_2)\frac{u^2}{q}\left[N(z + q - u) - N(z - u)\right]$$

$$+ c_2\left(\bar{v} + \frac{u - \bar{x}}{2} - z - \frac{q}{2}\right) + \frac{c_3}{w_p}\left[1 - \frac{u}{q}V(q - u)\right] \tag{1}$$

where

$$N(B) = \begin{cases} \sum_{S=0}^{B} W(S) = \sum_{S=0}^{B} \sum_{j=0}^{S} G(j) = \sum_{S=0}^{B} \sum_{j=0}^{S} \sum_{y=0}^{j} R(y) & B = 0, u, 2u, \ldots \\ 0 & B < 0 \end{cases}$$

(2)

where

$$R(y) = D(w) * E(v) = \sum_{v=0}^{y} D(y - v)E(v) \tag{3}$$

where

$$D(W) = \begin{cases} P(0) + \dfrac{u}{2} \sum_{x=u}^{\infty} \dfrac{P(x)}{x} & w = 0 \\ \dfrac{u}{2} \dfrac{P(w)}{w} + u \sum_{x=w+u}^{\infty} \dfrac{P(x)}{x} & w = u, 2u, \ldots \end{cases}$$

(4)

and where

$$V(k) = \sum_{j=0}^{k} F(j) = \sum_{j=0}^{k} \sum_{x=0}^{j} P(x) \tag{5}$$

The corresponding results for the continuous case are similar. By equations 14–2(7) and 14–1(6), the expected total-cost equation is

$$C(z, q) = (c_1 + c_2) \frac{K(z + q) - K(z)}{q} + c_2 \left(\frac{\bar{x}}{2} + \bar{v} - z - \frac{q}{2} \right)$$
$$+ \frac{c_3}{w_p} \left[1 - \frac{1}{q} V(q) \right]$$

(6)

where

$$K(S) = \begin{cases} \displaystyle\int_0^S T(Q)\, dQ = \int_0^S \int_0^Q M(r)\, dr\, dQ \\ \qquad = \displaystyle\int_0^S \int_0^Q \int_0^r m(y)\, dy\, dr\, dQ & S \geqq 0 \\ 0 & S \leqq 0 \end{cases}$$

(7)

where

$$m(y) = d(w) * e(v) = \int_0^y d(y - v)e(v)\, dv \tag{8}$$

where

$$d(w) = \int_w^{x_{\max}} \frac{f(x)}{x}\, dx \tag{9}$$

and where

$$V(q) = \int_0^q F(j)\, dj = \int_0^q \int_0^j f(x)\, dx\, dj \tag{10}$$

If we extend the results for continuous reviewing given by equations 14-2(30) and 14-1(13), we now obtain

$$C(z, q) = c_1\left(z + \frac{q}{2} - \bar{v}\right) + (c_1 + c_2)\frac{A(z) - A(z + q)}{q} + \frac{c_3 r}{q} \quad (11)$$

where

$$A(p) = \begin{cases} 0 & p \geq v_{\max} \\ \dfrac{\bar{v}}{2}\displaystyle\int_p^{v_{\max}}\frac{(v - p)^2}{v}\, e(v)\, dv & 0 \leq p \leq v_{\max} \\ \dfrac{(\bar{v} - p)^2}{2} & p \leq 0 \end{cases} \quad (12)$$

We can similarly extend the results of the discrete case and $x_{\max} = u$, which has been discussed in Sections 14-1 and 14-2. For type $(1, 2, 3)$ systems, by equations 14-2(38) and 14-1(21), the expected total cost is

$$C(z, q) = c_1\left(z + \frac{q}{2} - \bar{v} + \frac{u - \bar{x}}{2}\right) + (c_1 + c_2)\frac{A(z) - A(z + q)}{q}$$
$$+ \frac{c_3 r}{q} \quad (13)$$

where

$$A(p) = \begin{cases} 0 & p \geq v_{\max} \\ \dfrac{\bar{v}}{2}\displaystyle\sum_{v=p+u}^{v_{\max}}\frac{(v - p)^2}{v}E(v) & 0 \leq p \leq v_{\max} \\ \dfrac{(\bar{v} - p)^2}{2} + \dfrac{p(u - \bar{x})}{2} & p \leq 0 \end{cases} \quad (14)$$

All the expected total-cost equations (1), (6), (11), and (13) can be analyzed using the methods of Sections 13-3, 14-1, and 14-2. For a specified q the corresponding optimal z_o^q can be found with relative ease using the results of Section 14-2. But as in Section 13-3, for a given z it is only possible to specify necessary conditions for finding the corresponding optimal q_o^z. The conditions may not necessarily be sufficient.

14-4 PROBLEMS

1. Compare the probabilistic lot-size system of Section 14-1 with the probabilistic scheduling-period system of Section 9-1. In particular, compare the results given by equation 14-1(15) with those of equations 9-1(10) and 9-1(15).
2. Compare the probabilistic lot-size system with discrete units and $x_{\max} = u$ of Section 14-1 with the lot-size system with discrete units of Section 3-1.

Note the identical solution given by equations 14–1(22) and 3–1(16). Explain the difference between the cost equations 14–1(21) and 3–1(2).

3. Check the derivation of equation 14–2(30).

4. For a system with continuous reviewing, state the ranges for which the total-cost equations 14–2(7) and 14–2(30) always give identical results.

5. Check Table 14–2a for the results which are based on equation 14–2(7).

6. Solve Example 14–2a when the probability density of demand during lead-time is

$$e(v) = (1/b^2)ve^{-v/b} \qquad v \geqq 0 \tag{1}$$

7. The probability distribution of demand during the reviewing period is $P(x)$, $x = 0, 1, \ldots, x_{\max}$. Consider two reviewing periods only. At the beginning of the first there is an amount S in inventory. No replenishments are scheduled. Let y be the total demand during the two reviewing periods, so that $Q(y) = P(x) * P(x) = \sum_{x=0}^{y} P(y - x)P(x)$.

(a) Find the expected average amount in inventory and the expected average shortage assuming (i) demand x is uniform during each reviewing period, (ii) demand y is uniform during the interval composed of two reviewing periods. Show that assumptions (i) and (ii) may lead to different values for the respective averages. Then describe circumstances under which the results will be identical.

(b) Extend the results to Section 14–2 (and to Examples 14–2a and 14–2b).

8. Solve an extension of Example 14–2a when the optimal lot size has to be determined. Assume that the shortage cost is \$75 per unit per day and that the replenishment cost is \$20.

9. In an inventory system with a (z, q) policy, inventories are reviewed every week. Leadtime is 3 weeks. During any week there is a demand for one unit with the probability 0.6. Otherwise there is no demand. The carrying cost is \$1 per unit per week, the shortage cost is \$5 per unit per week, and the replenishing cost is \$2. Find the optimal reorder point, the optimal lot size, and the corresponding minimum expected total cost: (a) use equation 14–3(1), etc.; (b) use equation 14–3(13), etc.

10. The approximate solution of a (z, Z) system, in which the reviewing period is zero, is claimed to be

$$\int_{z_o}^{Z_o} (Z_o - y)(y - z_o)h(y) \, dy = \frac{2rc_3}{c_1 + c_2} \tag{2}$$

$$\left[\int_0^{Z_o} (Z_o - y)h(y) \, dy - \int_0^{z_o} (z_o - y)h(y) \, dy \right] \Big/ (Z_o - z_o) = \frac{c_2}{c_1 + c_2} \tag{3}$$

where z_o, Z_o are the optimal reorder point and order level respectively, y is the demand during leadtime, $h(y)$ is the probability density of y, r is the average rate of demand, and c_1, c_2, and c_3 are respectively the unit costs of carrying, shortage, and replenishing.

Discuss the following special cases: (a) demand is constant, (b) leadtime is zero, (c) $y_{max} \leq Z_o$ (d) $c_2 \to \infty$. In each case interpret the results and compare them with solutions of other pertinent systems.

11. Find the expected total cost of an inventory system with a (z, Z) policy in which demand is uniform and constant at a rate r, reviewing is continuous, and leadtime is variable. Assume that the density of leadtime is $g(L)$, $0 < a < L < b$.

Chapter 15

Probabilistic Reorder-Point–
Order-Level Systems without Leadtime

15–0 In this chapter we shall deal with probabilistic inventory systems with an (s, S) policy. The amounts in inventory in these systems may be described graphically as shown in Figure 15–0. We shall follow methods of analysis somewhat similar to the methods used in Chapter 13. The results, however, will be quite different.

As in Chapter 13, let Q be the amount on hand at the beginning of each reviewing period after a replenishment, if any, has been added to inventory. For discrete units, let $H(Q)$ be the probability distribution of Q. In Chapter 13 the distribution $H(Q)$ was the uniform distribution [equation 13–0(1)]. In the present system it is not too difficult to see that $H(Q)$ is not uniform, for each scheduling period always starts with an amount equal to the order level. To derive $H(Q)$, let $P(x)$ be the probability distribution of demand during the reviewing period w_p, let s be the reorder point, and let S be the order level.

We first consider the amount $Q = S - u$. To have this amount in inventory at some point of time T, the amount at time $T - w_p$ could only have been S or $S - u$. That is,

$$H(S - u) = H(S - u)P(0) + H(S)P(u) \tag{1}$$

Therefore,

$$H(S - u) = H(S)\frac{P(u)}{1 - P(0)} = H(S)R(u) \tag{2}$$

where

$$R(x) = \frac{P(x)}{1 - P(0)} \qquad x = u, 2u, \ldots, x_{\max} \tag{3}$$

274

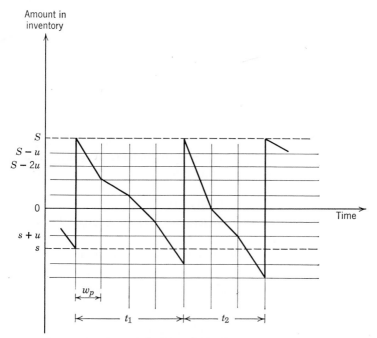

Figure 15-0 The probabilistic reorder-point–order-level systems.

Similarly,

$$H(S - 2u) = H(S - 2u)P(0) + H(S - u)P(u) + H(S)P(2u) \quad (4)$$

Therefore, by equations (2) and (3),

$$H(S - 2u) = H(S - u)R(u) + H(S)R(2u) = H(S)[R^2(u) + R(2u)]$$
$$= H(S)A(2u) \quad (5)$$

where the function A is defined recursively by

$$A(y) = \begin{cases} 1 & y = 0 \\ \sum_{x=u}^{y} A(y - x)R(x) & y = u, 2u, \ldots \end{cases} \quad (6)$$

It can be shown by induction that in general

$$H(S - y) = H(S)A(y) \qquad y = u, \ldots, S - s - u \quad (7)$$

Hence

$$H(Q) = H(S)A(S - Q) \qquad Q = s + u, \ldots, S - u \quad (8)$$

But

$$\sum_{Q=s+u}^{S} H(Q) = 1 \quad (9)$$

Therefore

$$H(S) = 1 \left/ \sum_{y=0}^{S-s-u} A(y) \right. \tag{10}$$

and

$$H(Q) = A(S - Q) \left/ \sum_{y=0}^{S-s-u} A(y) \right. \qquad Q = s + u, \ldots, S \tag{11}$$

Example 15–0a

The probability distribution of demand during the reviewing period is $P(0) = 0.20$, $P(0.5) = 0.24$, $P(1.0) = 0.40$, and $P(1.5) = 0.16$. The order level is 2.0. Derive $H(Q)$ for reorder points of 1.5, 1.0, . . . , −1.0, −1.5.

TABLE 15–0

Computations of $H(Q)$ of Equation (11) for Example 15–0a

s	x, b	$P(x)$	$R(x)$	$A(b)$	$\sum_{x=0}^{b-u} A(x)$	$H(2.0)$	$H(1.5)$	$H(1.0)$	$H(0.5)$	$H(0.0)$	$H(-0.5)$	$H(-1.0)$	$\bar{Q}$
2.0	0.	0.20		1.000		1.000							2.0000
1.5	0.5	0.24	0.3	0.300	1.000	1.000							2.0000
1.0	1.0	0.40	0.5	0.590	1.300	0.769	0.231						1.8845
0.5	1.5	0.16	0.2	0.527	1.890	0.529	0.159	0.312					1.6085
0.	2.0			0.513	2.417	0.414	0.124	0.249	0.218				1.3670
−0.5	2.5			0.535	2.930	0.341	0.103	0.201	0.180	0.175			1.1275
−1.0	3.0			0.522	3.465	0.289	0.087	0.170	0.152	0.148	0.154		0.8775
−1.5	3.5			0.527	3.987	0.251	0.075	0.148	0.132	0.129	0.134	0.131	0.6305

The computations are given in Table 15–0 and are self-explanatory. For example, when $s = 0.5$, then, by equation (10), $H(2.0) = 1/(1.000 + 0.300 + 0.590) = 1/1.890 = 0.529$. Therefore, by equation (11), $H(1.5) = A(0.5)/1.890 = 0.300 \times 0.529 = 0.159$, and $H(1.0) = A(1.0)/1.890 = 0.590 \times 0.529 = 0.312$. In addition, $\bar{Q} = 2.0 \times 0.529 + 1.5 \times 0.159 + 1.0 \times 0.312 = 1.6085$.

The Continuous Case

Let $f(x)$ be the probability density of demand during w_p. Let $g(Q)$ be the probability density of Q, and let h be the probability that Q equals S.

The function $g(Q)$ and the constant h can be derived from the simultaneous equations:

$$g(Q) = \int_Q^S g(y)f(y - Q)\,dy + hf(S - Q) \qquad s < Q < S \tag{12}$$

$$h = \int_s^S \int_{y-s}^\infty f(x)\,dx g(y)\,dy + \int_{S-s}^\infty hf(x)\,dx \tag{13}$$

These equations can be explained as follows.

The quantity Q at the beginning of a reviewing period can be reached in two ways, depending on the amount at the beginning of the previous period. Either the amount is y, where $Q < y < S$, and a demand $y - Q$ occurs, or the amount is S and a demand $S - Q$ occurs. Similarly, the quantity $Q = S$ can be reached in two different ways. Either the amount is y, where $s < y < S$, and a demand larger than $y - s$ occurs, or the amount is S and a demand larger than $S - s$ occurs. The corresponding probability considerations lead to equations (12) and (13).

The integral equation (12) can be solved explicitly for only a very limited number of probability densities $f(x)$. For other densities, it may be advisable to convert the continuous density to a discrete distribution and then use the methods applicable to discrete units given earlier in this section. Example 15–0b provides an illustration for the explicit solution of equation (12). Example 15–1b illustrates how discrete methods can be used to solve a continuous case.

Example 15–0b

The density of demand during a reviewing period is

$$f(x) = \frac{1}{b} e^{-x/b} \qquad x \geq 0 \tag{14}$$

For an (s, S) policy we wish to find the probability density of demand $g(Q)$ and the probability h of equations (12) and (13).

We first note that for the density in equation (14)

$$f(0) = \frac{1}{b} \tag{15}$$

and that

$$\frac{df(x)}{dx} = -\frac{1}{b} f(x) \tag{16}$$

Differentiation of $g(Q)$ of equation (12) with respect to Q now gives

$$\begin{aligned}
\frac{dg(Q)}{dQ} &= \int_Q^S g(y) \frac{df(y - Q)}{dQ} \, dy - g(Q)f(0) - h\frac{df(S - Q)}{dQ} \\
&= \frac{1}{b} \int_Q^S g(y)f(y - Q) \, dy - \frac{1}{b} g(Q) + \frac{1}{b} hf(S - Q) \\
&= \frac{1}{b}\left[\int_Q^S g(y)f(y - Q) \, dy + hf(S - Q) - g(Q) \right]
\end{aligned} \tag{17}$$

By equation (12) the term in the square brackets is zero. Hence

$$\frac{dg(Q)}{dQ} = 0 \tag{18}$$

and therefore

$$g(Q) = a \tag{19}$$

where a is a constant yet to be determined.

Equation (13), in general, can be stated as

$$h = \int_s^S \int_{y-s}^\infty f(x)\, dx\, g(y)\, dy \Big/ \int_0^{S-s} f(x)\, dx \tag{20}$$

Substituting in this equation the value of $g(Q)$ of equation (19) and that of $f(x)$ of equation (14) eventually leads to

$$h = ab \tag{21}$$

The constant a can now be determined from the general equation

$$\int_s^S g(Q)\, dQ + h = 1 \tag{22}$$

giving the result

$$a = \frac{1}{b + S - s} \tag{23}$$

Hence the solution of Example 15–0b is

$$g(Q) = \frac{1}{b + S - s} \qquad s < Q < S \tag{24}$$

$$h = \frac{b}{b + S - s} \tag{25}$$

THE PROBABILISTIC ORDER-LEVEL SYSTEM

15–1 In this section we examine the (s_p, S) policy in a type $(1, 3)$ system. We first consider the discrete case and then the continuous.

Let $P(x)$ be the probability distribution of demand during w_p. To avoid shortages the prescribed reorder point will be

$$s_p = x_{\max} - u \tag{1}$$

Let $D(r)$ be a probability distribution equivalent to $P(x)$. The expected average amount in inventory will then be

$$I_1 = \sum_{Q=s_p+u}^{S} \sum_{r=0}^{r_{\max}} (Q - r) D(r) H(Q) = \bar{Q} - \bar{r}$$
$$= \sum_{Q=s_p+u}^{S} Q A(S - Q) \Big/ \sum_{y=0}^{S-s_p-u} A(y) - \frac{\bar{x}}{2} \tag{2}$$

where the function H is given by equation 15–0(11) and the function A by equation 15–0(6).

The number of replenishments per unit time can be readily derived by considering the probability $H(S)$. This is essentially the fraction of the time in which the amount in inventory at the beginning of a reviewing period is S. To be in state S, either a replenishment has just occurred, or the previous state was S and no demand occurred. Thus the fraction of time corresponding to replenishments is $H(S)[1 - P(0)]$. Hence

$$I_3 = \frac{H(S)[1 - P(0)]}{w_p}$$

$$= 1 - P(0) \Big/ \left[w_p \sum_{y=0}^{S-s_p-u} A(y) \right] \tag{3}$$

The expected total cost of the system is then

$$C(S) = \left\{ c_1 \sum_{Q=x_{max}}^{S} QA(S - Q) + \frac{c_3}{w_p} [1 - P(0)] \right\} \Big/ \sum_{y=0}^{S-x_{max}} A(y) - \frac{c_1 \bar{x}}{2} \tag{4}$$

where the function A is defined by equation 15-0(6). Equation (4) can also be expressed in the form

$$C(S) = \frac{c_1 u K(S - x_{max} - u) + \frac{c_3}{w_p} [1 - P(0)]}{J(S - x_{max})} + c_1 \left(x_{max} - \frac{\bar{x}}{2} \right) \tag{5}$$

where the functions K and J are defined by

$$K(r) = \begin{cases} 0 & r < 0 \\ \sum_{i=0}^{r} J(i) = \sum_{i=0}^{r} \sum_{y=0}^{i} A(y) & r = 0, u, 2u, \dots \end{cases} \tag{6}$$

It can now be shown that for an optimal order level S_o the necessary conditions are

$$M(S_o - u) \leqq \frac{c_3[1 - P(0)]}{c_1 u w_p} \leqq M(S_o) \tag{7}$$

where

$$M(S) = \frac{[J(S - x_{max})]^2}{A(S - x_{max} + u)} - K(S - x_{max} - u) \tag{8}$$

where the functions J and K are defined by equation (6) and the function A by equation 15-0(6). The function M is not always an increasing function. Hence equation (7) may have more than one solution. If it does, we must use equation (5) to find which of the solutions gives the optimal S_o.

Example 15–1a

In an inventory system with an (s_p, S) policy the reviewing period is 2 weeks. Demand during the reviewing period is the same as in Example 15–0a, namely $P(0) = 0.20$, $P(0.5) = 0.24$, $P(1.0) = 0.40$, and $P(1.5) = 0.16$. The unit carrying cost is c_1 per unit per week. We wish to find the optimal order levels and the corresponding minimum expected total costs for replenishing costs of c_1, $3c_1$, $5c_1$, and $7c_1$.

TABLE 15–1a

Computation of the Functions J, K, and M of Equations (6) and (8)

x, y	$P(x)$	$A(x)$	$J(x)$	$K(y)$	S	$J(S - x_{max})$	$A(S - x_{max} + u)$	$K(S - x_{max} - u)$	$M(S)$
0	0.20	1.000	1.000	1.000	1.5	1.000	0.300	0.	3.333
0.5	0.24	0.300	1.300	2.300	2.0	1.300	0.590	1.000	1.864
1.0	0.40	0.590	1.890	4.190	2.5	1.890	0.527	2.300	4.478
1.5	0.16	0.527	2.417	6.607	3.0	2.417	0.513	4.190	7.198
2.0	0.	0.513	2.930	9.537	3.5	2.930	0.535	6.607	9.439
2.5	0.	0.535	3.465	13.002	4.0	3.465	0.522	9.537	13.463
3.0	0.	0.522	3.987	16.989	4.5	3.987	0.527	13.002	17.161
3.5	0.	0.527							

The computations needed to find the function M of equation (8) are given in Table 15–1a. The values of $A(x)$ were taken from Table 15–0. Since $s_p = x_{max} - u = 1.5 - 0.5 = 1.0$, the values chosen for S begin with $s_p + u = 1.5$.

The factor $c_3[1 - P(0)]/c_1 u w_p$ of equation (7) is $c_3 \times 0.8/(c_1 \times 0.5 \times 2) = 0.8 c_3/c_1$. For $c_3 = 7c_1$ the value of the factor is 5.6 and hence, by

TABLE 15–1b

The Expected Total Cost in Example 15–1a for Various Values of S and Various Values of c_3

S	$c_3 = c_1$	$c_3 = 3c_1$	$c_3 = 5c_1$	$c_3 = 7c_1$
1.5	$1.520c_1$	$2.320c_1$	$3.120c_1$	$3.920c_1$
2.0	$1.812c_1$	$2.428c_1$	$3.044c_1$	$3.660c_1$
2.5	$1.938c_1$	$2.362c_1$	$2.786c_1$	$3.210c_1$
3.0	$2.153c_1$	$2.485c_1$	$2.817c_1$	$3.145c_1$
3.5	$2.383c_1$	$2.657c_1$	$2.934c_1$	$3.205c_1$

equation (7), $S_o = 3.0$ and, by equation (5), $C_o = 3.145c_1$. When $c_3 = 5c_1$ the factor is 4.0 and hence $S_o = 2.5$ and $C_o = 2.786c_1$. When $c_3 = 3c_1$ the factor is 2.4 and hence S_o is either 2.5 of 1.5. But $C(1.5) = 2.320c_1$ and $C(2.5) = 2.362c_1$. Hence, for $c_3 = 3c_1$, $S_o = 1.5$ and $C_o = 2.320c_1$. Finally, when $c_3 = c_1$, the factor is 0.8 and hence $S_o = 1.5$ and $C_o = 1.520c_1$.

The expected total costs for various values of S are summarized in Table 15–1b.

Continuous Units

Let $f(x)$ be the probability density of demand during the reviewing period w_p. Let $k(r)$ be its equivalent density. By analogy with the discrete case we have here

$$s_p = x_{max} \qquad (9)$$

and

$$I_1 = \int_{s_p}^{S} \left[\int_0^{r_{max}} (Q - r)k(r)\, dr \right] g(Q)\, dQ + h \int_0^S (S - r)\, k(r)\, dr \quad (10)$$

where the function $g(Q)$ and the constant h are defined by equations 15–0(12) and 15–0(13). Since $S > s_p = x_{max} = r_{max}$, equation (10) can also be written as

$$
\begin{aligned}
I_1 &= \int_{s_p}^{S} (Q - \bar{r})g(Q)\, dQ + h(S - \bar{r}) \\
&= \int_{s_p}^{S} Qg(Q)\, dQ + hS - \bar{r}\left[\int_{s_p}^{S} g(Q)\, dQ + h \right] \qquad (11) \\
&= \bar{Q}(S) - \bar{r} = \bar{Q}(S) - \bar{x}/2
\end{aligned}
$$

where

$$\bar{Q}(S) = \int_{s_p}^{S} Qg(Q)\, dQ + hS = \int_{x_{max}}^{S} Qg(Q)\, dQ + hS \qquad (12)$$

(Note that $\bar{Q}(S)$ thus depends on the knowledge of $g(Q)$ and h. The function $g(Q)$ can rarely be expressed in a closed form, therefore in most cases $\bar{Q}(S)$, too, cannot be expressed explicitly.)

The expected number of replenishments per reviewing period is obviously h. Hence

$$I_3 = h/w_p \qquad (13)$$

Therefore the expected total-cost equation in the continuous case is

$$C(S) = c_1 \left[\bar{Q}(S) - \frac{\bar{x}}{2} \right] + \frac{c_3 h}{w_p} \qquad (14)$$

Example 15–1b

In an inventory system with an (s_p, S) policy, the probability density of demand during the reviewing period w_p is $f(x) = 6x(1 - x)$, $0 \leq x \leq 1$. What is the optimal order level as a function of the parameter $a = c_3/c_1 w_p$, where c_1 is the unit carrying cost in $[\$]/[Q][T]$ and c_3 is the replenishing cost in $[\$]$?

For the given density the integral equation 15–0(12) cannot be solved explicitly. We, therefore, convert the density to a discrete distribution.

Suppose we pick u as our discrete unit. We can then obtain the distribution

$$P(x) = \begin{cases} F\left(\dfrac{u}{2}\right) & x = 0 \\[2mm] F\left(x + \dfrac{u}{2}\right) - F\left(x - \dfrac{u}{2}\right) & u \leqq x \leqq x_{\max} - u \\[2mm] 1 - F\left(x_{\max} - \dfrac{u}{2}\right) & x = x_{\max} \end{cases} \quad (15)$$

where $F(x)$ is the cumulative distribution of $f(x)$.

The necessary computations for finding $P(x)$ and then $R(x)$ of equation 15–0(3), $A(y)$ of equation 15–0(6), and $J(i)$ and $K(r)$ of equation (6) are given in Table 15–1c. Since $s_p = x_{\max} - u = 0.9$, we now find $M(S)$ of

TABLE 15–1c

Computation of the Functions P, R, A, J, and K of Equations (15), 15–0(3), 15–0(6), and 15–1(6) for the Probability Density $f(x) = 6x(1 - x)$

x	$F(x + 0.05)$	$P(x)$	$R(x)$	$A(x)$	$J(x)$	$K(x)$
0.	0.00725	0.00725		1.000	1.000	1.000
0.1	0.06075	0.05350	0.054	0.054	1.054	2.054
0.2	0.15625	0.09550	0.096	0.099	1.153	3.207
0.3	0.28175	0.12650	0.126	0.137	1.290	4.497
0.4	0.42525	0.14350	0.145	0.168	1.458	5.955
0.5	0.57475	0.14950	0.151	0.193	1.651	7.606
0.6	0.71825	0.14350	0.145	0.211	1.862	9.469
0.7	0.84375	0.12550	0.126	0.220	2.082	11.551
0.8	0.93925	0.09550	0.096	0.219	2.301	13.852
0.9	0.99275	0.05350	0.054	0.204	2.506	16.358
1.0		0.00725	0.007	0.181	2.686	19.044
1.1				0.189	2.875	21.919

equation (8) for $S = s_p + u$, $s_p + 2u$, ... $= 1.0$, 1.1, ... The computations are given in Table 15–1d. Once again we note that $M(S)$ is not an increasing function. Hence equation 15–1(7) may have more than one solution.

The factor $b = c_3[1 - P(0)]/c_1 u w_p$ of equation (7) for $a = c_3/c_1 w_p$ is here $b = a(1 - 0.00725)/0.1 = 9.9275a$. Hence when $a = 0.5$, then $b = 4.96375$ and therefore $S_o = 1.0$. The corresponding minimum cost is then $1.246375c_1$. When $a = 1.0$, then $b = 9.9275$, and hence S_o is either 1.0 or 1.7. But $C(1.0) = 1.74275c_1$ and $C(1.7) = 1.68143c_1$. Therefore, for $a = 1.0$, $S_o = 1.7$ and $C_o = 1.68143c_1$. The pattern of the solution now becomes evident. For values of $a < a^*$ the optimal order level is 1.0. When $a = a^*$ the optimal order level is either 1.0 or S^*. When $a > a^*$ the optimal level is equal to or larger than S^*. It can then be determined uniquely from equation (7).

TABLE 15–1d

Computation of the Function M of Equation (8)

S	$J(S - 1.0)$	$A(S - 0.9)$	J^2/A	$K(S - 1.1)$	$M(S)$	$K/(J - 1)$
1.0	1.000	0.054	18.556	0.	18.556	
1.1	1.054	0.099	11.208	1.000	10.208	
1.2	1.153	0.137	9.708	2.054	7.654	
1.3	1.290	0.168	9.888	2.207	6.681	
1.4	1.458	0.193	11.009	4.497	6.512	
1.5	1.651	0.211	12.930	5.955	6.975	9.142
1.6	1.862	0.220	15.754	7.606	8.147	8.821
1.7	2.082	0.219	19.814	9.469	10.346	8.748
1.8	2.301	0.204	25.923	11.551	14.372	8.877
1.9	2.506	0.181	34.714	13.852	20.862	9.201
2.0	2.686	0.189	38.234	16.358	21.876	9.700

To determine a^* and S^* we must solve the simultaneous equations $C(x_{max}) = C(S^* > x_{max})$ and $M(S^* - u) \leqq a^*[1 - P(0)]/u \leqq M(S^*)$. The first equation, by equation (5), gives

$$a^*[1 - P(0)] = \frac{uK(S^* - x_{max} - u) + a^*[1 - P(0)]}{J(S^* - x_{max})} \qquad (16)$$

or

$$a^* = \frac{uK(S^* - x_{max} - u)}{[1 - P(0)][J(S^* - x_{max}) - 1]} \qquad (17)$$

The second equation and equation (17) now give

$$M(S^* - u) \leqq \frac{K(S^* - x_{max} - u)}{J(S^* - x_{max}) - 1} \leqq M(S^*) \qquad (18)$$

Inspection of Table 15–1d, in which the pertinent values of $K(S^* - x_{max} - u)/[J(S - x_{max} - 1]$ are given, immediately shows that $S^* = 1.7$ and hence, by equation (17), $a^* = 0.877194$.

THE PROBABILISTIC REORDER-POINT SYSTEM

15–2 In this section we are interested in analyzing a type $(1, 2)$ system with an (s, S) policy. We shall refer to this system as an (s, S_p) system. In this system we assume that

$$S_p = s + k_p \qquad (1)$$

where k_p is some prescribed amount. By prescribing k_p, we ensure that the cost of replenishing per unit time is a constant, independent of the reorder point s. Therefore we indeed have a type $(1, 2)$ system in which the optimal reorder point s_0 has to be determined.

We first consider the discrete case in which $P(x)$ is the probability distribution of demand during the reviewing period w_p and $K(r)$ is the equivalent distribution.

The Case $s \geqq 0$

The expected average amount in inventory and the expected average shortage can now be expressed as

$$I_1(s) = \sum_{Q=s+u}^{s+k_p} \sum_{r=0}^{Q} (Q - r)K(r)H(Q) \tag{2}$$

and

$$I_2(s) = \sum_{Q=s+u}^{s+k_p} \sum_{r=Q+u}^{r_{max}} (r - Q)K(r)H(Q) \tag{3}$$

where H is defined by equation 15-0(11). We can note that, by equation 15-1(2),

$$I_1(s) - I_2(s) = \sum_{Q=s+u}^{s+k_p} \sum_{r=0}^{r_{max}} (Q - r)K(r)H(Q) = \bar{Q}(s) - \frac{\bar{x}}{2} \tag{4}$$

Hence the expected total cost of the system is

$$C(s) = c_1 I_1 + c_2 I_2 = c_1 \left[\bar{Q}(s) - \frac{\bar{x}}{2} \right] + (c_1 + c_2)I_2(s)$$

$$= (c_1 + c_2)I_1(s) - c_2 \left[\bar{Q}(s) - \frac{\bar{x}}{2} \right] \tag{5}$$

This cost can also be expressed in the form

$$C(s) = (c_1 + c_2)u \sum_{Q=s+u}^{s+k_p} B(Q - u)H(Q) - c_2 \left[\sum_{Q=s+u}^{s+k_p} QH(Q) - \frac{\bar{x}}{2} \right] \tag{6}$$

where

$$B(Q) = \sum_{y=0}^{Q} G(y) = \sum_{y=0}^{Q} \sum_{r=0}^{y} K(r) \tag{7}$$

The necessary and sufficient conditions for finding the optimal reorder point are

$$N(s_0 - u) \leqq \frac{c_2}{c_1 + c_2} \leqq N(s_0) \tag{8}$$

where

$$N(s) = \sum_{Q=s+u}^{s+k_p} G(Q)H(Q) \tag{9}$$

where G is defined by equation (7)

The General Case for Any s

The results for $s \geq 0$ can readily be extended for any s. In equation (2), for the general case, the summation should apply only for positive values of Q. Therefore the first summations in equations (4) and (6) should be for positive Q, and we must therefore assume that $B(Q) = G(Q) = 0$ when $Q < 0$. In this way the expected total-cost equation (7) and the solution given by equation (8) hold for any s.

Example 15-2a

The probability distribution of demand during the reviewing period is the same as in Example 15-1a: $P(0) = 0.20$, $P(0.5) = 0.24$, $P(1.0) = 0.40$, $P(1.5) = 0.16$. Find the optimal reorder point s_o and the corresponding

TABLE 15-2a

Computations of the Functions K, G, B, and N of Equations (7) and (9) for Example 15-2a

x, s	$P(x)$	$\dfrac{P(x)}{x}$	$\sum\limits_{s+1} \dfrac{P(x)}{x}$	$K(x)$	$G(x)$	$B(x)$	$N(s)$
−3.0							0.1291
−2.5							0.2758
−2.0							0.4286
−1.5							0.5810
−1.0							0.7322
−0.5							0.8841
0.	0.20		0.9867	0.4467	0.4467	0.4467	0.9683
0.5	0.24	0.4800	0.5067	0.3733	0.8200	1.2667	0.9959
1.0	0.40	0.4000	0.1067	0.1533	0.9733	2.2400	1.0000
1.5	0.16	0.1067	0.	0.0267	1.0000	3.2400	1.0000
2.0	0.	0.	0.	0.	1.0000	4.2400	1.0000

minimum cost C_o when $k_p = S_p - s = 3.0$, and when $c_1 = \$5$ per unit per week and $c_2 = \$10$ per unit per week.

Table 15-0 can be used to find $H(Q)$. In this table $S = 2.0$. Hence the pertinent probabilities correspond to the row for which $s = -1.0$, for then $k_p = 2.0 - (-1.0) = 3.0$. Thus $H(s + 0.5) = 0.154$, $H(s + 1.0) = 0.148$, $H(s + 1.5) = 0.152$, $H(s + 2.0) = 0.170$, $H(s + 2.5) = 0.087$, and $H(s + 3.0) = 0.289$. The computations for the functions K, G, B, and N are given in Table 15-2a. Now $c_2/(c_1 + c_2) = 0.6667$. Hence, by equation (8), $s_o = -1.0$. The corresponding minimum cost is $C_o = (5 + 10)0.5(0.4467 \times 0.152 + 1.2667 \times 0.170 + 2.2400 \times 0.087 + 3.2400 \times 0.289) - 10[-0.5 \times 0.154 + 0 \times 0.148 + 0.5 \times 0.152 + \cdots + 2.0 \times 0.289 - (0.5 \times 0.24 + 1.0 \times 0.40 + 1.5 \times 0.16)/2] = \$5.634$.

Continuous Units

The results obtained for discrete units can also be extended to continuous units, but this will not be shown here. Instead, a somewhat different approach will be presented.

Let $J_1(s, k_p)$ be the expected total inventory carried during a scheduling period. Similarly, let $J_2(s, k_p)$ be the total shortage. The dimensions of both J_1 and J_2 are $[Q][T]$. Let $\bar{t}$ be the expected length of the scheduling period. Therefore the average amount in inventory and the average shortage are

$$I_1 = \frac{J_1(s, k_p)}{\bar{t}}$$

$$I_2 = \frac{J_2(s, k_p)}{\bar{t}} \tag{10}$$

But $\bar{t}$ only depends on $S - s$ which is equal to k_p, a prescribed quantity. Therefore the optimal reorder point which minimizes the expected total cost per unit time will also minimize the total cost per scheduling period. This latter cost is

$$K(s) = c_1 J_1(s, k_p) + c_2 J_2(s, k_p) \tag{11}$$

We can use this equation to find s_o.

Let $f(x)$ be the probability density of demand during a reviewing period and let $g(y)$ be its equivalent density.

The Case $s \geq 0$

The function J_1 can be obtained from the integral equation

$$J_1(s, k_p) = w_p \int_0^{s+k_p} (s + k_p - y)g(y)\, dy + \int_0^{k_p} J_1(s, m)f(k_p - m)\, dm \tag{12}$$

This equation can be explained as follows. The expected total inventory during a scheduling period is composed of essentially two quantities: first, the expected inventory in the reviewing period which starts with an amount $s + k_p$, and second, the expected inventory during the remaining portion of the scheduling period. This latter portion starts with an amount $s + m$ in inventory which results from a demand of $k_p - m$ occurring during the first reviewing period.

In a similar way, relations for the function J_2 can be obtained:

$$J_2(s, k_p) = w_p \int_{s+k_p}^{\infty} (y - s - k_p)g(y)\, dy + \int_0^{k_p} J_2(s, m)f(k_p - m)\, dm \tag{13}$$

The Case $s \leq 0$

Equations (12) and (13) do not hold when the reorder point is negative. In equation (12) it is assumed that $s + k_p \geq 0$ and that $s + m \geq 0$. But if

$s < 0$ then $s + m$ will be negative for certain values of m. Therefore equation (12) does not hold for $s < 0$. For a negative reorder point the expected total inventory can be obtained from

$$J_1(s, S_p) = w_p \int_0^{S_p} (S_p - y)g(y)\, dy + \int_0^{S_p} J_1(s, m)f(S_p - m)\, dm \quad (14)$$

This formulation assumes that the order level is not negative. Negative order levels are obviously of little interest; in other words, for an optimal policy we would never have $s_o < -k_p$.

Equation (13) does not hold when $s < 0$ for the same reasons that equation (12) does not hold. The expected total shortage can be derived from

$$J_2(s, S_p) = w_p \int_{S_p}^{\infty} (y - S_p)g(y)\, dy + \int_0^S J_2(s, m)f(S_p - m)\, dm$$
$$+ \int_s^0 B(s, n)f(S_p - n)\, dn \quad (15)$$

where $B(s, n)$ is the expected total shortage when $s < n < 0$. The function $B(s, n)$ can be derived from

$$B(s, n) = w_p(-n + \bar{y}) + \int_s^n B(s, r)f(n - r)\, dr \quad (16)$$

Example 15–2b

The probability density of demand during a reviewing period is $f(x) = (x/b^2)e^{-x/b}$, $x \geq 0$. The carrying and shortage costs are c_1 and c_2 per unit per unit time. The difference between the order level and the reorder point is k_p. What is the optimal reorder point?

The density equivalent to $f(x)$ is $g(y) = (1/b)e^{-y/b}$, $y \geq 0$. For this density and for $f(x)$ the following relations hold:

$$f(0) = 0 \qquad \frac{df(x)}{dx} = \frac{1}{b}[g(x) - f(x)]$$
$$g(0) = \frac{1}{b} \qquad \frac{dg(x)}{dx} = -\frac{1}{b}g(x) \qquad (17)$$

The Case $s \geq 0$

We consider equation (12) and write it in the simplified form

$$J = W + \int Jf \qquad (18)$$

where J stands for $J_1(s, k)$ or $J_1(s, m)$, as the case may be, where f stands for $f(k_p - m)$, and where

$$W = w_p \int_0^{s+k_p} (s + k_p - y)g(y)\, dy \qquad (19)$$

Differentiating equation (18) with respect to k_p, noting the relations in equation (17), and then using equation (18), we obtain

$$
\begin{aligned}
J' &= W' + Jf(0) + \int Jf' \\
&= W' + 0 + \frac{1}{b}\left(\int Jg - \int Jf\right) \\
&= W' + \frac{1}{b}\left(\int Jg - J + W\right) \\
&= W' + \frac{1}{b}\int Jg - \frac{J}{b} + \frac{W}{b}
\end{aligned}
\tag{20}
$$

Differentiating again, and using equations (17) and (20), leads to

$$
\begin{aligned}
J'' &= W'' + \frac{1}{b}\left(Jg(0) + \int Jg' - J' + W'\right) \\
&= W'' + \frac{1}{b}\left(\frac{J}{b} - \frac{1}{b}\int Jg - J' + W'\right) \\
&= W'' + \frac{1}{b}\left[\frac{J}{b} - \left(J' - W' + \frac{J}{b} - \frac{W}{b}\right) - J' + W'\right] \\
&= W'' + \frac{1}{b}\left(-2J'' + 2W' + \frac{W}{b}\right) \\
&= W'' + \frac{2W'}{b} + \frac{W}{b^2} - \frac{2J'}{b}
\end{aligned}
\tag{21}
$$

From equation (19) we readily ascertain that

$$
W'' + \frac{2W'}{b} + \frac{W}{b^2} = \frac{w_p(s + k_p + b)}{b^2}
\tag{22}
$$

Hence equation (21) now becomes

$$
J'' + \frac{2J'}{b} = \frac{w_p(s + k_p + b)}{b^2}
\tag{23}
$$

The general solution of this differential equation is

$$
J_1(s, k) = a_1 e^{-2k_p/b} + a_2 + \frac{w_p[k_p^2 + (2s + b)k_p]}{4b}
\tag{24}
$$

To establish the constants a_1 and a_2, we examine the values of J and J' when $k_p = 0$. From equations (12) and (24) we obtain

$$
W(s, 0) = w_p \int_0^s (s - y)g(y)\, dy = a_1 + a_2
\tag{25}
$$

And from equations (20), (19), and (24) we have

$$W'(s, 0) = w_p \int_0^s g(y) \, dy = -\frac{2a_1}{b} + \frac{w_p(2s + b)}{4b} \tag{26}$$

Equations (26) and (25) give the results

$$a_1 = \frac{w_p b}{8}\left(2\frac{s}{b} + 4e^{-s/b} - 3\right) \tag{27}$$

and

$$a_2 = \frac{w_p b}{8}\left(6\frac{s}{b} + 4e^{-s/b} - 5\right) \tag{28}$$

so that, by equation (24),

$$J_1(s, k_p) = \frac{w_p b}{8}\left\{4e^{-s/b}(1 + e^{-2k_p/b}) + 2\frac{s}{b}\left(2\frac{k_p}{b} + e^{-2k_p/b} + 3\right)\right.$$
$$\left. + \left[2\left(\frac{k_p}{b}\right)^2 + 2\frac{k_p}{b} - 3e^{-2k_p/b} - 5\right]\right\} \tag{29}$$

The integral equation (13) can be solved in a manner similar to that used in solving equation (12). As a matter of fact, equation (13) can also be written in the form of equation (18), except that now

$$W = w_p \int_{s+k_p}^\infty (y - s - k_p)g(y) \, dy \tag{30}$$

All the results given by equations (20) and (21) hold again. From equation (30) we obtain

$$W'' + \frac{2W'}{b} + \frac{W}{b^2} = 0 \tag{31}$$

Hence the general solution of equation (13) is

$$J_2(s, k_p) = a_1 e^{-2k_p/b} + a_2 \tag{32}$$

When $k_p = 0$, we have

$$W(s, 0) = w_p \int_s^\infty (y - s)g(y) \, dy = a_1 + a_2 \tag{33}$$

and

$$W'(s, 0) = -w_p \int_s^\infty g(y) \, dy = -\frac{2a_1}{b} \tag{34}$$

Equations (34) and (33) yield

$$a_1 = a_2 = \frac{w_p b}{2} e^{-s/b} \tag{35}$$

Hence the solution

$$J_2(s, k_p) = \frac{w_p b}{8} 4e^{-s/b}(1 + e^{-2k_p/b}) \tag{36}$$

The expected total cost per scheduling period for $s \geq 0$ is then

$$
\begin{aligned}
K(s) = {}& c_1 J_1 + c_2 J_2 \\
= {}& \frac{w_p}{8}\bigg((c_1 + c_2)4e^{-s/b}(1 + e^{-2k_p/b}) \\
& + c_1\bigg\{2\,\frac{s}{b}\bigg[2\,\frac{k_p}{b} + e^{-2k_p/b} + 3\bigg] \\
& + \bigg[2\Big(\frac{k_p}{b}\Big)^2 + 2\,\frac{k_p}{b} - 3e^{-2k_p/b} - 5\bigg]\bigg\}\bigg)
\end{aligned}
\tag{37}
$$

From this cost equation we readily obtain the solution

$$
e^{-s_0/b} = \frac{c_1}{c_1 + c_2}\,\frac{2(k_p/b) + e^{-2k_p/b} + 3}{2(1 + e^{-2k_p/b})}
\tag{38}
$$

or

$$
s_0 = b \ln \frac{[(c_1 + c_2)/c_1][2(1 + e^{-2k_p/b})]}{2(k_p/b) + e^{-2k_p/b} + 3}
\tag{39}
$$

Since the solution is based on the assumption that $s \geq 0$, it only holds when

$$
\frac{c_2}{c_1} \geqq \frac{2(k_p/b) - e^{-2k_p/b} + 1}{2(1 + e^{-2k_p/b})}
\tag{40}
$$

This solution can be compared with that of Example 8–2a. When $k_p = 0$, we have a (t_p, S) system where $t_p = w_p$ and $S = s$. And indeed, for $k_p = 0$, equation (39) gives $s_0 = b \ln [(c_1 + c_2)/c_1]$ as in equation 8–2(13). In addition, since the expected scheduling period is now $w_p = t_p$, then $C_o = K(s_0)/w_p$. Hence from equations (37) and (38), $C_o = (b/8)\{8c_1 + c_1[8(s_0/b) - 8]\} = c_1 s_0$, as in equation 8–2(14).

The Case $s \leqq 0$

Equation (14) can be written in the form of equation (18) where now

$$
W = w_p \int_0^{S_p} (S_p - y)g(y)\,dy
\tag{41}
$$

Differentiating with respect to S_p, etc., leads to equation (21). But

$$
W'' + \frac{2W'}{b} + \frac{W}{b^2} = \frac{w_p(S_p + b)}{b^2}
\tag{42}
$$

Hence equation (21) now becomes

$$
J'' + \frac{2J'}{b} = \frac{w_p(S_p + b)}{b^2}
\tag{43}
$$

The general solution is

$$J_1(s, S_p) = a_1 e^{-2S_p/b} + a_2 + \frac{w_p b}{4}\left[\left(\frac{S_p}{b}\right)^2 + \frac{S_p}{b}\right] \tag{44}$$

To find the constants a_1 and a_2 we examine J and J' when $S_p = 0$. This leads to

$$W(s, 0) = 0 = a_1 + a_2$$
$$W'(s, 0) = 0 = -\frac{2a_1}{b} + \frac{w_p b}{4}\frac{1}{b} \tag{45}$$

These simultaneous equations give

$$a_1 = \frac{w_p b}{8} \quad \text{and} \quad a_2 = -\frac{w_p b}{8} \tag{46}$$

Therefore

$$J_1(s, S_p) = \frac{w_p b}{8}\left[e^{-2S_p/b} - 1 + 2\left(\frac{S_p}{b}\right)^2 + 2\frac{S_p}{b}\right] \tag{47}$$

To find $J_2(s, S_p)$ we can use equations (15) and (16). Alternatively, we can derive the result from the general relation: $I_1 - I_2 = \bar{Q} - \bar{x}/2$. This relation leads to

$$J_1(s, S_p) - J_2(s, S_p) = J_1(s, k_p) - J_2(s, k_p) \tag{48}$$

Therefore, from equations (29), (36), and (46),

$$\begin{aligned}
J_2(s, S_p) &= J_1(s, S_p) - [J_1(s, k_p) - J_2(s, k_p)] \\
&= \frac{w_p b}{8}\Bigg(e^{-2S_p/b} - 1 + 2\left(\frac{S_p}{b}\right)^2 + 2\frac{S_p}{b} \\
&\quad - \left\{2\frac{s}{b}\left(2\frac{k_p}{b} + e^{-2k_p/b} + 3\right)\right. \\
&\quad \left. + \left[2\left(\frac{k_p}{b}\right)^2 + 2\frac{k_p}{b} - 3e^{-2k_p/b} - 5\right]\right\}\Bigg)
\end{aligned} \tag{49}$$

Hence the expected total cost per scheduling period for $s \leqq 0$ is

$$\begin{aligned}
K(s) &= c_1 J_1 + c_2 J_2 \\
&= \frac{w_p b}{8}\Bigg((c_1 + c_2)\left[e^{-2S_p/b} - 1 + 2\left(\frac{S_p}{b}\right)^2 + 2\frac{S_p}{b}\right] \\
&\quad - c_2\left\{2\frac{s}{b}\left(2\frac{k_p}{b} + e^{-2k_p/b} + 3\right)\right. \\
&\quad \left. + \left[2\left(\frac{k_p}{b}\right)^2 + 2\frac{k_p}{b} - 3e^{-2k_p/b} - 5\right]\right\}\Bigg)
\end{aligned} \tag{50}$$

It is important to remember that $S_p = s + k_p$ so that S_p is here a function of s.

From this cost equation we can find the solution

$$\frac{2(s_o + k_p)}{b} - e^{-2(s_o+k_p)/b} + 1 = \frac{c_2}{c_1 + c_2}\left(2\frac{k_p}{b} + e^{-2k_p/b} + 3\right) \quad (51)$$

We can readily ascertain that $s_o \leq 0$ when $c_2/c_1 \leq [2(k_p/b) - e^{-2k_p/b} + 1]/2(1 + e^{-2k_p/b})$. This result agrees with those for $s \geq 0$ [see equations (39) and (40)]. We also note that when the carrying cost is relatively much larger than the shortage cost, then $s_o = -k_p$, or $S_p = 0$, as expected.

THE PROBABILISTIC REORDER-POINT–ORDER-LEVEL SYSTEM

15-3 The results in Sections 15-1 and 15-2 can readily be extended to type (1, 2, 3) systems in which the optimal reorder point s_o and the optimal order level S_o have to be determined. For the discrete case, in which the probability distribution of demand is $P(x)$, the expected total cost of the system can be found directly from equations 15-2(6) and 15-1(4):

$$C(s, S) = (c_1 + c_2)u \sum_{Q=s+u}^{S} B(Q - u)H(Q) - c_2\left(\bar{Q} - \frac{\bar{x}}{2}\right)$$
$$+ \frac{c_3}{w_p} H(S)[1 - P(0)] \quad (1)$$

where

$$B(Q) = \begin{cases} 0 & Q < 0 \\ \sum_{y=0}^{Q} G(y) = \sum_{y=0}^{Q}\sum_{r=0}^{y} K(r) & Q \geq 0 \end{cases} \quad (2)$$

where

$$K(r) = \begin{cases} P(0) + \dfrac{u}{2}\sum_{x=u}^{\infty}\dfrac{P(x)}{x} & r = 0 \\ \dfrac{u}{2}\dfrac{P(r)}{r} + u\sum_{x=r+u}^{\infty}\dfrac{P(x)}{x} & r = u, 2u, \ldots \end{cases} \quad (3)$$

where

$$H(Q) = A(S - Q)\Big/\sum_{y=0}^{S-s-u} A(y) \qquad Q = s + u, \ldots, S \quad (4)$$

where

$$A(y) = \begin{cases} 1 & y = 0 \\ \sum_{x=u}^{y} A(y - x)R(x) & y = u, 2u, \ldots \end{cases} \quad (5)$$

and where

$$R(x) = \frac{P(x)}{1 - P(0)} \qquad x = u, 2u, \ldots \quad (6)$$

For some given k, where

$$k = S - s \tag{7}$$

the corresponding optimal reorder point $s_o{}^k$ can be found as in Section 15-2. That is, by equation 15-2(8),

$$N(s_o{}^k - u) \leq \frac{c_2}{c_1 + c_2} \leq N(s_o{}^k) \tag{8}$$

where

$$N(s) = \sum_{Q=s+u}^{s+k} G(Q)H(Q) \tag{9}$$

and where $G(Q)$ is as in equation (2).

As in other systems, we can derive necessary conditions (which may not always be sufficient) for $k_o{}^s$—the optimal k corresponding to some given reorder point s. This is left as an exercise [see problem 15-4(9)]. Once having found the necessary conditions, we can use the search procedure outlined in Section 13-3 to find the locally optimal values of $s_o{}^*$ and $k_o{}^*$.

Another search procedure is given in the following example.

Example 15-3a

In an inventory system with a reorder-point–order-level policy the reviewing period is 2 weeks. The probability distribution of demand during the reviewing period is the same as in Examples 15-0a, 15-1a, and 15-2a: $P(0) = 0.20$, $P(0.5) = 0.24$, $P(1.0) = 0.40$, $P(1.5) = 0.16$. The carrying cost is \$5 per unit per week. The shortage cost is \$10 per unit per week. The replenishing cost is \$40. What is the optimal reorder point s_o and what is the optimal order level S_o?

In this system the average demand during the reviewing period is $\bar{x} = 0.76$. Hence the rate of demand is $r = \bar{x}/w_p = 0.38$ units per week. In a deterministic system with this rate and the given unit costs, the minimum cost of the system, by equation 5-1(12), is $C_o{}^D = \sqrt{2rc_3c_1c_2/(c_1 + c_2)} = \sqrt{2 \times 0.38 \times 40 \times 5 \times 10/15} = \$10.07$ per week. We can thus reasonably assume that the minimum cost of the system under study will be larger than this amount.* The optimal lot size in the deterministic system, by equation 5-1(13), is $q_o = C_o{}^D/\bar{c} = 10/(5 \times 10/15) = 3.02$ units. This result suggests that the order of magnitude of $k_o = S_o - s_o$ may be about 3.0. But we should also recall that our analysis of the type $(1, 3)$ system in Section 15-1 indicates that the cost equation is not convex and that an optimal solution may also occur when $S_o - s_o$ is very small.

---

* This assumption is based on three reasons. In the deterministic system reviewing is continuous, units are continuous, and demand is constant. In the present system the reviewing period is 2 weeks, units are discrete, and demand is probabilistic.

These preliminary observations suggest the following search procedure. Successive values of k are evaluated, beginning with $k = u$ and ending about $k = q_o$. For each value of k, the corresponding $s_o{}^k$ is found by using equation (8). Then the corresponding expected total cost $C(k)$ is computed by equation (1). The various $C(k)$ are observed. When $C(k^* + u) > C(k^*)$ for $k^* \approx q_o$, the search is terminated. The local optimal k, $k_o{}^*$, is that k giving the minimum $C(k)$.

For the present system the search is recorded in Table 15-3a.

TABLE 15-3a

Computation of $s_o{}^k$ of Equation 15-3(8) and the Corresponding $C(k)$ of Equation 15-3(1) for Various Values of $k = S - s$

k	$s_o{}^k$	I_1	I_2	I_3	$C(k)$
0.5	0.	0.223	0.103	0.400	18.150
1.0	−0.5	0.172	0.167	0.308	14.835
1.5	−0.5	0.371	0.142	0.211	11.737
2.0	−0.5	0.597	0.110	0.166	10.705
2.5	−1.0	0.492	0.245	0.136	10.362
3.0	−1.0	0.707	0.210	0.116	10.258
3.5	−1.0	0.932	0.181	0.100	10.488

The values of $s_o{}^k$ were found by computing $N(s)$ of equation (9) as in Table 15-2a. The function G is given in the table and the function H was obtained with relative ease from Table 15-0. For example, if $k = 0.5$ then $N(-0.5) = 0.4467$ and $N(0) = 0.8200$. But $c_2/(c_1 + c_2) = 10/15 = 0.6667$. Hence, by equation (8), $s_o^{0.5} = 0$. Similarly, for $k = 1.0$, $N(-1.0) = 0.3435$, $N(-0.5) = 0.7338$; hence $s_o^{1.0} = -0.5$, etc.

The expected average inventory carried was obtained from equation (1):

$$I_1 = u \sum_{Q=s+u}^{s+k} B(Q - u)H(Q) \tag{10}$$

The function B is given in Table 15-2a and the function H can be obtained from Table 15-0. Thus, for example, when $k = 0.5$ then $I_1 = 0.5 \sum_{0.5}^{0.5} B(Q - 0.5)H(Q) = 0.5 \times 0.4467 \times 1.0 = 0.223$. Similarly, for $k = 1.0$, $I_1 = 0.5 \sum_0^{0.5} B(Q - 0.5)H(Q) = 0.5 \times 0 \times 0.231 + 0.5 \times 0.4467 \times 0.769 = 0.172$, etc.

The expected average shortage was computed from

$$I_2 = I_1 - \bar{Q} + \bar{x}/2 \tag{11}$$

as in equation 15-2(4). Here $\bar{x}/2 = 0.38$ and $\bar{Q}$ can be obtained from Table 15-0. For example, if $k = 0.5$ then $I_2 = 0.223 - 0.5 + 0.38 = 0.103$. Similarly, when $k = 1.0$ then $I_2 = 0.172 - 0.1155 + 0.38 = 0.167$, etc.

The expected number of replenishments per week, by equation 15-1(3), is

$$I_3 = \frac{H(S)[1 - P(0)]}{w_p} \qquad (12)$$

This reduces to $I_3 = H(S)0.8/2 = 0.4H(S)$. But $H(S)$ is only a function of k and can be readily obtained from Table 15-0. Thus, for $k = 0.5$, $H(S) = 1.0$ and hence $I_3 = 0.4$. Similarly, for $k = 1.0$, $H(S) = 0.769$ and $I_3 = 0.308$, etc.

The expected total cost can now be obtained from

$$C(k) = c_1 I_1 + c_2 + I_2 + c_3 I_3 \qquad (13)$$

The results for $k = 0.5, \ldots, 3.5$ are given in Table 15-3a, from which we note that $k_o = 3.0$.

The solution of the system is thus $s_o = -1.0$, $S_o = 2.0$, and $C_o = \$10.26$ per week.

It is interesting that the minimum expected cost of the system is close to the minimum cost of a similar but deterministic system. Moreover, the difference $k_o = S_o - s_o$ is very close to the optimal lot size in the deterministic system.

Continuous Units

The expected total cost of the (s, S) system for continuous units can also be obtained as an immediate extension of Sections 15-0, 15-1, and 15-2. For a probability density $f(x)$ the cost is

$$C(s, S) = (c_1 J_1 + c_2 J_2 + c_3)/\bar{t} \qquad (14)$$

where, by equations 15-2(12) and 15-2(14),

$$J_1(s, S) = \begin{cases} w_p \displaystyle\int_0^S (S - y)g(y)\,dy + \int_0^{S-s} J_1(s, m)f(S - s - m)\,dm & s \geq 0 \\[4mm] w_p \displaystyle\int_0^S (S - y)g(y)\,dy + \int_0^S J_1(s, m)f(S - m)\,dm & s \leq 0 \end{cases} \qquad (15)$$

where

$$g(y) = \int_y^\infty \frac{f(x)}{x}\,dx \qquad (16)$$

where, by equations 15–2(13), 15–2(15), 15–2(16), and 15–2(30),

$$
J_2(s, S) = \begin{cases} w_p \int_S^\infty (y - S)g(y)\, dy + \int_0^{S-s} J_2(s, m)f(S - s - m)\, dm & \\ \hspace{6cm} s \geqq 0 & \\ w_p \int_S^\infty (y - S)g(y)\, dy + \int_0^S J_2(s, m)f(S - m)\, dm & \\ \hspace{5cm} s \leqq 0 & \\ \hspace{1cm} + \int_s^0 B(s, n)f(S - n)\, dn & \end{cases}
$$

(17)

and where

$$
B(s, n) = w_p(-n + \bar{y}) + \int_s^n B(s, r)f(n - r)\, dr \tag{18}
$$

The expected length of the scheduling period $\bar{t}$ depends only on the difference $S - s = k$. It can be determined from

$$
\bar{t}(k) = w_p + \int_0^k \bar{t}(v)f(k - v)\, dv \tag{19}
$$

Only for some very special probability densities $f(x)$ can the integral equations (15), (17), (18), and (19) be solved explicitly. For most systems it may be best to use the discrete methods described earlier in this section.

Example 15–3b

In an inventory system with an (s, S) policy, the reviewing period is w_p. The density of demand during the reviewing period is $f(x) = (x/b^2)e^{-x/b}$, $x \geqq 0$. The carrying and shortage costs are c_1 and c_2 per unit per unit time, and the replenishing cost is c_3. Find the optimal s_o and S_o.

This example is an extension of Example 15–2b. The functions J_1 and J_2 in equation (14) have already been determined. It therefore remains to find $\bar{t}(k)$ of equation (19). This equation is in the form of equation 15–2(18), where J stands for $\bar{t}(k)$ and $W = w_p$. Therefore, by equation 15–2(21),

$$
\bar{t}''(k) + \frac{2\bar{t}'(k)}{b} = \frac{w_p}{b^2} \tag{20}
$$

The general solution of this differential equation is

$$
\bar{t}(k) = a_1 e^{-2k/b} + a_2 + \frac{w_p k}{2b} \tag{21}
$$

The constants a_1 and a_2 can be determined from the simultaneous equations:

$$
W(0) = w_p = a_1 + a_2 \tag{22}
$$

$$
W'(0) = 0 = -\frac{2a_1}{b} + \frac{w_p}{2b}
$$

Hence $a_1 = w_p/4$ and $a_2 = 3w_p/4$, so that

$$\bar{\imath}(k) = \frac{w_p}{4}\left(\frac{2k}{b} + e^{-2k/b} + 3\right) \tag{23}$$

The Case $s \geqq 0$

From equation 15–2(37) and equations (14) and (23) we have

$$C(s, k) = \left(\frac{w_p b}{8}\right)\left\{(c_1 + c_2)4e^{-s/b}(1 + e^{-2k/b}) + c_1\left[2\frac{s}{b}\left(2\frac{k}{b} + e^{-2k/b} + 3\right)\right.\right.$$
$$\left.\left. + 2\left(\frac{k}{b}\right)^2 + 2\frac{k}{b} - 3e^{-2k/b} - 5\right]\right\} + c_3\right) \Big/ \frac{w_p}{4}\left(2\frac{k}{b} + e^{-2k/b} + 3\right) \tag{24}$$

Let us now define the following auxiliary variables and functions

$$\begin{array}{ll}
x = s/b & H(y) = 2y^2 + 8y + 4 \\
y = k/b & n = c_2/c_1 \\
J(y) = e^{-2y} + 1 & A = 8c_3/bw_p c_1 \\
G(y) = 2y + e^{-2y} + 3 &
\end{array} \tag{25}$$

Equation (24) can then be written in the form

$$C(x, y) = \frac{bc_1}{2}\left[\frac{(1 + n)4e^{-x}J(y) + H(y) + A}{G(y)} + 2x - 3\right] \tag{26}$$

Differentiating with respect to x and y, etc., leads to the necessary condition for the minimum cost,

$$e^{-x_o} = \frac{1}{1 + n}\frac{G(y_o)}{2J(y_o)} \tag{27}$$

and

$$[(1 + n)4e^{-x_o}J'(y_o) + H'(y_o)]G(y_o) = [(1 + n)4e^{-x_o}J(y_o)$$
$$+ H(y_o) + A]G'(y_o) \tag{28}$$

where J', H', and G' indicate derivatives with respect to y.

Substituting the result of equation (27) in equation (28) and rearranging gives

$$G(y_o)\frac{2G(y_o)J'(y_o) + J(y_o)H'(y_o)}{J(y_o)G'(y_o)} - 2G(y_o) - H(y_o) = A \tag{29}$$

Thus y_o can be found from equation (29) and then x_o from equation (27), so that the desired solution is $s_o = x_o b$ and $S_o = s_o + y_o b$.

The Case $s \leqq 0$

From equation 15-2(49) and equations (14) and (23) we have, for $S \leqq k$,

$$C(k, S) = \left\{ \frac{w_p b}{8} (c_1 + c_2) \left[e^{-2S/b} - 1 + 2\left(\frac{S}{b}\right)^2 + 2\frac{S}{b} \right] \right.$$

$$- c_2 \left[2\frac{S-k}{b}\left(2\frac{k}{b} + e^{-2k/b} + 3 \right) + 2\left(\frac{k}{b}\right)^2 + 2\frac{k}{b} \right.$$

$$\left. - 3e^{-2k/b} - 5 \right] + c_3 \right\} \bigg/ \frac{w_p}{4}\left(2\frac{k}{b} + e^{-2k/b} + 3 \right) \quad (30)$$

Let us now define the following

$$y = k/b \qquad\qquad\qquad H(y) = 2y^2 + 8y + 4$$
$$z = S/b \qquad\qquad\qquad m = c_1/c_2$$
$$I(z) = 2z^2 + 2z + e^{-2z} - 1 \qquad B = 8c_3/bw_p c_2 \qquad (31)$$
$$G(y) = 2y + e^{-2y} + 3$$

Equation (30) can then be written as

$$C(y, z) = \frac{bc_2}{2}\left[\frac{1 + m)I(z) - H(y) + B}{G(y)} + 2(y - z) + 3 \right] \quad (32)$$

Differentiating with respect to z, etc., we have

$$I'(z_o) = \frac{2}{1 + m} G(y_o) \quad (33)$$

or

$$2z_o - e^{-2z_o} = \frac{2y_o + e^{-2y_o} + 3}{1 + m} - 1 \quad (34)$$

Differentiating equation (32) with respect to y and using the result in equation (34) eventually leads to the simple relation

$$(y_o + 2)^2 = (1 + m)(1 + z_o)^2 + \frac{B}{2} + 1 - m \quad (35)$$

The simultaneous equations (34) and (35) can be used to find the optimal y_o and z_o, and hence we also obtain the solutions $S_o = z_o b$ and $s_o = S_o - y_o b$.

For example, let $w_p = 2$ weeks, $b = 3$ units, $c_1 = \$2$ per unit per week, $c_2 = \$21$ per unit per week, and $c_3 = \$333$.

In a deterministic system with a mean of $r = 2b/w_p = 3$ units per week the optimal lot size, by equation 5-1(5), is

$$q_o = \sqrt{2 \times 3 \times 333(2 + 21)/(2 \times 21)} = \sqrt{1094.1} \approx 33$$

The optimal order level, by equation 5-1(6), is $S_o \approx 33 \times 21/23 \approx 30$. Hence we may first check for a solution using equations (34) and (35). Here we may expect that $y_o \approx 33/3 = 11$ and $z_o \approx 30/3 = 10$, making both e^{-2z_o} and e^{-2y_o} in equation (34) negligible. Here also $m = 2/21$ and $B = 148/7$. Equations (34) and (35) thus give the simultaneous equations $23z_o = 21y_o + 20$ and $21(y_o + 2)^2 = 23(z_o + 1)^2 + 241$. From these equations we obtain the solution $y_o = 10$ and $z_o = 10$. And therefore, by equation (32), the minimum cost of the system is $63 per week.

Since $y_o = z_o$ then $x_o = 0$, which means that the solution could have also been obtained by using equations (27) and (29). And, indeed, we have here $n = 21/2$ and $A = 222$. From equation (29), for large values of y_o, we can obtain the equation $y_o^2 + y_o - 110 = 0$, from which we have the result $y_o = 10$. And then, by equation (27), for $y_o = 10$, we obtain $e^{-x_o} = 1$ or $x_o = 0$. Thus the complete solution for the numerical values selected is $s_o = 0$, $S_o = 30$, and $C_o = 63$ per week.

15-4 PROBLEMS

1. Show that equation 15-1(4) reduces to the total-cost equation of the lot-size system when demand is constant.
2. Compare the solution of Example 15-1a with the solution of a similar but deterministic system.
3. Solve Example 15-1a for a type (2, 3) system.
4. Show that equations 15-2(14) and 15-2(15) do not hold when $s > 0$.
5. In Example 15-2b, for $s \leqq 0$, show that $B(s, n)$ of equation 15-2(16) is given by

$$B(s, n) = \frac{w_p b}{8}\left[\left(3 - \frac{2s}{b}\right)e^{-2(n-s)/b} + 2\left(\frac{s}{b}\right)^2 - 4\frac{s}{b} - 2\left(\frac{n}{b}\right)^2 - 2\frac{n}{b} + 5\right] \quad (1)$$

6. Compare Example 15-2b with the system of Section 5-1 when b is relatively very small is relation to k_p. In particular, examine the solution given by equation 15-2(39) or 15-2(51) and compare it with the solution given by equation 5-1(15).
7. Solve problem 6, when b is relatively very much larger than k_p.
8. In an inventory system with an (s, S) policy, demand occurs at the beginning of each reviewing period w_p. The probability density of demand is $f(x) = (1/b)e^{-x/b}$. The unit carrying and shortage costs are c_1 and c_2 in $[$]/[Q][T]$.

The unit replenishing cost is c_3 in [$]. Let m and n be dimensionless quantities defined by

$$m = c_2/\sqrt{2c_1c_3/(bw_p)} \tag{2}$$

$$n = \frac{c_2/c_1}{m} = \sqrt{2c_3/(w_p b c_1)} \tag{3}$$

Show that
(a) For $m \geq 1$

$$s_o = b \ln [(mn + 1)/(n + 1)] \tag{4}$$

$$S_o = s_o + nb \tag{5}$$

(b) For $m \leq 1$

$$s_o = -b[\sqrt{(1 + n/m)(1 + mn)} - 1] \tag{6}$$

$$s_o = mn(-s_o + b) \tag{7}$$

(c) For any m

$$C_o = c_1 S_o \tag{8}$$

(Compare this problem with Karlin's model in Arrow et al. [4], pp. 229–233.)

9. Find the necessary conditions for determining $k_o{}^s$ of Section 15–3 in an inventory system with discrete units and an (s, S) policy.

10. For $s = -1.0$ simulate the (s, S) system of Example 15–0a over a period of 25 reviewing periods. Find the probability distribution of the amount on hand at the beginning of each reviewing period. Compare the results with the theoretical results in Table 15–0.

11. *The (s, S) policy as delayed recurrent events.*[*] In an inventory system with an (s, S) policy, let p_i be the probability of the occurrence of a demand i, let $n = S - s$, and let u_n be the expected length of the scheduling period. Show that u_n can be expressed in the form of the renewal equation

$$u_n = b_n + \sum_{i=0}^{n} p_i u_{n-i} \tag{9}$$

Hence show that

$$U(s) = \frac{B(s)}{1 - P(s)} = \frac{s}{(1 - s)[1 - P(s)]} \tag{10}$$

where $P(s)$, $B(s)$, and $U(s)$ are respectively the generating functions of p_i, b_n, and u_n. Check the results numerically for $n = 0, 1, 2, 3, 4$, and 5 if $p_0 = 0.0$, $p_1 = 0.5$, $p_2 = 0.3$, and $p_3 = 0.2$.

12. In an inventory system with an (s, S) policy, $s = 0$ and $S = 2$. During any day the probability of no demand is 0.5 and the probability of a demand for one unit is 0.5. At time 0 there is one unit in inventory. Let u_n be the probability that a replenishment occurs at time n, let b_n be the probability that a replenishment occurs for the first time at time n, and let f_n be the probability

---

[*] Details on delayed recurrent events can be found in Feller [17], pp. 293–296. Details on probability generating functions can be found in Feller [17], pp. 218–267.

that a replenishment occurs for the first time at time $m + n$, given that a previous replenishment occurred at time m. Let the corresponding generating functions* be $U(s)$, $B(s)$, and $F(s)$. Show that

$$B(s) = \frac{s}{2 - s}$$

$$F(s) = B^2(s) \tag{11}$$

$$U(s) = \frac{s(2 - s)}{4(1 - s)}$$

13. In an inventory system with an (s, S) policy, $s = 2$ and $S = 5$. The probability distribution of demand is $P(0) = 0.5$, $P(1) = 0.3$, $P(2) = 0.1$, and $P(3) = 0.1$.

(a) Show that on the average there will be 227/54 units in stock at the beginning of each day

(b) Show that the probability of a replenishment on any day is 25/108.

* See previous footnote.

Chapter 16

Extensions of Reorder-Point–
Order-Level Systems

16–0 This chapter deals with two classes of reorder-point–order-level systems. The first is the dynamic inventory model of Arrow, Harris, and Marschak. This model has received much attention since its publication in 1951. We shall treat it as an extension of the system of Section 15–3.

The second class of systems to be covered in this chapter concerns systems with leadtime. We shall see how the analysis of the previous chapter, in which leadtime is zero, can be readily extended to systems in which leadtime is significant.

THE ARROW, HARRIS, AND MARSCHAK
DYNAMIC MODEL

16–1 In 1951 Arrow, Harris, and Marschak published the now famous paper, "Optimal Inventory Policy" [3]. In this paper they analyze an inventory system which they call "a dynamic model with uncertainty." This model has since become closely identified with systems with an (s, S) policy.*

Using the terminology and notation of this book, the properties of the dynamic model can be stated as follows: the probability density of demand during a reviewing period w_p is $f(x)$, $x \geqq 0$. Demand occurs at the end of the period (i.e., the pattern index is zero). The carrying cost is c_1 per unit per unit time. The shortage cost is c_2 whenever there is any shortage during the reviewing period. The replenishing cost is c_3.

* See, for example, Dvorstzky, et al. [16].

302

In the original paper the authors assume that $w_p = 1$. They denote the cumulative distribution of demand by F and the unit costs by c, A, and K respectively. They also use a present value factor α. We shall assume that this factor is equal to 1. The method of analysis used by the authors can be classified as that of dynamic programming. We shall use another approach which is essentially the one used in Chapter 15. The authors have only examined the case when $s \geq 0$. We shall examine this case and also the case when $s \leq 0$. (In what follows the order level S is assumed to be non-negative, since for an optimal solution S_o would never be negative.)

Let the variable k be defined by

$$k = S - s \tag{1}$$

Let $K(s, k)$ or $K(s, S)$, as the case may be, represent the expected total cost of the system during a scheduling period. Let $\bar{t}(k)$ represent the expected length of the scheduling period. The expected total cost of the system can then be expressed as

$$C(s, S) = \frac{K(s, S)}{\bar{t}(k)} \tag{2}$$

From this equation we can determine the optimal s_o, S_o, and k_o.

The expected length of this scheduling period can be determined from

$$\bar{t}(k) = w_p + \int_0^k \bar{t}(v) f(u - v)\, dv \tag{3}$$

The expected total cost during the scheduling period will depend on whether $s \geq 0$ or $s \leq 0$. When $s \geq 0$ it can be determined from

$$K(s, k) = c_1(s + k)w_p + c_2 \int_{s+k}^{\infty} f(x)\, dx + c_3 \int_k^{\infty} f(x)\, dx$$
$$+ \int_0^k K(s, v) f(u - v)\, dv \tag{4}$$

When $s \leq 0$ then

$$K(s, S) = c_1 S w_p + c_2 \int_S^{\infty} f(x)\, dx + c_3 \int_{S-s}^{\infty} f(x)\, dx$$
$$+ \int_0^S K(s, v) f(S - v)\, dv + \int_0^{-s} B(v) f(S - s - v)\, dv \tag{5}$$

where $B(v)$ is the expected total cost during that portion of the scheduling period over which only shortages exist. The function B can be determined from

$$B(v) = c_2 + c_3 \int_v^{\infty} f(x)\, dx + \int_0^v B(w) f(v - w)\, dw \tag{6}$$

Example 16–1

In the Arrow, Harris, and Marschak dynamic model let $f(x) = (1/b)e^{-x/b}$, $x \geq 0$. Find s_o and S_o for any of the parameters w_p, b, c_1, c_2, and c_3.

Equations (3), (4), (5), and (6) can all be expressed in the simplified form

$$J(z) = W(z) + \int_0^z J(y)f(z - y)\, dy \tag{7}$$

In addition, for the specific density $f(x) = (1/b)e^{-x/b}$, we have

$$f(0) = \frac{1}{b}, \quad \frac{df}{dx} = -\frac{1}{b}f(x), \quad \int_z^\infty f(z)\, dz = bf(z) \tag{8}$$

Differentiating equation (7) with respect to z, and noting the relations in equation (8), we obtain

$$J'(z) = W'(z) + J(z)f(0) - \frac{1}{b}\int_0^z J(y)f(z - y)\, dy$$

$$= W'(z) + \frac{1}{b}\left[J(z) - \int_0^z J(y)f(z - y)\, dy\right] \tag{9}$$

Hence, from equation (7),

$$J'(z) = W'(z) + \frac{1}{b}W(z) \tag{10}$$

The solution of the differential equation (10) will now depend on the specific form of the function $W(z)$. This solution will always have a constant which can be determined from equation (7) for $z = 0$, namely,

$$J(0) = W(0) \tag{11}$$

For $\bar{t}(k)$ of equation (3), $W(z) = w_p$, and hence

$$\bar{t}'(k) = \frac{w_p}{b} \tag{12}$$

Therefore

$$\bar{t}(k) = w_p\frac{k}{b} + a \tag{13}$$

But $\bar{t}(0) = w_p$; hence

$$\bar{t}(k) = \frac{w_p k}{b} + w_p = w_p\left(\frac{k}{b} + 1\right) \tag{14}$$

For $K(s, k)$ of equation (4)

$$W(k) = c_1(s + k)w_p + c_2\int_{s+k}^\infty f(x)\, dx + c_3\int_k^\infty f(x)\, dx \tag{15}$$

Hence, from equations (10) and (8),

$$K'(s, k) = c_1 w_p - c_2 f(s + k) - c_3 f(k)$$
$$+ \frac{1}{b}[c_1(s + k)w_p + c_2 bf(s + k) + c_3 bf(k)] \qquad (16)$$
$$= c_1 w_p \left(\frac{k}{b} + \frac{s}{b} + 1 \right)$$

Therefore

$$K(s, k) = c_1 w_p \left[\frac{k^2}{2b} + \left(\frac{s}{b} + 1 \right) k \right] + a \qquad (17)$$

But, by equations (11), (15), and (8),

$$K(s, 0) = c_1 s w_p + c_2 bf(s) + c_3 \qquad (18)$$

so that equation (17), after rearranging, becomes

$$K(s, k) = c_1 w_p \left[\frac{k^2}{2b} + \left(\frac{s}{b} + 1 \right) k + s \right] + c_2 e^{-s/b} + c_3 \qquad (19)$$

To find $K(s, S)$ of equation (5), we first have to find $B(v)$ of equation (6). By equation (10) we have

$$B'(v) = -c_3 f(v) + \frac{1}{b}[c_2 + c_3 bf(v)] = \frac{c_2}{b} \qquad (20)$$

And since $B(0) = c_2 + c_3$, we have

$$B(v) = c_2 \left(\frac{v}{b} + 1 \right) + c_3 \qquad (21)$$

For equation (5) we now have

$$W(S) = c_1 w_p S + c_2 bf(S) + c_3 bf(S - s)$$
$$+ \int_0^{-s} \left[c_2 \left(\frac{v}{b} + 1 \right) + c_3 \right] f(S - s - v)\, dv \qquad (23)$$
$$= c_1 w_p S + c_2 (b - s)f(S) + c_3 bf(S)$$

Therefore, by equation (10),

$$K'(s, S) = c_1 w_p - \frac{c_2(b - s)f(S)}{b} - \frac{c_3 bf(S)}{b}$$
$$+ \frac{1}{b}[c_1 w_p S + c_2(b - s)f(S) + c_3 bf(S)] \qquad (24)$$
$$= c_1 w_p \left(\frac{S}{b} + 1 \right)$$

Hence

$$K(s, S) = c_1 w_p\left(\frac{S^2}{2b} + S\right) + W(0)$$

$$= c_1 w_p\left(\frac{S^2}{2b} + S\right) + c_2\left(1 - \frac{s}{b}\right) + c_3 \tag{25}$$

Equations (2), (14), (19), and (25) now give the expected total cost of the system. When $s \geq 0$ it is

$$C(s, k) = \frac{c_1 w_p[k^2/2b + (s/b + 1)k + s] + c_2 e^{-s/b} + c_3}{w_p(k/b + 1)} \tag{26}$$

and when $s \leq 0$ it is

$$C(s, S) = \frac{c_1 w_p(S^2/2b + S) + c_2(1 - s/b) + c_3}{w_p[(S - s)/b + 1]} \tag{27}$$

We first consider equation (26). Differentiating with respect to s, etc., leads to

$$s_o = b \ln \frac{c_2}{c_1 w_p(k_0 + b)} \tag{28}$$

Using this result we then obtain

$$k_o = \sqrt{\frac{2(b/w_p)c_3}{c_1}} \tag{29}$$

and

$$C_o = c_1(s_o + k_o + b) \tag{30}$$

These results only hold when $s \geq 0$, that is, when

$$b \ln \frac{c_2}{c_1 w_p(k_o + b)} \geq 0 \tag{31}$$

or when

$$\frac{c_2}{w_p} \geq \sqrt{2(b/w_p)c_1 c_3} + bc_1 \tag{32}$$

Otherwise, $s_o = 0$ or possibly $s_o < 0$.

We now consider equation (27) which was based on $s \leq 0$. It can be rearranged and expressed in the form

$$C(s, S) = \frac{c_2}{w_p} + \frac{c_1 w_p(S^2/2b + S) - c_2 S/b + c_3}{w_p[(S - s)/b + 1]} \tag{33}$$

If the numerator in the second term on the right side of equation (33) is positive, this immediately implies that

$$s_o = -\infty \quad \text{and} \quad C_o = \frac{c_2}{w_p} \tag{34}$$

If the numerator is negative then $s_o = 0$ or possibly $s_o > 0$. But this can occur only if

$$\frac{c_2}{w_p} \geq bc_1 + \frac{c_1 S}{2} + \frac{bc_3}{w_p S} \geq bc_1 + \sqrt{2(b/w_p)c_1 c_3} \qquad (35)$$

which, by equation (32) and its preceding equations, is the condition for $s_o \geq 0$. Therefore when equation (32) holds, the solution of the system is given by equations (28), (29), and (30).

In summary, then, the complete solution can be stated as follows. Let

$$c_2 = a[\sqrt{2(b/w_p)c_1 c_3} + bc_1]w_p \qquad (36)$$

Then, when $a \geq 1$,

$$k_o = \sqrt{\frac{2(b/w_p)c_3}{c_1}}, \qquad s_o = b \ln a \qquad (37)$$

$$S_o = s_o + k_o, \qquad C_o = c_1(s_o + k_o + b) = c_1 b \ln a + \frac{c_2}{a w_p}$$

When $a \leq 1$, the solution is

$$s_o = -\infty, \qquad S_o = 0, \qquad C_o = c_2/w_p \qquad (38)$$

THE PROBABILISTIC REORDER-POINT–ORDER-LEVEL SYSTEMS WITH LEADTIME

16–2   In this section we deal with all systems with a (z, Z) policy. It will be recalled that systems with a (z, q) policy can be analyzed relatively easily as extensions of (s, q) systems. These extensions also apply to (z, Z) systems.

Let Q be the amount on hand and on order in a system with a (z, Z) policy. In a system with discrete units the probability distribution of Q will be the same as in a corresponding (s, S) system. Let $P(x)$ be the probability distribution of demand during the reviewing period. Then, by equation 15–0(11), we have

$$H(Q) = A(Z - Q) \Big/ \sum_{y=0}^{Z-z-u} A(y) \qquad Q = z + u, \ldots, Z \qquad (1)$$

where

$$A(y) = \begin{cases} 1 & y = 0 \\ \sum_{x=u}^{y} A(y - x)R(x) & y = u, 2u, \ldots \end{cases} \qquad (2)$$

and where

$$R(x) = \frac{P(x)}{1 - P(0)} \qquad x = u, 2u, \ldots \qquad (3)$$

Let L be the leadtime, let v be the demand during leadtime, and let $N(v)$ be the probability distribution of demand. Let Q' be the amount on hand at the beginning of a reviewing period. Obviously,

$$Q'(T + L) = Q(T) - v \tag{4}$$

That is, if there is an amount Q on hand and on order at time T, there will be an amount $Q' = Q - v$ on hand at time $T + L$, since any amount on order at time T will have been added to stock by time $T + L$. In the steady state the random variables Q', Q, and v are therefore related by

$$Q' = Q - v \tag{5}$$

Let $M(Q')$ designate the probability distribution of Q'. Then

$$M(Q') = \sum_{Q=Q'}^{Z} H(Q)N(Q - Q') \qquad z + u - v_{\max} \leqq Q' \leqq Z \tag{6}$$

Once $M(Q')$ is known the system can then be treated as in Chapter 15.

Example 16–2a

In an inventory system with a reorder-point–order-level policy the reviewing period is 2 weeks. The probability distribution of demand during the reviewing period is $P(0) = 0.20, P(0.5) = 0.24, P(1.0) = 0.40, P(1.5) = 0.16$. Leadtime is 2 weeks. The carrying cost is \$5 per unit per week, the

TABLE 16–2a

The Probability Distribution $M(Q')$ of Equation (6) for Example 16–2a

Q' / k	Z	$Z - 0.5$	$Z - 1.0$	$Z - 1.5$	$Z - 2.0$	$Z - 2.5$	$Z - 3.0$	$Z - 3.5$	$Z - 4.0$	$Z - 4.5$
0.5	0.200	0.240	0.400	0.160						
1.0	0.154	0.231	0.363	0.205	0.037					
1.5	0.106	0.159	0.312	0.223	0.150	0.050				
2.0	0.083	0.124	0.244	0.218	0.170	0.126	0.035			
2.5	0.068	0.103	0.201	0.180	0.175	0.146	0.099	0.028		
3.0	0.058	0.087	0.170	0.152	0.148	0.154	0.121	0.085	0.025	
3.5	0.050	0.075	0.148	0.132	0.129	0.134	0.131	0.106	0.074	0.021

shortage cost is \$10 per unit per week, and the replenishing cost is \$40. What are the optimal reorder point z_o and the optimal order level Z_o?

This example is identical with Example 15–3a except that we now have a 2-week leadtime. The probability distribution of the amount on hand and on order $H(Q)$ is essentially the same as in Table 15–0. The probability distribution of demand during leadtime is the same as demand during the reviewing period. Using equation (6), the distribution $M(Q')$ is given in Table 16–2a. In this table the variable k is defined by

$$k = Z - z \tag{7}$$

For example, let $k = 1.0$. The variable Q' then has the range $Z - k + u - v_{max}$ to Z, or $Z - 2.0$ to Z. By equation (6) $M(Z) = H(Z)N(0) = 0.769 \times 0.20 = 0.154$, $M(Z - 0.5) = H(Z - 0.5)N(0) + H(Z)N(0.5) = 0.231 \times 0.20 + 0.769 \times 0.24 = 0.231$, etc., and $M(Z - 2.0) = H(Z - 2.0)N(0) + \cdots + H(Z)N(2.0) = 0 \times 0.20 + 0 \times 0.24 + 0 \times 0.40 + 0.231 \times 0.16 + 0.769 \times 0 = 0.037$.

We can now proceed as in Section 15–3 by replacing s with z, S with Z, Q with Q', and $H(Q)$ with $M(Q')$. All the other results are unchanged. As

TABLE 16–2b

Computation of $z_0{}^k$ of Equation 15–3(8) and the Corresponding $C(k)$ of Equation 15–3(1) for Example 16–2a

k	$z_0{}^k$	I_1	I_2	I_3	$C(k)$
0.5	1.0	0.4653	0.1053	0.4000	19.3795
1.0	0.5	0.2915	0.0465	0.3076	14.2265
1.5	0.5	0.5972	0.1282	0.2116	12.7320
2.0	0.0	0.4765	0.2495	0.1656	11.5015
2.5	0.0	0.6892	0.2017	0.1364	10.9190
3.0	0.0	0.9102	0.1732	0.1156	10.9070
3.5	−0.5	0.7892	0.3002	0.1004	10.9640

in Example 15–3a, we search for the optimal difference k_o starting with $k = u = 0.5$, etc. The principal results are given in Table 16–2b which is quite similar to Table 15–3a. From the table we conclude that $Z_o = 3.0$ and $z_o = 0$. The minimum expected total cost is $10.91 per week. The introduction of a 2-week leadtime has thus increased the cost from $10.26 per week to $10.91 per week.

Continuous Units

Let $f(x)$ be the density of demand during the reviewing period, and let x_{max} be the maximum possible demand. Let Q be the amount on hand and on order at the beginning of a reviewing period. Let $g(Q)$ be the probability density of Q and let h be the probability that Q equals Z. Then, by equations 15–0(12) and 15–0(13),

$$g(Q) = \int_Q^Z g(y)f(y - Q)\, dy + hf(Z - Q) \qquad z < Q < Z \qquad (8)$$

and

$$h = \int_z^Z \int_{y-z}^\infty f(x)\, dx\, g(y)\, dy + \int_{Z-z}^\infty hf(x)\, dx \qquad (9)$$

Let $n(v)$ be the probability density of demand during leadtime. Let Q' be the amount on hand at the beginning of a reviewing period. Let $m(Q')$ be the probability density of Q'. This density can be determined from

$$m(Q') = \begin{cases} \int_{Q'}^{Z} g(Q)n(Q - Q') \, dQ + hn(Z - Q') & z < Q' < Z \\[2em] \int_{z}^{Z} g(Q)n(Q - Q') \, dQ + hn(Z - Q') & z - x_{\max} < Q' < z \end{cases} \tag{10}$$

Now let $k(r)$ be a density equivalent to $f(x)$. Then

$$I_1 = \int_{z-x_{\max}}^{Z} \left[\int_0^{Q'} (Q' - r)k(r) \, dr \right] m(Q') \, dQ' \tag{11}$$

and

$$I_2 = \int_{z-x_{\max}}^{Z} \left[\int_{Q'}^{x_{\max}} (r - Q')k(r) \, dr \right] m(Q') \, dQ' \tag{12}$$

The value of I_3 is not affected by leadtime and is the same as it was in Chapter 15, namely,

$$I_3 = \frac{h}{w_p} \tag{13}$$

It should be noted that I_1 and I_2 can be computed by another method. Let w be a demand defined by

$$w = v + r \tag{14}$$

and let its density be

$$p(w) = n(v) * k(r) = \int_0^w n(v)k(w - v) \, dv \tag{15}$$

Then

$$I_1 = \int_z^Z \left[\int_0^Q (Q - w)p(w) \, dw \right] g(Q) \, dQ + h \int_0^Z (Z - w)p(w) \, dw \tag{16}$$

$$I_2 = \int_z^Z \left[\int_Q^\infty (w - Q)p(w) \, dw \right] g(Q) \, dQ + h \int_Z^\infty (w - Z)p(w) \, dw \tag{17}$$

Example 16–2b

In an inventory system with a (z, Z) policy demand is instantaneous at the beginning of each reviewing period. The probability density of demand is $f(x) = (1/b)e^{-x/b}$, $x \geq 0$. Leadtime is one reviewing period. What is the expected total cost of the system for non-negative reorder points?

Equations (8) and (9) have already been solved for the given density (Example 15–0b). Hence, by equations 15–0(24) and 15–0(25),

$$g(Q) = \frac{1}{b + Z - z} \qquad z < Q < Z \tag{18}$$

and

$$h = \frac{b}{b + Z - z} \tag{19}$$

Hence equation (10) now becomes

$$m(Q') = \begin{cases} \displaystyle\int_{Q'}^{Z} \frac{1}{b + Z - z} \frac{1}{b} e^{-(Q - Q')/b} \, dQ + \frac{b}{b + Z - z} \frac{1}{b} e^{-(Z - Q')/b} \\ \qquad\qquad\qquad\qquad\qquad\qquad\qquad\qquad\qquad z < Q' < Z \\[6pt] \displaystyle\int_{z}^{Z} \frac{1}{b + Z - z} \frac{1}{b} e^{-(Q - Q')/b} \, dQ + \frac{b}{b + Z - z} \frac{1}{b} e^{-(Z - Q')/b} \\ \qquad\qquad\qquad\qquad\qquad\qquad\qquad\qquad\qquad -\infty < Q' < z \end{cases} \tag{20}$$

Evaluation of the definite integrals leads to

$$m(Q') = \begin{cases} 1/(b + Z - z) & z < Q' < Z \\ [1/(b + Z - z)]e^{-(z - Q')/b} & -\infty < Q' < z \end{cases} \tag{21}$$

Since demand is instantaneous, the equivalent distribution $k(r)$ is identical with $f(x)$. Therefore, by equations (11) and (21),

$$\begin{aligned} I_1 &= \int_0^z \int_0^{Q'} (Q' - r) \frac{1}{b} e^{-r/b} \, dr \frac{1}{b + Z - z} e^{-(z - Q')/b} dQ' \\ &\quad + \int_z^Z \int_0^{Q'} (Q - r) \frac{1}{b} e^{-r/b} \, dr \frac{1}{b + Z - z} \, dQ' \\ &= b \Bigg[e^{-z/b} \left(\frac{z}{b} + 3 \right) - e^{-Z/b} + \frac{(Z/b)^2 - (z/b)^2}{2} \\ &\quad - \frac{Z}{b} + \frac{2z}{b} - 2 \Bigg] \bigg/ \left(1 + \frac{Z - z}{b} \right) \end{aligned} \tag{22}$$

Similarly, by equations (12) and (21),

$$\begin{aligned} I_2 &= \int_{-\infty}^0 \int_0^{\infty} (r - Q') \frac{1}{b} e^{-r/b} \, dr \frac{1}{b + Z - z} e^{-(z - Q')/b} \, dQ' \\ &\quad + \int_0^z \int_{Q'}^{\infty} (r - Q') \frac{1}{b} e^{-r/b} \, dr \frac{1}{b + Z - z} e^{-(z - Q')/b} \, dQ' \\ &\quad + \int_z^Z \int_{Q'}^{\infty} (r - Q') \frac{1}{b} e^{-r/b} \, dr \frac{1}{b + Z - z} \, dQ' \\ &= b \left[e^{-z/b} \left(\frac{z}{b} + 3 \right) - e^{-Z/b} \right] \bigg/ \left(1 + \frac{Z - z}{b} \right) \end{aligned} \tag{23}$$

These results for I_1 and I_2 can also be obtained from equations (16) and (17). From equation (15) we obtain

$$p(w) = \int_0^w \frac{1}{b} e^{-v/b} \frac{1}{b} e^{-(w-v)/b} \, dv = \frac{w}{b^2} e^{-w/b} \tag{24}$$

Therefore equation (16) gives

$$\begin{aligned} I_1 &= \int_z^Z \int_0^Q (Q - w) \frac{w}{b^2} e^{w/b} \, dw \, \frac{1}{b + Z - z} \, dQ \\ &+ \frac{b}{b + Z - z} \int_0^Z (Z - w) \frac{w}{b^2} e^{-w/b} \, dw \end{aligned} \tag{25}$$

This leads to the result in equation (22).

Similarly, equations (17), (18), (19), and (24) lead to the result in equation (23).

The expected total cost of the system for $z \geqq 0$ can now be determined, namely by equations (22) and (23) and equations (13) and (19):

$$C(z, Z) = c_1 I_1 + c_2 I_2 + c_3 I_3$$

$$= \frac{b\left\{ (c_1 + c_2)\left[e^{-z/b}\left(\dfrac{z}{b} + 3\right) - e^{-Z/b} \right] + c_1\left[\dfrac{1}{2}\left(\dfrac{Z}{b}\right)^2 - \dfrac{1}{2}\left(\dfrac{z}{b}\right)^2 - \dfrac{Z}{b} + 2\dfrac{z}{b} - 2 \right] \right\} + \dfrac{c_3}{w_p}}{1 + \dfrac{Z - z}{b}} \tag{26}$$

In a similar manner the expected total cost can be determined for $z \leqq 0$. Then the optimal z_o and Z_o can be computed for any of the parameters w_p, b, c_1, c_2, and c_3.

16–3 PROBLEMS

1. Find the expected total cost of the Arrow, Harris, and Marschak dynamic model when $S < 0$.
2. Compare the solution of the system of Section 16–1 with the solutions of the following systems: (a) Section 5–4, (b) Section 8–1 (Case 8–1a), (c) Section 8–3 (Example 8–3a).
3. How is the solution of the system of Section 16–1 affected as the unit of replenishing costs decreases? In particular, analyze the system for $c_3 = 0$.

4. Show algebraically that when $a \geq 1$ in equation 16–1(36) then

$$c_1 b \ln a + c_2/aw_p \leq c_2/w_p \qquad (1)$$

What is the significance of this statement?

5. Verify the results given by equations 16–1(28), 16–1(29), and 16–1(30).

6. Check the results given in Table 16–2b for (a) $k = 2.5$, (b) $k = 3.0$, and (c) $k = 3.5$.

7. In Section 16–2 it is possible to find the expected average amount in inventory I_1 and the expected average shortage I_2 without first computing the distribution $M(Q')$ of equation 16–2(6). Let $D(w)$ be a probability distribution equivalent to $P(x)$ and let $R(y)$ be defined by

$$R(y) = D(w) * N(v) = \sum_{v=0}^{y} D(y - v)N(v) \qquad (2)$$

Show that

$$I_1 = \sum_{Q=z+u}^{Z} \sum_{y=0}^{Q} (Q - y)R(y)H(Q) \qquad (3)$$

and that

$$I_2 = \sum_{Q=z+u}^{Z} \sum_{y=Q+u}^{\infty} (y - Q)R(y)H(Q) \qquad (4)$$

where $H(Q)$ is defined by equation 16–2(1). Verify the result by computing I_1 and I_2 for $k = 3.0$ in Example 16–2a.

8. Interpret equations 16–2(11) and 16–2(12) when $z < x_{max}$ and when $z < 0$.

9. What is the significance of the approach leading to the results of equations 16–2(16) and 16–2(17) as compared with the results of equations 16–2(11) and 16–2(12).

10. Verify the results given by equation 16–2(22) and 16–2(23). Show that identical results can be obtained using equations 16–2(16) and 16–2(17).

11. Solve example 16–2b when $w_p = 1$ week, $b = 2$ units, $c_1 = \$8$ per unit per week, $c_2 = \$24$ per unit per week, and $c_3 = \$18$ per replenishment. Show that the optimal reorder point and the optimal order level are 3.3 units and 6.7 units respectively, and that the minimum expected total cost is \$40.04 per week.

12. Simulate the (z, Z) system of Example 16–2a over 25 reviewing periods for $z = 0$ and $Z = 3.0$. Find the probability distribution of the amount on hand at the beginning of each reviewing period. Compare the results with the theoretical results in Table 16–2b.

13. What is the extension of the model of Section 16–1 to discrete units and significant leadtime? How would you use simulation to solve the extended model? Illustrate your method of solution for the system in which $w_p = 1$ week, $P(1) = 0.4$, $P(2) = 0.3$, $P(3) = 0.2$, $P(4) = 0.1$, $L = 2$ weeks, $c_1 = \$1$ per unit per week, $c_2 = \$100$, and $c_3 = \$15$.

14. Solve problem (13) when leadtime is zero and when (a) $c_2 = \$10$ and (b) $c_2 = \$100$.

Chapter 17

Comparison of Inventory Policies

17-0 Three principal inventory policies have been discussed in this book, the (t, S) policy, the (s, q) policy, and the (s, S) policy. A number of other policies were also mentioned (e.g., in Section 7–2 and in Chapter 12). It is only natural to ask how these various policies compare with one another and which, if any, is the best policy.

In Section 7–1, for example, we saw that the minimum cost of the system for an (s, q) policy was larger than the minimum cost for a (t, S_i) policy. We also saw that the best policy was a (t_i, S_i) policy. Another example is provided by the systems of Section 3–5 and problem 3–6(13) in which several items have a common replenishment cost. In this example the policy of replenishing items independently with different scheduling periods is more costly than the policy of replenishing all items simultaneously with the same scheduling period.

In this chapter we shall show that for a certain class of inventory systems the (s, S) policy is always better than or equal to an (s, q) policy. We shall also show that an (s, q) policy is always better than or equal to a (t, S) policy. It should be emphasized, however, that these results do not hold in general for all inventory systems. Section 17–3 provides a number of illustrations in which a (t, S) policy may be the best policy.

The problem of finding optimal policies is in general a rather difficult one. It is fairly safe to say that we cannot even prescribe a general method which will lead to the determination of an optimal policy for every inventory system. At best the following procedure may be adopted.

1. Several different policies are formulated [e.g., (s, q), (t, S), etc].

2. For each policy the optimal values of the controllable variables are found (e.g., s_o, q_o or t_o, S_o, etc.).

3. The minimum cost for each policy is ascertained [e.g., $C(s_o, q_o)$, $C(t_o, S_o)$, etc.].

4. On the basis of the results of step 3 the optimal policy is selected [i.e., if $C(s_o, q_o) < C(t_o, S_o)$, the (s, q) policy is chosen].

Of course, for certain policies it may be possible to go from step (1) to step (4) directly. (We shall do this for the (s, S), (s, q), and (t, S) policies of Sections 17–1 and 17–2.) Generally, however, we are not so fortunate, particularly with complex inventory systems that include many items. Section 17–3 provides two illustrations of systems with several items.

COMPARISON OF (s, q) AND (s, S) POLICIES

17–1   In an inventory system with an (s, q) policy let the optimal reorder point be designated by $s_o{}^q$ and let the optimal lot size be q_o. Let the corresponding minimum expected total cost of the system be $C_o{}^q$. In the same system, but with an (s, S) policy, let the corresponding quantities be designated by $s_o{}^S$, S_o, and $C_o{}^S$. In addition, for any s and q, or s and S, let the corresponding expected total costs be $C^q(s, q)$ or $C^S(s, S)$. Hence, by definition, for any s and q, or s and S,

$$C_o{}^q \leqq C^q(s, q)$$
$$C_o{}^S \leqq C^S(s, S) \tag{1}$$

We now propose to show that in general

$$C_o{}^S \leqq C_o{}^q \tag{2}$$

We shall give the proof for the discrete case. The continuous case can be proved in a similar way.

The inventory system with an (s, q) policy is described graphically in Figure 13–0. Under this policy the amount Q at the beginning of any reviewing period may be any amount between $s + u$ and $s + q$. At the beginning of any scheduling period the amount Q will also be between $s + u$ and $s + q$. Now consider the same system with an (s, S) policy as in Figure 15–0. Here the amount Q in inventory at the beginning of any reviewing period may be between $s + u$ and S, but the amount at the beginning of any scheduling period is always S. Thus for the (s, q) policy the amount at the beginning of each scheduling period is not necessarily the same from period to period, whereas for the (s, S) policy it is the same. This simple observation will form the basis of our proof.

The term $C^S(s, S)$ has been defined as the expected total cost of the inventory system with an (s, S) policy. This means that if we start a scheduling period with S and replenish when the reorder point is reached, the expected total cost per unit time is $C^S(s, S)$. Therefore if we start any scheduling period with Q and replenish when the reorder point s is reached, the expected total cost per unit of time will be $C^S(s, Q)$. It is now evident that the expected total cost of the system with an (s, q) policy can be stated as

$$C^q(s, q) = \sum_{Q=s+u}^{s+q} w_Q C^S(s, Q) \tag{3}$$

where the w_Q are weighing factors which depend on how frequently the scheduling period starts with Q and how long it then is. Obviously,

$$w_Q \geq 0 \quad \text{and} \quad \sum_{Q=s+u}^{s+q} w_Q = 1 \tag{4}$$

From equations (1), (3), and (4) we now obtain the desired result

$$C_o^q = C^q(s_o^q, q_o) = \sum_{Q=s_o^q+u}^{s_o^q+q_o} w_Q C^S(s_o^q, Q) \geq \sum_{Q=s_o^q+u}^{s_o^q+q_o} w_Q C_o^S = C_o^S \tag{5}$$

Example 17–1

In an inventory system the reviewing period is 1 week. Demand during the reviewing period has the distribution $P(0) = 0.2$, $P(1) = 0.4$, $P(2) = 0.4$. The carrying cost is \$1 per unit per week, the shortage cost \$1 per unit per week, and replenishing cost \$1 per replenishment. Compare the costs of the system for an (s, q) policy with those for an (s, S) policy.

TABLE 17–1a

The Expected Total Costs for an (s, q) Policy

q \ s	−2	−1	0	1	2
1	2.40	1.40	1.40	2.20	3.20
2	1.70	1.20	1.60	2.50	3.50
3	1.33	1.27	1.87	2.80	3.80

Using the methods of Chapter 13, we can determine with relative ease the expected total cost of the system for various reorder points and various lot sizes. They are given in Table 17–1a. Similarly, using the methods of Chapter 15, we can obtain the results in Table 17–1b. Tables 17–1a and 17–1b can be compared in several ways. First, the results are identical when $q = u$ and $S - s = u$. This is not a surprising result. The (s, q) policy is in general identical with the (s, S) policy whenever this occurs.

The second comparison should be regarded as qualitive rather than quantitative. It appears that under an (s, q) policy the total costs are about as sensitive to changes in the controllable variables as in the (s, S) policy, probably because of the particular distribution of demand and the unit costs.

The third comparison deals with the minimum expected total costs. As has been proved, we do indeed have* $C_o^q = 1.20 > 1.13 = C_o^S$. The pertinent weighing factors w_Q of equations (3,) (4), and (5) are $w_0 = \frac{1}{4}$ and

TABLE 17–1b

The Expected Total Costs for a (s, S) Policy

$S - s$ \ S	−1	0	1	2	3
1	2.40	1.40	1.40	2.20	3.20
2	2.47	1.47	1.13	1.67	2.60
3	2.84	1.84	1.29	1.31	1.93

$w_1 = \frac{3}{4}$. Hence, by equation (3) and from Tables 17–1a and 17–1b, we indeed have

$$C_o^q = C^q(-1, 2) = \sum_{Q=0}^{1} w_Q C^S(-1, Q)$$
$$= w_0 C^S(-1, 0) + w_1 C^S(-1, 1) \qquad (6)$$
$$= (\tfrac{1}{4})1.40 + (\tfrac{3}{4})1.1\dot{3} = 1.20$$

We shall now show how the factors w_0 and w_1 can be computed from first principles. Let p_0 be the probability that under the (s, q) policy there is an amount $Q = 0$ in inventory at the beginning of a scheduling period. Let $\bar{t}_0$ be the corresponding expected length of the scheduling period. Similarly, let p_1 and $\bar{t}_1$ be defined for $Q = 1$. By the reasoning leading to equation (3), we would expect that

$$w_0 : w_1 = p_0 \bar{t}_0 : p_1 \bar{t}_1 \qquad (7)$$

In the present example, for $s = -1$, $q = 2$, the probability $H(Q)$, by equation 13–0(1), is $H(0) = \frac{1}{2}$ and $H(1) = \frac{1}{2}$. Therefore $p_0 = H(0)P(2) = (\frac{1}{2})0.4 = 0.2$. And $p_1 = H(0)P(1) + H(1)P(2) = (\frac{1}{2})0.4 + (\frac{1}{2})0.4 = 0.4$. The expected scheduling period $\bar{t}_0$ can be determined from

$$\bar{t}_0 = 0.8 \times 1 + 0.2(1 + \bar{t}_0) \qquad (8)$$

Hence $\bar{t}_0 = 1.25$. The expected scheduling period $\bar{t}_1$ can now be determined from

$$\bar{t}_1 = 0.4 \times 1 + 0.4(1 + \bar{t}_0) + 0.2(1 + \bar{t}_1) \qquad (9)$$

Hence $\bar{t}_1 = 1.875$. Therefore, by equation (7), $w_0 : w_1 = 0.2 \times 1.25 : 0.4 \times 1.875 = 1 : 3$. Hence, by equation (4), $w_0 = \frac{1}{4}$ and $w_1 = \frac{3}{4}$.

* Note that the precise value of C_o^S is $\frac{17}{15} = 1.1\dot{3}$.

Extensions

The result expressed by equation (2) is quite general. It does not depend, for example, on the specific cost parameters used or on the structure of the costs. The result holds whenever the cost of the system with an (s, q) policy can be expressed in the form of equation (3).* For similar reasons, we can extend the result to systems with leadtime. That is,

$$C^q(z_o{}^q, q_o) \geqq C^Z(z_o{}^Z, Z_o) \tag{10}$$

The notation in this equation is self-explanatory, and the details for proving this assertion are left as an exercise [problem 17–4(3)].

COMPARISON OF (t, S) AND (s, q) POLICIES

17–2   The comparison of inventory systems with (t, S) policies and (s, q) policies is considerably simpler than the comparison of the systems in the previous section. The major clue in the comparison is the nature of the (s, q) policy when q approaches zero. In the discrete case the smallest value q can have is u. What does an (s, u) policy mean? It is quite evident that in such a case we have a (t, S) policy, where $t = w_p$ and $S = s + u$. Thus a system with a (t, S) policy is a special case of the (s, q) policy. We can therefore assert that the minimum cost of a system with a (t, S) policy is larger than, or equal to, the minimum cost of a system with an (s, q) policy.

For a formal proof we can proceed as follows. Let the expected total cost of an inventory system with a (t, S) policy and a reviewing period w^t be denoted** by $C^t(w^t, t, S)$. Let the optimal reviewing period be $w_o{}^t$, let the optimal scheduling period be t_o, and let the optimal order level be S_o. Obviously

$$w_o{}^t = t_o \tag{1}$$

Let the corresponding minimum cost be $C_o{}^t$, that is,

$$C_o{}^t \leqq C^t(w^t, t, S) \tag{2}$$

Similarly, let the expected total cost for a (s, q) policy be $C^q(w^q, s, q)$, let the optimal reviewing period, reorder point, and lot size be respectively $w_o{}^q$, s_o, and q_o, and let the minimum cost be $C_o{}^q$. That is,

$$C_o{}^q \leqq C^q(w^q, s, q) \tag{3}$$

We shall now show that

$$C_o{}^q \leqq C_o{}^t \tag{4}$$

---

* This is, of course, true even when the w_Q are very difficult to compute. The mere knowledge that the w_Q exist suffices to prove equation (5).

** Obviously, t will always be an integer multiple of w^t.

This can be done immediately from the definitions and equation (1):

$$C_o{}^t = C^t(w_o{}^t, t_o, S_o) = C^t(t_o, t_o, S_o)$$
$$= C^q(t_o, S_o - u, u) \geqq C^q(w_o{}^q, s_o, q_o) = C_o{}^q \quad (5)$$

The Optimal Reviewing Period

In order to obtain the proof in equation (5) it was convenient to think of the reviewing period as a controllable variable. When there is no cost associated with reviewing, we would expect w to be as small as practically possible. But when there is such a cost, it is certainly meaningful to speak of the optimal reviewing period. In any case, for the (t, S) policy the relation in equation (1) must hold, for decisions can only be made every t units of time and it would never pay to review more frequently. In systems with an (s, q) policy, on the other hand, when there is a cost associated with reviewing, the finding of the optimal reviewing period is a very meaningful problem. Problem 17–4(9) provides an illustration of such a case.

Example 17–2

Consider Example 17–1. Assume that the unit of time is 1 week. Compare the costs of the system for a (t, S) policy with those of an (s, q) policy and an (s, S) policy.

The costs of the latter policies are given in Tables 17–1a and 17–1b. The costs for a (t, S) policy can readily be computed using the methods of Chapter 8 and are given in Table 17–2.

TABLE 17–2
The Expected Total Cost for a (t, S) Policy

t \ S	-1	0	1	2	3
1	2.40	1.40	1.40	2.20	3.20
2	2.68	1.68	1.28	1.56	2.32
3	3.13	2.13	1.54	1.47	1.88

Comparing Table 17–2 with Tables 17–1a and 17–1b, we note that, first, the results for $t = 1$ in Table 17–2 are identical with the results for $q = 1$ in Table 17–1a and for $S - s = 1$ in Table 17–1b. The three policies are one and the same under these circumstances. Next we note that the sensitivity of costs to changes in the controllable variables is about the same in the regions about the minimum costs. Finally, as expected, the minimum cost for the (t, S) policy is larger than the minimum cost for the (s, q) policy, which in turn is larger than the minimum cost for the (s, S) policy.

COMPARISON OF POLICIES IN SYSTEMS WITH SEVERAL ITEMS

17-3   The results of the last two sections do not necessarily hold for all inventory systems. In particular, they may not hold in systems with several items in which one replenishment cost may apply to several items. The results do hold (even in systems with several items) whenever the unit costs and demands associated with any item are independent of the unit costs of all other items.

In this section we shall illustrate by examples the solutions of two inventory systems, each with several items. The methodology suggested in Section 17-0 will be used.

Example 17-3a

An inventory system comprises N items. The demand for each item varies; during any period t

$$\frac{x_{\max,i}(t)}{\bar{x}_i(t)} = 1 + \frac{b_i}{t} \tag{1}$$

where b_i is some known constant of dimension $[T]$ pertaining to item i. The average rate of demand of item i is r_i, and its carrying cost is c_{1i} per unit per unit time. The replenishing cost is c_3; this cost applies whenever one or more items are ordered. Leadtime is zero, and no shortages are allowed. Inventories are reviewed continuously (i.e., $w_p = 0$). What is the optimal inventory policy?

Essentially only two policies are available, an (s_i, q_i) policy and a (t, S_i) policy. Under the (s_i, q_i) policy, which will be referred to as policy A, item i is replenished whenever inventory is at s_i; then an amount q_i is immediately added to stock. Under the (t, S_i) policy, policy B, decisions regarding replenishments are made every t time units; at these times the amount in inventory of item i is raised to the level S_i.

For policy A it is obvious that

$$s_{io} = 0 \tag{2}$$

The total cost of the system is then given by*

$$C^A = \sum_{i=1}^{N} \left(\frac{c_{1i}q_i}{2} + \frac{c_3 r_i}{q_i} \right) \tag{3}$$

The minimum cost is then

$$C_o^A = \sqrt{2c_3} \sum_{i=1}^{N} \sqrt{c_{1i}r_i} \tag{4}$$

* We assume here that it is unlikely that two or more items will be replenished at the same time.

Under policy B, in order to avoid shortages

$$S_{io} = \left(1 + \frac{b_i}{t}\right) r_i t \tag{5}$$

Hence the total cost is

$$C^B = \sum_{i=1}^{N} c_{1i}\left(S_{io} - \frac{r_i t}{2}\right) + \frac{c_3}{t} \tag{6}$$

The minimum cost is then

$$C_o^B = \sqrt{2c_3}\sqrt{\sum_{i=1}^{N} c_{1i} r_i} + \sum_{i=1}^{N} b_i c_{1i} r_i \tag{7}$$

It is now relatively simple to see that for all values of r_i, c_{1i}, b_i, and c_3 one policy is not necessarily better than the other. For some values of the parameters policy A is better, and for others policy B is better.

Example 17–3b

In an inventory system with only two items inventories may be reviewed every week, 2 weeks, etc. The reviewing cost is $0.20 per review. This cost is incurred whether one item is reviewed or both. The replenishment cost is $3.00. This cost, too, is incurred whether one item is replenished or both.

TABLE 17–3a

The Probability Distributions and Unit Costs in Example 17–3b

	$P(0)$	$P(1)$	$P(2)$	$P(3)$	c_1	c_2
Item 1	0.2	0.1	0.0	0.7	$1.00	$5.00
Item 2	0.0	0.3	0.4	0.3	1.00	4.00

The probability distribution of weekly demand for each item and the unit carrying and shortage costs are given in Table 17–3a. The problem is to compare the (t, S_i^t) policy with the (s_i, S_i^s) policy* and to choose the policy with the least expected total cost.

The (t, S_i^t) Policy

Suppose $t = 1$ week. To find the corresponding optimal S_{io}^t we must first establish the equivalent distributions. The work is displayed in Table 17–3b. For item 1, $c_2/(c_1 + c_2) = \frac{5}{6} = 0.833$; hence $S_{1o}^t = 1$. For item 2 $c_2/(c_1 + c_2) = \frac{4}{5} = 0.8$; hence $S_{2o}^t = 2$. When $t = 1$, reviewing will be

---

* The order levels bear superscripts to indicate the policy to which they refer. The subscript i refers to the item. It can be either 1 or 2.

TABLE 17-3b

The Equivalent Distributions for $t = 1$ *week*

Item	x, y	$P(x)$	$\dfrac{P(x)}{x}$	$\displaystyle\sum_{y+1}^{\infty} \dfrac{P(x)}{x}$	$G(y)$	$\displaystyle\sum_{x=0}^{y} G(x)$
	0	0.2		0.733	0.567	0.567
1	1	0.7	0.700	0.033	0.383	0.950
	2	0.0	0.000	0.033	0.033	0.983
	3	0.1	0.033	0.	0.017	1.000
	0	0.0		0.600	0.300	0.300
2	1	0.3	0.300	0.300	0.450	0.750
	2	0.4	0.200	0.100	0.200	0.950
	3	0.3	0.100	0.	0.050	1.000

every week. Moreover, since there is always some demand for item 2, there will also be a replenishment every week. The total cost for $t = 1$ week is then

$$C^t = [(1 \times 0.567)1.00 + (1 \times 0.033 + 2 \times 0.017)5.00]$$
$$+ [2 \times 0.300 + 1 \times 0.450)1.00 + (1 \times 0.050)4.00] \qquad (8)$$
$$+ 3.00 + 0.20 = \$5.35 \text{ per week}$$

Suppose now that $t = 2$ weeks. The detailed computations are given in Table 17-3c. From the table we conclude that $S_{1o}^t = 2$ and that $S_{2o}^t = 3$.

TABLE 17-3c

The Equivalent Distributions for $t = 2$ *weeks*

Item	x, y	$P(x)$	$\dfrac{P(x)}{x}$	$\displaystyle\sum_{y+1}^{\infty} \dfrac{P(x)}{x}$	$G(y)$	$\displaystyle\sum_{x=0}^{y} G(x)$
	0	0.04		0.5750	0.3275	0.3275
	1	0.28	0.2800	0.2950	0.4350	0.7625
	2	0.49	0.2450	0.0500	0.1725	0.9350
1	3	0.04	0.0133	0.0367	0.0433	0.9783
	4	0.14	0.0350	0.0017	0.0192	0.9975
	5	0.00	0.0000	0.0017	0.0017	0.9992
	6	0.01	0.0017	0.	0.0008	1.0000
	0	0.00		0.273	0.1365	0.1365
	1	0.00	0.000	0.273	0.2730	0.4095
	2	0.09	0.045	0.228	0.2505	0.6600
2	3	0.24	0.080	0.148	0.1880	0.8480
	4	0.34	0.085	0.063	0.1055	0.9535
	5	0.24	0.048	0.015	0.0390	0.9925
	6	0.09	0.015	0.	0.0075	1.0000

Inventories will be reviewed only once every 2 weeks and replenishments, too, will be made once every 2 weeks. Hence the total cost is

$$
\begin{aligned}
C^t = {} & [(2 \times 0.3275 + 1 \times 0.4350)1.00 + (1 \times 0.0433 \\
& + 2 \times 0.0192 + 3 \times 0.0017 + 4 \times 0.0008)5.00] \\
& + [(3 \times 0.1365 + 2 \times 0.2730 + 1 \times 0.2505)1.00 \qquad (9) \\
& + (1 \times 0.1055 + 2 \times 0.0390 + 3 \times 0.0075)4.00] \\
& + 3.00/2 + 0.20/2 = \$5.17 \text{ per week}
\end{aligned}
$$

In a similar way we can obtain results for $t = 3$ weeks. It can be shown that $S_{1_o}^t = 3$, $S_{2_o}^t = 5$, and that the corresponding cost is \$6.03 per week. Thus the minimum total cost for a (t, S_i^t) policy is \$5.17 per week.

The (s_i, S_i^s) Policy

Let the difference k_i be defined by

$$
k_i = S_i^s - s_i \qquad (10)
$$

We can use the methods of Section 15–0 to find the probability distribution $H(Q)$ of the amounts in inventory at the beginning of each reviewing period. The computations are displayed in Table 17–3d. In this table the

TABLE 17–3d
Determination of the Distribution $H(Q)$ of Equation 15–0(11)

Items	x, k	$P(x)$	$R(x)$	$A(x)$	$\sum_{x=0}^{k-1} A(x)$	$H(S)$	$H(S-1)$	$H(S-2)$	$H(S-3)$	I_3
	0	0.2		1.000						
	1	0.7	0.875	0.875	1.000	1.000				0.800
1	2	0.0	0.000	0.766	1.875	0.533	0.467			0.426
	3	0.1	0.125	0.795	2.641	0.379	0.331	0.290		0.303
	0	0.0		1.000						
	1	0.3	0.3	0.300	1.000	1.000				1.000
2	2	0.4	0.4	0.490	1.300	0.769	0.231			0.769
	3	0.3	0.3	0.567	1.790	0.559	0.167	0.274		0.559
	4	0.0	0.0	0.456	2.357	0.424	0.127	0.208	0.241	0.424

computations for $H(Q)$ are based on equation 15–0(11) and the several equations which precede it. I_3 comes from equation 15–1(3).

Next, Table 17–3e is prepared. In this table are displayed the expected average inventory and the expected average shortage during a reviewing period. The corresponding costs are also given. Table 17–3e also describes the system for a (t, S_i^t) policy when $t = 1$ week. Note that the table gives the previously obtained results, $S_{o1}^t = 1$ and $S_{o2}^t = 2$. The table will now be used to evaluate costs for the (s_i, S_i^s) policy for various k_i and various S_i^s.

TABLE 17–3e

The Expected Average Inventory and Average Shortage and Their Costs during a Reviewing Period

Item	Q	$I_1(Q)$	$I_2(Q)$	$C_1(Q)$	$C_2(Q)$	$C_{12}(Q)$
	−1	0.	1.500	0.	7.500	7.500
	0	0.	0.500	0.	2.500	2.500
1	1	0.567	0.067	0.567	0.335	0.902
	2	1.517	0.017	1.517	0.085	1.602
	3	2.500	0.	2.500	0.	2.500
	0	0.	1.000	0.	4.000	4.000
	1	0.300	0.300	0.300	1.200	1.500
2	2	1.050	0.050	1.050	0.200	1.250
	3	2.000	0.	2.000	0.	2.000
	4	3.000	0.	3.000	0.	3.000
	5	4.000	0.	4.000	0.	4.000

The sum of the expected carrying and shortage costs for given k and S can be expressed as

$$C_{12}(k, S) = \sum_{Q=S-k+1}^{S} C_{12}(Q)H(Q) \tag{11}$$

where the $H(Q)$ are as given in Table 17–3d and the $C_{12}(Q)$ as given in Table 17–3e. The pertinent costs are listed in Table 17–3f. From the table we can immediately infer what is the minimum sum of carrying and shortage costs for any given difference k. These costs are marked with asterisks in the table.

TABLE 17–3f

The Sum of Carrying and Shortage Costs for Various k and S

Item	S / k	0	1	2	3	4	5
	1	2.500	0.902*	1.602	2.500	3.500	4.500
1	2		1.648	1.275*	2.095	3.033	
	3		3.344	1.631*	1.739	2.619	
	1	4.000	1.500	1.250*	2.000	3.000	4.000
2	2		2.078	1.308*	1.827	2.769	
	3			2.045	1.738*	2.354	
	4				2.283	2.148*	2.794

The expected number of replenishments per reviewing period is given in Table 17-3d. Let $I_3{}^i$ designate this number for item i. It follows that the expected cost of replenishing per week is given by

$$C_3 = [1 - (1 - I_3{}^1)(1 - I_3{}^2)]c_3 + c_4 \qquad (12)$$

where, in our case, $c_3 = \$3.00$ and $c_4 = \$0.20$.

We can now tabulate the total expected costs of the inventory system for the various choices of k_1 and k_2. They are given in Table 17-3g and are

TABLE 17-3g

The Total Expected Cost for the $(s_i, S_i{}^s)$ Policy

k_1 \ k_2	1	2	3	4	
	0.902	0.902	0.902	0.902	C_{12}^1
1	1.250	1.308	1.738	2.148	C_{12}^2
	3.200	3.061	2.935	2.854	C_3
	5.352	5.271	5.575	5.904	C
	1.275	1.275	1.275	1.275	C_{12}^1
2	1.250	1.308	1.738	2.148	C_{12}^2
	3.200	2.802	2.441	2.208	C_3
	5.725	5.385	5.454	5.631	C
	1.631	1.631	1.631	1.631	C_{12}^1
3	1.250	1.308	1.738	2.148	C_{12}^2
	3.200	2.668	2.185	1.875	C_3
	6.081	5.607	5.554	5.654	C

based on Tables 17-3d and 17-3f and on equation (12). From this table we conclude that for the $(s_i, S_i{}^s)$ policy the minimum cost is $5.27 per week. This cost is larger than the minimum cost for a $(t, S_i{}^t)$ policy. We therefore conclude that a $(t, S_i{}^t)$ policy is better for this inventory system.

17-4 PROBLEMS

1. In Section 7-1 we have seen that the minimum cost of the system for an (s, q) policy is in general larger than the minimum cost for a (t, S_i) policy. This result seems to be in contradiction with the statements in Section 17-2. Explain this apparent contradiction.

2. In Example 17–1 express the total cost $C^q(-1, 3) = 1.27$ in terms of the costs $C^S(-1, 0) = 1.40$, $C^S(-1, 1) = 1.13$, and $C^S(-1, 2) = 1.31$ as in equation 17–1(3). Find the weighing factors by extending the results given by equations 17–1(7), 17–1(8), and 17–1(9).

3. Prove the assertion given by equation 17–1(10).

4. Compare the (s, q), (s, S), and (t, S) policies in Examples 17–1 and 17–2 if the reviewing period is 2 weeks and the scheduling periods must be integer multiples of 2 weeks.

5. Prepare a numerical example of an inventory system in which the reorder point under an (s, q) policy is different from the reorder point under an (s, S) policy. Compare the minimum expected total costs of the system for the two policies.

6. In an inventory system the probability distribution of weekly demand is $P(x)$, where $P(0) = 0.6$ and $P(1) = 0.4$. Whenever a demand for one unit does occur, it is equally likely to be at any time during the week (i.e., the pattern of demand is uniform). The reviewing period is 1 week.

   The carrying cost is $6 per unit per week, the shortage cost is $30 per unit per week, and the replenishing cost is $4. Leadtime is zero.

   Find the optimal decisions and the corresponding minimum total costs for each of the policies: (a) (t, S), (b) (s, q), and (c) (s, S).

7. In an inventory system the reviewing period is either 1 week or 2 weeks. If the (t, S) policy is used, the minimum total cost is $C_o{}^t$. For a 1-week reviewing period and an (s, q) policy the minimum total cost is $C_o{}^{q_1}$, and for for a 2-week reviewing period it is $C_o{}^{q_2}$.

   Prepare a numerical example of such a system for which the optimal scheduling period for a (t, S) policy is 2 weeks and for which

$$C_o{}^{q_1} < C_o{}^{q_2} < C_o{}^t \tag{1}$$

8. How do policies A and B in example 17–3a compare when $b_i = 0$.

9. Find the minimum expected total cost of the system of Example 17–3b for an $(s_i, S_i{}^s)$ policy if the reviewing period is 2 weeks. Compare the result with Example 17–3b in which the reviewing period is 1 week.

10. Verify the results given by equations 17–3(4) and 17–3(7).

11. In Example 17–3b for the $(t, S_i{}^t)$ policy and for $t = 3$ weeks, show that the minimum expected total cost is $6.03 per week.

12. Explain the reasoning behind equation 17–3(12).

13. The year is composed of two periods, T_1 and T_2. During T_1 months customers demand r_1 units per month. During T_2 months they demand r_2 units per month. Inventory carrying costs are c_1 per unit per month. The cost of placing and handling an order is c_3 per order. No shortages are allowed.

   (a) Solve the inventory system for three ordering policies: (1) the lot size is constant, (2) the scheduling period is constant, and (3) no restrictions are placed on the lot size or on the scheduling period.

   (b) Give numerical answers for $T_1 = 4$ months, $T_2 = 8$ months, $r_1 = 67.5$ lb per month, $r_2 = 20.25$ lb per month, $c_1 = $10 per pound per month, and $c_3 = $45 per order.

14. Solve problem 13 for $T_1 = 3$ months, $T_2 = 9$ months, $r_1 = 300$ parts, $r_2 = 500$ parts, $c_1 = \$0.12$ per part per year, and $c_3 = \$2.25$ per order.

15. An inventory system comprises three different items. For each item and for any period t the ratio of the maximum demand to the average demand is $1 + 2/t$. The average annual demands are respectively 640, 1620, and 960 parts. The unit carrying costs are respectively $\$0.10$, $\$0.05$, and $\$0.15$ per part per year. The ordering cost is $\$50.00$ per order. This cost is independent of the number of items on the order or of the amounts ordered. Leadtime is zero. No shortages are allowed.

Determine the optimal ordering policy.

References and Bibliography

The following list is composed mainly of references cited in this book. Extensive bibliographies and articles on inventory systems and related subjects can be found in Whitin [55], pp. 329–342 (over 220 items); Gourary, Lewis, and Neeland [22] (over 150 items); Arrow, Karlin, and Scarf [4], pp. 337–340 (over 60 items); and Hanssmann [24], pp. 237–249 (over 240 items). A general bibliography on operations research which includes hundreds of items on inventory systems is available in the Case Institute's *Operations Research Group Comprehensive Bibliography* [46] and in Batchelors' *Annotated Bibliography* [5].

Periodical abstracts, digests, and reviews of operations research literature appear in *International Abstracts in Operations Research* (IAOR) and in *Operations Research/Management Sciences* (OR/MS). IAOR is published by the Operations Research Society of America for the International Federation of Operational Research Societies. OR/MS is published by Executive Sciences Institute, Inc., Whippany, New Jersey.

Surveys of literature on inventory systems and related subjects can be found in Simon and Holt [52], Whitin [56], Ackoff [1], and Hanssmann [25].

[1] Ackoff, Russell L., "The Development of Operations Research as a Science," *Operations Research*, Vol. 4, No. 3, June 1956, pp. 271–273.

[2] Arora, Sant Ram, "Determination of Optimal Decision Parameters with Distribution Functions Not Completely Known," Doctor of Engineering dissertation, The Johns Hopkins University, Baltimore, 1963.

[3] Arrow, Kenneth J., Theodore Harris, and Jacob Marschak, "Optimal Inventory Policy," *Econometrica*, Vol. 19, No. 3, July 1951, pp. 250–272.

[4]   Arrow, Kenneth J., Samuel Karlin, and Herbert Scarf, *Studies in the Mathematical Theory of Inventory and Production*, Stanford University Press, Stanford, 1958.

[5]   Batchelor, James H., *Operations Research Annotated Bibliography*, St. Louis University Press, St. Louis, Vol. 1, second edition, 1959, Vol. 2, 1962, Vol. 3, 1963.

[6]   Battersby, Albert, *A Guide to Stock Control*, Sir Isaac Pitman and Sons, London, 1962.

[7]   Bowman, Edward H., and Robert B. Fetter, *Analysis for Production Management*, Richard D. Irwin, Homewood, Ill., 1957.

[8]   Bowman, Edward H., and Robert B. Fetter, editors, *Analyses of Industrial Operations*, Richard D. Irwin, Homewood, Ill., 1959.

[9]   Brenner, Michael E., "Correlated and Selective Sampling Applied to the Simulation of Some Inventory Systems," Doctor of Engineering dissertation, The Johns Hopkins University, Baltimore, 1963.

[10] Brenner, Michael E., "Selective Sampling—A Technique for Reducing Sample Size in Simulation of Decision-Making Problems," *The Journal of Industrial Engineering*, Vol. 14, No. 6, November–December 1963, pp. 291–296.

[11] Brown, Robert G., *Statistical Forecasting for Inventory Control*, McGraw-Hill, New York, 1959.

[12] Brown, Robert G., *Smoothing, Forecasting and Prediction of Discrete Time Series*, Prentice-Hall, Englewood Cliffs, N.J., 1963.

[13] Buchan, Joseph and Ernest Koenigsberg, *Scientific Inventory Management*, Prentice-Hall, Englewood Cliffs, N.J., 1963.

[14] Churchman, C. West, Russell L. Ackoff, and E. Leonard Arnoff, editors, *Introduction to Operations Research*, John Wiley and Sons, New York, 1957.

[15] Dvoretzky, A., J. Kiefer, and J. Wolfowitz, "The Inventory Problem," *Econometrica*, Vol. 20, No. 2, April 1952, pp. 187–222; No. 3, July 1952, pp. 450–466.

[16] Dvoretzky, A., J. Kiefer, and J. Wolfowitz, "On the Optimal Character of the (s, S) Policy in Inventory Theory," *Econometrica*, Vol. 21, No. 4, October 1953, pp. 586–596.

[17] Feller, William, *An Introduction to Probability Theory and Its Application*, Vol. 1, second edition, John Wiley and Sons, New York, 1957.

[18] Fetter, Robert B., and Winston C. Dalleck, *Decision Models for Inventory Management*, Richard D. Irwin, Homewood, Ill., 1961.

[19] Flagle, Charles D., William H. Huggins, and Robert H. Roy, editors, *Operations Research and Systems Engineering*, The Johns Hopkins Press, Baltimore, 1960.

[20] Galliher, Herbert P., "Simulation of Random Process," Chapter 11 in *Notes on Operations Research*, M.I.T. Press, Cambridge, Mass., 1959.

[21] Gaver, D. P., Jr., "On Base Stock Level Inventory Control," *Operations Research*, Vol. 7, No. 6, November–December 1959, pp. 689–703.

[22] Gourary, M., R. Lewis, and F. Neeland, "An Inventory Control Bibliography," *Naval Research Logistics Quarterly*, Vol. 3, No. 4, December 1956, pp. 295–303.

[23] Hadley, G., and T. M. Whitin, *Analysis of Inventory Systems*, Prentice-Hall, Englewood Cliffs, N.J., 1963.

[24] Hanssmann, Fred, *Operations Research in Production and Inventory Control*, John Wiley and Sons, New York, 1962.

[25] Hanssmann, Fred, "A Survey of Inventory Theory from the Operations Research Viewpoint," Chapter 3 in *Progress in Operations Research*, Vol. 1, edited by Russell L. Ackoff, John Wiley and Sons, New York, 1961.

[26] Holmes, John M., Jr., "Inventory Control in a Telephone Company," Master of Science in Engineering essay, The Johns Hopkins University, Baltimore, 1962.

[27] Holt, Charles C., Franco Modigliani, John F. Muth, and Herbert A. Simon, *Planning Production, Inventories and Work Force*, Prentice-Hall, Englewood Cliffs, N.J., 1960.

[28] Kemeny, John G., Hazleton Mirkil, J. Laurie Snell, and Gerald L. Thompson, *Finite Mathematical Structures*, Prentice-Hall, Englewood Cliffs, N.J., 1959.

[29] Kemeny, John G., and J. Laurie Snell, *Finite Markov Chains*, D. Van Nostrand, Princeton, N.J., 1960.

[30] Laderman, J., S. B. Littauer, and Lionel Weiss, "The Inventory Problem," *Journal of the American Statistical Association*, Vol. 48, No. 264, December 1953, pp. 717–732.

[31] Magee, John F., *Production Planning and Inventory Control*, McGraw-Hill, New York, 1958.

[32] Messer, H. Donald, "Theoretical and Practical Solution of a Class of Dynamic Inventory Models with No Constraints on Demand Distribution Structure," Doctor of Engineering dissertation, The Johns Hopkins University, Baltimore, 1962.

[33] Meyer, Herbert A., editor, *Symposium on Monte Carlo Methods*, John Wiley and Sons, New York, 1956.

[34] Mills, Edward S., *Price, Output, and Inventory Policy*, John Wiley and Sons, New York, 1962.

[35] Morse, Philip M., *Queues, Inventories, and Maintenance*, John Wiley and Sons, New York, 1958.

[36] Morse, Philip M., and George E. Kimball, *Methods of Operations Research*, M.I.T. Press, Cambridge, Mass., 1951.

[37] Naddor, Eliezer, "Elementary Inventory Models," Chapter 8, pp. 199–234 in [14].

[38] Naddor, Eliezer, "Elements of Inventory Systems," Chapter 12, pp. 311–364 in [19].

[39] Naddor, Eliezer, "Some Models of Inventory and an Application," *Management Science*, Vol. 2, No. 4, July 1956, pp. 299–312; and Chapter 24, pp. 429–443 in [8].

[40] Naddor, Eliezer, and Sidney Saltzman, "Optimal Reorder Periods for an Inventory System with Variable Cost of Ordering," *Operations Research*, Vol. 6, No. 5, September–October 1958, pp. 676–685.

[41] Naddor, Eliezer, "On the Equivalence of Some Inventory Systems," *Management Science*, Vol. 9, 1963, pp. 482–489.

[42] Naddor, Eliezer, "Comparison of (t, Z) and (z, Z) Policies," *Operations Research*, Vol. 10, No. 3, May–June 1962, pp. 401–403.

[43] Naddor, Eliezer, "Markov Chains and Simulations in an Inventory System," *Journal of Industrial Engineering*, Vol. 14, No. 2, March–April 1963, pp. 91–98.

[44] Naddor, Eliezer, "Economic Lot Sizes for Some Elementary Inventory Systems," *Bolletino del Centro per la Ricerca Operativa*, No. 4, pp. 1–10, 1957.

[45] Naddor, Eliezer, "Evaluation of Inventory Control," pp. 255–297 in *Proceedings of the Second International Conference on Operations Research*, J. Banbury and J. Maitland, editors, English University Press, London, 1961.

[46] Operations Research Group, Case Institute of Technology, *A Comprehensive Bibliography on Operations Research*, Vol. 1, through 1956, with supplement for 1957, Vol. 2, 1957–1958, John Wiley and Sons, New York, 1958 and 1963.

[47] Pipes, Louis A., *Applied Mathematics for Engineers and Physicists*, McGraw-Hill, New York, 1958.

[48] Pratt, John W., Howard Raiffa, and Robert Schlaifer, *Introduction to Statistical Decision Theory*, McGraw-Hill, New York, 1965.

[49] Raymond, Fairfield E., *Quantity and Economy in Manufacturing*, McGraw-Hill, New York, 1931 (out of print).

[50] Saaty, Thomas L., *Mathematical Methods of Operations Research*, McGraw-Hill, New York, 1959.

[51] Sasieni, Maurice, Arthur Yaspan, and Lawrence Friedman, *Operations Research—Methods and Problems*, John Wiley and Sons, New York, 1959.

[52] Simon, Herbert A., and Charles C. Holt, "The Control of Inventories and Production Rates—A Survey," *Operations Research*, Vol. 2, No. 3, August 1954, pp. 289–301.

[53] Starr, Martin, and David W. Miller, *Inventory Control: Theory and Practice*, Prentice-Hall, Englewood Cliffs, N.J., 1962.

[54] Wagner, Harvey M., *Statistical Management of Inventory Systems*, John Wiley and Sons, New York, 1962.

[55] Whitin, Thomson M., *The Theory of Inventory Management*, Princeton University Press, Princeton, N.J., second edition, 1957.

[56] Whitin, Thomson M., "Inventory Control Research: A Survey," *Management Science*, Vol. 1, No. 1, October 1954, pp. 32–40; and in Appendix 1, pp. 230–241 in [55].

INDEX